The
Parallel Curriculum
in the Classroom
Book 2

*With gratitude to the educators whose interest in the Parallel
Curriculum Model has provided an impetus to explore its
possibilities further, whose questions have caused us to deepen our thinking,
and whose work in schools and classrooms has given legs to curriculum dreams.*

The Parallel Curriculum in the Classroom

Book 2

Units for Application Across the Content Areas K-12

A Joint Publication With the
National Association for Gifted Children

Carol Ann Tomlinson ◆ Sandra N. Kaplan ◆ Jeanne H. Purcell
Jann H. Leppien ◆ Deborah E. Burns ◆ Cindy A. Strickland

CORWIN PRESS
A SAGE Publications Company
Thousand Oaks, California

For information:

Corwin Press
A Sage Publications Company
2455 Teller Road
Thousand Oaks, California 91320
E-mail: order@corwinpress.com

Sage Publications Ltd.
1 Oliver's Yard
55 City Road
London EC1Y 1SP
United Kingdom

Sage Publications India Pvt. Ltd.
B-42, Panchsheel Enclave
Post Box 4109
New Delhi 110 017 India

Printed in the United States of America.

Library of Congress Cataloging-in-Publication Data

The parallel curriculum in the classroom / Carol Ann Tomlinson . . . [et al.].
        2 v. cm.
"A Joint Publication of the National Association for Gifted Children and Corwin Press."
Includes bibliographical references and index.
    Contents: bk. 1. Essays for application across the content areas, K-12 — bk. 2. Units for application across the content areas, K-12.
ISBN 0-7619-2971-1 (cloth : v. 1) — ISBN 0-7619-2972-X (pbk. : v. 1) — ISBN 1-4129-2527-4 (cloth : v. 2) — ISBN 1-4129-2528-2 (pbk. : v. 2) 1. Gifted children—Education—Curricula.
2. Curriculum planning. I. Tomlinson, Carol A. II. National Association for Gifted Children (U.S.)
LC3993.2.P344 2006
371.95'3—dc22

                                                                    2005007504

This book is printed on acid-free paper.

05 06 07 08 09 10 9 8 7 6 5 4 3 2 1

Acquisitions Editor:	Robert D. Clouse
Editorial Assistant:	Jingle Vea
Project Editor:	Tracy Alpern
Copy Editor:	Mary L. Tederstrom
Proofreader:	Theresa Kay
Typesetter:	C&M Digitals (P) Ltd.
Indexer:	Sylvia Coates
Cover Designer:	Michael Dubowe

Contents

Acknowledgments

Corwin Press gratefully acknowledges the contributions of the following manuscript reviewers:

Sherri S. Jarrett
GATE Resource Specialist
Peter Muhlenberg Middle School
Woodstock, VA

Sandy Marzec
GATE Teacher
Twin Lakes Elementary School
Federal Way, WA

Pamela Lyle-Walton
GATE Teacher
Nautilus Elementary School
Federal Way, WA

Kathleen M. Pierce
Assistant Professor
Graduate Department of Education &
    Human Services
Rider University
Lawrenceville, NJ

Gillian I. Eriksson Sluti
Instructor
Educational Studies, College of
    Education
University of Central Florida
Orlando, FL

Vicki Vaughn
Instructor of G/T Grad Courses
Codirector of Gifted/Talented
    Licensure
Purdue University
West Lafayette, IN

Marsha Sobel
Executive Director, Curriculum and
    Instruction
Newburgh Enlarged City School
    District
Newburgh, NY

About the Authors

 **Carol Ann Tomlinson**'s career as an educator encompasses 21 years as a public school teacher, including 12 years as a program administrator of special services for struggling and advanced learners. She was Virginia's Teacher of the Year in 1974. More recently, she has been a faculty member at the University of Virginia's Curry School of Education, where she is currently Professor of Educational Leadership, Foundations, and Policy and was named Outstanding Professor in 2004. Also at the University of Virginia she is codirector of the university's Summer Institute on Academic Diversity. She is author of more than 150 books, articles, and chapters on differentiation and curriculum.

 **Sandra N. Kaplan** has been a teacher and administrator of gifted programs in an urban school district in California. Currently, she is Clinical Professor in Learning and Instruction at the University of Southern California's Rossier School of Education. She has authored articles and books on the nature and scope of differentiated curriculum for gifted students. Her primary area of concern is modifying the core and differentiated curriculum to meet the needs of inner-city and urban gifted learners. She is a past president of the California Association for the Gifted (CAG) and the National Association for Gifted Children (NAGC). She has been nationally recognized for her contributions to gifted education.

 **Jeanne H. Purcell** is the consultant to the Connecticut State Department of Education for gifted and talented education. Prior to her work there, she was an administrator for Rocky Hill Public Schools, where she coordinated a staff-development initiative on curriculum differentiation; a program specialist with the National Research Center on the Gifted and Talented (NRC/GT), where she worked collaboratively with other researchers on national issues related to high-achieving young people; an instructor of Teaching the Talented, a graduate-level program in gifted education; and a staff developer to school districts across the country and Canada. She has been an English teacher, community service coordinator, and teacher of the gifted, K–12, for 18 years in Connecticut school districts. She is the author of two books and has

published many articles that have appeared in *Educational Leadership, Gifted Child Quarterly, Roeper Review, Educational and Psychological Measurement, National Association of Secondary School Principals' Bulletin, Our Children: The National PTA Magazine, Parenting for High Potential,* and *Journal for the Education of the Gifted.* She is active in her local community and in the National Association for Gifted Children (NAGC) as a member of the executive board and board of directors. She served on the awards committee and the curriculum committee where she cochaired the annual Curriculum Awards competition.

Jann H. Leppien is an associate professor at the University of Great Falls in Great Falls, Montana, where she teaches coursework in curriculum and instruction, gifted education, assessment and learning, educational research, and methods in social sciences. In addition, she teaches curriculum courses and thinking skills courses online and in the Three Summers program at the University of Connecticut. Before joining the faculty at the University of Great Falls, she worked as a research assistant for the National Research Center on the Gifted and Talented (NRC/GT). She has been a classroom teacher, enrichment specialist, and coordinator of a gifted education program in Montana. She is the coauthor of *The Multiple Menu Model: A Practical Guide for Developing Differentiated Curriculum* and *The Parallel Curriculum: A Design to Develop High Potential and Challenge High-Ability Students.* She conducts workshops for teachers in the areas of differentiated instruction, curriculum design and assessment, thinking skills, and program development. She has served on the board of the National Association for Gifted Children (NAGC) and currently serves on the Association for the Education of Gifted Underachieving Students (AEGUS).

Deborah E. Burns is a curriculum coordinator for the Cheshire, Connecticut, schools. Previously, she worked for 15 years as an associate professor and an administrator in educational psychology at the University of Connecticut, where she taught courses in curriculum design, differentiation, assessment, talent development, and thinking skills instruction. Her related professional experience includes K–8 classroom teaching, work as a gifted education specialist, and work as a remedial reading and math specialist. As a consultant and program evaluator, she works with school districts nationwide. Her publications include journal articles, chapters, and books based on her research and work with teachers and in classrooms. She graduated from Michigan State University in 1973 with her BS, from Ashland University in 1978 with her MEd, and from the University of Connecticut in 1987 with her PhD.

 **Cindy A. Strickland** is currently pursuing her doctorate in Educational Psychology with an emphasis in gifted education at the University of Virginia, where she serves as teaching assistant to Carol Ann Tomlinson. She is an international consultant in the areas of differentiation of instruction, the Parallel Curriculum Model, and gifted education. Her publications include *Differentiation in Practice: A Resource Guide for Differentiating Curriculum, Grades 9–12* and *In Search of the Dream: Designing Schools and Classrooms That Work for High Potential Students From Diverse Cultural Backgrounds*. She has been a teacher for more than 20 years. She has taught music, French, humanities, and gifted education to elementary- through college-age students.

Introducing the Parallel Curriculum Model in the Classroom

Carol Ann Tomlinson and Sandra N. Kaplan

ABOUT THE BOOK

The Parallel Curriculum Model in the Classroom is published in two books. The first book presents five essays that are intended to clarify and expand upon the key ideas presented in *The Parallel Curriculum* (Tomlinson et al., 2002; see the Introduction to Book 1 for more detail). This second book contains eight units that apply the Parallel Curriculum Model (PCM) in varied subjects and at varied grade levels. The two books can stand alone, but they are designed to work in tandem to extend a reader's understanding of the PCM and to illustrate some ways in which the model can be used in classrooms.

In Book 2, we have made a special effort to link the PCM information and guidelines in Book 1 with the creation of exemplary units. The following introduction to the units offers the rationale, methods, and resources that are important to consider while reading the eight PCM curriculum units and applying the concepts and principles gained therein to a reader's own curriculum and instruction.

The Units

Book 2 presents curriculum units developed by using the PCM. We were fortunate to have many high-quality educators volunteer to create units for the book. In fact, ultimately we had to eliminate several useful units because of space limitations. The units included in this book represent primary, elementary, middle school, and high school levels of instruction. They represent several disciplines as well: social studies, science, art, math, and language arts. Some were written by PCM authors, and some were written by classroom teachers. Some of the units include all of the model's parallels, and some do not. In other words, we have selected units that reflect a variety of applications of the PCM.

Each unit has three key components. First, background material provides readers with a "big picture" of the unit, grade level and subject, goals, and standards incorporated in the unit. Second, the unit is "unpacked" or explained step-by-step in a left-hand column. Third, the unit developer's reasoning about her work is provided in a right-hand column. We elected to retain the voices of the units' authors, so you will "hear" the thinking of a number of curriculum developers about how and why they crafted the units based on the PCM, the requirements of their teaching context, and the needs of the students they teach. In some cases, the book editors modified units to ensure that the collection of units offered here corresponds to a variety of the key ideas and applications of the PCM. Application of PCM principles is shaped—as it always is with crafting thoughtful curriculum—by the author's own journey as a human being and as a professional. One PCM author notes that the units all reflect the essential elements of PCM, but those elements "rotate" somewhat like the elements in a kaleidoscope, depending on who holds the kaleidoscope and at what angle.

As the editors began compiling units that would appear in the book, we asked ourselves the question, "What *is* necessary in the design of a Parallel Curriculum unit?" There are many characteristics we would like to see in effective curricula. For the purposes of this book and this model, we concentrated on these essential traits. We believe that the units included here (1) explicitly lead to a conceptual understanding of the topics and disciplines on which they are based, (2) persistently honor the intent of the parallel(s) they represent, (3) appropriately utilize and extend the questions designated in the original PCM book as critical to achieving the goals of a particular parallel, (4) use the essential components of curriculum as a framework for ensuring coherence in the units, and (5) apply Ascending Intellectual Demand in a way that escalates students toward expertise.

We debated—and continue to debate—whether every PCM unit must reflect all four of the model's parallels. We have not yet reached unanimity about that issue. Certainly a key contribution of the PCM is insistence that learners profit from examining the world they study through a varied set of high-quality lenses. Thus all of us *do* agree that through the course of a year—and over the course of a number of years—PCM units should challenge students to examine topics and issues through the curricular perspectives of Core, Connections, Practice, and Identity. To do less is to shortchange students and to raise the question of why one "buys" interchangeable lenses if not to examine the world more richly. At the same time, it may be useful for students at some points to concentrate in a more focused way on perspectives provided by one of the lenses—or two, or three—rather than making imperative the use of all four lenses on each "learning excursion." Further, it may be useful to teachers to craft some units that require their extended attention to the nature and goals of one of the parallels—especially in early explorations and applications of the model. It is on the issue of whether *all* parallels must be used in *all* units in order to address the intent of the model about which the authors of the PCM continue to have vigorous debates.

Our solution is to offer some units that probe (for both teacher and students) the possibilities of one parallel, some that enlist the possibilities of two or three, and some that draw on all four parallels. Were we given the opportunity to present a full year of curriculum for any subject, we would unanimously concur that all four parallels would need to be utilized over the course of the year in ways that serve the learning goals of the various units, the learning needs of students, and the growth of teachers. In any case, our experience leads us to offer the caution that transitory, shallow, or surface applications of a parallel neither represent the possibilities of the parallel nor extend the possibilities of students. In other words, we would not suggest that a lesson is an example of the Curriculum of Practice just because a student looked at a slide through a microscope and drew what he or she saw. We would not claim that a lesson represents the Curriculum of Identity just because a student wrote an opinion about a current event. In neither case does the activity address core concepts and principles of the discipline. In neither case does the activity address the deep intent of any of the parallels.

We do not envision the units included in this book as off-the-shelf selections a teacher would pick up and teach. Rather, we see them as professional development tools helpful to any educator who wants to reflect on the process of creating thoughtful curriculum—particularly, thoughtful curriculum based on the PCM. We hope you find your experiences with this book to be a positive catalyst in your own development as an educator.

USING THE MODEL AND UNITS FOR PROFESSIONAL DEVELOPMENT

To maximize the usefulness of the PCM and the units and essays included in Book 1 and Book 2, we suggest the following guidelines for professional development based on the model. The guidelines should help you ensure the integrity of the model and maximize the likelihood that work produced using the model addresses the intellectual needs of the students the model was designed to serve.

- Study the PCM (see *The Parallel Curriculum,* Tomlinson et al., 2002), as well as the PCM essays in Book 1, to ensure that educators understand its philosophy and intent.

- Examine this model in comparison with other curriculum models. It is often through such a comparison that the value of a particular design becomes clear.

- Discuss the relationship between the PCM and current issues in both general and gifted education. Among those issues might be the changing nature of student populations, the evolving and expanding understanding of intelligence, the need to have many students exposed to high-quality curriculum, the possibility that high-quality curriculum can be a catalyst for both identifying and developing potential in learners, the need to balance equity and excellence in our schools, and the need to develop standards-based curriculum that honors our best knowledge about dynamic teaching and learning.

- Demonstrate learning experiences based on the PCM as a preface to using the model to develop curriculum for larger groups of students. Observing the model in practice is likely to be far more powerful than only reading or hearing about it.

- Propose a set of criteria to ensure that the integrity of the model is maintained as curriculum is developed. Such a list should help curriculum implementers make sure that their work is synchronized with the intent of the various parallels and the model as a whole. Just as stages of review accompany the process of writing for publication, reviews in the curriculum writing and implementation process need to precede "publication" for one or many groups of students.

- Field test units developed with the PCM. For example, two teachers might design a unit together. They may then try out the unit with their students and compare responses of students during the unit as well as examine student products from the unit. It is then possible for the two teachers to engage in a grounded discussion about the degree to which the unit seemed to facilitate student attainment of goals reflected in the unit and the model.

- Create a systematic plan to review PCM-based work in a school or district. This is likely to be most useful if done intermittently throughout the year so that in-process adjustments are possible.

- Develop a plan for disseminating the newly designed curriculum that includes ample opportunity for teachers who will use the curriculum to understand the PCM and the intent of the authors. Teachers also need ample opportunity to ask questions about implementation at various stages of teacher comfort with using the unit.

- Develop a plan to ensure that a wide range of stakeholders understands the model and benefits of using it with a wide range of learners. Helping teachers, administrators, parents, and community members understand and appreciate the goals and potential benefits of the model is paramount to application and efficacy of the model and curriculum developed using the model.

There is an unfortunate tendency in educators to revise or reconstruct a new model or approach so that it fits their previous practices rather than adopting the model in a way that honors the "nonnegotiables" of the model. Effective professional development plans with the PCM—or any other worthwhile educational approach—will challenge educators to understand the approach and support them in using the approach so that its integrity is paramount in their thinking and practice.

We wish you well on your journey of discovery, reflection, exploration, and refinement of the PCM in your own schools and classrooms.

Your Story, My Story, History

A Unit for Kindergarten Students

Deborah E. Burns

BACKGROUND FOR UNIT

The study of history is a characteristic part of an intermediate or secondary school curriculum. However, beyond attention to national holidays and key historical figures, the typical kindergartener rarely participates in a history-based curriculum. Can children this young learn discipline-based history content and skills? We think so, as long as we offer them lessons and content that will demonstrate the relationship between what they already know and the new information they are about to discover. Young students' natural curiosity and intrinsic motivation for learning also provide us with compelling reasons for teaching discipline-based content and skills in the primary grades.

This chapter provides seven lessons from a larger Parallel Curriculum Model (PCM) history unit for kindergarteners that incorporates the Core, Connections, Practice, and Identity Parallels. We developed this particular set of lessons to illustrate the four PCM parallels, Ascending Intellectual Demand (AID), and the integral role of ongoing assessment and student observation. Each of the lessons was structured to address one main idea (concept, principle, generalization, or skill) inherent to the study of history and to explore one or more of the facets of history knowledge emphasized in the different PCM parallels. As a result, each lesson requires anywhere from one to six hours to implement. As a whole, the lessons in this chapter unit require about 20 hours of class time to implement.

Students learn about the discipline of history as they study the Core concepts of time, era, change, continuity, story, perspective, artifact, museum, and historian. They practice the Core skills of listening, recalling, retelling, time sequencing, comparing and contrasting, cause and effect, finding relationships, asking questions, making inferences, recording information, and making a presentation. Within the Connections parallel, they explore one of the National Council of Social Studies history themes, namely "time, change, and continuity." The Identity parallel is used as an opportunity for students to find relationships between the history stories of their friends and elders and their own lives. Students come to understand that history is a collection of stories and interpretations about events and objects from the past through their involvement in read-alouds, class discussions, center activities, and think-pair-shares. The Practice parallel is used to investigate and practice the role of a historian. After visiting with a local historian and practicing how to ask and answer inferential questions about historical objects and events, the children assume the role of historians by collecting and sharing a historical artifact from their own family. The students also ask inferential questions about the historical artifacts of their classmates that are stored in the classroom. As a culminating activity, each student contributes to the development of a class museum and a historical book that contains students' historical questions, pictures of the artifacts they analyzed, and their conclusions and answers to their own history questions.

A postassessment is used to evaluate student learning, and a large-group debriefing discussion helps students understand and articulate what they have learned. They discuss what the unit has meant to them and how they see themselves as students of history or as historians. We anticipate a major change in students' knowledge, skills, and expertise as a result of their participation in this unit, but most important, we hope this unit instills a lifelong curiosity and interest in all things historical.

The teachers at Darcey Elementary School in Cheshire, Connecticut, have a long history of working collaboratively to develop and implement teaching and learning activities in the various curriculum areas. The majority of the existing curriculum units incorporate fiction and nonfiction literature; information about holidays and celebrations, science, and social studies content; arts and crafts, music, games, center activities, and field trips; and grade-level math, reading, and writing skills and concepts. The previous social studies curriculum addressed topics and events, such as a trip to a local apple orchard; a trip to local farms; and stories, books, and activities about colonial times, the holidays, and famous people in U.S. history.

The social studies unit from which these lessons are drawn is a revision of an existing set of lessons and activities that provided students with background information about the presidents of the United States and Martin Luther King Jr. The previous curriculum also gave students the opportunity to collect and share a historical family artifact. When revising this unit to emphasize state and national content standards and the Core parallel, the committee wanted to retain and embellish the collecting and sharing of historical artifacts because of their authenticity and motivational value for students.

The committee of four teachers and two administrators who developed this PCM history unit, as part of a federal Javits grant project, began their work by informally surveying all of the kindergarten teachers at Darcey to identify the lessons and activities they currently provided and the time typically allocated for social studies instruction. They discovered that, although the topics in social studies were usually common across classrooms, the teaching methods, student activities, resources, and time allocations varied widely. Few of the teachers were familiar with the state or national standards for history or social studies, and they had no formal training with constructivist learning theory, the PCM, concept-based teaching methods, or constructivist teaching methods and learning strategies. Nevertheless, all of the teachers who implemented the unit had intuitive understanding of each of these concepts and practices.

The first step in the revision process was to review the state and national standards for primary grade history. Concepts such as time, events, inquiry, questioning, change, cause, and evidence were prominent in the standards—concepts that are also core to the discipline of history. All of the committee members agreed with the relevance of these concepts, but they believed their greatest challenge lay in deciding how to address these standards in a coherent and developmentally appropriate manner.

We next introduced the committee of curriculum writers to the steps and procedures for revising and authoring curriculum units and, in particular, to the components and goals of the PCM. We began our work with a discussion of the importance of beginning the curriculum development process with an emphasis on content, followed by discussions about time allocations, assessment, and teaching and learning methods.

Initially, this progression appeared to be counterintuitive. Teachers with little time to work and plan together preferred to use precious meeting time to discuss materials and activities instead. Subsequent conversations resolved these concerns, and we continued the development process with a brainstorming session that identified the key concepts and principles we wanted to stress in this unit. The concepts of history and time; the role of historians, events, people, places, artifacts, and perspectives; and the skills of asking questions, collecting and observing evidence, making inferences, and sharing conclusions emerged from these conversations. Compared with the existing social studies content we had previously offered to our kindergarteners, the challenge level seemed immense.

We spent several meetings discussing how to sequence this content and how much time would be required to implement related activities that would assure student understanding and connections to their own lives, experiences, and families. We decided that no matter what we created this year, we would convene our own lesson study group to discuss the impact of our unit and make appropriate changes.

The printed unit and lessons that resulted from those meetings are living documents. As I write, we are analyzing our students' postassessment tests and revising our first draft of the unit. Our teachers met weekly to compare notes, share anecdotes and student work, and consider changes they would like to implement next year.

CONTENT FRAMEWORK

Organizing Concepts

> **Discipline-Specific Concepts.** History, Story, Timeline, Era, Event, Artifact, Historian, Museum
>
> **Macroconcept.** Time, Continuity, Change

Principles and Generalizations

G1 History is a collection of people's stories about events, people, places, and things from the past.

G2 We can learn new things about the past by reading and listening to history stories.

G3 History stories took place at different times in the past.

G4 All generations of people have their own stories about the events in their lifetime.

G5 Different generations of people have different lifestyles.

G6 History stories help us find similarities and differences, changes, and causes.

G7 Most objects we use today existed in the past in another form.

G8 History stories often tell about continuity and change over time and the reasons for changes.

G9 Historians ask questions, gather evidence, and share their learning with others.

G10 Museums are one of the places where historians share their knowledge with others.

History Standards

SD1 Identify historical data from multiple sources.

SD2 Engage in reading challenging primary and secondary historical source materials.

SD3 Create timelines that sequence events and people, using days, weeks, and months.

SD4 Write short statements of historical ideas and create other appropriate narrative presentations from investigations of source materials.

SD5 Locate people, places, and events in time and place.

Skills

S1   Attending
S2   Listening
S3   Remembering
S4   Retelling
S5   Describing
S6   Sequencing
S7   Asking questions
S8   Making inferences
S9   Comparing and contrasting
S10 Using evidence
S11 Categorizing
S12 Drawing conclusions

MAKING SURE THE PARALLELS REMAIN CENTRAL IN TEACHING AND LEARNING

Curriculum Component	Component Descriptions and Rationale
Content	Learning objectives for this unit address Core parallel concepts, skills, generalizations, and principles and attend to related content standards in the discipline of history. Additional objectives in the Connections parallel address the macroconcepts of time, continuity, and change, a major theme in all of the social sciences. A third set of skill and application objectives is closely tied to the Practice parallel; students are expected to learn and apply the questioning, reasoning, and product development skills of a historian. Objectives from the Identity parallel are also incorporated in this unit; students have numerous opportunities to see themselves as historians, to develop and display curiosity and enthusiasm for history, to empathize with historical figures, and to find relationships among historical events, their own lives, and contemporary lifestyles.
Assessments	The preassessment and postassessment for this unit measure students' summative knowledge of a sample set of Core content and skill objectives, specifically the concept of history, the ability to retell a history story, the ability to ask a historical question, and the ability to make a historical inference.
	Student assignments, products, and behaviors are used as formative assessments of student learning and progress. Rubrics and assignments provide a way for teachers to measure the Core parallel concepts of history, artifacts, and the past as well as a few basic thinking skills. In addition, assessments address the Connections concepts of time, change, and continuity, the skills and products of a historian in the Practice parallel, and the extent to which students demonstrate curiosity and can empathize with historical figures and see relationships among historical people, events, and their own lives in the Identity parallel.
Introductory activities	There are three introductory activities in this unit. First, a stratified, random set of students participates in a preassessment using a scripted set of interview questions designed to measure a sample set of Core concepts, skills, and generalizations. Teachers use this information to make minor adjustments to the lesson plans or as a forewarning about the need to modify the content and activities or to add Ascending Intellectual Demand (AID) opportunities. Next, all of the students have the opportunity to share their understanding of the Core concept of history

(Continued)

(Continued)

Curriculum Component	Component Descriptions and Rationale
	and learn about the ideas of other students in the class. Then the children participate in a read-aloud using the book *Who Came Down That Road?*, which introduces the concept of era and time from the Core parallel. A visual analogy of time as a path down a winding road further reinforces this Core concept. Later, students participate in a think-pair-share activity that introduces some of the Identity parallel objectives and helps them share their perspectives about the history story and attend to the perspectives of their partners in the class. Last, the teacher shares a brief overview of the unit's activities in order to enhance student motivation to learn, curiosity, and enthusiasm.
Teaching strategies	The teaching methods in this unit range from direct instruction to mentoring. Each teaching method was selected purposefully to attend to a specific learning objective and the students' current levels of expertise. Whenever possible, teachers use questioning, feedback, discussion, dialogue, and coaching to encourage students to think for themselves, to learn from each other, and to build their own understanding of the content objectives and skills within this unit. However, if preassessment data suggest that a skill or concept is new for most students, direct instruction is used to explain, model, or practice the content with the novice learners. A visit by a community historian and the development of a simulated class museum, under the mentoring of the classroom teacher, fosters the Practice parallel learning objectives. Read-alouds, class discussion, and partner dialogues are used to address Core parallel objectives. Read-alouds, Socratic questioning, and cognitive coaching are used to foster Core, Practice, and Connections parallel learning objectives.
Learning activities	The learning activities for this PCM unit were designed using a three-part format. For each activity, (1) the content or skill objective (e.g., understand the concept of history, estimate the era of a historical event, make a historical inference, empathize with a historical figure) was carefully aligned with (2) the thinking skill(s) that students would use to achieve that objective (e.g., attend, observe, find characteristics, compare and contrast, recall, find a relationship, make an analogy, etc.) and (3) the activity students would do (e.g., listen, read, draw, discuss, share, watch, question, touch, talk) to input, process, and transfer new information and skills before, during, and after learning.

Curriculum Component	Component Descriptions and Rationale
	For this reason, opportunities for active participation, thinking, and application are crucial to student achievement. Although students listen to stories, watch a videotape, and participate in a presentation and demonstration, they never act as passive learners. Journaling, think-pair-shares, sketching, presenting, discussions, and opportunities to ask their own questions, make inferences, and draw conclusions are ongoing and frequent.
	Thinking skills, such as finding relationships and making analogies and generalizations, are used more frequently with Connections parallel content objectives. Skills such as planning, problem solving, and decision making facilitate Practice parallel objectives. Analytical skills are used more frequently with Core parallel learning objectives, and critical thinking and decision-making skills are used more often with Identity parallel learning objectives.
Grouping strategies	This unit provides opportunities for students to work in various sized groups (e.g., whole-class groups, pairs, small groups, tutoring with parents, conferencing with the teacher, and working independently). The learning objectives and students' level of proficiency dictate the nature of the grouping practices. For example, large-group activities, partnering, conferencing with a teacher, and opportunities for independent reflection facilitate Identity parallel objectives regarding empathy. Given the age of these students, the Practice parallel objectives that ask students to practice the skills of a professional historian are best addressed in small groups and during tutoring and conferencing sessions with the teacher.
	The Core parallel concepts, skills, and generalizations are introduced, demonstrated, and practiced during large-group teacher-led discussions, with large-group teacher modeling and examples, and during small-group center time. The Connections parallel macroconcepts of time, continuity, and change are most easily facilitated during large-group discussions and during individual conference time between the teacher and students.
Products	Decisions about the nature of student products and assignments are closely tied to the age and ability level of our students and our desire to collect and analyze evidence of their new learning. Drawings with "invented spelling" captions, lists, whole-class chart stories, whole-class and personal reflections, time-sequenced illustrations, storytelling, and presentations are all incorporated into the unit.

(Continued)

(Continued)

Curriculum Component	Component Descriptions and Rationale
	Parents' favorite student assignment requires parent participation and cooperation. We ask them to share a personal story about a historical event in their lives that demonstrates the concept of change. The parents are asked to tell the story to their child, and the children retell the story to the teacher and their classmates. The teacher takes verbatim notes from each child's retelling. The results are fascinating, funny, and joyful. Of course, they are shared with the parents and probably saved in a vault for all of posterity!
	Parents also help by providing a historical artifact from their family that students bring to school and display in a class museum. Students ask and answer historical questions about classmates' artifacts and "write" related reports for their artifact display. The museum is clearly a highlight of the unit and for the students.
Resources	A dozen different picture books about history concepts, events, and historical people provide the backbone for this unit. We were lucky enough to find an age-appropriate, commercial videotape about history for students to watch. Teachers, parents, and community members graciously supplied a wonderful assortment of historical artifacts and stories, and the school principal, her friend and colleague at a local university, and the student technology department at the high school kindly agreed to create and produce a videotape about the nature and purpose of a museum and the role of a curator and historian. We depend on Google image searches and laminating film to create poster-size and 8- × 10-inch enlargements of historical pictures. Chart paper is used extensively to record students' comments and reflections and to create a giant historical timeline for the class. We also created parent letters, assessments, rubrics, and reflection journals for the unit. Sketch paper, markers, crayons, and story paper are used for story retelling and the labeling of artifacts for the class museum.
	It was time-consuming, but not impossible, to locate picture books that dealt with Core parallel concepts and generalizations, although it was always easier to find a picture book about a historical event or person than one with a historical idea or generalization related to the Core parallel. We also experienced a shortage of books for primary-grade students that addressed people, cultures, or events before the nineteenth century. The use of pictures and teacher explanations helped bridge both gaps. The books and videotape used in this unit came from either

Curriculum Component	Component Descriptions and Rationale
	the school or the town library. The unit requires only one book of each kind per teacher. The type of book used is more important than the specific title.
Extension activities	Given the typical time constraints of a kindergarten program that serves children for only 2.5 hours a day, many of the unit's extension activities are offered to parents and students as suggestions in parent-teacher notes, e-mails, and newsletters. Several of the parents stopped by the classroom at the end or the beginning of the day, and that contact provided teachers with additional opportunities to share ideas with parents for extension activities that might be of special interest to their child, activities he or she could pursue at home or within the community. In some cases, teachers were able to create additional, optional center activities for students with special or intense interest in certain topics or activities. Some of the extension activities encouraged students to tell additional family history stories or to illustrate some of the history stories they had heard from other students. Some students became interested in making their own historical timelines to show how transportation, toys, clothing, telephones, or games had changed over time.
Modifications for learner need, including Ascending Intellectual Demand (AID)	Our introductory discussions at the beginning of the unit make it easy to identify those students who are ready for more complex learning. We use differentiated questioning strategies, tiered assignments, and opportunities to conference with the teacher to support students' advanced abilities. Advanced students have the opportunity to learn in-depth information about historical figures and events, develop a sophisticated understanding of time, decades, and centuries, and produce lengthy invented spelling stories about history. One or two students in each class had cursory knowledge of some historical information at the beginning of the unit, several more exhibited strong interest and curiosity in history, and at least 30 percent of the class demonstrated advanced vocabulary and analytic thinking skills. Several of these students were able to learn in-depth information about historical figures and events, and they developed a sophisticated understanding of time, decades, and centuries that other students weren't quite ready to learn. Some of them produced lengthy invented spelling stories about history, and many of their parents reported long and involved dinner conversations about historical topics discussed at school. We anticipate a great deal more interest in museum experiences from all of the children.

UNIT SEQUENCE, DESCRIPTION, AND TEACHER REFLECTIONS

Lesson 1: Preassessment of Students' Prior Knowledge

(90 minutes for the teacher and 10 minutes for each student)

Unit Sequence	Teacher Reflections
Concepts. History, Stories, Events, Artifact G1, G3, P7, SD1, SD4–5, S1–2, S5 Select a group of six students for the interviews. Choose three with advanced abilities, two with average achievement, and one student with below-grade-level achievement. Review the set of interview questions (below) that sample the major skills, concepts, generalizations, and principles embedded in this unit. These questions are meant to elicit students' current understandings about the concepts of history, time sequences, change, historical events, and historical artifacts. Each interview requires approximately 10 minutes. The teacher must pose each of the 11 open-ended questions and script the main ideas in each student's response. Printing copies of the interview questions with three to five inches of response space supports this process. A five-point summated rating (5 = correct response with elaboration; 4 = accurate and complete response; 3 = partially correct response; 2 = incorrect or tangential response; 1 = no response, or student responds that she or he does not know) should be used to assess varied students' present degree of understanding. Be sure to explain to the students why you are asking the questions and why you are talking to them in private. If necessary spend two to three minutes making each student feel comfortable and confident before asking any of the interview questions.	This preassessment does not measure all of the unit's learning objectives. Like any assessment, it samples only some of the more important concepts, generalizations, and skills. We knew that we didn't have the time or the personnel to preassess every student in each of the kindergarten classes. Since our major goal was to measure the extent to which our new curriculum unit fostered student learning and challenged our students, we decided to preassess and postassess only a sample of the students in each class. Because our district serves a high number (40 percent) of students with advanced cognitive skills and academic achievement, we decided to preassess a representative sample of our student body. In each class, we randomly selected three students working above grade level, two students at grade level, and one student below grade level. We repeated the preassessment procedures in 6 of our 19 kindergarten classrooms. One of our instructional specialists, Kay Rasmussen, and the building principal, Barbara Stern, volunteered to conduct the assessments so that the classroom teachers could spend more time with their students. None of our students appeared uncomfortable or frightened during the interviews. In fact, they were all eager to spend some one-on-one time with the adults who conducted the assessments. We think we got valid and reliable responses from all of the children with whom we worked.

Unit Sequence	*Teacher Reflections*

The interview questions include the following:

1. What does the word *history* mean?

2. Can you tell me a history story about something or someone from the past?

3. Can you tell me what historians do? What is their job?

4. Why do you think people learn about history?

5. Do you like history? What do you like about it?

6. When people talk about history and about things that happened in the past, what do they mean by the "past"?

7. Where do people go or what do they do when they want to learn about history?

8. I am going to show you a picture of a historical object. Can you tell me some questions you might like to ask about this object? (Repeat with pictures of two different historical objects, e.g., a wringer washing machine and a wooden pitchfork.)

9. I am going to show you a picture of a historical object. Can you use the information in the picture and what you know about objects we use today to make some guess about what this object is, how it was made, or how it was used? (Repeat with pictures of two historical objects, e.g., Conestoga wagon and a 1920s vintage typewriter.)

As soon as possible after the last interview, spend a few minutes scoring the assessments and jotting notes about your reflections regarding differences among students.

Most of our students had no idea what the world *history* means, and they were very comfortable in saying, "I don't know."

Others told us that history was "about dinosaurs."

One young lady said, "I went to the Museum of Natural History in New York. I don't know what it means!"

Another student told us, "Jesus died 2,000 years ago."

Yet another, with a very serious look on his face, told us, "History means something you can't see. People think it's real, but we don't actually know yet."

One child said, "History is stuff from a long time ago that was really important, like the war on Bunker Hill. I saw it on *Liberty Kids*."

All of the students in the preassessment group were ready to take a guess about how a pitchfork, a wringer washing machine, and a Conestoga wagon were used. From their responses, we knew that we probably had only to encourage their historical inferences and give the skill of "inferencing" a name. They showed no hesitation about using whatever available information they had to draw a logical conclusion.

On the other hand, the ability to ask a historical question was more difficult for most students. It occurred to us that many of them had repeated opportunities to respond to adults' questions, but few of them appeared comfortable asking their own questions. We knew this skill would be one that we would need to emphasize during the unit.

The preassessment made it easy to see that we needed to adjust some of our questions, information, and tasks to address the wide range of skills and prior knowledge in our class. The need for AID was apparent, and early on we recognized the need to share more sophisticated examples and encourage more abstract questions from some of the students. There was no shortage of enthusiasm, however, from any of the students, and we left the preassessment task convinced that all of the children would retain or increase their curiosity for history content.

Lesson 2: What Is History?

(60 minutes)

Unit Sequence	Teacher Reflections
Concepts. History, Stories, Events, Artifact G1–3, G8, SD1–2, SD5, S1–2, S5 In preparation for the introductory lesson, find and set up an easel chart, chart paper, markers, blank paper, and at least three sticky notes for each student. Set aside a crayon and a marker for each student to use in the history center after they have listened to your read-aloud story. Write the word *history* in large manuscript letters on the chart paper and locate a copy of the picture book *Who Came Down That Road?* by George Lyon, 1992, Barton Press. Ask opened-ended questions, attuned to the varying levels of prior knowledge, language skills, or social skills of your students, to help them communicate what they already know about history and their insights about each page of the picture book.	With time so short in most kindergarten classes, advanced preparation can be a real asset. We knew the kindergarteners at Darcey School were already comfortable with the use of centers in the classrooms, but the introduction of a new center, a history center, required some advanced preparation on our part. We also had to consider how best to orient the students to the purpose for this center. The preassessment task forewarned us of the need to prepare examples, tasks, and questions that would challenge all of our students, regardless of their level of prior knowledge. We purposely chose a picture book (*Who Came Down That Road?*) that could be enjoyed by children who demonstrated various levels of experience and abstraction.
If you have not already done so, teach students how to sit on the reading or meeting rug for a read-aloud. Teach them how to participate in a think-pair-share by listening to and thinking about a question posed by the teacher and pivoting to face their assigned or selected partners with legs crossed. Everyone on the rug should take turns sharing a response to the teacher's first question with his or her partner and listening to the partner's response.	We wanted to make sure that we allocated enough time for the discussion and read-aloud to provide all students with an opportunity to share their ideas. Even more important, we wanted to begin the unit with clear expectations regarding students' role as learners. Some kindergarten students, like some adults, are so eager to share their experiences with others that they forget to listen, enjoy, and learn from the experiences of others. The first part of this lesson was designed to teach them how to listen to adults and peers and how to respond to others' ideas.

Unit Sequence	*Teacher Reflections*

Modifications for Learner Need. Advanced pairs should be encouraged to find similarities and differences in their two sets of responses. Convene the class on the meeting rug in front of the easel and chart paper. Tell students that the class is about to begin a new set of activities about *history,* the word that is printed in the chart paper. Repeat the word slowly and ask students if any of them has ever heard the word before. Allow students an opportunity to share their ideas about the word's meaning.

Share the correct, but age-appropriate, definition of *history* as a story about past events, people, places, or objects. Use the word *artifact* and explain that it describes any old or historical objects that people might find or save to help them understand history or to tell history stories. Ask students if they have any old history objects in their home or in their family. Give them a chance to share the names of these artifacts. List them and the corresponding names of the students who shared the artifacts.

Tell students that during the next few weeks they will be learning about history events, the names of artifacts, people, objects, and places by listening to stories, watching a video, and collecting and sharing their own artifacts and history stories. Remind them that their job during the lessons is to listen carefully to other people's ideas, share their own ideas, and talk with their parents about what they are learning. Tell them that they will have the chance to act like historians by collecting and sharing their own set of historical stories and artifacts. They will also be involved in creating a classroom museum that they can visit to ask and answer their own history questions and create their own history stories.

We were surprised at the number of students who had never heard the word *history* before. We were just as surprised to find that several students had extensive background knowledge of history, much more than any of us had anticipated. In the future, we plan to use another sheet of chart paper to record students' responses and the names of the students who shared each idea.

We think it is important that all students have an opportunity to contribute, even if their concept of history is inaccurate. Other students might be asked to help the class name the letters or the sounds in the word so that everyone has a chance to contribute to the lesson.

One of the ten kindergarten teachers in our school district, Terri LaChance, had a clever idea. She decided to videotape a class discussion during the first day of the unit. Before the beginning of the discussion, she printed the word *history* on chart paper, showed it to the students sitting in front of her, and asked them to take turns explaining to the "camera" the meaning of the word. Each of the students was eager to share her or his ideas. At the end of the unit, Terri made another videotape of a class discussion. Again, she asked the students to describe the meaning of the word history. The difference between their earlier and later responses was nothing short of amazing.

Providing students with an opportunity to find and share examples of history stories and artifacts from their own life offered a wonderful occasion to personalize students' learning.

(Continued)

(Continued)

Unit Sequence	Teacher Reflections
Draw two sketches, one of a winding dirt road with four bends in it and one of a clock, underneath the word *history* on the chart paper. Tell students that studying history is like taking a trip by traveling down a road to the past; the longer we travel back into time, the more we can learn about the past, the people, the events, and the objects from long ago. Tell students that some history stories are about events that happened only a short distance down the time road (such as their first birthday). Draw a birthday candle before the first bend in the road to represent their first birthday.	Some of the teachers on the staff were unsure about the extent to which kindergarten children could grasp the abstract concept of time, especially when we started to talk about time spans of hundreds and thousands of years. Drawing a concrete analogy of time as a long road, and history as a way of traveling down this road, seemed to help the children understand these two abstract concepts. We will search for additional ideas to explain time sequencing to the children as we revise the unit next year. Throughout the unit, we will continue to use this analogy of history as travel down the road of time. During the next few lessons, the class will create a simple, but large timeline using the same winding road and icons (e.g., birthday candle, astronaut, horse and wagon). As we read and discuss various stories about historical people and events, the children will draw related pictures and glue their pictures near the appropriate era of the class timeline. We hope these repeated experiences will lead to a deeper understanding of the Core parallel concepts of time and era.
Tell them that some history stories are farther down the road, such as the history stories about their parents' childhood or when astronauts first traveled to the moon. Draw a picture of a moon or a stick figure of an astronaut after the first bend in the road.	
Tell students that other history stories are even farther down the time travel road (point to a place after the second bend in the road), such as the stories about people who rode in carriages and wagons before there were cars. Draw a corresponding picture of a horse and wagon after the second bend in the road.	
Tell students that there are still other, older, history stories that tell of times when only the Native Americans lived in this country. Draw a corresponding picture of a Native American after the third bend in the road.	We discovered that several children wanted to share their knowledge of related events that occurred during each "bend" in the time travel road. Again, allowing them an opportunity to talk about and sequence these events provided the initial practice needed to advance their skills in a topic important to practicing historians. We kept watching for students with an advanced sense of time and sequencing, as such students would be prime candidates for AID activities.
Mention that the oldest of history stories tell of a time when there were only plants and animals but no people living on the Earth. Draw a corresponding picture of a dinosaur after the fourth bend in the road.	
Tell students that they are going to listen to a story that shows them what would happen if they were to walk down that history road and travel back in time. Ask them to listen to the story and see if they can discover what the mother and her son learn as they travel back in time along the history road.	

Unit Sequence	Teacher Reflections

Read *Who Came Down That Road?* to the students, pausing at each page to show them the pictures, and point out how long ago each event occurred. Make reference to the picture of the bends in the road that you drew earlier. Pause as appropriate after a page or two to share your own reflections about a picture or passage. At other times ask students to raise their hands and share their reflections with the class or let them conduct a think-pair-share with one or two of the questions printed below:

  a. Have you ever wondered who was in your house before you lived there? What do you wonder or know about this?

  b. Have you ever wondered where your parents lived or what they did when they were in kindergarten? What do you wonder or know about this?

  c. Have you ever wondered who lived in this town or who went to Darcey School before you were born? What do you wonder or know about this?

Debriefing. After you finish the book, ask students to think-pair-share with each other to summarize the sequence and the main ideas in the book. As they talk with each other, walk around the rug with a clipboard, a checklist, or sticky notes listening to students' comments to each other, and record notes about their present levels of understanding. You may want to use **Lesson 2 Rubric: Conceptual Understandings of History** to help you in these determinations.

Several years ago, Carol Tomlinson shared this wonderful book with a group of educators. I enjoyed it when she read it to us and marveled at the author's and illustrator's ability to explain such a difficult idea to young children. When I read the book to children in my family, in our neighborhood, and in our district, the experience convinced me to suggest it as the centerpiece for the introduction of this unit. Maybe it's the fact that I've always found visual analogies and metaphors personally appealing that made me so enthusiastic about using the book in this unit. Thank goodness I work with a group of people who, although apprehensive that the book's ideas might be too sophisticated for five-year-olds, were willing to try it anyway.

This lesson also provides an opportunity to teach content, pose a question, conduct an activity, and make an assignment that asks students to extend the discipline-based Core knowledge they are learning. Students are asked to identify how this content relates to their own attitudes, experiences, and interests (Identity). They are also asked to make interdisciplinary Connections and to become involved in activities in which their Core learning can incorporate the Practice or tools of real-world professionals in this field.

Using the think-pair-share strategy also seemed to help listening comprehension a great deal.

A checklist, with students' names in the first column and the four concepts in the columns to the right, supports ongoing assessment. During the course of the unit the teacher can engage in conversations with individual students to assess their understanding of these concepts and use the rubric to document progress and change. This is also a good time to identify those students who could benefit from more challenging content, questions, or tasks because of their prior knowledge or cognitive abilities.

(Continued)

(Continued)

Unit Sequence	*Teacher Reflections*
Before you dismiss students from the rug to begin other activities, explain to them that sometime in the next few days you want each of them to visit the history center that you have organized in the classroom. Show them the picture of the winding road and tell them that this picture will help identify where this center is in their room. Show them the word *history* again and tell them that the word will also be on the sign indicating the history center. Tell them that when they visit the history center, they are to use their new learning about history, the past, events, and artifacts to draw a picture of a winding road with the crayons. Then, direct them to draw three smaller pictures from history, artifacts, people, events, or places and to place them in the appropriate sequence on their history road.	If possible, ask an aide to work with the students when they visit the history center. The aide can record the students' dictation and the names they offer for each of the pictures they draw on the sticky notes. We also suggest dating and keeping the pictures the students draw as part of their work portfolio for this unit. Parents will appreciate this record of their child's learning, and teachers can later refer to these portfolios as they work in groups to revise the unit for next year.
Close the lesson by telling students what excites you about the upcoming history unit and what pleased you about their work today. Ask them what excites them or makes them happy about the new history unit. If time permits, record their responses and names on chart paper.	The ideas and information that students mention during this discussion can be shared with parents by e-mail, on a teacher's Web site, or during parent conferences.
Last, ask them to think about what they will tell their parents when they get home about what they learned in school today. Try to elicit these responses in a round-robin brainstorming session.	The teachers who use this unit again next year will probably continue to meet as a group once or twice a month to compare notes, share experiences, discuss student learning, and brainstorm ways to improve the unit. It is important to remember that what works in one place may need to be revised to succeed in a classroom that has different expectations, time frames, groups of students, content goals, or levels of resources. By evaluating student similarities and differences across classrooms or from year to year, we can more easily predict and identify the curriculum components (e.g., the content objectives, assessments, teaching methods, learning activities, grouping practices, resources, student assignments, differentiation strategies, pacing recommendations, and
After the students have left for the day, take a minute to record your own reflections about the lesson using sticky notes, and place them in the appropriate section of the lesson for future use and revision.	
If possible, spend some time making informal notes or observations about each student's current level of expertise with regard to the learning objectives for the unit. Again, the Lesson 2 rubric might be	

Unit Sequence	*Teacher Reflections*

useful. Unlike the summative unit assessment we used at the beginning of this unit, the assessment rubric is designed to provide formative information about students' understanding and learning. It should be used to signal a need for lesson revision or for AID opportunities. It can also be used as an ongoing assessment to measure and report the progress students make and their gains in expertise from the beginning to the end of the unit.
 	
The objectives for this lesson are all conceptual in nature. Use questions, discussions, conversations, and students' responses to assess student learning with regard to these Core parallel guiding questions:
 	
    What is history?
 	
    What is the "past"?
 	
    What is an event?
 	
    What is an artifact (historical object)? (AID)
	parallels) that may need to be revised to best suit the needs of students in other classrooms.
	
	Teachers in Japan often use a technique called "lesson study" to examine and revise an existing set of lessons to make them more efficient, effective, or appropriate. We plan to meet together to revise this unit for several years to come. We may add or delete learning objectives, change the parallels, modify the time expectations, or use different questions, activities, or resources to make the unit more successful with our students. In addition to improving the appropriateness of the unit, our team's lesson study, personal attention, and creative alterations are also likely to enhance our shared vision, ownership, and curriculum fidelity. Nothing works better than "doctoring" a recipe to create pride for the cook and satisfaction for the taste-testers.

Lesson 3: Tools We Use to Learn History

(60 minutes for group lesson and 30 minutes for individual center activities)

Unit Sequence	*Teacher Reflections*
Concepts. History, Stories G1, SD2, S1–6 Exposing young students to history stories is no guarantee that they will attend to these stories, understand them, be able to remember them, or be able to use the story content in a relevant application. To learn through listening, the listener must employ at least five different thinking skills. This short, 60-minute lesson and related center activities provide students with an opportunity to review the attending, listening, sequencing, visualizing, and retelling skills that improve their ability to learn and remember new history content.	One of the strategies that helped us design appropriate PCM lessons for this unit was the use of guiding questions. We reviewed the reflection questions in *The Parallel Curriculum* (Tomlinson et al., 2002) for each of the four parallels. We used these reflection questions as "prompts" to identify our Core, Practice, Identity, and Practice questions and to frame each lesson and its AID opportunities.

(Continued)

(Continued)

Unit Sequence	Teacher Reflections
Draw and post five pictures on large paper that will serve as visual cues for the following thinking skills: a. **Attending** (a picture of a horse with blinders) b. **Listening** (a picture of a person cupping his or her ear) c. **Sequencing** (a picture of a hand and its five fingers) d. **Visualizing** (a picture of person with a thought bubble above the head) e. **Retelling** (a picture of a tape recorder) Write the corresponding thinking skill underneath each picture. Create a one-page, 8- × 11-inch sheet of paper that contains miniature versions of the five drawings and words. Duplicate these miniatures for the students' use. You will need one pair of scissors for each student. Gather three to five brief history stories (that require two to three minutes to read aloud) for use during the lesson. Place the history story audiocassettes, tape player, and headphones in the listening or history center. Gather all students together on the rug and in front of the place where you have mounted the five pictures. Have the easel, markers, and chart paper handy.	For example, because this lesson focuses primarily on the Core parallel and on AID, we reviewed the Core focusing questions on pages 20–21 of *The Parallel Curriculum* and the related AID focusing questions on page 22. We quickly chose the last question on page 20 as central to this lesson: How can I use these ideas and skills? The first, third, and eighth bullets from page 22 seemed to be appropriate ways to provide AID for those students who were ready to work with these ideas and skills at more expert levels: • Using more advanced reading, resources, and research materials • Developing rubrics for tasks and/or products that articulate levels of quality that include expert-level indicators • Designing work that requires continuing student reflection on the significance of ideas and information and causes students to generate new and useful ways to represent ideas and information
Tell students that this is the beginning of their second history lesson. Ask the students if any of them remembers what he or she did during the first lesson. Ask if anyone is willing to share what she or he remembers or thinks was new learning or most important about the lesson. If appropriate, clarify the meaning of the term *history*, and respond to any new history examples students might share. Ask two to three volunteers to summarize how to conduct a think-pair-share. Ask other students to offer their reflections about what was new, interesting, or puzzling about the think-pair-share strategy or about the last lesson in general.	A quick review is a useful strategy to help students attend to instruction and link new learning to their prior knowledge. The trick is asking the right questions and allowing time for students to comment and reflect. Consider writing the students' reflections and comments on a piece of chart paper and/or making notes related to student ideas as you listen to their reflections. **Optional Extensions** • Ask if students can describe history questions they might want to explore or investigate during this unit.

Unit Sequence	Teacher Reflections
As a segue to the second lesson, tell students that the reason the class is going to continue studying history is to learn new ideas and information that will be useful and interesting to them.	• If time permits, ask interested students to share any examples or reasons that explain why or how history is interesting or exciting to them.
Ask students if they know what a person has to do or use in order to learn history. Elicit ideas from individuals. Reinforce the idea that we learn by thinking.	• A sketch or diagram of a human brain might be an interesting additional resource for this part of the lesson. Some children may not know that thinking occurs in the brain. Others may be interested in learning that they can control and monitor their own thinking. Still others might find it interesting to discover that we can learn how to be better thinkers.
Tell students that today they are going to learn how to use their "thinking caps" to help them become wonderful history learners. Ask them if they know where their "thinking cap" is. Allow one to two minutes for various students to describe what they believe "thinking" is, how they go about thinking, or examples of their own thinking.	A decorated or gaudy cap might also make an interested prop and visual example of a "thinking cap."
Tell students that good history learners have a set of at least five thinking "tricks" they use to help them learn about history. Tell them that today you will show these "tricks" to them and help them decide if they already know how to use them.	
Show students each of the five thinking tricks posters, in order. Explain how each of the graphics depicts the skill. Create a hand cue that represents each of the skills (e.g., cup your hands on each temple to represent blinders; cup your hand to your ear to represent listening; hold up each of five fingers, in order, to represent sequencing; point a finger to the back of your head while you gaze upward to represent visualizing; and hold your hand in front of your mouth while bending your fingers to touch your thumb in rapid succession to represent talking). Explain and demonstrate the hand cues to the students. Make sure each student understands what the graphic or hand cue represents, the name of the skill, why that thinking skill is useful, how to use that thinking skill, and when to use the skill.	This lesson incorporates the use of visual and hand cues, examples, modeling, reflection, and short practice activities to help students remember and use the five skills that enhance aural learning and comprehension. Students should practice each hand signal and its related skill in preparation for the various history stories they will listen to and discuss during the next four lessons.

(Continued)

(Continued)

Unit Sequence	Teacher Reflections
Provide an opportunity for students to share stories about when they used one or more of these skills. Tell students that you are going to demonstrate how to use of each of these skills, as you read a brief history story to them. As you read the story aloud, pause briefly at the beginning, in the middle or during, and at the end of the story to tell students which of the five thinking skills you are using. Ask volunteers to point to the appropriate cue picture and poster.	**Modifications for Learner Need.** Observe students carefully to identify anyone who seems confused about the words that are used to describe the skills. Use synonyms or encourage the students to ask clarifying questions to help them identify the kind of thinking you are describing. ESL students may benefit from a translation of the English word into their own language. If you notice that some students still don't grasp the skill or the terminology after you have explained it, demonstrated it, and reflected on your use of the skill while reading the story, you can be pretty sure that you will need to work with these students in a small group. Consider scheduling this group to meet during center time, when other students are working with the taped stories. If you can identify which of the thinking skills are more difficult for some of the students, plan to have your small-group work focus more attention on these skills.
Ask students to find a partner in the room and to spend one to two minutes with their partner reviewing each of the posters, in order, and telling each other what they should do when they see or hear that cue from the teacher. Rotate around the room and provide feedback and coaching as needed. Reconvene the large group on the rug and tell students that they are going to practice using these thinking skills with a new history story that you are going to read to them. Begin to read the first two to three sentences from one of the brief history stories. As you begin the story, pause and point to the picture poster of the horse with blinders. Ask students to tell you which thinking skill (attending) they should be using as they begin to listen. As you read the remainder of the story aloud, pause briefly at appropriate parts in the story, point to the appropriate cue poster, and ask students to stop, think, and use the skill you indicate.	**Modifications for Learner Need.** If necessary, the teacher should become partners with the students in the room who are experiencing the most difficulty. If you notice that some students catch on quickly, be sure to note this in the skill rubric that accompanies this lesson. You may want to consider adding an alternate skill for these students to practice. Expert listeners, comprehenders, and readers also make "text-to-self" connections while they are listening or reading. This skill is especially appropriate for advanced students of this age. Add a related graphic and cue card to your set of posters if you do decide to add this additional skill for some learners.

Unit Sequence	Teacher Reflections

Repeat the process with another history story. This time, ask a student volunteer to stand next to the posters and point to the appropriate poster as you prompt students to use each of the five skills during the reading of the story.

If you notice that the children are beginning to lose focus and can't attend to instruction, end the lesson after one story. Begin the lesson again tomorrow or after a stretch break, a special activity, or center time.

Repeat the practice a third time, with a new history story, but instead of prompting the students, pause five to seven times during the course of the reading and ask volunteer students to tell the rest of the class which thinking skill they are using in their minds at that particular point in time. Ask volunteers to point to the appropriate cue picture and poster.

Modifications for Learner Need. You may discover that some of the advanced students have difficulty waiting and watching your demonstration. They are eager to share an anecdote about their use of the skill or to tell you that they used a different listening and thinking skill than the one you just demonstrated. It's fine to acknowledge their contributions and to let all students know that different people use these skills at different times, but they need to remember that by interrupting your demonstration they may be making it harder for other students to focus on your examples or to learn from the demonstration. Tell them that they will have a chance to reflect on their own thinking during the next activity. Remind them that good learners must also be patient as other people engage in the learning process.

Give students a copy of the miniature cue cards and a pair of scissors and ask them to cut out the cue cards and place them in front of them. Read a fourth history story and point to various cue posters while asking students to hold up the appropriate cue card and use that skill in their mind to help them learn the content of the history story you are reading. At the end of this practice session, ask volunteers to evaluate their use of the skill (e.g., Did you use this skill? Which skill is the easiest? Which skill is the hardest? Which skill did you forget to use?).

You might also convene a small group of students who already know how to retell the details and main idea of the story while the rest of the class works with a partner on the fifth skill, retelling. Ask the advanced students to try to retell only the "most important" parts of the story. Encourage them to think before they share with their partner. Ask them to try to "summarize" the story with as few words as possible.

Here is an opportunity for advanced learners to work together and use a think-pair-share strategy to practice making text-to-self connections.

Again, if you notice that the students are restless after the story, end the session and continue the lesson tomorrow.

(Continued)

(Continued)

Unit Sequence	Teacher Reflections
For the fifth and last practice session, tell students to turn again to their partners, keeping their pile of cue cards in front of them. Tell them that you are going to read one more history story and that you will prompt them to use each of the five thinking skills. When you prompt them, they are to hold up the correct thinking card and use that skill to learn the content and ideas in the story. As you finish the story, point to the last poster (retelling) and ask students to take turns retelling the history story to their partners.	**AID.** Be careful about assuming that students who have initial difficulties with the skills will continue to have difficulty or that the skills are not "developmentally appropriate" for them. The "power law of learning" (see, e.g., Erev & Roth, 1998, 1999; Roth & Erev, 1995) suggests a steep learning curve at the beginning of instruction. With enough practice opportunities, many of the students who are novices at the beginning of the lesson will reach expert status after 12 to 15 practice opportunities. Stay the course and give them the practice, feedback, and encouragement they need to succeed.
	Modifications for Learner Need. If you notice that a few of the students are already active listeners and don't need your prompting to use the skills, consider having these students meet together, with a parent volunteer or a teacher's aide, in a corner of the room. Ask the aide or volunteer to read a different story to these students, possibly a longer story, one with more sophisticated content (e.g., *Pompeii . . . Buried Alive*, by Edith Kunhardt-Davis, a Step Into Reading book by Random House).
	Modifications for Learner Need. If more practice is needed to help students attend, listen, sequence, visualize, or retell, consider extending the use of the practice sessions to include your daily read-alouds in language arts, using picture books and fiction books that aren't related to history. Still more practice could be provided by using the picture cues and your own prompting during daily or weekly show-and-tell sessions. Either way provides an excellent opportunity to show students how these skills can transfer to other subject areas.

Unit Sequence	*Teacher Reflections*

Provide an opportunity for students to become independent users of these five thinking skills and to monitor and describe their own thought processes (metacognition) by asking them to use center time to listen again to the five history stories, using the audiocassettes, audiocassette player, headphones, and miniature cue cards. As the students listen to one or more of the stories, they should point to the appropriate cue cards as they realize they are using that skill. Of course, the retelling skill should be used last, ideally, by asking the student to retell the story to a partner at the center.

Optional Extension. You may also want to duplicate the miniature pictures of the cues for each of the five thinking skills and send the paper home with a brief note to parents describing how they could reinforce the use of these skills when they are watching television, telling a story, or reading to their children. If parents model and help their children practice these skills at home and with varied content (e.g., dinner table stories, bedtime books, television, videotapes), the likelihood that the skills will be generalized and transferred to other subject areas is increased.

Many schools have parent volunteers who might be willing to help you locate and record appropriate nonfiction history stories for use during these center activities.

Depending on the needs of your students, you might want to have them use the audiocassettes to listen to the stories you already read during the lesson. With other groups, you might prefer to let them practice with new stories that they have not yet seen, read, or heard.

Conduct a short debriefing session with the entire class and ask volunteers to tell you in their own words what each of the five cue posters represent, why they should use these thinking skills, and how these skills help them become good learners.

These debriefing and reflection opportunities may also be a chance for the teacher, the aide, and any parents in the room to discuss their observations about students' behaviors and reactions to the lesson.

We designed another formative assessment for the Core skills that were introduced in this lesson. Like the trait rubric used in the last lesson, the **Lesson 3 Rubric: Retelling a Story** has four levels. The "satisfactory" level can be considered grade-level expectations. We recommend using student performances and application activities, teacher observation, and student and teacher conferences to measure the extent to which each student understands these skills and can use them with prompting by the teacher.

The use of a leveled rubric provides an opportunity for teachers to measure standards-based (Core) grade-level expectations. It also allows teachers to communicate learning progress to parents over the course of the unit or during the marking period or school year. The rubric can also be used to evaluate the curriculum and make appropriate adjustments.

A checklist, with students' names in the first column and the five skills in the

(Continued)

(Continued)

Unit Sequence	Teacher Reflections
The objectives for this lesson reinforce the use of thinking skills to learn historical content: • Attending • Listening • Sequencing • Visualizing • Retelling	columns to the right, supports ongoing assessment. It is not necessary to assess these skills only during this lesson. Instead, the teacher can conduct ongoing assessment during the course of the unit by watching students' behaviors as they are asked to listen to and recall the history content they are learning.
Note that the rubric for this lesson measures only the last of the five skills in this lesson, retelling. This is the skill that appears to lend itself most readily to rubric assessment.	Practicality won out! The other four skills are important, but time just doesn't permit the assessment of every student on every objective in this unit.

Lesson 4: History Stories Over Time

(Two to three hours)

Unit Sequence	Teacher Reflections
Concepts. History, Stories, Events, Era G1–4, G8, SD1–3, SD5, S1–3, S6 A few days prior to this lesson, visit the town or school library and select six to eight different picture books that describe historical events or people. Try to find books that span several generations or even centuries. Our favorites were the following: *Seven Brave Women,* by Betsy Hearn *The Copper Tin Cup,* by Carole Lexa Schaefer *Homeplace,* by Anne Schelby *Amelia and Eleanor Go for a Ride,* by Pam Munoz Ryan *Pompeii . . . Buried Alive,* by Edith Kunhardt-Davis *When I Was Little,* by Toyomo Igus *Peppe the Lamplighter,* by Elisa Barton	We had a hard time finding books that address several different time periods, especially anything prior to the twentieth century. This is probably due to some authors' perception that history stories about ancient times or distant centuries might be uninteresting or too difficult for young students to understand. **AID.** Students who seem to be working at greater levels of expertise in historical understandings and analysis would benefit from books about less familiar times and cultures, such as pre-Columbian Native Americans, the Greeks and Romans, dinosaurs and wooly mammoths, the Gold Rush, immigration in the twentieth century, the colonies, westward expansion, the explorers, Lincoln, Kennedy, Rembrandt, George Washington, and Coronado.
Convene the class for a meeting on the rug or in the center of the room.	It might be helpful to post the charts, pictures, and icons that you used during the last two lessons before convening the group on the rug.

Unit Sequence	*Teacher Reflections*
Review the activities, concepts, and skills from the last two lessons. Ask review questions, such as "Can anyone remind us of the meaning of the word *history*? What about the meaning of the word *past*? Can you turn to your learning partner and share what you think the word *artifact* means? Please turn to another partner and share your understanding of the word *event*."	These four questions allow students an opportunity to review the four concepts that were the focus of the introductory lesson. Some students seem to find it easier to review and remember the content from the last two lessons if they have a chance to discuss some of the concepts and skills with a partner. Using the think-pair-share format also saves time. Every student has a chance to respond and contribute, but the rest of the students don't have to wait for a turn to speak.
Tell students that the stories you will be reading to them during the next few days will be about different events, artifacts, people, and time periods from the past.	
Explain that history is always about the past, but that not all history events happened at the same time. Explain that the past can be divided into segments: the recent past, the past, and the distant past. Explain the difference between recent or near and distant. Give examples (e.g., yesterday was the recent or near past) for clarification.	**Modifications for Learner Need.** Students who have difficulty with the grade-level concepts of past, near past, or distant past might have better success with the phrases "now," "when my mom was a child," and "when my grandmother was a child." Provide these students with opportunities to draw pictures of several examples of an event or an artifact. Or the teacher or aide might draw picture examples of the four concepts and ask students to match a picture with one of the names of the four concepts.
Make an analogy between the bends in the time travel road you drew and discussed in the introductory lesson and the time segments (now, near past, past, and distant past) you just explained. Tell students that one way to keep track of history events and stories is to place a picture or caption about the event or person on a timeline. Explain that a timeline is like the history road the students drew in the last story, but without the bends in the road. Use the analogy of a yardstick or measuring tape or chart they might have at home on which they mark their height at each birthday. Students need to understand the purpose of the marks on the timeline as icons that stand for a certain event and when it occurred in time.	Use the actual chart picture from the last lesson as a visual reminder.

(Continued)

(Continued)

Unit Sequence	Teacher Reflections

Show students roll paper, rulers, scissors, and markers. Ask them to think about how the class might create its own timeline that would be a straight "road" down the path of time. Encourage students to volunteer a variety of answers, products, and solutions. As a class, decide on one format for making your timeline. Consider the floor and wall space available in the room before making a final decision.

Have students work alone, with partners, or in small groups to draw and cut a rectangle for their timeline. The length of the timeline is restricted only by available space. Be sure to have the students use the appropriate intervals and spacing to segment the timeline.

If possible, each individual student or each small group of students should create a three-foot timeline, and the class should create one long, 10- to 12-foot timeline. The class timeline should remain visible for the rest of the unit. Students can add marks at appropriate intervals and glue pictures to the appropriate mark as they add more events to their timeline during the course of the unit.

Convene students on the rug again and explain the purpose for the segments and the marks on a timeline. Choose an appropriate sequence (e.g., near past, past, distant past; seventeenth, eighteenth, nineteenth, and twentieth century; 1900s, 1920s, 1930s) and have students work in small groups to mark their timelines accordingly.

Modifications for Learner Need.
Students who demonstrate an advanced understanding of time as it relates to history should be encouraged to learn the names and numbers that represent the centuries and decades. Their timeline can include these advanced terms.

Bring the students back to the rug or meeting area. Display the completed timeline for the class to see. Ask students to speculate how the class might be able to use a timeline to "map" the events or setting in a history story. Encourage numerous students to share their ideas.

If appropriate, end the lesson now and complete the last half of this lesson on the following day.

Tell students that during the second half of this lesson they are going to use the listening, thinking, and remembering parts of their "thinking caps" to learn about the people and events in several different history stories that you are going to read to them. The stories they hear and the pictures they observe will be about people and events from different periods of time in history. As they listen to the story, they should also be thinking about the time period in which the story events occurred.

Some of these stories occurred during several different time periods.

Throughout the rest of the lesson, encourage students to compare and contrast the characteristics of the various time periods in the different stories.

For our own amusement, we asked, "Do you think the dinosaurs were alive when your grandmothers

Unit Sequence	Teacher Reflections
Read one story and pause for students to discuss the events in the story and to speculate about the time period. Encourage them to use the appropriate time sequence words to describe the setting of the story.	and grandfathers were little children?" Some students were sure they were, and others, approximately 30 percent, knew that people and dinosaurs did not live at the same time in the past.

Continue to reinforce the various time words and concepts introduced earlier in the lesson during the read-aloud, the discussion, and during the center activities. In addition, reinforce the principle that historical inferences and conclusions should always be supported with evidence.

Show students the cover of the book and ask students to guess about the time period of the story. Ask them to support their hunch with information in the picture and reasons for their guess. As you finish a story, or a segment of a story, pause and encourage student reflections about the characters' actions and the characteristics of the time period.

Tell students that the culminating activity for each story will be a center activity that provides an opportunity for students to draw a small picture that represents a main idea in the story. Each should have the opportunity to glue his or her picture to the appropriate time segment of the timeline.

As students complete the illustrations for each book and place them on their timeline, hold a sharing session so that they can show their work to others and comment on the similarities and differences.

Have students work together to complete the larger illustration for each story that will be placed on the class timeline.

Consider taking digital photos of the timeline as it progresses and incorporates more stories, events, people, eras, and time periods. Share the work in progress on the class Web site.

Repeat this cycle over several days with stories from different time periods. After each story, convene a class meeting time to put a representative drawing on the correct place of the class timeline. Continue adding new stories (four to six) until you are sure that most of the students have improved their ability to describe and sequence an event in time. Convene the entire class at the end of the last story or timeline activity to discuss its observations about the similarities and differences in the timeframes, events, people, and behaviors.

AID. Encourage students with a more advanced understanding of time to document the timeframe of each story using more advanced vocabulary and concepts.

This final discussion provides an opportunity for synthesis of unit ideas and concepts, such as time, continuity, and change. It also gives an opportunity to see how far the children have progressed in the skills and understandings related to history.

(Continued)

(Continued)

Unit Sequence	Teacher Reflections
Ask students to speculate about the cause of the differences across the stories and time periods. **Assessment.** Refer to the **Lesson 4 Rubric: Categorizing Historical Eras**. Write the objective for this lesson on the left-hand column of a chart that includes four other columns, one for each level of mastery. As you observe the students during the read-aloud, during center time, or during project time, informally confer with each of them, assess their proficiency with the objective, and mark the appropriate column of the chart.	This discussion also provides another opportunity to spot growth and talent for historical analysis in students and to foreshadow upcoming lessons. Use the data you collect to inform instruction (AID, modifications, or reteaching opportunities) and to inform parents of progress, work habits, and effort.

Lesson 5: Time, Continuity, and Change About Our Own Families

(Two hours of classroom time, one hour of homework)

Unit Sequence	Teacher Reflections
Concepts. History, Stories, Events, Time, Evidence, Continuity, Change G1–6, G8, SD1–3, SD5, S2, S5, S7–11 In this lesson, students are asked to gather, retell, listen to, and compare their own and each other's family history stories in order to sequence and locate the events in time and place and categorize the stories or aspects of each story as examples of time, continuity, and/or change.	This lesson provides an opportunity for students to learn about one of the important themes in history—all historical events involve aspects of time, continuity, and change. For this reason, we have identified this lesson as an example of the Connections parallel. **AID Opportunity.** Given the teacher's prompting, coaching, and support, some students may also be able to find and cite evidence in the stories that explains or infers the reasons for the historical continuity or the change.
Preparation. In preparation for the introduction to this lesson, locate and preread two picture books, both of which illustrate historical events over time.	Some of the books that were read to students during the preceding lessons will make excellent resources for this lesson as well. Do not worry about the fact that the students have already heard the story. You can say that they are revisiting an "old favorite" to see it from a different perspective and to learn even more about the story than they learned the first time that they heard it.

Unit Sequence	Teacher Reflections

One of the books should be an example of the concept of change over time, and the other book will act as an example of continuity over time. We used *When I Was Little,* by Toyomi Igus, as an example of a history story with the theme of change over time, and *The Copper Tin Cup,* by Carole Schaefer, as an example of continuity over time. You might also choose books that provide an opportunity for students to hear and discuss examples of the place and location content standard, as well as the time, continuity, and change theme, across different cultures and lifestyles and different eras of time.

Locate a map of the United States and prepare a blank copy of a historical timeline that covers three to five generations or decades. This will be used during the introductory activity and the teaching and learning activities. In addition, the teacher should make four 4- × 6-inch cards for each child in the class. Write a word—*time, continuity, change,* and *location*—on each card. Add an appropriate picture or icon to remind nonreaders of the meaning of each word. For example, a clock; a sketch of twins; a picture of two coins, one heads and one tails; and a picture of a globe should be drawn on the appropriate card before it is reproduced for all students.

Modifications for Learner Need.
If you have families and grandparents of students in your classroom who were born outside of the United States, you might also want to locate a map of those countries in preparation for this lesson.

Modifications for Learner Need.
If necessary, prepare this letter in alternative languages to meet the needs of families who speak and read something other than English as their first language.

Last, prepare an introductory letter to parents that overviews the lesson schedule, learning objectives, resources, activities, and assignments for this lesson. Ask for parents' help in supporting one of the major learning activities for the unit, the collection of historical event stories from different eras, locations, cultures, and time periods or family generations. Explain to parents that stories exemplify change and/or continuity over time and across cultures. Give them an example of such a story and encourage them to be creative when selecting a brief but age-appropriate and motivating historical story to tell to their children. Encourage parents to emphasize aspects of time, change, continuity, and culture with their child as they share the story of a historical event that occurred in their family.

Parents may write or call with questions about how to help with this assignment. Some parents may be unsure about how to select an appropriate story or how to share the story with their child. Others may question how the teacher or their child is going to use the story. All of these questions provide wonderful opportunities for parent communication, coaching, and the development of shared responsibilities for learning and education.

The stories that the parents shared with their children and that the children retold at school were all fascinating. My two personal favorites were one about the effects

(Continued)

(Continued)

Unit Sequence	Teacher Reflections

Introduction. Display the two books you have selected for the introduction on an easel or a chalk tray. Gather the students together on the rug or in the meeting place. Remind them of the skills they need to use to listen, think, and share during history lessons.

Ask them to recall and think-pair-share what they did and learned during the last history lesson (i.e., listened to history stories and put each of the events on a timeline).

Through questions and conversation, review with students what they already know, or think they know, about history, events, time, and eras.

Tell students that in this lesson they are going to collect, listen to, timeline, map, and think about more history stories—but this time the stories will be about their own families, not just about characters in a book or people they have never met.

Ask them to think about which of their family members (and which generation of family members) might have an interesting history story or event to share with the class. Tell them to keep thinking about this idea until they get home that night. Tell the students that you will show them how to collect and share this story in the next part of the lesson.

Teaching and Learning Activities. Tell students that you are going to show them how to do their work in this lesson by using two examples from stories that all of them already know.

But first, tell them that you want to review some ideas that they have already learned about history in the previous lessons. Review the concepts of history, event, time, timeline, and era with the students.

of a major snowstorm on a family (The child told us that the snowfall at night was so heavy, fast, and deep that in the morning, when they awoke, the family could not get out of their front door of their home. In a dramatic voice the kindergartener turned to me and said, "Do you get it? My grandpa had to climb out of his upstairs bedroom window to get out of the house!") and a story about an exploring, curious child (the kindergartener's grandmother at age 3) who climbed into a milk box on the neighbor's porch and fell asleep ("And her parents looked and looked all over the neighborhood to find my little grandma, and they couldn't find her anywhere. And then a policeman came, and he looked and looked all over too, and he found her asleep in the milk box and he woke her up and gave her ice cream and carried her home.").

Some parents who shared these stories with their children created a rebus-based set of pictures and stick figures to help their children remember and be able to retell the story in the appropriate sequence and with the important content when the children repeated the oral story independently at school.

Unit Sequence	*Teacher Reflections*
Tell them that now you are going to teach them about four new concepts that they will use in this lesson. Print the words *time, continuity, change,* and *location* on the board. Say each word, one at a time, and spend two minutes with each concept, soliciting students' definitions and examples of the word, inventing and drawing an icon for the concepts, and sharing your own definitions and examples of each concept.	Printing the words on the board, drawing a rebus picture for each word, and quickly reviewing examples of each idea should help with the effectiveness of the review process.
Tell students that some history stories take place at different times and in different locations. Tell students that some history stories are examples of continuity and that some stories are examples of change.	Don't be worried about the seemingly abstract nature of these concepts. Kindergarteners already have experience with abstract concepts, such as love, hate, share, rules, learning, reading, night, fear, and happiness. The concepts in this lesson will be learned just as readily with appropriate opportunities for conversation, relevant synonyms, and numerous, related examples.
Tell students that today they are going to be listening to history stories, finding the location of the history event, finding clues (evidence) in the stories that are examples of change, and other clues (possibly in other stories) that are examples of continuity. Remind students that the authors of these stories may not use the words *history, event, location, time, continuity,* or *change* within the story. The students will have to listen carefully to the words in the story, remember the key ideas they are looking for, and try to find examples of the ideas in the story. Encourage them to consider many words and parts of the story as possible examples of time, continuity, change, and location.	Remind them of the role of location by recollecting one or two history stories (from previous lessons) that took place at different times and in different locations. If time permits, place these events on the timeline and find these locations on the map.
Tell students that, often, good listeners and thinkers use evidence, clues, and their own questions and thinking to draw a conclusion about whether the history event or story is mostly about change or mostly about continuity.	Hold up the two picture books to indicate the next activity to students and their role in the activity.
Tell students that some people think that *all* history events and stories have examples of location, time, change, or continuity. Ask students to keep their eyes open for examples of these ideas in all of the history stories they hear and read and to share these examples and ideas with others so that they can see them too.	**Modifications for Learner Need.** Drawing a picture of a detective and/or clues on the board as you speak may reinforce the ideas that you are trying to convey to students.
	Consider using the metaphor of a treasure hunt to describe the students' role in this lesson. Not everything a treasure hunter finds is valuable, just like not every story item a student hears

(Continued)

(Continued)

Unit Sequence	Teacher Reflections
	or remembers will be an example of time, continuity, change, or location. Advise students that good thinkers often "try on" many examples and clues in a story to find out which ones are the "best fit" for the kinds of ideas they are searching for.
Tell students that in this lesson they are going to be good detectives and find out if that rule—that all history stories and events are about location, time, continuity, and change—is really true for *all* history stories. Tell students that they are going to start their detective work and investigation by looking at history stories that come from a book; later, they will do the same detective work with their own history stories.	If you pose this principle and theme as a question to students, you challenge them to accept or refute it. Students often love the idea of proving a group of adults to be wrong or, better yet, joining forces with them to solve a mystery. This challenge also puts the children in the role of an active learner. It is a prime example of how a teacher can attend to the tenets of constructivist learning theory using a deductive, not inductive, method of teaching.
Show students the two books, and do a fast, two-minute "picture walk" with each book. Ask them to recall, if appropriate, what they remember about this book.	The use of preliminary book examples permits a common learning experience to be shared by all students. This prerequisite experience should provide a scaffold to support students' individual and independent thinking and learning work with the lesson's guiding principle. Allow about one minute for volunteers from the class to spontaneously contribute their shared memories of the storylines in each book.
Distribute a set of four concept cards with each card having one of the following words and an appropriate icon (*time, continuity, change,* and *location*) to each child before you begin reading. Read the cards to each student, explain the icons, and ask students to hold up any of the cards if they think they might have found an example of that idea in the story. Read each story, one at a time. Pause frequently when you discern an example of one the four concepts of change, continuity, time, or location. Encourage	Tell students that you expect that several students might think they each have found an example, but the examples might be different ones. These differences are to be expected. In fact, the differences provide a wonderful opportunity for students to talk about the evidence they used to support their examples of change, continuity, time, or location. Students should be encouraged to change their minds when confronted with different evidence or reasons from their peers. When appropriate, share your own thoughts about the theme of each story and the evidence that supports your conclusion.

Unit Sequence	Teacher Reflections

students to hold up the appropriate theme card to identify an example of that concept in the story. Provide sufficient time for students to discuss the similarities, differences, and reasons for their choices.

Convene the next section of this lesson on a new day. Remind students that you asked them to think about which of their family members—parents, grandparents, aunts, or uncles—they might ask to tell them a family history story. Tell students that you have prepared a letter for them to take home to tell their parents about this story. Students are to listen to a history story from a family member, practice retelling it, and come to school ready to draw the story and tell it to the other students in the class. Then, in small or large groups, the students will decide whether each story is an example of change or continuity. In addition, students will draw conclusions about the time and location for each story.

If appropriate, share an example of one of your own family's history stories. Make sure you choose to tell a story that is an example of time or location and either change or continuity. To accomplish this, make sure your story covers two or more time periods within the same culture and within the same family. As a model for this type of storytelling and thinking, make sure you mention the time period(s) for your story and locate the setting on a map or globe for your students.

Have students work in centers to retell each of the stories they bring to school to the teacher or to an aide. The child can draw related pictures while other children are giving dictation to the teacher.

During daily large-group meetings, ask two to three students at a time to share their pictures and retell their stories as the other students listen with their cue cards (location, time, change, and continuity) in their laps. Ask the other students to listen and look for clues in each story that identify the themes of time, continuity, or change. After each story is retold, spend time in a large-group discussion or think-pair-share discussing pertinent examples of the themes.

It was wonderful to have the help of aides and parent volunteers to work with children as they practiced their story retelling before presenting in a large group. The illustrations also made it easier for students to remember the beginning, middle, and endings of their stories. Some parents also helped children create PowerPoint illustrations or rebus drawings to accompany the storylines.

(Continued)

(Continued)

Unit Sequence	Teacher Reflections
Reflection Opportunities. Ask students to discuss their conclusions about the principle you shared with them at the beginning of this portion of the lesson: Is it true that *all* history stories contain examples of time, change, continuity, or location? Do you think we found more examples of one of these concepts than the others?	The teacher may need to prompt students with questions at appropriate points in the story to help them identify examples of the history themes.
Assessment Opportunities. To determine the extent to which students grasped the concepts of time, continuity, and change, ask four to six students, chosen at random or as a stratified sample, to meet with you in conference for two to three minutes. At the conference, retell one of the history stories collected by one of the students in the class. Ask students to tell you if and when they identify an example of time, change, continuity, or location. Use the **Lesson 5 Rubric: Time, Continuity, and Change** to assess student performance.	The class may want to post the illustrations of each story with a sticky note that identifies the story as an example of time, location, change, or continuity. **AID.** Students who demonstrate advanced knowledge in history may be asked to speculate on the reasons for (causes of) the patterns they discovered.

Lesson 6: Historians, Museums, and the Work They (We) Do

(Three hours of classroom time, one hour of homework)

Unit Sequence	Teacher Reflections
Concepts. Historian, Museum, Curator, Artifact, Question, Evidence, Inference, Conclusion G7, G9–10, SD 4–5, S7–8, S10–12 This lesson provides an opportunity for students to link their Core parallel content knowledge about history to the Practice parallel and the work of historians. **Preparation.** Gather a collection of three to five historical artifacts (photographs, documents, tools, objects, text, etc.) from your own family to bring to school and share with your students during the introduction to this lesson. If possible, bring related artifacts that provide clues to a historical era, event, culture, or lifestyle.	Students view history from the perspective of a historian in this lesson. They learn about the work of a historian, the purpose and nature of a museum, and the role of questions, inference, artifacts, and evidence in the work of a historian. In addition to learning about historians and museums, the students work as practicing historians to collect, display, and describe their own collection of historical artifacts by creating a class history museum. As a culminating exercise for this module, students tour their own museum, examine the artifacts and historical descriptions collected by other students, and ask and answer their own history questions using historical evidence, artifacts, and their inference skills.

Unit Sequence	Teacher Reflections
Locate two boxes that contain 25- to 50-piece picture puzzles. These will be used during the lesson to build an analogy to the work of a historian.	Being able to understand a picture when many of the puzzle pieces are missing is much like the work of a historian. As an additional resource, find a magazine photograph of an active scene and tear holes and remove segments of the photo in strategic places that are key to understanding the actions in the scene. This provides an opportunity for student viewers to make inferences in order to draw conclusions about the nature of the photograph.
Ask a docent to arrange a behind-the-scenes tour of a local museum for the students in your class. If that is not possible, try to locate a virtual tour on a Web site or look for a video tour of a national museum, such as the Smithsonian.	
During the course of this lesson, find photographs of various museums and display them in the classroom to add authenticity to your classroom museum.	If possible, try to find other photographs of historians at work. Be sure to include work places other than a museum (e.g., a university, interviewing a small group of people, examining a photograph, cleaning an artifact, writing at a computer, taking field notes, thinking, creating a display, analyzing note cards, researching in a library and on the Web).
Schedule a local historian to visit the classroom and talk about his or her work.	
	AID. During this lesson, keep your eyes open for students who display a keen interest in history and in artifacts. As the lesson progresses, you may want to ask a visiting docent to speak with a small group of such students and train them in how to act as a docent during parent and class tours of your own history museum.
Compose a parent letter that describes this lesson and its learning goals and asks for parents' help in locating and loaning a family historical artifact for the class museum that students will create. You may also want to suggest local museum exhibits in your area or pertinent History Channel offerings that may be of interest to the students in your class.	Other students and their parents might be prime candidates for the development of a historical display, similar to the one that you collect for this lesson. It will contain a set of family artifacts, all related to the same era, event, culture, or cultural universal.
	Be sure to encourage parents to support the children's questioning and inference skills and strategies during family conversations about history.

(Continued)

(Continued)

Unit Sequence	Teacher Reflections

Introduction. Gather students on the meeting rug or in the meeting circle. Remind them that during the last five lessons they have been learning about history by listening and telling history stories, finding the location of history stories on a map, and making a timeline to show the era when a history event occurred. Tell them that during this lesson they are going to extend their knowledge by learning how to think and act like a historian.

Keep this review segment of the lesson as short as possible to permit enough time for the essence of the lesson—learning the skills of the practicing historian.

Next, show students the first item in your set of historical family artifacts. Tell them to whom it belonged and ask them to speculate about its purpose, meaning, age, construction, history, and so on. Allow five to ten minutes for paired or small-group student dialogue about the artifact.

Repeat this activity with the second, third, fourth, and fifth artifact from your set.

Make sure that all students have sufficient opportunity to look at each artifact, touch it, hold it, and so forth. If necessary, caution students about the rules for proper handling and remind them to take turns.

As students examine the artifacts, in turn, encourage them to ask questions of themselves and their peers about the artifacts. Ask them to create "wondering" questions that begin with the words "I wonder."

After students have had sufficient opportunity to examine the artifacts, formulate questions, make inferences, and draw conclusions about the individual artifacts, bring the students back together as a large group. Synthesize this experience by telling students that the artifacts they just examined were part of a collection and a set. Ask them to use their observations and analysis of the artifacts to decide how they think all of these artifacts might be related. Encourage them to create their own oral "history story" that explains the relationship among the artifacts, the era, and the individuals who used them.

Modifications for Learner Need. The most difficult part of this activity asks students to see each artifact as part of a unified set and to make inferences and assumptions about missing, but crucial, elements in your history artifact collection. To succeed, students must view the artifacts as partial clues to a scene, action, or event from the past. Teachers can scaffold this activity by asking supportive connection-to-self questions such as the following:

- Have you ever seen anything that looks like this?
- What does this remind you of?
- What do we have/do today that is like this?

Other supportive questions might include:

- What is happening here?
- What is this for?
- What is this made of?
- Who might have used/done this?
- Why did they use/do this?
- How did they use/do this?

Next, show students the magazine photograph in which you have made holes. Ask them to look at the partial photograph in the same way that they looked at the collection of your family's artifacts. Tell them that each of the artifacts, like each section of the photograph, provides clues

Unit Sequence	*Teacher Reflections*
to a history story. In the same way that they acted like history detectives in the preceding part of the lesson, they have to look at each part of the photograph and use any clues to make good guesses about the missing pieces.	• What might be missing from this collection? • What else is going on in this family or during this event or time period that is missing from this collection of artifacts? • Can you make up a story that has all of these artifacts in it? • What artifacts might be missing from this collection? • What parts of your story are you sure are true? • Which parts of your stories are wild guesses?
Give them an opportunity to view the existing photo segments and to make guesses about the content of the missing pieces. As a final task, ask students to describe the whole picture, even though they only had the opportunity to look at pieces of it. Explain to them that you have just asked them to think and act as a history detective who uses artifacts as clues to the stories of the past.	
If students seem to need another learning experience to build the analogy between a photograph with missing pieces and the task of a historian, try showing them a cardboard picture puzzle box with a photograph of the entire puzzle on the front of the box. Then show them a partially completed puzzle (from a different box), using only 30 to 50 percent of the puzzle pieces, and ask them to infer the picture that might be on the front of the second puzzle box.	Students may enjoy a brief pause-and-reflect opportunity at the close of this activity to think and talk about their own experiences while putting together puzzles. Encourage them to make a link between putting a puzzle together without a picture to guide them, and the kind of thinking that a history detective must do. It's probably a good idea to recognize students' success with the last three activities before moving on to the next segment of the lesson. This builds efficacy for the hard work of question formation and inferencing with evidence that follows.
Tell students that during the remaining days of this lesson they are going to use the thinking skills they just practiced with the artifacts, the photograph, and the puzzle to learn to act like an adult who has a job and career studying history, asking history questions, and conducting history investigations.	This is a good time to share the photographs that you have collected of historians at work. We found that a search of www.google.com, looking for "images only," provided a wealth of photographs that could be put into a PowerPoint presentation or viewed on the school's or classroom's television through a technology interface connection.
Introduce the word and concept *historian* to the students. Print the word on the board. Ask students if they have ever heard the word before and to	

(Continued)

Unit Sequence	Teacher Reflections
speculate on the meaning of the word. Help students define the word, find synonyms, draw a picture of a historian at work, and speculate on how this person would spend his or her workday.	
Explain to students that during the next few days, a historian will visit the class to discuss her or his work. In addition, students will have the opportunity to visit a museum and see how some historians share their work with other people. Provide an opportunity for students to share their prior experiences with historians and museums.	Encourage the students to begin thinking about the questions they would like to ask the historian about his or her work, the tools used to study history, and the way historians share their work with others.
Before the close of this segment of the lesson, explain to students that the ultimate purpose for the visit by the historian and the visit to the museum is to prepare students to act like historians themselves. Ask students to think about these visits as an opportunity to work with a mentor who will help them prepare to do similar work in their own classroom. Provide time for students to discuss their interest in acting like "real" historians and in creating their own history museum.	This is an important segue to the remaining portions of this lesson. Students should come to a firm understanding of their role as interns who are learning and practicing the skills, processes, and strategies of a practicing professional: a historian. Students might enjoy talking about internships and the relationship between high school and college career explorations, internships, and what they are about to do.
This is a prime opportunity to introduce a working historian to the class. The visit can last as few as 20 to 30 minutes and be extremely effective if you can ensure that the historian understands beforehand that your target learning objective for this visit and for your students is *not* to share or learn about history stories or artifacts but to explain how she or he got interested in history, does his or her work, finds questions to ask, views his or her research and product development, and undertakes the role of problem solving and thinking in his or her career. Ideally, this person will not emphasize the role of a curator, but the profession and discipline of history.	Time spent on a phone call or conference with your invited historian is time well spent. If the individual is a frequent volunteer in elementary and secondary classrooms, he or she may make assumptions about how to interact and what to say to your students. If the person is a college professor, he or she may be inclined to try a minilecture as a teaching strategy. If you want to increase the effectiveness of this visit, make sure that your visitor is able to play a mentoring role and emphasize age-appropriate history skills and methodologies over content and information when working with students. In addition, provide your guest with guidelines about how much adult talk time (one to two minutes)

Unit Sequence	Teacher Reflections
If appropriate, coach students to ask the visiting historian questions such as the following:	should be sandwiched in between students' conversation and active learning time (one to two minutes). Encourage the use of anecdotes, artifacts, and tools to illustrate the skills and strategies that will be shared with students.

- How did you get interested in history?
- What did you study in history as a student?
- What is the difference between studying history and being a historian?
- How does a historian do his or her work?
- What do you do with history?
- How do you ask history questions?
- What kinds of history questions do you ask?
- Are you a history detective?
- What do you use as clues to answer your history questions?
- What is the hardest part about being a good historian?
- What mistakes have you made?
- Do you think we could act like historians?
- Can you show us how you create a history question about an artifact?
- How should we answer our history questions?
- Can you show us how you make a good guess and a bad guess about your history question?

After the historian's visit and after the students have sent thank-you notes and made promises to share their history work with their "visiting expert," be sure to allow enough time for students to "debrief" and reflect upon the visit. Again, the most important thing for them to learn from the historian's visit is how to ask questions, use evidence, make inferences, and draw conclusions as a practicing historian.	With kindergarten students, it is usually a good idea to conduct the debriefing as soon as possible after the conclusion of the visit. Be sure to allow time for the students to share their personal reflections about the visit, what was new and most interesting to them, and what skills and ideas they thought would be most useful to them when they begin their work as historians.
The historian's visit can be followed with a trip to a local museum, preferably a children's history museum or a section of a history museum that has a special exhibit for children. During the museum trip, the	History museums are often housed at historical sites (e.g., homes, worksites, communities, or the location of historical events) or in historical buildings. Students may tell the story of an event, a culture,

(Continued)

Unit Sequence	Teacher Reflections
children should focus on the purpose, structure, and organization of a museum. For this reason, it is probably a good idea to conduct a focusing session with the students prior to their visit.	an era, a lifestyle, a person's life, a technology, or the nature of change over time.
Help students understand the difference between the work of a historian and the purpose of a museum. Explain to students that you want them to enjoy the exhibits in the museum, but as they are doing so, you also want them to concentrate on these guiding questions:	Make a copy of these guiding questions to share with your parent chaperones during the trip. The chaperones can use these questions as prompts and guiding questions as they converse with their small groups during their tour of the museum.
• What is a museum? • Why do people build museums? • What is in a museum? • How are museums organized? • What is inside a museum display?	Ask one of the museum curators to chat with students near the end of their trip to the museum. If the curator knows beforehand of your visit and its purpose, he or she might be able to support students' understanding and give some tips about how to design and arrange their own history displays.
	If you are unable to visit a local museum, then a related video or pictures from a www.google.com search will provide an adequate substitute, assuming you can moderate the visual images by spotlighting important features and offering your own explanations.
	Teachers, aides, and chaperones on the trip should take note of the way that the artifacts are arranged, displayed, labeled, and explained. This information will be useful when you return to school and help students create their own displays. Develop your own criteria for judging the quality of a display and its effectiveness and impact on young viewers and visitors.
After the trip to the museum, convene the students for another reflection and debriefing session. This is a good opportunity to display and discuss the pictures and videos of museums and their displays and components.	Remind students of the artifacts display that you shared with them several days ago, at the beginning of the lesson.
The purpose of the reflection discussion is to segue from the visit to the museum to the creation of students' individual	**AID.** As mentioned earlier, students with intense interest in history may want to create a more elaborate display that has more than one "puzzle piece." With parents' help, these children may be able to create a display with multiple, related artifacts that

Unit Sequence	*Teacher Reflections*

museum displays. For this reason, the discussion questions should focus on the following:

- What is a museum?
- Why do people make museums?
- What is inside a museum?
- How do people decide what to display in a museum?
- What are the parts of a museum display?
- How do people make a museum display?
- Should adults and children visit museums? Why?
- What do visitors do in a museum?
- Can kids make museum displays? If so, how would they do it?
- What might you want to display in a museum? Why?
- How can your parents, teacher, and friends help you make a museum display?

Tell students that you would like to give them an opportunity to create their own history display, with an artifact of their own choosing and their own class history museum.

Give students sufficient opportunity to brainstorm potential artifacts that they may be able to bring to school and use as their historical display. Remind them that their parents and relatives may be a big help to them with this project because they probably have more knowledge of family history than the children do.

Set an expected "send-in date" for the artifact and send the related letter and directions home to parents. In the letter, explain that students and parents have the option of working together at home to create their display and add the labels, written explanations, and guiding questions that will accompany the artifact in the class history museum. Or, the child can do this work with peer and teacher support at school. If appropriate, tell

visually tell a story and paint a picture of an era, a lifestyle, an occupation, or a cultural universal.

Other children may prefer to create a historical display about a technology and its use, or about a historical event, occupation, lifestyle, or place.

(Continued)

(Continued)

Unit Sequence	Teacher Reflections

parents that you have an example at school that they might like to view if they need more information about how to help their child create an artifact display.

As the students' artifacts drift into school, you may notice that some or all of them do not contain the related display components. Other children may not be able to bring in display items. In the former situation, we recommend making the displays at school during center time, with the help of an aide or parent volunteer. Be sure to stock plenty of paper, pens, scissors, and glue at the center for this purpose. In the latter situation, we suggest providing students with artifacts (available at tag sales or from parent volunteers) that might be especially relevant for youngsters, such as old toys, magazines, tools, or equipment.

If possible, ensure that each artifact has an accompanying display with a name label, a date, a location, an explanation, and an appropriate guiding question. Some teachers may prefer to house each artifact and related information in a shoebox. Others might use shelving, trays, cloth "fluff," or an empty table in one section of the classroom.

When everyone has finished his or her display, work together as a class to decide where and how to arrange each student's display. Ask students to use their classification and pattern-finding skills for this purpose.

You have created your own class history museum. The students are likely to be amazed and proud. Now, it's time to invite the public to learn from your study and labor.

We have added the component of a guiding question as part of the children's museum display to encourage more active learning (e.g., thinking, reflection, analysis, and connections to self and world) as peers tour their museum. The use of a guiding question is similar to the interactive experiences many contemporary museums create to encourage visitors to do more than merely walk by and observe the objects in a display. A guiding question encourages a visitor to pause and reflect on the display, its contents, and how it illustrates major concepts, principles, and patterns about the time period, events, people, issues, and their culture. Guiding questions might include any of the following:

- What does this remind you of?
- Why do you think it was made this way?
- How do you think it would feel to use this?
- What would it be like to live here?
- What does this make you wonder?

Unit Sequence	Teacher Reflections
	Some schools and classrooms may find that they are able to leave their displays in place for an extended period of time. Librarians often volunteer to donate shelf space or space on the tops of low-level bookcases for this purpose. Other schools have scant space and must make the displays temporary. In these cases, you might want to arrange for an evening showing of the museum for interested parents. If you want other students in the school to view the museum, or if this is part of an interclass or intergrade project, then a touring schedule needs to be organized and distributed.
In most cases, classroom teachers themselves can select and train student "docents" to give the public, other students, parents, and other classrooms a tour of your class museum.	You may want to assign student docents to specific displays so that they have an opportunity to study their assignment, rehearse their information, and practice their presentations.
Remind students that a docent is a volunteer who studies an exhibit or section of the museum in order to answer visitors' questions and to provide additional information that the guests can't get by reading the print material in the exhibit.	
While the training is in progress, the public notices about the museum and its "hours of operation" can be printed and distributed to parents and other classrooms.	You may even want to invite a local newspaper reporter.
Once the docent training is finished, you are ready to give the tours and stand back and marvel at the way your students perform and demonstrate their understandings.	
Don't forget to reflect on the experience with your students after the tours have ended. Debriefing questions might include the following: • What surprised you most about the visitors to our museum? • What was the hardest thing about being a docent?	The assessment rubric that accompanies this lesson may be useful to have on hand while you conduct the debriefing session with the students. If you used the rubric to gather and analyze preassessment information about students' prior knowledge, you can compare that level of knowledge with their postassessment achievement.

(Continued)

(Continued)

Unit Sequence	Teacher Reflections
• Did you have enough time to tour our museum yourself, as a guest and visitor? • What else could we do to make our museum a better learning experience for our guests and visitors? • How would you suggest we improve our museum? • How might we improve our displays? • If you were to make another class museum, can you think of a theme for our museum that would help us select and organize our artifacts? • Now that you have experienced museums, exhibits, and being a docent, how would you define a museum? • Why do people create museums? It is best to wait a few days after the museum tour to begin the next segment of the lesson. Students need time to reflect on that experience and to tour their own museum as guests and not merely as docents for one exhibit.	Of course, the last part of this lesson, which involves teaching students to ask and answer historical questions using evidence, inference, and conclusions, has yet to be conducted. For this reason, consider any data you collect at this point to be formative, not summative, evaluation data.
This last phase provides an opportunity for students to take on the role of practicing historians. Although the role of a historian was introduced and addressed in an earlier segment of this lesson, the class museum needed to be created before we could act on this set of skills. Ask students to recall the class visit by the local historian. Review the definition of a historian and the skills and processes they use. Emphasize the role of historians as people who ask and attempt to answer history questions by collecting, observing, and examining evidence. Remind students of the advice and training that the historian provided to them. Discuss the importance of evidence, inference, and the drawing of tentative conclusions.	For this phase of the lesson, the teacher will need to locate and display the photos of historians at work. The photos will add an air of authenticity to the students' work and serve as a fitting finale to the lesson.

Unit Sequence	Teacher Reflections

Remind students that they have already acted as both museum curators and docents. Tell them that, as a group, they have an entire collection of artifacts in the classroom. In fact, there are so many wonderful objects in the room that it seems a shame not to "have a go at them" and use the artifacts the way that a real historian would use them— that is, like the people in the pictures they see around them in the room would use the artifacts.

Now students will be asked to act not as museum curators or docents, but as historians working "behind the scenes" at a history museum. They will take on the role of researchers who attempt to ask and answer new questions about history through an examination of artifacts and the use of observation, analysis, identification, pattern-finding, and inference skills.

Invite students to put on their "thinking caps" again to act like real historians. Tell them that you want them to choose, ask questions about, observe, study, describe, and draw conclusions about one of the artifacts in the room.

Ask each child to take one of the artifacts in the class history museum that is interesting and intriguing to him or her. Encourage students to take an artifact that is unfamiliar to them so that they can act, as closely as possible, like a "real" historian.

Again, remind students to take special care of the artifacts and to remember two very big rules for historians—preservation and safety.

The following process may aid students in their historical work:

1. Observe the artifact carefully.
2. Think about where and when the artifact was found.
3. Find three to four things that really intrigue you about your chosen artifact.
4. Turn these ideas into a few questions.
5. Select your best question.
6. Use evidence, your own thinking, and conversations with your friends to help you answer your history question.
7. Take your time and think carefully. Don't be in a big hurry to answer your question.
8. Share your history question and your answer with others. See if they agree or disagree with you. Use their thoughts to help you do even more thinking about your artifact.

These steps should mirror the advice and process shared by your visiting historian but need to be written in language the children can understand. Icons may help students "read" and remember the steps and process you want them to use.

AID. Some students may be ready to ask history questions that need to be answered with multiple artifacts or with interviews with a variety of people who have different perspectives.

Modification for Learner Need. Other students may find it quite challenging to locate a new and interesting artifact, to observe it, analyze it, describe it, and draw conclusions about its composition and use. These students may not yet be ready to ask and answer inferential questions about an artifact.

(Continued)

(Continued)

Unit Sequence	Teacher Reflections
Provide enough time for students to work alone, with a partner, or in small groups to choose, observe, formulate questions, and make inferences about a new artifact. Rove throughout the room to support students' work and take dictation if necessary. If time permits, hold a historians' "conference" and allow students to share their "research" with their peers.	Other students may need your help or the help of a parent volunteer to think their way to a conclusion. Making a video of students' think-alouds or their "conference" presentation allows them to view their own work process and make related reflections.
Last, conduct a final reflection session for the entire lesson and assess students' understanding of the major concepts and skills in this lesson. **Lesson 6 Rubric: Artifacts and Inferences** supports that assessment.	The most important objective for this lesson is for students to come to an understanding of the work of historians, museums, curators, docents, and the process of asking questions, making observations, and drawing conclusions.

Lesson 7: What Does History Mean to Me?

(60 minutes)

Unit Sequence	Teacher Reflections
Concepts. Interests, Plans, Goals G1–10, SD1–5, S3–5, S10 This lesson focuses on the Identity parallel of the PCM. It provides an opportunity for students to reflect on their experiences in this curriculum unit and make connections to themselves, their interests, future plans, actions, values, and goals. The title for this lesson is also the essential question that students should ponder as they reflect on their learning during this unit.	The Identity parallel provides an opportunity for students to consider the connection between themselves and the academic discipline they are studying. In this unit, kindergarteners are asked to think about their learning experiences in light of their own identity as history scholars and history makers. They have an opportunity to reflect on their interest in history and their place in history. Guiding questions, such as those described on page 215 of *The Parallel Curriculum Model*, can be used by lesson designers to support the development of their own Identity questions for a particular lesson or unit. Questions such as the following might guide the use of the Identity parallel in this kindergarten history unit:
Preparation. Use a blank 8- × 11-inch sheet of paper to draw a silhouette of a child. Make a copy for each student.	
Find a hand mirror that students can use to "reflect" on what history means to them.	
Locate one of the pictures of a historian at work and a picture of a museum that was used earlier in the unit.	• Is there a piece of history that is interesting to me? • What parts of history are/will be mine to tell?
Find some kind of a prop that could serve as a pretend microphone and/or television camera.	• Will I grow up to be a person who visits history museums and reads about history?

Unit Sequence	Teacher Reflections

Find a pearl- or gray-colored balloon that you can use as a prop for a crystal ball to allow students to see into their future.

Last, make enough copies of a blank list that contains five numbered lines.

Stock pencils and crayons at the tables or desks.

- Am I a historian?
- What history stories might people tell about me?
- Who will I become in history?
- Can I identify with people in history?

If possible, you may want to inflate a balloon for each student and make a cardboard mirror for each student to use.

Introduction. Call the students to the meeting area. Begin the lesson with the provocative and essential question that is also the title for this lesson. Provide a minute or two for students to think-pair-share their initial reaction to the question, "What does history mean to me?"

It might be a good idea to keep the **Lesson 7 Rubric: What Does History Mean to Me?** and a list of the students ready and available so that you can assess their level of interest, self-knowledge, and personal involvement as you listen and observe their responses.

Tell students that this is the closing lesson for the unit. Explain that this final lesson provides an opportunity for each of them to think back on what they have done, created, and learned during this unit.

Explain that this time for reflection and remembering will make it easier for all of the students to select which memories they want to save and store in their minds. Reflection also allows us to set goals and make plans for the future based on what we have learned.

Don't worry if some students have difficulty answering this question during the introductory section of this lesson. You will be providing several activities that will scaffold their thinking and allow them to successfully answer this essential question by the end of the lesson.

This is a good time to use parent volunteers or aides to take dictation for the students that have difficulty with writing or with invented spelling.

Learning Activities. Ask the students to return to their desks or tables. Distribute the copies of the silhouettes to them. Ask students to think about the conversation they just had with their partner and the memories they discussed. Show them the silhouettes and ask them to write or draw on the outline of the head all of the things that are now in their mind about history and this unit.

As students finish their drawings, ask them to share their work with the other students at their table. Comment on the similarities and the differences among students' memories and assure them that it is a good thing that different people are storing different memories in their minds and that these differences are what makes each of them special and unique.

(Continued)

(Continued)

Unit Sequence	Teacher Reflections
Next, show students the pictures of the museum and the historian and tell them that you would like them to role-play their thoughts about visiting a museum and acting like a historian. Tell them that you will act as a newspaper or television reporter who wants to interview them to get their thoughts and feelings and to share these ideas with all of the people in town.	If parent volunteers are available, they could help with this role-play by acting as television camerapersons.
Ask one of the more outgoing students to help you model this role-playing scenario. Hold up the photo of the museum when you are asking interview questions about the students' thoughts about a museum. Use the photograph of the historian when you inquire about their interests in doing historical work.	
Then allow two to three student volunteers to perform the role play with you in front of the rest of the class.	If students become restless or if time is short, pair the remaining students and let them use a spoon to simulate the microphone so that each pair can take turns interviewing each other.
When the role-playing has finished, ask students to return to their tables or desks. Give each student a balloon and ask him or her to pretend it is a crystal ball. If necessary, explain to students that some people pretend that they can see the future by looking into a glass ball. Using the markers on the table, ask students to gently draw a picture of themselves in the future. Ask them to illustrate what they think they might be wondering, doing, investigating, or learning about history in the future.	**AID.** If appropriate, ask the students with a deep understanding of the concept of history or an intense involvement in history to draw a picture and make a prediction based on one of these questions: • What kind of history will I make? • What parts of history will be mine to tell? • What history stories might people tell about me? • Who will I become in history?
For the last activity in this lesson, ask the students to remain at their tables or desks. Distribute the blank lists and pencils. Tell students that if they want to make their predictions of their future come true, they will need to set some goals and have a plan of action.	If necessary, give students the definition, examples, and synonyms for the words and concepts related to memories, goals, plans, and decisions.
Ask them to think about five goals, actions, or plans they would like to set for their future with history, historians, history stories,	Be sure to save enough time to congratulate students on their learning and their accomplishments and to let them know how proud you are of their achievements, work habits, knowledge, and skills.

Unit Sequence	*Teacher Reflections*
and museums. Rotate around the room and help them think about their options and ideas before they begin to write.	

Provide time for students to share their plans and ideas with each other. Comment on their plans and give students their work products to take home and share with their parents.

As a culminating activity, repeat the interview you conducted with a random set of students during the preassessment. Compare their preassessment and postassessment responses and estimate the level of growth they have undergone.

Lesson 2 Rubric: *Conceptual Understandings of History*

Objective	Beginning	Satisfactory	Competent	Proficient
Students will be able to define the concepts of history, the past, events, and an artifact and give an example of each.	Students provide an example of a natural history or social history event, person, object, or story.	Students can define history and give an appropriate example.	Students can define all four concepts and give an example of one or two concepts.	Students can define all four concepts and give an example of one or two concepts.

Lesson 3 Rubric: *Retelling a Story*

Objective	Beginning	Satisfactory	Competent	Proficient
The student will be able to attend to an oral reading, a brief conversation, or a presentation by peers for at least ten minutes and be able to retell the major points.	Student attends to a brief oral presentation and makes related remarks.	Student attends to presentation and can mention three to four details she or he remembers from an oral presentation.	Student attends to an oral presentation and can identify its main idea and related details.	Student can retell the major points and related details in an oral presentation with the appropriate sequence.

Lesson 4 Rubric: *Categorizing Historical Eras*

Objective	Beginning	Satisfactory	Competent	Proficient
The student will be able to attend to an oral reading and be able to identify the time period of the story as near past, past, or distant past.	Student attends to a brief oral presentation and accurately describes the setting of the story as past or present.	Student attends to the story and correctly identifies the time period as past, near past, or distant past.	Student attends to the story, correctly identifies the time period, and can give an example of another event that occurred during that time period.	Student attends to the story, correctly identifies the time period, can give an example of another event that occurred during that time period, and can name the century or decade when the story occurred.

Lesson 5 Rubric: Time, Continuity, and Change

Objective	Beginning	Satisfactory	Competent	Proficient
Students will demonstrate their understanding of the social studies macroconcept (theme) of time, continuity, and change.	The student is able to describe the similarities and the differences between two historical stories or events.	The student is able to describe the similarities and the differences between two or more historical stories or events. The student is able to identify the historical similarities as examples of continuity and the examples of differences across time as evidence of historical change.	The student is able to describe the similarities and the differences among three or more historical stories or events. The student is able to identify the historical similarities as examples of continuity and the examples of differences across time as evidence of historical change.	The student is able to describe the similarities and the differences among three or more historical stories or events. The student is able to identify the historical similarities as examples of continuity and the examples of differences across time as evidence of historical change. The student is able to use evidence to infer the reasons for the change or the historical continuity.

Lesson 6 Rubric: Artifacts and Inferences

Objective	Beginning	Satisfactory	Competent	Proficient
The student can explain the concepts of historian, artifacts, and museums. The student can ask history-oriented questions. The student can make inferences about artifacts and historical evidence. The student displays interest in historical exhibits.	The student can provide an age-appropriate definition for an artifact, a museum, or a historian. The student can respond to a history question with a plausible response. The student attends to historical displays and exhibits.	The student can provide an age-appropriate definition for two of the following: an artifact, a museum, or a historian. The student can describe a historical artifact. The student can respond to a history question with a plausible response. The student attends to historical displays and exhibits.	The student can provide an age-appropriate definition for all of the following: an artifact, a museum, and a historian. The student can describe a historical artifact. The student can ask a question about a historical event, era, artifact, or person. With prompting, the student can make a historical inference. The student displays interest in historical exhibits.	The student can provide an age-appropriate definition for all of the following: an artifact, a museum, and a historian. The student can describe a historical artifact and make inferences about it. The student can ask a question about a historical event, era, artifact, or person. The student seeks out opportunities to visit historical exhibits and museums.

Lesson 7 Rubric: What Does History Mean to Me?

Objective	Beginning	Satisfactory	Competent	Proficient
The student can reflect upon his or her own interests about history and demonstrates an appreciation for history in his or her own life.	The student attends to history lessons and presentations and his or her behavior suggests at least topical or temporal interest.	The student can describe his or her present interest in history, historical thinking, museums, or historians.	The student can verbalize his or her specific interest in history. The student acts on his or her interest voluntarily. The student values and appreciates at least some historical topics.	The student can verbalize his or her specific interest in history. The student acts on his or her interest voluntarily and in a manner that increases proficiency and expertise. The student values and appreciates at least some historical topics.

Wind—The Unequal Heating of the Earth's Surface

A Core Unit on Weather for Elementary Students

Jeanne H. Purcell

BACKGROUND FOR UNIT

This Core parallel unit on weather has unusual origins. It began with a search for weather materials that were both developmentally appropriate and true to the discipline. The search yielded little that addressed the learning needs of 10- and 11-year-olds *and* that addressed the Core content of this complex topic in a systematic fashion. This Earth science curriculum unit about weather was written to fill those needs.

Weather: The Never-Ending Story contains four modules. The first module, I Can Be a Meteorologist Too, is designed to engage students with the subject matter. They begin to realize that they can create weather instruments, gather important weather data, and make their own predictions that rival the accuracy of professional meteorologists. Module 2 includes learning activities that allow young people to understand how local winds are formed. The third module provides students with multiple opportunities to understand the water cycle, and the fourth module addresses the relationship between geography and daily weather.

This unit answers—in two ways—a major focusing question for the Core Curriculum: How is the information organized to help people use it better? First, the unit contains a concept map (see Lesson 1). A concept map is a graphic, two-dimensional, hierarchical representation of a circumscribed set of concepts. The concepts are linked together with prepositional statements, words, or phrases that express the relationship among concepts. The propositional statements are a most important component in the map because they express the principles—or structure—of the field. These principles are the heart of the Core parallel.

In addition, the map arranges concepts in hierarchical form with categories and subcategories. Students can readily see the structure of the discipline and that any particular concept can be related to many others. When students understand deeply the structure of a subject, they can remember and retrieve knowledge with greater ease.

Second, the principles and facts in this curriculum unit are organized in a unique manner. They are "storyboarded," or sequenced, to ensure that they are coherent for all learners. When learning is organized in logical steps—rather than disconnected episodes—students are able to construct their own deep knowledge and understanding about the core principles of a discipline. As such, the storyboarding enables students to remember the core of a subject, make meaning about it, and use what they know in unfamiliar situations.

This unit provides the teacher with varied opportunities to provide for the unique learning needs of students: those at grade level, those below grade level, and those above grade level. Many whole-group learning activities are included, as well as opportunities for teachers to flexibly meet the needs of a wide range of learners. Preassessments are described to help teachers pinpoint students' unique learning needs. A variety of teaching strategies help teachers coach students through some of the abstract content in meteorology. Extensions are described to accommodate the interests of students, as are techniques for intensifying the content to meet the needs of students who require more demanding learning opportunities, sometimes referred to as Ascending Intellectual Demand (AID).

Module 2 of the larger unit, Weather: The Never-Ending Story, is featured here. It includes a preassessment and seven lessons that deal with local winds resulting from the unequal heating of the Earth. If you are interested in viewing the other modules, please contact the author at jeanne.purcell@po.state.ct.us.

CONTENT FRAMEWORK

Organizing Concepts

Discipline-Specific Concepts. Light Energy, Heat Energy, Unequal Heating, Wind

Macroconcept. System

Principles and Generalizations

G1 The sun is the source of radiant energy that drives our weather.
G2 When sunlight is absorbed by the earth, it is transformed into heat energy, which causes changes to Earth's surfaces.
G3 The darker surfaces (e.g., dark soil, asphalt roadways, forests) absorb more sunlight than lighter-colored substances (e.g., snow, glacier ice) and, as a result, release more heat than the lighter-colored surfaces.
G4 (AID) The absorption of gases in the atmosphere influences the temperature of the earth. The enhanced greenhouse effect is caused by human activity.
G5 Water gains and loses heat more slowly than land.
G6 Warm air is lighter than cold air and rises into the atmosphere.
G7 When warm air rises, cooler, denser air rushes in to take its place.
G8 The movement of warm and cool air causes local winds.

National Standards for Science

SD1 The sun provides light and heat necessary to maintain the temperature of the earth.

SD2 The sun is a major source of energy for phenomena on the earth's surface, such as the growth of plants, winds, ocean currents, and the water cycle. Seasons result from variations in the amount of the sun's energy hitting the surface, due to the tilt of Earth's rotation on its axis and the length of the day.

SD3 Light travels in a straight line until it strikes an object. Light can be reflected by a mirror, refracted by a lens, or absorbed by an object.

SD4 Describe the sun as the source of energy that causes weather to change.

SD5 Air is a substance that surrounds us, takes up space, and whose movement we feel as wind.

SD6 Global patterns of atmospheric movement influence local weather. Oceans have a major effect on climate, because water in the oceans holds a large amount of heat.

Skills

S1 Making observations

S2 Estimating the amount of land and water on Earth

S3 Displaying data (i.e., fractions, percentages, pie charts)

S4 Reading a thermometer

S5 Determining cause and effect (e.g., places near large bodies of water are cooler in the summer and warmer in the winter than places that are inland)

S6 Comparing and contrasting

MAKING SURE THE CORE REMAINS CENTRAL IN TEACHING AND LEARNING

Curriculum Component	*Component Description and Rationale*
Content	In spite of its complexity, our daily weather can be reduced to a series of core principles and generalizations that can be easily understood by students in Grades 4 and 5. We focus here on the sun and how it heats the surface of Earth unequally to create wind. The lessons help the teacher and students focus on a principle that is at the heart—or core—of meteorology. An essential goal of this unit is to answer one of the focusing questions for the Core parallel: How is information—or content—organized? When we use this question to guide us, student understanding about the structure of content becomes critically important. To support students' learning about the structure of knowledge in this unit, the teacher will use a concept map to help young people understand the organization of the essential concepts and principles related to this module's content. While it is important to share a concept map with students at the beginning and end of any unit of instruction—to introduce the structure of knowledge and then later to reflect upon and assess growth—the concept map can also be used at any time

(Continued)

Curriculum Component	Component Description and Rationale
	throughout the unit to deepen student understanding about any individual concept and/or the relationship(s) among them.
Assessments	Although a variety of assessment formats are included in this weather unit, most are designed to assess students' conceptual understanding of the concepts and principles that are at the heart of this Core Curriculum unit.
Introductory activities	The introductory activities in a Core Curriculum unit may contain as many as six components: a focusing or guiding question, a preassessment, a hook to motivate students, information about the relevancy of the unit, the learning objectives students are to acquire, and consideration for students' interests.
	This unit contains a preassessment; a concept map that depicts the components of our Earth's weather system, as well as the relationships among the elements (the "big ideas" behind weather); prompts for teachers to share the lesson objectives; and several hooks using a variety of multimedia sources.
Teaching strategies	Teaching strategies are used to make clear to students—in both whole and small groups—the key concepts and principles in this weather unit. A variety of teaching strategies, including lecture, Socratic questioning, and the concept-attainment model, are used throughout this unit to respond to the learning needs of the entire class, as well as to the unique learning needs of individuals and small groups of students.
Learning activities	Because this is a Core Curriculum unit, the majority of student learning activities are designed to help students learn deeply about critical concepts and acquire a thorough understanding of essential principles. Students complete experiments and demonstrations that require them to draw conclusions about the effects of the unequal heating of Earth's surfaces.
Grouping strategies	In a Core Curriculum unit, grouping strategies are selected purposefully to ensure that all students have acquired the essential concepts and skills. Grouping strategies may also be used to support the unique learning needs of individuals and small groups within the class. Small and individual groupings are used, for example, to assess the degree to which students have acquired major concepts and principles, provide individualized feedback and coaching, and analyze examples and information that support concept acquisition.
Products	All products are selected to illustrate students' acquisition of the concepts, principles, and skills of the Core Curriculum.
Resources	Resources include weather journals, raw data from weather observations, graphic organizers, clear directions for data analysis, thinking protocol worksheets, and concept maps.
Extension activities	Extension activities in this unit stem from the unit content and are interest based. Individuals or small groups of students can complete these activities, and they can be of short or long duration.
Modifications for learner need, including Ascending Intellectual Demand (AID)	Ascending Intellectual Demand (AID) is designed specifically for students who need more intense cognitive tasks because they have greater prior knowledge than their grade-level peers, can learn at a faster pace, or have greater facility to make inferences with the content. These learners may be invited to (1) learn more complex content, (2) work at more expert skill levels, or (3) create products that approximate the work of professionals in the field.

UNIT SEQUENCE, DESCRIPTION, AND TEACHER REFLECTIONS

Preassessment: How Are Local Breezes Formed?

(20 minutes)

Unit Sequence	Teacher Reflections
SD1–5 The preassessment is a simple prompt: Explain how local breezes are formed. Invite students to share their thinking in a short paragraph at the beginning of the unit.	It is important to gather baseline information about students' prior knowledge. It will help you (1) target where you need to begin with the module, (2) determine which content to emphasize and which content to stress less, and (3) measure student growth over the course of the module. I have spent a great deal of time with students talking about the importance of a preassessment. By now, they realize that this prompt is not a test, nor will they be graded on it. They know that I will use the information in their paragraphs to help me tailor my teaching around their learning needs. Furthermore, I will review each student's answer and make brief notes about his or her level of understanding. I will refer back to my notes to evaluate the extent of student growth exhibited in the postassessment (see **Lesson 7 Worksheet: Tiny Tornados**).

Lesson 1: Hot Spots, the Sun

(about 40 minutes)

Unit Sequence	Teacher Reflections
Concepts. Sun, Energy, Weather G1, SD1, SD4 **Introduction**. Begin this module by explaining to students that they will be learning about the sun and its role in our daily weather. Show students the **Unit Concept Map: The Driving Force in Weather** for their study of this unit. Point out that the sun is at the very top of the concept chart because it is the driving force in weather. Also point out the other components that make up the weather system: the unequal heating of the Earth and the water cycle.	I have already taught students about concept maps in general. I will spend time sharing this concept map about weather for several reasons. First, its use will help young people understand how the concepts and principles of this module are organized. In doing so, it will help them to answer a Core focusing question for the module: How is this information organized? Second, it will serve as an advanced organizer for their learning. As such, it will help them make sense of the new learning that will occur in this module, thereby increasing the likelihood of student achievement gains.

(Continued)

(Continued)

Unit Sequence	Teacher Reflections
Discussion. Pose a question to students, who are convened as a whole class, but are sitting in small groups: What is so important about the sun as it relates to our weather? Ask students to talk quietly about the answer to this question for a minute or two, and then invite them to write down their answers, individually, on **My Thinking Sheet: The Most Important Thing About the Sun.**	While students discussed this question in their small groups, I took the opportunity to rove around the room listening to students' conversations. I knew I had some students who were very interested in weather. In addition, I had some students who possessed a great deal of prior knowledge about the role of the sun and the water cycle as elements of the weather system. Finally, I knew I had other students who had very little interest in this earth science topic. I created **Lesson 1 Rubric: Assessing the Question, "What Are the Most Important Things About the Sun?"** to assess students' conceptual understanding of the role of the sun as it relates to weather. I created it with a high ceiling and a low baseline to capture the range of learners in my classroom.
Ask students to put their Thinking Sheets aside for now. Invite them to listen as you read Margaret Wise Brown's (1990) book, *The Important Book*. At the end of your reading, ask students once again to think about what is so important about the sun as it relates to our weather? If they have new ideas about the sun, ask students to record any new thinking on their **My Thinking Sheet.**	This beginning unit is all about concept attainment. I want students to understand that we all construct knowledge one step at a time. For this reason, I chose Margaret Wise Brown's children's book. She makes the point that there are lots of reasons why common, everyday objects are important, but that there is always one reason why the object is most important.
	I have used **My Thinking Sheet** with students because I want them to practice what scientists do every day. Scientists think and rethink their observations, data, and "learnings" in order to come to new understandings about the world around them. It is part of scientific habits of mind to think about the world, make observations, draw conclusions, listen to the thinking of others, and perhaps change one's initial thinking.
Examining Pictures of the Sun. Switch gears and ask students to join you at the computer. Show them live pictures of the sun from Project SOHO, which stands for Solar and Heliospheric Observatory, a satellite that studies the sun 24 hours a day,	Not only do I have students interested in technology, but I also have above-grade-level readers with interests in the solar system and weather. In addition, I am hoping that these remarkable images will capture the attention of some of my more

Unit Sequence	*Teacher Reflections*
365 days a year (see http://sohowww.nas com.nasa.gov). Explain to them that scientists are fascinated by the sun and have hundreds of unanswered questions about it, such as the following:	reluctant students. I invite everyone to complete this extension activity.
• How big is it? • How hot is it? • What is it made of? • How does it work? • Why does it shine? • How much light gets to Earth? • What is sunshine?	I want students to leave today knowing that the sun is the most important element in our weather system: It is the energy source for all daily weather activity.
Make a point of referring back to any student-generated questions about the weather. Highlight matches between the students' questions and those that scientists are studying. Underscore the importance of personal questions; they are at the heart of scientists' work. Explain to students the importance of questions in science. Sometimes scientists study just one or two questions throughout their entire professional lives.	I couldn't help but compare this Core Curriculum unit with other, more traditional curriculum materials about meteorology. Hardly any of the traditional materials talk about the sun at the outset of the unit. This is astonishing because the sun is the driving force of our weather. By beginning with the sun, I know that I am getting to the core ideas about weather, as well as the structure of the discipline.
Show students other sites about the sun too. The following Web sites have photographs of the sun, the birth of stars, solar flares, and sunspots: http://soho.nascom.nasa.gov/hotshots http://umbra.nascom.nasa.gov/images	
Ask the students to return to their groups and, in a think-pair-share, reflect a couple of minutes about the importance of the sun in our daily weather. Why is the sun important? What does it do for us?	Think-pair-share is one of the most common cooperative learning strategies. The teacher asks students to think about a topic, pair with a partner to discuss it, and share their ideas with a group.
Debriefing. Reconvene students to engage them in a dialogue about what they have learned. Ask them to tell you what they now believe are the most important things about the sun.	I recognize that students have only a superficial grasp of these concepts and principles, but I know that I have helped move their thinking forward in this first lesson. We will have plenty of opportunities to deepen their understanding as the unit progresses.
As you record their responses and "second thinkings," weave in some of the concepts and definitions that are featured in this lesson: sun, star, light energy, work.	

(Continued)

(Continued)

Unit Sequence	Teacher Reflections
Using Socratic questioning, help students think their way to understanding that the sun is the source for all interactions in our weather: It heats the land; it causes air to warm and rise (wind); it causes water to move; and wind moves water in the atmosphere.	
Reinforce the facts that our daily weather is a system and that the system begins with the sun. The most important thing about the sun is its light, the energy source for our weather.	
Optional Extension. Invite interested students to visit any of the Web sites that were used in class and to submit any of their questions to the scientists at the SOHO laboratory.	

Lesson 2: Sun Power

(35 minutes)

Unit Sequence	Teacher Reflections
Concepts. Sunlight, Absorbed, Energy, Observation, Cause, Effect G2, SD1–3, S1 **Introduction.** Convene a whole-class meeting. Explain to students that in this lesson they will be studying a different but related aspect about the sun: its tremendous power. Ask them to remember the session in which they looked at pictures of the sun and answered the question, "What is the most important thing about the sun?" Explain that one of the most important things about the sun is its light and that students will have a chance to see the tremendous power of its light in action in	In this lesson, students will extend their understanding of the power of the sun as a source of energy. They will witness light energy being transformed into heat energy. In addition, they will apply their skill of observation to a demonstration about the power of the sun. This session reinforces Principle 2: When sunlight is absorbed by the earth, it is transformed into heat energy, which causes changes to Earth's surfaces. This lesson, like the last, is focused on concept attainment. Specifically, students need to understand that light energy is turned into heat energy when it is absorbed by Earth's surfaces. The lesson is a dramatic one, designed purposefully to capture students' attention and interest in the sun.

Unit Sequence	*Teacher Reflections*
just a few moments. Their job in this lesson is to make detailed and accurate observations.	In this introduction, I am doing two things. First, I am activating prior knowledge by reiterating one of the important principles that students learned earlier. Namely, the sun is a source of energy that drives all our weather. Second, I am creating some drama about what is to come in the lesson.
Lab Activity. Arrange students into pairs for this activity. Ask them to read through the lab sheets to make sure that they understand what they will be doing in the **Lesson 2 Worksheet: Focusing Attention on Sunlight**.	I arranged students into pairs so that all students would have a partner with whom to discuss the sophisticated and abstract concepts and principles in this Core lesson. Students can also use their partner to check the comprehensiveness of the observations that they will make in the upcoming demonstration.
When students have read the sheets, show them the magnifying glass and the piece of paper that are placed on a nonflammable surface. Hold the magnifying glass so that it captures light but does not focus it on the paper.	**Modifications for Learner Need.** While they were reading, I rotated through the pairs to support students who may have experienced difficulty with the reading. I pointed out the headings, explained what they meant, and showed them how they could use their sticky notes to write down questions about the content. (I try to provide students with sticky notes most of the time because it helps them remember their questions and thoughts. Students' notes are especially helpful during whole-class debriefings because they help students remember the questions they have not had a chance to ask.)
Invite students to guess what they will see, hear, and/or smell as you continue to hold the magnifying glass so that the light remains unfocused on the paper. Ask students to place their guesses on the appropriate places on their **Lesson 2 Lab: Black and White—My Guesses and Observations**. Continue to hold the magnifying glass so that light shining through the glass remains unfocused. Ask students to complete their observations (versus predictions or guesses).	
Then, change gears. Say this time, "I am going to hold the magnifying glass so that the light is focused tightly on the paper." Invite students to guess what will happen and record their guesses on their lab sheet. They can talk over their guesses with their partner.	
Do the demonstration again. This time focus the light tightly enough so that smoke begins to rise from the paper that is	I have tissues handy to use if the sun is not shining brightly. Tissues will smolder more quickly than paper.

(Continued)

Unit Sequence	Teacher Reflections

being heated by the focused rays of sunlight. If necessary, repeat the demonstration so that students have the opportunity to make their observations one more time.

When students have finished their observations, ask them to complete **Beyond the Data** at the end of the **Lesson 2 Lab**. Tell students that they can talk over the questions with their partner, but that they must each submit a completed lab sheet.

Debriefing. Explain to students that they have observed how powerful just a few rays of the sun can be. Engage them in a discussion about what they saw.

- What changes did you observe in the paper in the second demonstration?
- Based on your observations, what can you infer about the way light affects surfaces?
- What is the sun's energy?
- How do you think the sun's light affects Earth?
- If the sun is this powerful, how might it affect our weather?
- Which of your questions have yet to be answered?
- In what ways do you see your powers of observation improving?

Share with students that they will be looking more closely at this interaction among the sun, air, land, and water over the next few lessons. Close by saying that in the next session they will explore the effect of sunlight on land, which has many different kinds of surfaces.

Emphasize with students the concepts and principles that they witnessed in this small model of the interaction between the sun and Earth. Light energy comes from the sun. It is absorbed by all surfaces on Earth and transformed or changed into heat energy. The Earth's surfaces release some of the heat into the air nearby, warming the air, our atmosphere. The sun's light is what causes all of the effects just mentioned: the heating of Earth's surface, the release of some of the heat, and the warming of the atmosphere.

Lesson 3: Unequal Heating of Earth's Surfaces

(80 minutes)

Unit Sequence	*Teacher Reflections*
Concepts. Dark Surfaces, Light Surfaces, Absorb, Release, Light Energy, Heat, Weather, Enhanced Greenhouse Effect (AID) G3, G4 (AID), SD2–4, S1, S3–4, S6 **Introduction.** Convene a whole-class meeting. Remind students that they have been studying about weather, which is the study of the interactions among the sun, land, air, and water. Explain that today they will look at how sunlight is absorbed by Earth's surfaces. Ask the guiding questions so that students have a focus for their work: Do all substances absorb (take in) the same amount of heat? Do all substances release (give off) the same amount of heat?	In this session, the teacher will develop students' understanding of Principle 3: The darker surfaces of Earth (e.g., dark soil, asphalt roadways, forests) absorb more sunlight than lighter surfaces (e.g., snow, glacier ice) and, as a result, release more heat. Students will participate in a simple experiment with black and white paper that will provide them with the opportunity to construct their own understanding of the absorption rates of different colored surfaces. The black paper represents the darker surfaces on Earth, while the white paper represents the lighter surfaces. This session also provides an alternate experiment for students who may already be familiar with the absorption rates of different surfaces and need increasing levels of challenge.
Preassessment. Ask students, either orally or in writing, what happens when sunlight shines on dark and light substances. Use the **Lesson 3 Rubric: Assessing Answers to the Question "What Happens When Sunlight Shines on Different Colored Substances of Earth?"** which ascertains students' knowledge level. If some students understand differing absorption rates, arrange them into a separate group (Group 2) that will work on the enhanced greenhouse effect experiment that follows.	**Modifications for Learner Need.** Based upon earlier preassessments and "kid watching" over the past several lessons, I know that I have students at different levels of understanding about this principle. Some of my students already understand that dark clothing makes you feel warmer than light-colored clothing. I am pretty sure that some of my students have a more sophisticated understanding of the absorption rates of different surfaces, namely that darker surfaces absorb more light energy and give off more heat than do light surfaces. As a double check on my hunches, I designed a quick preassessment that uses a rubric. I wasn't surprised when some students were able to articulate that dark surfaces on Earth give off more heat than do lighter surfaces. They are pretty good thinkers and observers of the world around them!
Lab Activity. Ask all students, in both Group 1 and Group 2, to read through their lab instructions. Explain that students in Group 1 will be exploring how different surfaces, represented by white and black paper, will absorb different amounts of sunlight and give off different amounts of heat. Students in Group 1 will be going outside to record the temperatures of black and white paper over a ten-minute period of time. They will use their **Lesson 3 Lab: Black and White—What Happens When**	**AID.** As I designed AID in this Core Curriculum lesson, it was of paramount importance to build in increasing levels of

(Continued)

Unit Sequence	Teacher Reflections
Sunlight Shines on Different Colored Objects? to record their data. Remind them to also complete the Beyond the Data questions after they have finished the lab. Students in Group 2 will be exploring another aspect of daily temperature, on the **Lesson 3 Lab: Enhanced Greenhouse Effect**. They will be going outside and recording the temperatures of two chambers: one that has a lid and one that does not have a lid. They will use their lab sheets to record their data. Share with students that they will reconvene during their next session together to share the findings of the two experiments. While students conduct the experiments, rotate from group to group. **Debriefing.** Reconvene students and ask Group 1 students to form small groups of four students. Have Group 2 students work as a small group. Ask Group 1 students to summarize how surfaces absorb sunlight differently. Ask Group 2 students to summarize what happens when heat does not escape and is instead absorbed by gases in our atmosphere. When students have had a chance to summarize their findings, provide them with the opportunity to share their findings with the entire class. Then, engage students in a discussion of Group 1's summary statements. What was similar among the findings? What differences exist? In what ways might the black and white paper model what happens on Earth? Provide students in Group 2 with the same opportunities. At the conclusion of their presentation, emphasize that our	cognitive intensity for my learners with prior knowledge. From reading *The Parallel Curriculum* (Tomlinson et al., 2002), I knew that I could (1) use more advanced materials, (2) offer instruction at a brisker pace, (3) offer content with greater depth or breadth, (4) provide more or less scaffolding to support concept attainment, or (5) require more expert level of quality in products (p. 91). In addition, I had to ensure that the content for AID stemmed directly from the content of this lesson, namely the heating of Earth's surfaces and atmosphere. I decided to alter the depth of students' learning. I had a good hunch that I wanted to focus the content for AID around the enhanced greenhouse effect because it is a contemporary issue that stems directly from the release of heat from surfaces of Earth. The only question in my mind was whether I would find background reading material suitable for my students on this sophisticated and theoretical topic. I did an Internet search. I entered "exploring greenhouse effect" to locate sites that were educational in nature and quickly found thousands. Within ten minutes, I located a site written just for young people, and at three reading levels: beginning, intermediate, and advanced (see www.windows.ucar.edu/tour/link=/earth/interior/greenhouse_effect.html). It was easy to make up the experiment for Group 2 to stay within the time frames of the experiment for Group 1. Group 1 students were recording the temperatures of two different colored papers over ten minutes. I constructed Group 2's experiment so that students could record the temperatures in open and closed containers over the same ten-minute interval.

Unit Sequence	Teacher Reflections

Unit Sequence

atmosphere is, indeed, fragile. Some scientists believe that radiated heat is being absorbed by human-created pollutants in our atmosphere. When this happens, the temperatures may be higher than normal. The enhanced greenhouse effect may have harmful effects, such as melting glaciers and ice caps, which, in turn, raise the sea level.

Review with students the connection between the absorption rates of dark and light substances and our weather. Daily temperatures are affected by the heat released from Earth's surfaces. Some scientists believe that our daily weather may be warmer as a result of the enhanced greenhouse effect.

Teacher Reflections

To summarize, the enhanced greenhouse experiment for advanced learners addressed two different "Core Curriculum pathways." As a learning alternative, it required above-grade-level students to use a different, more advanced resource and work at a much greater depth and level of complexity.

As I roam from group to group, I often see things that I have never noticed before. First, the kids really like working in groups and being responsible for their learning and behavior. Second, when I listen carefully to the group members' dialogue, I can figure out where they are stuck in their thinking. I've discovered that if I ask just the right question or provide just the right hint, kids get the answer by thinking their way through the problem. I can vary the amount of feedback and the kinds of questions that I ask, depending on whether I've got struggling learners or advanced thinkers.

I want to listen intently to students' findings. I want to make sure that they tie their learning back to the Core principle we are investigating in this experiment, namely that darker substances (e.g., dark soil, asphalt roadways, forests) absorb more sunlight than lighter substances (e.g., snow, glacier ice) and, as a result, release more heat than the lighter surfaces. If students do not relate their learning back to the principle, this is my opportunity to weave their findings back to our Core. I emphasize that different substances do, indeed, absorb sunlight differently. The darker surfaces absorb more light than lighter surfaces. With respect to the Earth, darker substances are forests, dark soils, and asphalt. Lighter substances include sand, fresh snow, glacial ice, and ice caps.

Dark and light substances release different amounts of heat. The heat, in turn, warms the nearby air, our atmosphere. The interaction of the sun, land, and air all contribute to weather.

Lesson 4: Estimating Percentages of Land and Water

(40 minutes)

Unit Sequence	Teacher Reflections
Concepts. Estimation, Reasonable, Percentage SD6, S2	In the next two lessons, the teacher will be developing students' understanding of the fact that there is a great deal more water on Earth than there is land. Students will learn explicit skills for making an estimate.
Introduction. Divide students into small, heterogeneous groups of three students each. Ask students to generate a list of the things that have surprised them since they began their discussion about the weather. Provide students with time to share their thinking with the class. Students' responses will vary. Show them the **Unit Concept Map** again and make sure that students have a clear understanding of the organization of knowledge so far.	I take my time in this introduction because I want students to see the connection between their learning so far and the new learning that this set of two lessons includes. Students have learned that the sun is the driving force behind all our weather, sunlight is transformed into heat energy, and different surfaces on Earth absorb different amounts of light and, by extension, give off different amounts of heat.
Explain that students are in for another surprise. They will spend time talking about a very important fact about weather. It is something that they probably all know about but have not, until now, connected with the weather. It is that the Earth is covered mostly by water. If this is so, how might the idea of our vast oceans be connected to weather? Ask students to talk for a minute in their groups to come up with a possible connection.	These principles and concepts are a critical foundation for the next fact: Earth is 75 percent water and 25 percent land. This realization has tremendous implications for understanding the next lessons about wind, because air moves as a result of the unequal heating of Earth's surfaces. Water and land absorb and give off different amounts of heat. This is a critical juncture for students. I want to make sure that they are all "with me" before I proceed.
Elicit responses from the groups and record their answers on flip chart paper.	
Hang the flip chart paper containing students' ideas and explain that they will return to these ideas over the next two days. Explain that before we address this important question, we need to talk about how we estimate, a very important skill that all scientists use.	
Lab Activity. Arrange students into small, heterogeneous groups. Explain that they will be learning a thinking protocol for estimation during this session.	
Invite students to read through their **Lesson 4 Lab: Estimation—It's Easier Than You Think!** Work through the first estimation problem together as a whole class: How much water will you drink in a lifetime? Make sure to verbalize with students all the steps in your thinking. Then move on to the	I know that my students will be at very different levels with respect to their ability to think their way through an estimation problem and reflect metacognitively on their own thinking processes. I make a point to rotate through the groups and pay special attention to the students who need more

Unit Sequence	*Teacher Reflections*

next estimation problem: How tall is the flagpole? Use the second example for students to try the estimation protocol on their own in their small groups, using guided practice as an instructional strategy. Finally, have students work through the last problem: About what percentage of the Earth's surface is covered by land? By water? Make sure that students have estimates that are reasonable.

scaffolding. I provide hints and suggestions to students who have trouble breaking down the maps into smaller, more workable sections (from six to nine sections will probably be ideal).

While students work, use Socratic questioning to help them develop a line of reasoning once they have estimates for each of the smaller portions of the map. Students will need to make an overall estimate of the amount of land and water on Earth based on each of the six to nine estimates that resulted when they broke down the map into smaller, more manageable sections.

Modifications for Learner Need. I vary the number of questions that I ask, the degree of inference embedded within the questions, and the amount of feedback that I provide.

Remind students to also complete the **Lesson 4 Lab: What Percentage of Earth's Surface Is Water? Is Land?** questions after they have finished the lab.

Debriefing. Make sure that students understand the thinking process that is the foundation for estimation. Explain that we can all be better thinkers if we understand the "thinking procedures" behind commonly used thinking skills.

I highlight two things in this debriefing. First, I underscore the importance of estimation. Second, I make sure that students see the connection between their learning about estimation and our study of weather. We need to be able to estimate the amount of land and water on Earth to better understand how the earth absorbs sunlight and gives off heat unequally.

Equally important, make sure that students have generated a reasonable estimate of the amount of water and land on Earth's surface.

1. Ask students to explain out loud the thinking steps involved with estimation.

2. Ask if students checked their answer to make sure it was reasonable.

3. Ask students, "Which strategy did you use to tell if your answer was reasonable?"

4. Listen to students' responses to check the "reasonableness" of their strategies.

5. Talk about the slight variations in students' estimates. Is it OK to have slightly different estimates? Why or why not?

Tell students to clean up, store their work, and be prepared for the next session in which they will make a visual representation of their answer. Share that students' visual representations will help them understand more about the unequal heating of Earth's surfaces.

Lesson 5: Using Pie Charts to Represent Information

(40 minutes)

Unit Sequence	Teacher Reflections

Concepts. Estimation, Percentage, Pie Chart

SD6, S3, S5

Introduction. Request that students collect their work from before and return to the groups from the earlier session. To prompt students' thinking, ask them—in their small groups—to recall their estimates of the amount of land and water on the Earth. Make sure the estimates are reasonable.

In this session students will be making a visual representation of their estimate of the amount of water and land on Earth. This session, like the one preceding it, addresses the idea that there is a great deal more water on Earth than there is land. To construct their own meaning of what a percentage or fraction means, they will make a pie chart of the surface of Earth using one hundred 1-inch squares of blue and brown construction paper.

Because I know that fractions and percentages are abstract concepts to students, I have made a collection of graphs from *USA Today*. I have brought examples of pie charts from the paper with me so that I can show students how accessible visual displays of data are and that many people, including scientists, use graphs to display and describe their findings. This lesson especially appeals to my more visual learners.

Learning Activities. Based on your knowledge of students' background knowledge, facility with fractions and percents, and ability to graph data, assign them to Task 1 or to Task 2 (AID).

Task 1. Explain that today students will be creating a particular kind of graph, called a pie chart, to make a visual representation of their estimate of water and land on Earth's surface.

To begin this activity in creating pie charts, ask the groups of students to place one of the large pieces of white paper at the center of their tables.

Next, demonstrate how students should draw a large circle, about 10 inches in diameter, on the paper with the pencil that is at their table.

Invite students to imagine that the lightly drawn circle represents the whole of the Earth. Ask them to look at their estimate from yesterday. Think about the whole of Earth as 100 percent. If that is so, then we can use a fraction or percentage to represent the amount of land and water making up the "whole" of Earth.

Modifications for Learner Need. I noticed that different groups of students needed varying levels of support for their work with fractions and percentages. I rotate from group to group, providing students with hints and questions that forward their estimates and progress.

Unit Sequence	*Teacher Reflections*

Tell the students that they will be selecting a total of 100 small blue and brown paper squares to represent their estimate. Ask students, "How many brown pieces will you select to represent your estimate? How many blue ones will you need to illustrate your estimate?" For example, if they believe that one-half of Earth is covered by land and one-half by water, then they would select 50 pieces of blue and 50 pieces of brown paper, and so forth. If they believe that the parts are three-fourths and one-fourth, respectively, they will select 75 pieces and 25 pieces, respectively.

Ask students to place and paste their colored pieces of paper in the circle. They may have to tear some of the pieces so that the edges fit within the circle. Invite students to hang their pie charts when they are done.

Task 2 (AID). Invite students to read a very short selection, "The Water Cycle," which contains information in percentages about the availability and distribution of fresh water, at http://earthobservatory.nasa.gov/Library/Water/

Upon completion of their reading, ask students to make a pie chart showing the sources of water, including freshwater, and their percentages that are available in the world. You might also want to limit the number of water sources because some of them are too small to show on a pie chart. Thus the following list of sources would be more than adequate for students to understand that a very limited amount of freshwater is available—oceans and bays (96 percent); ice caps, glaciers, and permanent snow (1.5 percent); groundwater (1.5 percent); lakes and rivers (0.5 percent); and other (0.5 percent).

Students who already know the meaning of a fraction, that 75 percent of the Earth is covered with water, and who can represent their data in a pie chart should be assigned to Task 2.

My challenge in creating this activity was to simultaneously ground these students' learning within the context of the lesson and extend their learning in a meaningful way. I had a number of choices. I could have required these students to do more in-depth reading about any aspect of the oceans, or I could have asked students to work with a computer application that allowed them to make more colorful pie charts. I decided that these options "missed the mark" because they did not stem directly from the content of the unit or address the students' need for greater depth related to percentages and fractions.

Instead, I decided to alter only the resources that these above-grade-level students would use. The easy-to-read article about the availability of water on Earth was a perfect fit for the content of the unit. The pie chart students were asked to create from the data in the article required them to make much finer discriminations in their graphs. Instead of representing one-fourth and three-fourths as percentages, this assignment

(Continued)

(Continued)

Unit Sequence	Teacher Reflections
	required students to represent 1/100 or 1 percent. By using this pathway to AID, I required my advanced learners to work at a greater level of depth and abstraction.
	Equally important, by altering the resource and maintaining a similar product, I simultaneously kept my AID manageable and required my advanced learners to read in more depth about water on Earth and create products with more expertlike qualities.
Debriefing. In this debriefing, reinforce three important points with students: • Estimation is an important skill used by all people, especially scientists. • Estimation involves a series of thinking steps that will help ensure that estimates are reasonable: find the unknown; identify what one does know about the unknown, usually by breaking it into smaller, more knowable pieces; establish a line of reasoning; and check the answer for reasonableness. • There is a great deal more water than land on Earth. Bring students back to the last guiding question in this module: How does the amount of water on the Earth's surface affect our weather? Return to the flip chart paper that includes students' thinking about the connection between the large amount of water on Earth and weather. (This was done in the introduction of Lesson 4.) Query students to see if anyone has thought more about this question. Listen to students' thinking and share that they will be looking more closely at the connection between the large amount of water on Earth and the weather in the sessions to come.	I make a point of bringing the conversation full circle in the lesson. Students need to revisit the reason for their work in estimation. They may not fully understand the connection between percentages of water and land on Earth and wind, but I will begin "to set the stage" for students' subsequent investigations into wind, one of the key components of weather.

Lesson 6: Absorption Rates of Land and Water

(50 minutes)

Unit Sequence	Teacher Reflections
Concepts. Gains, Losses, Weather G5, SD6, S1, S4, S6	Students have spent time learning about the interaction of the sun on land surfaces. Most recently, they have learned about Earth as the water planet, whose surface is about 75 percent water. In this session, students will learn about the different absorption rates of land and water. Specifically, water gains and loses heat more slowly than does land. Students will see this important principle at work in an experiment. They will use graphing to see the different rates of warming and cooling in water and soil. At the end of this experiment, students will be invited to think about how this difference in absorption rate affects daily weather.
Introduction. Convene a whole-class meeting and arrange students into groups of two. Ask students to close their eyes and think about a hot summer afternoon when they are at a lake or the ocean. The temperature is well up into the 90s. They are walking on the sand. How do their feet feel? They are so hot that they jump into the water. How do their feet feel now? Tell students that today they will be exploring why the lakes and oceans stay cooler than land. Their job during today's experiment is to learn why water and land have different temperatures. In addition, their job is also to continue their thinking about the guiding question, "What effects do the different temperatures of land and water have on our weather?"	
	In this introduction, I am setting the stage for students' investigation. I am also trying to establish relevance. By providing them with a scenario that is familiar, I hope that they will see that the principle underlying this lesson influences and affects their lives.
Lab Activity. Students are asked to complete a lab experiment in which they place equal amounts of soil and water in the sun or under a lamp. During **Lesson 6 Lab: Sunlight on Land and Water**, they are asked to record the temperatures of two samples: water (oceans and lakes) and soil (earth). When students display their raw data in line graph form, they see that water loses and gains heat much more slowly than does land. Next, have students answer the Lesson 6 Lab questions in the Beyond the Data section.	The resources are easy to collect for this Core Curriculum unit and much less expensive than the consumables in many commercial kits. The local newspaper weather maps are easy to cut out, as is the temperature information for different locations. Kids love the authentic nature of the resources.
Debriefing. Arrange students in small groups of four. Show students the temperature readings from places that are close to large bodies of water and places that are nearby, but inland. Ask students to draw conclusions based upon the data from their experiments and the weather data. Ask each group to develop an explanation for the differences between the temperatures at the two locations. Invite students to share their thinking.	This debriefing will be an assessment of students' understanding of the effect of the unequal heating of Earth's surfaces. It requires students to apply their learning from the lab experiment. If students understand the different absorption rates well, they will be able to draw the conclusion that places near large bodies of water stay warmer in the winter and cooler in the summer. If students have difficulty drawing this conclusion, use Socratic questioning to guide their thinking to the explanation.

Lesson 7: Tiny Tornados
(80–100 minutes)

Unit Sequence	Teacher Reflections
Concepts. Lighter, Rises, Local Winds, Air Movement G6–8, SD5, S1, S3–5, S6	In this lesson, using a heated lamp bulb and some talcum powder, you will "make visible" the fact that warm air rises. Concurrently, cooler air rushes in to take its place. When this happens, local winds are formed.
Introduction. Begin this session by reading aloud "Who Has Seen the Wind?" by Christina Rossetti, available at either of the following Web sites: www.recmusic.org/lieder/r/rossetti/wind.html www.grc.nasa.gov/www/K-12/Summer_Training/Elementary97/WhoHasSeenThe Wind.html Ask students the following questions: a. Have you seen the wind? b. How do you observe the wind if you can't see it? What other senses might you use? c. What is wind? Explain to students that today their job is to learn what causes wind and what makes it move fast. In addition, they will come to understand that it is an important feature of our daily weather.	I designed this introduction so that students could see the far-reaching effects of the weather. I wanted them to understand that artists of all kinds—visual artists, poets, fiction writers, dancers—feature weather in their work. I will make a point to "kid watch" during this introduction to see if any students might be interested in pursuing the way artists have depicted weather. Be sure to make works from varied cultures available to all students.
Lab Activity. Assign students to heterogeneous pairs. Explain that they will be observing two demonstrations. Their job is to make careful observations with all their senses. Invite them to read through **Lesson 7 Lab: It's All About Hot Air**. If you believe some students will need help with the observation process, put out copies of **My Thinking Sheet**, which was used in Lesson 1. These sheets will serve as a reminder for students to use all their senses when they are observing.	One of the challenges in teaching the Core principles in science is getting students to construct their knowledge of the principles. I chose these two demonstrations to illustrate that warm air rises and cool air rushes in to take its place. I also built in plenty of time for students to think about what is happening and to draw their own conclusions about the movement of air. These concepts and principles are very abstract, and students need time to build their own understanding.

Unit Sequence	*Teacher Reflections*

Begin with a regular lamp with a bare bulb. It should be off. Shake some talcum powder on a cloth. Then, shake the cloth over the cold bulb. Let students make observations. Then, turn the lamp on and let it warm up so that it is hot.

Shake the cloth again. Students should be able to observe some of the particles rising upward in the air that is warmed above the bulb.

In a think-pair-share, ask students to dialogue about what has happened to the particles of talcum powder. Then, have them discuss what inferences they can draw about the warm air. They should all be able to explain that warm air rises.

Show them two balloons that have been stretched over the mouths of two soda bottles. One bottle has been immersed in ice water for about 30 minutes; the other has been in hot water for the same amount of time.

Students will see that the balloon on the bottle in hot water has inflated. The air inside the bottle is warmed, has expanded, and is actually lighter than unwarmed air. So it inflates, as in this demonstration.

In the same think-pair-share format, ask students to talk about what replaced the warm air that rose. Reconvene the class and engage students in a discussion about their theories. Using Socratic questioning, lead them to understand that something had to replace the warm air, and it is cooler air that is denser than warm air.

Explain to students that the same air exchange happens continually on a much larger scale in Earth's atmosphere. When sunlight warms Earth, the surface releases heat energy, which in turn warms the nearby air. That warm air then rises up into the atmosphere. Cooler air rushes in to take its place, thereby causing local winds. The greater the temperature difference, the stronger the wind.

I know that I will need to scaffold for my students in a number of ways. For my grade-level learners, I will need to make sure they draw the right conclusions. For my below-grade learners, I know I will need to prompt them with questions that will help them think their way through this lesson. I might even need to work with them in a small group to reteach some of the material and redo the demonstration. I developed the **Graphic Organizer: Cause and Effect—Wind** as a way to help these learners understand this principle.

In addition, I know I will need to do a great deal of scaffolding for all my students as we make the leap from the lightbulb experiment to how convection works in the atmosphere.

I am already thinking that students may have a hard time understanding that cool air "sinks." I may need to extend this module by one lesson to provide students with another demonstration that allows them to "construct" their own understanding of this abstract scientific principle.

I have already tried at home a simple kitchen demonstration that will illustrate for students that cool air sinks. It involves (1) holding a smoldering piece of incense next to a refrigerator freezer door, (2) opening the freezer door, (3) watching the incense smoke be carried downward with the cool air.

If I need to add this lesson about the behavior of cool air, I will replicate my kitchen demonstration in the classroom. I will replace the refrigerator with an ice chest that holds a container of frozen coolant or ice.

Optional Extensions. Interested students can be encouraged to visit the Mount Washington Observatory Web site at

(Continued)

(Continued)

Unit Sequence	Teacher Reflections
Remind students to also complete the **Lesson 7 Lab: Beyond the Data** questions after they have finished their lab.	www.mountwashington.org/observatory/index.html. It was at this spot that the highest wind gust on earth was recorded on April 12, 1934. Despite its relatively low elevation (6,288 feet), Mount Washington is located at the confluence of three major storm tracks, and being the highest point in New England, it generally takes the brunt of passing storms. The steepness of the slopes, combined with the north-south orientation of the range, causes the winds to accelerate dramatically as they rise up from the valleys.
	Students may also be interested in looking for more information about the following:
	• Locations and events *Windiest place:* Gale winds reaching 200 miles an hour *Place:* Commonwealth Bay, Antarctica
	• Fastest tornado winds—286 miles an hour *Place:* Wichita Falls, Texas *Date:* April 2, 1958
	• Hurricane with the highest wind gusts—175–80 miles per hour *Place:* Central Keys and lower southwest Florida coast *Date:* August 29–September 13, 1960
Unit Postassessment. Assign students to work in pairs. Explain that they will be given an assignment in class to complete about the unequal heating of the earth. Review the worksheet **Lesson 7 Worksheet: Tiny Tornados** with them. Tomorrow they will work in pairs to discuss the assignment. Although pairs can talk about the answer to the tiny tornado puzzle, each student will be responsible for turning in an assignment.	I crafted this performance assessment carefully. It had to sample the concepts and principles addressed in this unit because I could not assess everything that I taught. In addition, I had to make sure that my postassessment was a "fraternal twin" to the preassessment. I am pleased that students will have to apply their newly acquired knowledge in a different context, because this will give me a true indication about what they really learned. I think they will find it fun, too, because everyone has seen a tiny tornado and wondered about it.
Debriefing. In this concluding session on wind, once again show students the **Unit Concept Map** for the unit. Trace with them their new understanding about the unit principles:	I created **Lesson 7 Rubric: Assessing Answers to Tiny Tornados Worksheet** for

Unit Sequence	*Teacher Reflections*
• Sunlight is the source of energy for weather. • When sunlight is absorbed unequally by different surfaces, they release different amounts of heat energy into the air nearby. • Warm air rises, cool air sinks. • When cool air rushes in to take the place of warm air, local winds are created. • Local winds influence our weather. Remind students that weather is a result of the complex interaction among the sun, air, land, and water. In today's lesson they looked at air movement, which is called wind. Local winds are based on a cause and effect relationship between warm air and cool air. Wind speed and direction are key features of our daily weather.	the performance assessment. It has a high ceiling and a low baseline. I will be eager to see students' assignments and compare their learning with preassessment data gathered earlier. I knew it would be important for me to return to the Concept Map in this last session for two reasons. First, I wanted another opportunity to reinforce the structure of the content—concepts and principles—so important to the Core parallel. With my finger, I will trace the concepts and principles carefully on the map to make sure that students understand the relationships among the concepts and clear away any lingering misconceptions. The second reason for returning to the Concept Map at the conclusion is to underscore for students how much they have learned since the outset of the unit. I derive such pleasure when I see the amazed looks on some students' faces. They frequently share that they have "come a long way!" By working with the Core parallel in this unit, I am now able to describe this parallel in one sentence: It cuts to the chase. The principles we focused on are the most important ones there are in this discipline. There is no wasted time in these lessons, and they "pack a punch" with the way they are sequenced. I think the sequenced principles are one of the best things about this Core Curriculum; the principles are the perfect, most logically ordered bits of information for my students. It makes me realize how episodic and sometimes "off the mark" my former teaching about weather was. I'll never again have my students study the Coriolis effect as a "stand-alone unit." Nor will I have my students make dioramas with cotton ball clouds ever again. Cotton balls simply do not tap into students' conceptual understanding. And remember those tornados in a bottle? It was a nice activity, but I never taught the science behind it. No more tornados in a bottle, either.

Unit Concept Map: The Driving Force in Weather

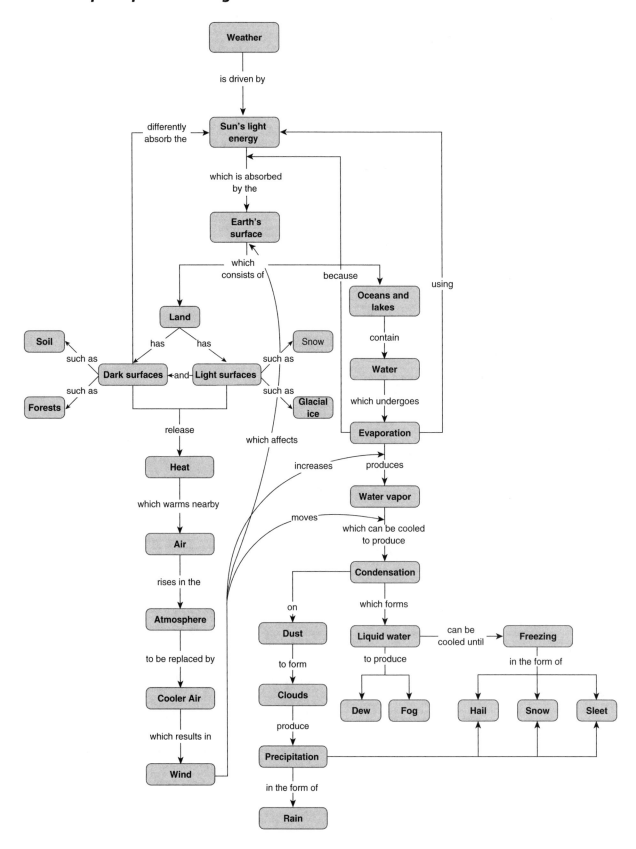

My Thinking Sheet: The Most Important Thing About the Sun

My First Reasons

1.
2.
3.
4.
5.

The Reasons I Added to My First List

1.
2.
3.
4.
5.
6.

I Changed/Did Not Change My Thinking Because

_____

_____

_____

_____

_____

_____

❖　❖　❖

Lesson 1 Rubric: Assessing the Question
"What Are the Most Important Things About the Sun?"

Novice	Intermediate	Advanced	Expert
The sun is big and shines when the weather is nice.	The sun is a ball of fire that warms the earth.	The sun provides Earth with energy. Its energy helps plants to grow, laundry to dry, our house to be warm, and puddles to dry.	The sun is a source of energy that sets into motion the interaction among the elements that create our weather: the land, the air, and the water.

Lesson 2 Worksheet: Focusing Attention on Sunlight

Name: _____

Date: _____

Background

We see the sun in the sky almost every day. Because it is such a regular object in the sky, we probably don't take the time to stop and think about sunlight and how it affects Earth and our weather. In this experiment, you will have a chance to focus your thinking about the effects of sunlight on objects.

You will be making some guesses about what will happen in this experiment and also making observations. Space is provided on your lab sheet to explain what you think will happen in this experiment.

You will also have the opportunity to record your observations. Do you remember that observations are made with our eyes (sight), ears (sound), nose (smell), and fingers (touch)? In the Data Charts below, you have four columns, one for each sense that you may use to make your observations. When you make your guesses and observations, make sure that you use the correct column.

❖   ❖   ❖

Lesson 2 Lab: Black and White—My Guesses and Observations

What Will Unfocused Sunlight Do to Paper?

My Observations—What Does Unfocused Sunlight Do to Paper?

My Guesses—What Will Focused Sunlight Do to Paper?

My Observations—What Does Focused Sunlight Do to Paper?

Beyond the Data

1. In what ways were your guesses accurate?

_____

_____

_____

2. What questions do you still have?

_____

_____

_____

3. Review your observation charts. Which sense did you use the most to make your observations? The least?

_____

_____

_____

4. What is so important about the sun?

_____

_____

_____

5. How might the power of the sun influence our weather?

_____

_____

_____

Lesson 3 Rubric: Assessing Answers to the Question "What Happens When Sunlight Shines on Different Colored Substances on Earth?"

Novice	Intermediate	Advanced	Expert
Sunlight shines every day on all surfaces.	More sunlight is absorbed by the darker things. That's why I don't wear dark clothes in the summer. It's too hot!	Darker substances on Earth absorb more sunlight. When the dark surfaces absorb lots of sunlight, they get hot, like asphalt in the summertime.	Darker substances on Earth absorb more sunlight. When the dark substances absorb more sunlight, they have more heat that they release into the air. Lighter substances can't absorb as much sunlight as the darker ones, and so they have less heat to release into the air. That's why in the summer it's hotter in cities than in the country.

Lesson 3 Lab: Black and White—What Happens When Sunlight Shines on Different Colored Objects?

Name: _____

Date: _____

Background

For the last couple of days we have been talking about what happens when sunlight falls upon objects. You've already noted that sunlight seems to increase the surface temperature of objects. But there is a twist to this experiment. Today you will have a chance to see what happens when the rays of the sun fall upon different colored objects. Will the black paper absorb the sunlight in the same way that it is absorbed by the white paper?

Materials

To conduct this experiment, you will need the following materials for each pair of students:

- 2 pieces of paper, one black and one white
- 2 thermometers
- A lab sheet

Procedures

1. Take your pieces of paper to a sunny window or place outside in the sunlight.

2. Place your papers out of the sunlight.

3. Put both thermometers in a shady place for a few minutes until they read approximately the same temperature.

4. While you are waiting, make predictions about what will happen when you place your thermometers on the white and black pieces of paper and expose them to the sunlight.

5. When your teacher says "begin," place your papers in the sunlight. Then, put one thermometer on the white paper and the other one on the black paper.

6. Take your first reading of each thermometer and place the temperature readings on your data chart.

7. Your teacher will prompt you to make your remaining readings. You will take one reading a minute for the next nine minutes.

8. After each reading, you can talk about your observations with your partner. Place your observations on your data sheet. Although you can talk with your partner about your experiment and your observations, you will each be asked to turn in a lab sheet.

My prediction about what will happen to the temperatures on the white and black sheets of paper:

_____

_____

_____

Data Table

Observation #	Temperature Reading on the White Paper	Temperature Reading on the Black Paper	Observations
1			
2			
3			
4			
5			
6			
7			
8			
9			
10			

Beyond the Data

1. What information did you use to make your prediction?

_____

_____

_____

2. What did you notice about the surface temperature of the white paper? The black paper?

_____

_____

_____

3. How do you explain the fact that one piece of paper had a higher surface temperature?

_____

_____

_____

4. Think about what you know about the light paper and the dark paper. What conclusions can you draw about the absorption rates of the different surfaces of Earth (e.g., soil, forests, asphalt surfaces, sand, ice, glacial ice, and snow cover)?

_____

_____

_____

Lesson 3 Lab: Enhanced Greenhouse Effect

Name: _____

Date: _____

Background

To many people, the term "greenhouse effect" brings to mind unpleasant images of Earth's future. Yet without it, Earth would be a very cold planet. We would be experiencing an average temperature around 0 degrees Fahrenheit, instead of the 59 or 60 degrees of today's weather.

How can the term "greenhouse effect" create both good and bad images in our mind? How can it both protect the Earth and threaten it at the same time? The contradiction lies in the proper understanding of this principle.

The greenhouse effect that keeps our planet warm is really the "natural greenhouse effect." As the sun's energy reaches Earth's surface, some of it is reflected back and some is absorbed. The absorbed energy warms the earth, which in turn radiates heat back toward space. Water vapor, carbon dioxide, and other gasses in the atmosphere absorb some of the outgoing energy, which heats them. The molecules of these substances from Earth then radiate the energy in all directions, including back to Earth. In effect, some of the energy remains in our atmosphere, warming the planet. This warming protects us and the earth.

The greenhouse effect that could cause climate change is the "enhanced greenhouse effect." It works the same way as the natural greenhouse effect, but the extra carbon dioxide and other gases that we release into the atmosphere help increase the amount of energy that is absorbed. Sometimes we refer to the enhanced greenhouse effect as global warming.

Global warming refers to an average increase in the earth's temperature. Some scientists think that our earth's average temperature may be rising. In fact, they think Earth has warmed by about 1 degree Fahrenheit over the past 100 years. A warmer Earth may lead to unwelcome changes in rainfall patterns and a rise in sea levels, among other things. Scientists think that the earth could be getting warmer on its own, but they think it is more likely that people and their activities on our planet are contributing to the rise in temperature.

If you would like to read more about these terms, you can visit the following Web site: www.epa.gov/globalwarming/kids

Materials

You can do a simple experiment with a lab partner that will help you understand global warming. You will need the following materials:

- 2 jars, one with a lid and one without
- 2 thermometers
- 2 small balls of clay for anchoring the thermometers

Procedures

1. Take your materials to a sunny window or place outside if the weather is nice.

2. Place a small ball of clay on the inside of each jar on any side. Then, anchor a thermometer in the clay so that the bottom of the thermometer is suspended off the bottom of each jar by about 1 inch.

3. Wait 5 minutes until both thermometers have come to about the same temperature.

4. While you are waiting, predict what will happen to the temperatures in each jar once you have placed the lid on one of them and waited for ten minutes.

5. Place the lid on one of the jars.

6. Every minute, for ten minutes, record the readings for both thermometers on the data chart below. Don't disturb the thermometers.

My Predictions

My prediction about what will happen to the temperature in each jar once the lid is placed on one of the jars:

_____

_____

_____

Data Table

Time	Observation #	Temperature Jar 1	Temperature Jar 2	Observations
	1			
	2			
	3			
	4			
	5			
	6			
	7			
	8			
	9			
	10			

Beyond the Data

1. What information did you use to make your prediction?

_____

_____

_____

2. How accurate is your prediction?

_____

_____

_____

3. Why do you think the temperature rose in the jar with the lid?

_____

_____

_____

4. What is the difference between the natural greenhouse effect and the enhanced greenhouse effect?

_____

_____

_____

5. How can this experiment be used as a model of the enhanced greenhouse effect on Earth?

_____

_____

_____

6. What might be some limitations of this model? What doesn't it show clearly?

_____

_____

_____

7. If scientists are correct in their thinking about the enhanced greenhouse effect, how might it influence our weather?

_____

_____

_____

Lesson 4 Lab: Estimation—It's Easier Than You Think!

Name: _____

Date: _____

Background

Estimating is a thinking process that we use to make skillful and reasonable judgments about questions that, at first, seem unknowable. It involves five stages: (1) figuring out the different unknowns in the problem, (2) thinking about or writing down what you already know about the unknowns, (3) developing an accurate chain of reasoning, (4) using the reasoning to generate your estimate, and (5) checking your answer to make sure it is sensible.

For example, you might want to estimate how much water you will drink in a lifetime. How would we ever estimate such a large quantity?

First, you will need to figure out the different "unknown" parts of the question. In this example, there are two unknowns. The first one is how much you drink, and the other is how long you will live.

Second, write down what you already know about each of the unknown parts of the problem: how much you drink and how long you will live. In problems that seem unknowable, it is advisable to break the unknown parts into smaller, "knowable" units. For example, if you think about what you drink in one day, rather than in a lifetime, the problem will be easy to solve:

"On average, I drink three glasses of milk (8 oz), one glass of juice (8 oz), some milk on my cereal (1/2 a cup or 4 oz), and one can of soda (8 oz)."

So, write down: "On average, I drink about 44 oz of fluid a day."

Now address the other unknown part of the estimation problem: How long you will live. How long do we think most people live? Many scientists believe that people live, on average, about 75 years.

So, write down: "I think I will live to be about 75 years old."

Third, create a line of reasoning with your information to help you solve the problem: "I will have to multiply what I drink in 1 day times 365 (days in a year) times 75 (the average number of years I will live)."

Fourth, using your line of reasoning, generate the answer to the problem:
44 oz × 365 × 75 = 1,204,500 oz

To make it easier to understand the answer, you can convert it to 8 oz cups or gallons:

Cups in a lifetime: 150,562.5

Gallons in a lifetime: 18,820.3

Fifth, check whether your answer seems reasonable: "If I continue to drink about the same amount of liquid each day as I do now, and I live to an average age, I think my estimate is pretty reasonable."

To summarize, estimation is an important thinking skill that is used in science, mathematics, and many other areas to solve seemingly unknowable problems. Used correctly, estimation can help people make reasoned and sound decisions and avoid guessing. Those who are skilled at estimation structure and sequence their thoughts in a thinking protocol that includes five stages:

1. Find the unknown(s) in the problem.

2. Identify what you do know about the unknowns, which usually involves breaking down the larger "unknown" into smaller, more knowable units.

3. Develop a line of reasoning.

4. Generate an answer based on the line of reasoning.

5. Check the answer to make sure it is sensible.

Lesson 4 Lab: What Percentage of Earth's Surface Is Water? Is Land?

At first, this problem appears unknowable. Earth's surface is just too big to make an estimate of the amount of water and land it contains. Some might give up and say that they will need to use reference books to arrive at an answer. You think, however, that you might be able to estimate an answer to the problem by using the five steps in the estimation thinking protocol:

1. What appears hard or unknowable in this problem?

_____

_____

_____

2. Using the map of Earth, how might we break down the problem into smaller, more "knowable" parts?

_____

_____

_____

(Hint: Can you divide the map into smaller sections so that it is easier to estimate how much is land and how much is water? Once you have a small section of the map to look at, think to yourself: Is half, or 50 percent, of this small section water? Maybe it is 75 percent water? Write down a percent to represent the amount of water and land that you believe is in each section. You can use the table below to help you keep track of your estimates. When you have finished your estimates, look over all your percentages and estimate the total proportion of land on the map and the total proportion of water. Then check your final answer for reasonableness.)

Percentages

	Water	Land
Example:		
Section 1	50% (½)	50% (½)

3. What reasoning or thinking will you use to develop an estimate of all the water and land on Earth?

_____

_____

_____

4. Using your line of reasoning, develop a percentage to represent water and land on the entire map.

   Percentage of water on Earth's surface: _____

   Percentage of land on Earth's surface: _____

5. How might you check your estimate to make sure it is sensible or reasonable?

_____

_____

_____

Lesson 6 Lab: Sunlight on Land and Water

Name: _____

Date: _____

Background

You have recently learned that Earth's surface contains a great deal more water than land. Do you think that the large amount of water on Earth's surface affects our weather? In this next experiment, you will see that sunlight affects land and water differently. You will also have the chance to hypothesize how the different absorption rates of land and water influence our weather.

Procedures

1. Listen to your teacher, who will explain how to use the graph that is attached to your lab sheet.

2. When your teacher tells you, gather your two cups, which are labeled "land" and "oceans and lakes." Be careful to hold them as steady as you can so that you do not spill the water or dislodge the thermometers.

3. Go with your teacher outside to a place in the sun, or move the cups to a sunny window location.

4. Your teacher will tell you when to begin recording the temperature on each of your thermometers. Make sure to read both thermometers and record the temperature of each in a different color on your graph.

5. Your teacher will tell you when to make your observations.

6. When your teacher tells you to move your cups out of the sun, carefully move them to a shady location.

7. Continue to make your recordings at the designated times.

8. When you have finished your observations, complete Beyond the Data, which is attached to this lab. You can talk over the answers to the questions with your partner, but you will each be responsible for handing in a completed lab sheet.

(Continued)

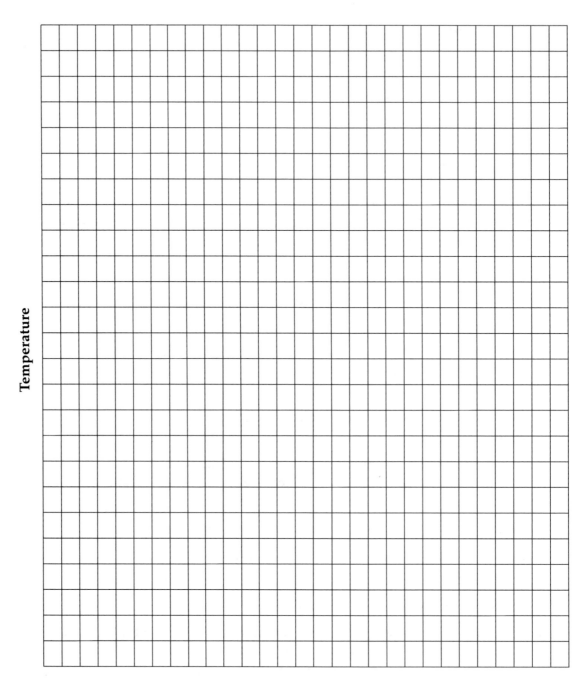

Beyond the Data

1. Look at the data for sunlight on land and on water. Which Earth features warmed more quickly?

    _____

    _____

    _____

2. How much warmer did one get than the other?

    _____

    _____

    _____

3. Which feature cooled more quickly?

    _____

    _____

    _____

4. Think back to the hot summer day at the beach that we talked about at the beginning of the lesson. Why is land near the ocean cooler than land that is inland?

    _____

    _____

    _____

Lesson 7 Lab: It's All About Hot Air

Name: _____

Date: _____

Background

The sun is the most powerful source of energy in our universe. It is so powerful that it is able to move both air and water through our atmosphere. As the sun moves air and water, these two forces interact to create our changing weather.

In the past, you explored how sunlight heats objects and warms the air in the atmosphere nearby. What happens to warm air? That is the question you are going to answer today.

Procedures

Your teacher will be doing a demonstration for you. Work with your partner to make observations about the demonstration, using the observation sheet that is provided. While you can talk with your partner about your observations, you will each be responsible for turning in your own lab sheet.

My Observations

Sense	Observation
	• • • • •
	• • • • •
	• • • • •
	• • • • •

Beyond the Data

1. What did you observe in the demonstration?

_____

_____

2. Think about the demonstration as a small model of Earth's atmosphere. What can you conclude happens when the sun warms air in our atmosphere?

_____

_____

3. Thinking further: When warm air in our atmosphere rises, where does it go? What takes its place?

_____

_____

❖ ❖ ❖

Graphic Organizer: Cause and Effect—Wind

Name: _____

Subject: _____

Cause	Effect
(When . . .)	**(These events or conditions happen . . .)**
Examples:	
• When warm air rises . . .	•
• When cool air rushes in to take the place of warm air . . .	•
• When the temperature between the warm air and the cool air is large . . .	•

Lesson 7 Worksheet: Tiny Tornados

You have just been asked to be the expert in a local TV show about the weather. Your job is to answer questions about the weather that are sent in by readers. Here's your first question:

To: Weather Expert

From: Salvatore and Jasmine

My sister and I were walking down the street the other day toward the park. It was a very warm day and the asphalt streets were really hot. You could see the heat shimmering off the black surfaces. As we got closer to the park and the shade provided by its tall trees, we saw something funny happen. We saw a bunch of papers and leaves get picked up and whirled around like a top. My sister said the whirling papers were a result of the cars whizzing by. I don't believe her. I think it looked more like a little tornado. Please answer this so I can tell my sister the *real* story.

Lesson 7 Rubric: Assessing Answers to Tiny Tornados Worksheet

Novice	Intermediate	Advanced	Expert
The wind is just blowing all around in the city. It is made by the cars and the warm air.	The whirling top is caused by the wind. Wind is caused by the meeting of warm air and cool air.	The tiny tornado was caused by the heat in the city. Cool air came rushing in to take the place of warm air that rose up in the air.	You really did see a tiny tornado. The heat, released from the asphalt streets, warmed the air nearby. The warm air rose and cooler air, probably from under the shady trees, rushed in to take its place. When the cool air rushed in, it picked up the papers and leaves in its path.

Adaptation

A Social Studies Unit on Cultures for Elementary Students

Sandra N. Kaplan

BACKGROUND FOR UNIT

This unit has been designed to attain three goals: (1) teach social studies content standards related to the development and nature of cultures, (2) reinforce the relationship between content and pedagogy, and (3) provide a format to guide the process of curriculum design and decision making. This unit is also designed to meet the needs of gifted students in a heterogeneous class setting while providing *all* students in the classroom with the opportunity to have access to high-quality curriculum. Modifications in time for learning, the amount and type of teacher and peer assistance, and the types of learning resources used provide options to individualize the curriculum and accommodate the needs and strengths of diverse students in a heterogeneous classroom.

The relationship between content and pedagogy (see Kaplan essay, Book 1, Chapter 3) is crucial to students' understanding of the subject matter at the levels of sophistication that both a differentiated curriculum demands and intellectual growth requires. Attempts to increase students' subject matter knowledge using didactic teaching methods often dilute a curriculum that is based on advanced content. Students need to apply critical, creative, and problem-solving processes in order to become self-directed, independent thinkers. The lessons in this unit of study emphasize instructional strategies that:

- stress open-ended tasks;
- use multiple and varied references as the basis for discussion and dialogue;
- promote divergent points of view;
- focus on generalizations, principles, and theories as the impetus for acquiring factual and conceptual learning; and
- underscore a belief that students can and should acquire learning-to-learn skills as they attain comprehension of the content standards.

The successful interaction between content and pedagogy also depends on teaching strategies that enhance motivation to learn. This unit's teaching strategies include investigative prompts, advance organizers, retrieval charts to express and synthesize information, and research tasks that facilitate the inquiry process.

The content goals of each of the four Parallel Curricula suggest a need to align these goals with relevant instructional strategies. This unit of study focuses on the use of a variety of instructional strategies that are similar to the following chart.

Curriculum	Goals	Instructional Strategies
Core Curriculum	Learn the essential concepts, generalizations, principles, and skills within a discipline.	Use inductive teaching methods and ask students to use analytic thinking skills to investigate artifacts, representative topics, examples, and evidence to infer the essential understandings in the discipline.
Curriculum of Practice	Assume the role of a practitioner as a means of studying the discipline. Function as a practitioner and researcher in the discipline.	Use an advance organizer to describe the varied roles of a disciplinarian in order to prompt student problem solving and research. Adopt research methodology such as historical or case studies.
Curriculum of Connections	Use essential concepts, generalizations, principles, and skills to make connections across the disciplines, time, locations, or cultures.	Identify a principle such as "adaptation is necessary for survival" as a motivator and prompt that helps students make associations across cultures.
Curriculum of Identity	Understand how personal interests serve as a means to further understanding.	Introduce personal profiles to stimulate the inquiry process: state problem, hypothesize, etc.

The concept of AID can also prompt the use of specific instructional strategies.

Elements of AID	Instructional Strategies
Help students represent, solve, and generalize from problem-solving situations.	Acquire problem-solving methodologies and strategies.
Provide greater depth of knowledge aligned to student expertise.	Provide investigative prompts, such as identifying the language of the discipline, trends affecting the discipline, and unanswered questions in the discipline.
Examine and critique the organization of concepts and principles in a topic or discipline.	Ask students to assume the role of a reviewer, critic, and/or evaluator of complex content knowledge.
Identify patterns, relationships, and interactions among areas of study.	Use the advance organizer as a conduit to link bodies of knowledge.

This unit is based on both conventional wisdom about curriculum and theoretical constructs governing curriculum development. The principles include the following:

1. The use of all four Parallel Curricula in a single unit of study is essential to create a qualitatively differentiated curriculum.

2. Curricula should cater to the needs of students and society as well as create new visions of what students can and should know.

3. Curricula should provide opportunities to increase specific clarity of understanding while increasing generalizability of the subject matter.

4. Curricula should uncover as well as respond to the potential of the learners.

The instructional elements described in this unit provide the key points for curriculum decision making. The elements are arranged in order of sophistication, each providing a different orientation to learning the standards or attaining the objectives. In addition, each element has been selected to address a particular parallel in this unit. The purpose and function for each element is explained below:

Engage—refers to learning activities that "open the stage" for learning. This element serves as the motivation and provides the readiness for learning. In some cases, this element also serves as the statement of the lesson's objective and is an informal assessment of students' previous knowledge and skill mastery.

Excavate—refers to learning activities that allow students to "dig deeper into understanding." This element serves as the source for input at a more advanced level of understanding. In most cases, this element requires research, interpretation, and synthesis.

Exaggerate—refers to "selecting a part of the whole" to examine closely. This element allows for individualization of the subject matter under study by students. It also allows for students to specialize in one of the aspects of the total curriculum unit.

Extend—refers to encouraging students to "move beyond the topic." This element allows students, as individuals or a group, to define and explore a pathway from the study to other related areas of potential study.

The use of these four elements within the Parallel Curriculum Model (PCM) allows the curriculum designer to determine the emphasis given to each parallel within the context of a unit of study. For example, the association of the element of engagement with a parallel would imply that this parallel would be used as motivation for the unit. Using the element of excavation with a parallel implies that this parallel would be used to provide an opportunity for an in-depth study of some aspect of the topic or discipline. Using these four elements and the four parallels, the following curriculum design worksheet illustrates how this unit on adaptation was formulated.

Curriculum Design Worksheet

Area: Social Studies   **Subject:** Culture   **Theme:** Adaptation

Standards: Students will understand the relationship between culture and geography.

Overarching Objective: Students will prove, with evidence, that culture reflects multiple environments. They will use print and nonprint resources and demonstrate understanding in an essay.

Curricular Elements	Parallel Curriculum			
	Core	*Practice*	*Connections*	*Identity*
Engage		Introduce the study of the disciplines and disciplinarians, such as anthropology and anthropologist, ecology and ecologist, etc.		
Excavate	Present the big idea "Culture is a reflection of multiple environments" to teach the standards-based curriculum.			
Exaggerate			Introduce the big idea "Adaptation is necessary for survival" as the connector to understand how adaptation occurs across the disciplines.	
Extend				Provide an opportunity for self-selected independent study about one's abilities, style, and need to become a scholar or disciplinarian.

CONTENT FRAMEWORK

Organizing Concepts

Discipline-Specific. Culture, Environment (Social, Physical, Economic, Aesthetic), and Change

Macroconcept. Adaptation

Principles and Generalizations

G1   A culture is a reflection of multiple environments.
G2   Adaptation is necessary for survival.
G3   Many types of environments (physical, social, economic, aesthetic) affect or influence a culture.
G4   Under certain conditions, some environments exert more influence over the culture than do others.
G5   Artifacts represent the materials, work, technology, habits, time, and so on of the culture.
G6   Information is organized into formal branches of knowledge, called disciplines. One who studies the specific knowledge of the discipline is labeled a scholar, expert, and/or disciplinarian.
G7   Change is a stimulus for adaptation to occur.
G8   History repeats itself.
G9   Learners, students, and scholars are a reflection of their environments.
G10   Change is inevitable.

Standards for Social Studies

SD1   Describe the effects geography has on societies.
SD2   Compare and contrast various aspects of different cultures to meet human needs and concerns.
SD3   Investigate how the disciplines and disciplinarians contribute to the interpretation of data, records, and so on of a culture.
SD4   Identify and use various sources to reconstruct the past.
SD5   Demonstrate an understanding that people in different times and places perceive events, conditions, work, and so on differently.
SD6   Exemplify the importance of cultural unity and diversity within and across groups.

Skills

S1   Define
S2   Describe
S3   Prove with evidence
S4   State and test assumptions
S5   Interpret
S6   Summarize
S7   Relate
S8   Compare and contrast
S9   Substantiate, verify, and/or validate an idea
S10   Debate informally

MAKING SURE THE PARALLELS REMAIN CENTRAL IN TEACHING AND LEARNING

Curriculum Component	*Component Description and Rationale*
Content	The standards-based content is the study of *culture*. The interaction of the study of culture with the concepts of adaptation, change, and environment provide the student with more advanced understanding of the social studies standards related to culture. In addition, the introduction to the disciplines and role of disciplinarians are used to enhance the basic core content.
	The Core Curriculum, Curriculum of Practice, Curriculum of Connections, and Curriculum of Identity are used to provide the understandings of the unit's content. Each of these Parallel Curricula contributes to the development of an advanced understanding of the standards related to culture. Each Parallel Curriculum fosters a different and unique perspective on the content.
Assessments	Each learning experience in the unit affords the teacher with an opportunity to assess student achievement informally. The level of responses in a discussion or the data points recorded on a retrieval chart is a typical example of "in-process of learning" informal assessments.
	The activities in the Curriculum of Identity are fundamental for the teacher to discern the individual progress achieved by each student. This is achieved by using formal and/or informal individual or group conferences. In addition, maintaining a learning log facilitates an analysis of the student's development as a learner, scholar, and/or expert in an area.
Teaching strategies	The majority of the learning experiences designed for this unit are best described as using deductive reasoning (proving the meaning of a theory or principle) and inductive reasoning (using new information to develop a theory or principle). The use of an advance organizer or prompts as the anticipatory set for researching and organizing information is replete within the various lessons.
	The activities designed for the Curriculum of Connections reinforce deductive and inductive reasoning strategies. The activities also stress the need for investigative skills and methods as students work independently or cooperatively. Working deductively requires students to gather evidence from various disciplines to support or confirm an existing or given principle. Working inductively enables students to amass information from the disciplines and organize it to state a principle.
Learning activities	The learning activities in this unit include four basic types, and they serve to engage, excavate, exaggerate, and extend. Each type of activity requires a specific orientation to learning.
	Engage: motivation providing readiness to learn
	Excavate: general in-depth understanding of the topic

Curriculum Component	Component Description and Rationale
	Exaggerate: specific analysis of a part of a subject *Extend*: relating learned subject matter to new areas of study While each type of learning activity (engage, excavate, exaggerate, and extend) can be used in all the Parallel Curricula, some types of learning activities are best matched to a particular parallel. *Core Curriculum*: excavate *Curriculum of Practice*: excavate, exaggerate *Curriculum of Connections*: extend *Curriculum of Identity*: engage, exaggerate
Grouping strategies	The learning activities in this unit can be taught in any type of instructional setting. They were designed to allow for flexible grouping. The type of group setting selected by the teacher for instruction should be dependent on the nature of how students best learn rather than on the nature of the learning activity. The basic issue undergirding the decision to use large- or small-group settings or independent work or study is determining the relationship between the students and the defined outcomes expected of them. The instructional or teaching strategy selected is a means to the end or outcome. Classroom experience with the PCM has indicated that some Parallel Curricula are more appropriately taught in certain group settings. For example, the Curriculum of Connections appears to lend itself to independent work as well as whole-group settings. The need for personalized inquiry as a preface to the group sharing of ideas has proven to be very successful while involving students in this parallel. The Curriculum of Identity requires intellectual solitude or independent learning time.
Products	The ways in which students synthesize and transmit their knowledge acquisition and skill mastery can assume different forms. The major products developed by students as a consequence of their involvement in this unit are a debate and an essay. While these are the formalized and anticipated products from the students' endeavors in this unit, there are numerous opportunities for teachers to include a variety of written, oral, and kinesthetic products to culminate the lessons. There is no specific alignment of products to a particular Parallel Curriculum. However, the Curriculum of Identity appeared to require a more personal rather than general form of expression of a student's synthesis of learning. Personal forms of expression are those that provide opportunities for students to ponder how they acquired the methods to learn and the results of such methods. Logs, journals, profiles, and discussions are products affording these personal forms of expression.
Resources	A range of resources is paramount to the success of this unit for all students in the heterogeneous classroom. Following are suggested types of resources to be made available to the class:

(Continued)

(Continued)

Curriculum Component	Component Description and Rationale
	• Many and varied print materials, such as a range of text material including picture books, specialized dictionaries and encyclopedias for the disciplinarian, and journal articles and newspapers providing contemporary information on the subject • Many and varied nonprint materials, such as pictures, charts, videos, models, and so on • Raw materials to facilitate expression of ideas, including cereal boxes, craft sticks, and swatches of fabrics and materials • Play materials to dramatize or model conceptual understandings, such as Legos or wooden blocks The use of different resources to accommodate different learning styles, preferences, and abilities is valuable in order to make the *same* curricular task accessible to all students. Too often the task is adjusted rather than adjusting the materials used to achieve the task. In this unit, teachers are encouraged to modify the means (materials) to attain the end (curricular task).
Extension activities	The possible extensions in this unit align with the concept of AID: • *Introduction*: Provide students with the opportunity to relate the concept of *culture* across the disciplines of *science* and *social studies*. Ask students to investigate how a "culture" assumes different meanings in different contexts: school culture, professional culture, and so on • *Replication*: Introduce students to the study of sociology and anthropology. Encourage students to gather information from various courses of study documents as well as to conduct interviews with professionals to determine "how professionals study cultures." • *Extension*: Engage students in a "follow the footsteps" study of a culture by selecting an individual who is noted for his or her study of a culture of people or animals. • *Transformation*: Provide the opportunity for students to respond to a futuristic problem about a culture or to respond to a "request for proposal" by an agency to conduct a cultural study.
Modifications for learner need, including AID	Among the members of the heterogeneous student population are those who are experientially and linguistically diverse. Both types of students need a set of readiness activities or activities that provide a background of prerequisite understandings. Such activities might include the introduction of artifacts representative of different cultures. The teacher could plan and conduct a "meet and greet" event, where students can interact with adults and children from other cultures. A "word wall" of terms that describes the concept of culture facilitates the language development needed for learners within this unit of study. A large and permanent Venn diagram kept in the classroom can be used to illustrate how cultures are alike and different. It also provides the academic comfort levels vital to the participation of experientially and linguistically diverse students.

UNIT SEQUENCE, DESCRIPTION, AND TEACHER REFLECTIONS

Preassessment

Unit Sequence	Teacher Reflections
Overarching Objective. Students will prove with evidence that a culture is a reflection of multiple environments. They will assume the role(s) of an anthropologist and/or ecologist to gather information from print and nonprint references and to summarize the evidence into an essay accompanied by nonlinguistic representation, such as an illustration, graph, or model. An overarching objective is prepared by the teacher and drives, so to speak, the unit and lessons within it.	Overarching objectives delineate major areas of a curricular learning experience: thinking skills (prove with evidence), content (culture is a reflection of the environment), resources, research skills, and culminating product. The components of the overarching objective thread through all four lessons.

Directions:

1. Read the two columns.

2. Match the items in Column 1 to the items in Column 2.

3. Review the matches you made.

4. Describe briefly the reasons for making these matches.

Column 1	Column 2
• The group of people fished for their food.	• The people live in the forest.
• The group of people made their homes out of mud.	• The people live in the desert.
• The group of people believed in the "magic" of cactus.	• The people live by the sea.

Reason(s) for making the matches:

_____

_____

_____

_____

The preassessment worksheet is designed to determine the student's previously acquired knowledge about the relationship between culture and environment. In addition, it provides the teacher with knowledge regarding the student's skill in supporting knowledge or using evidence to "prove" a point.

The subjective nature of the preassessment tool requires criteria against which teachers can determine the level of a student's ability to complete the task and to recognize the relationship between culture and the environment by connecting the culture to the appropriate geographic setting. Criteria to be considered in assessing students' abilities to make matches are that (1) relationships are logical, and (2) relationships are verified by previously learned knowledge.

CURRICULUM OF PRACTICE LESSON

Lesson 1: Engage

(2–3 hours, approximately)

Unit Sequence	Teacher Reflections
Concepts. Culture, Environment G4–6, SD3–5, S1–5, S8–9 **Introduction.** Present a collection of illustrations or actual pictures of different types of museums.	The curricular element "engage" provides the motivation or stimulus for students to learn, introduces them to the dominant concepts of the unit (i.e., discipline, museology, sociology, environment, culture, and artifact), and provides the frame of reference for students to assume the roles of an anthropologist, sociologist, and ecologist.

Art	Natural History	Space
Museum	Museum	Museum

Unit Sequence	Teacher Reflections
Discuss the purposes for a museum and the commonalities among the various types of museums. Describe a museum as "a place devoted to the exhibition and study of objects that have scientific, historic, and/or artistic value."	
Define the reasons for *specialized* versus *general* museum collections. Define the word *museology* as the specific "study of design, organization, and management of a museum."	The introduction to the correct nomenclature of the disciplines is an important feature that supports student readiness to learn sophisticated and abstract content. English as a Second Language (ESL) learners need to be taught the appropriate language of the disciplines using Sheltered English instructional strategies. Gifted emergent English language learners often are denied access to sophisticated content when the appropriate lexicon is withheld from them.
Introduce the concept of a *discipline* or a specific branch of knowledge. Discuss the difference between a *subject* and a *discipline*.	

Unit Sequence	*Teacher Reflections*

Demonstrate the relationship between *subject* and *discipline* by showing the following diagram to illustrate how subjects fit within a discipline.

The Discipline of Sociology

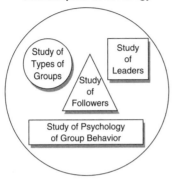

Introduce the discipline-based concepts *anthropology* and the role of the disciplinarian called an *anthropologist*, using the following graphic as a reference:

DISCIPLINARIAN	**DISCIPLINE**
Anthropologist	Anthropology
One who is an expert or specialist in the study of anthropology	The study of the political, social, and cultural development of people

Discuss the concepts and skills used by anthropologists to do their work by examining the following job description:

> As an anthropologist, I am concerned about the habits, work, and beliefs of people within a culture. I examine the books and art they create, the tools they use to do their work, and the religion they practice. I also interview and observe them.

The students can be given 3- × 5-inch cards with subject areas written on them: Native Americans, the community, our state, and so on. They can match a current classroom subject to one or more of the discipline-related descriptors in the model to the left.

There is controversy about if and when to introduce students to the various disciplines. Educators who have introduced students to the study of the disciplines or branches of knowledge state that such understandings facilitate a deeper understanding of content and skills and enhance students' abilities to make meaningful connections within and across disciplines.

The study of *disciplinarians* is not to be confused with the study of *careers*. The intent in this study of the disciplines is to value and understand the nature of specialized work in organized bodies of knowledge.

An introduction to the role and work of the disciplinarian can also be accomplished using biographies and autobiographies.

Some educators question the emphasis on discussion as opposed to spending time developing tangible products, such as models, murals, and editorials. Learning how to listen and respond to discussion are both an art and product to be appreciated as well as developed. Discussions can be enriched when teachers ask students to define their responses and provide examples that augment their responses and to illustrate the relationship between their responses and the real world.

(Continued)

(Continued)

Unit Sequence	Teacher Reflections

Introduce another discipline, for example, *ecology* and the role of the *ecologist.*

DISCIPLINARIAN	DISCIPLINE
Ecologist	Ecology
One who specializes in the study of the environment	The study of the use and conservation of an environment

Introduction of the Problem. Introduce this problem to students:

> The curator at the Museum of Cultures is trying to organize an exhibition of objects from different cultures. The objects or artifacts must be placed in the environment in which they were used by the culture: forest, desert, plains, ocean, and so forth. What evidence is needed to sort these objects correctly into the environments?

Discuss the meaning of the problem and clarify concepts, such as *curator, cultures, artifact,* and *environment.*

Discuss how an examination of an artifact yields evidence about the culture. Direct students to use these attributes of artifacts to reference and formulate questions needed to gather information:

→ Materials
→ Purpose
→ Technology
→ Time
→ Weather

The use of some form of a puzzle activates students' interest and promotes readiness for pursuing the content and skills for the unit.

Modifications for Learner Need. Responses to the problem could help teachers make decisions about how to group students, select resources, and utilize time for the other lessons in the unit. For example, students whose responses indicate a lack of understanding about the features distinguishing a forest from a desert could be placed in a small group to review topography. Students who indicate sophisticated responses to the problem could be accelerated with lessons related to geography (AID).

Unit Sequence	Teacher Reflections

Learning Activities. Help students apply the study of the *disciplines* and the roles of the *disciplinarians* to solve the curator's problems, using real-world illustrations of artifacts from the different environments:

Picture of basket	Picture of wooden bour	Picture of straw hat for shade

Picture of tool for cutting	Picture of hooks for fishing

Follow the pattern of questioning below to facilitate students' identification and sorting of evidence into its appropriate environment (desert, forest, ocean, plains), where it might have been used by a culture:

What is the artifact?

As an *anthropologist*, what attributes of the artifact do you notice that reveal where it was used?

As an *anthropologist*, where do you think the artifact was made and used?

As an *ecologist*, what do you think is the relationship among the artifact, the culture, and the environment?

As an *anthropologist* and *ecologist,* in which environment was the artifact most likely to be used?

Record the responses onto a chart similar to the one below:

ARTIFACT	ENVIRONMENT	EVIDENCE
Hooks for fishing	Ocean ——— Forest	Fish are used as a source of food.
Straw hat for shade	Plains ——— Ocean	The summer sun is hot. Farmers need protection.

Retrieval charts are an important aid to collect and synthesize information during a lesson. They can be a focal point for discussions and a means to develop further questions to research or design a journal of what has been studied.

(Continued)

Unit Sequence	Teacher Reflections

Ask students to determine *why* the information from the study of anthropology and ecology helps solve the problem posed by the curator.

Discuss the information derived from the *disciplines* and *disciplinarians* that is needed to determine the relationship between *cultures* and the *environment*.

Review the relationships among artifacts, cultures, and environments to define the dominant factor among the three elements.

Use the following illustrations to depict the possible relationships among the elements:

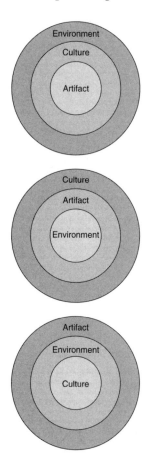

Open-ended tasks provide the backdrop for the development of creative and independent thinking. The purpose of these three circles is to illustrate the varied relationships that can be made among artifacts, culture, and environments. Each set of circles illustrates how the same factors can be dominant or subordinate in different contexts to define the meaning of the concept of adaptation.

Discuss which graphic representation best summarizes the discussion. Ask students to justify their individual or group selection of a graphic representation as the most significant one to synthesize the relationship among environment, culture, and artifacts.

Discussions do not always have to be conducted in a large-group setting. Students could be assigned to a discussion group, or they can form their own discussion groups. In some situations, conversations among peers can be the appropriate context for a discussion to take place.

CORE CURRICULUM LESSON

Lesson 2: Excavate

(3–4 hours, approximately)

Unit Sequence	Teacher Reflections

Concepts. Culture, Environment

G1, G3–5, SD2, SD4–5, S1–10

Introduction of the "Big Idea." Present a theory on a chart as the puzzle to initiate the lesson.

> A culture is a reflection of multiple environments.

Instruct students to write their interpretation of the statement on 3- × 5-inch cards. Collect the cards and place them in an envelope.

Learning Activities. Define the meaning of *environment* by soliciting students' responses to key categories of environments: social, physical, economic, and aesthetic. Make and use these keys to stimulate inquiry and comprehension of the different environments.

The introduction to a "big idea" serves as the puzzle for the lesson. It is analogous to a provocative question used to initiate the learning process. Students use the big idea as the frame of reference to gather evidence that will define, clarify, support, and substantiate the theory during the lesson.

Social Environment

interaction peer pressure

Economic Environment

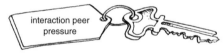

supply/demand goods/services

Physical Environment

climate/location resources

Aesthetic Environment

art/music/ architecture

Create a brief scenario depicting "life in a culture." Use the keys to probe understanding as to how the culture was responsive to the different environments identified by each key.

(Continued)

Unit Sequence	Teacher Reflections

Distribute a set of topographical maps. Instruct students to analyze the topography to hypothesize the customs, arts, and so on of the culture inhabiting the area. Provide the resources for students to validate or restate their hypothesis. Discuss the cues most beneficial to confirm that physical environments affect a culture.

Inform students that they will be focusing on a selected culture to examine how the *behaviors, arts, beliefs, institutions,* and *products of the culture* reflect or are influenced by multiple environments. Practice using either prior knowledge of a particular culture or the contemporary culture to which the students currently belong to explain how a facet of the culture reflects one or all environments.

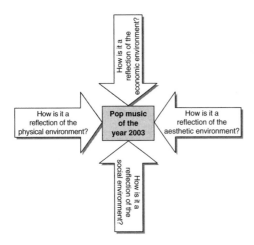

Optional Extension. Bring into the classroom a collection of contemporary newspaper articles describing "life in the current year." Ask students to read the newspaper articles to determine which environments affect contemporary cultures. Graph the environments' influences over culture. Decide if any one environment exerts more influence than another on a culture.

AID. Studying contemporary cultures, such as a social culture, professional culture, or economic culture, can be part of the challenge identified with AID.

Divide students into groups to

- study the cultures designated for the grade. For example, each group of students could study a tribe of Native Americans.

Working in a group is an "art" and requires prerequisite skills of understanding how to be a collaborator or colleague while still retaining individuality of thought. This can be a subtle means of reinforcing the Curriculum of Identity.

Unit Sequence	*Teacher Reflections*

- study different environments affecting a single culture.
- study the same culture using different types of resources, such as an atlas, picture, travel book, encyclopedia, or textbook.

Instruct groups of students that they are to conduct research to prove, with evidence, this theoretical statement: "A culture is a reflection of multiple environments." Use the following retrieval chart as the format to represent and summarize the data collected by the students.

Retrieval charts can be dated and stored by the teacher. They can be reintroduced to the students and used to prompt new discussions, research questions, independent study, or self-selected assignments.

Culture:			
Social Environment	*Physical Environment*	*Economic Environment*	*Aesthetic Environment*

Analyze the information written on the chart to answer these questions:

- Which environment exerts the most and least influence on the *needs* of the culture?
- What is meant by "a single environment having a ripple effect on all other environments and then on the culture's needs"?

Retrieve the envelope that contains the 3- × 5-inch cards with the students' original assumptions about the meaning of the theory, "A culture is a reflection of multiple environments." Ask students to reread their original statements. Ask students to what degree their original assumptions were accurate or faulty. Why and how can they prove, with evidence, that their original ideas were or were not correct, based on the current information they have accumulated?

The most beneficial discussions require students to substantiate or validate their comments with both an example and a citation or reference. Teachers often use these questions in response to a student's answer or statement to cause the student to probe or "excavate" deeper into the topic or subject under study:

1. How do you *define* that idea?

2. What *examples* can you give us of that idea?

3. What *reference* or *citation* was used to develop or support that idea?

CURRICULUM OF CONNECTIONS LESSON

Lesson 3: Exaggeration

(2–3 hours, approximately)

Unit Sequence	Teacher Reflections

Concepts. Culture, Environment, Change, Adaptation

G1–4, G7–8, G10, SD2, SD4–6, S3–10

Introduction. Present students with the word sets below, which depict forms of the change process.

sudden—slow

evolutionary—revolutionary

natural—person made

orderly—chaotic

helpful—harmful

Use these word sets to describe historic or current changes in a culture that they have studied or are studying currently. These descriptions will provide *evidence* of one or more of these changes.

Introduce the following principle:

Adaptation is necessary for survival.

Reinforce the meaning of *adaptation* as a concept of change and review synonyms that can be used to discuss *adaptation*: namely *alter, modify, adjust,* and so on.

Learning Activities. Develop four learning stations, each related to an area of study and a set of content standards within the area.

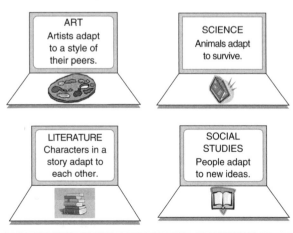

Learning stations provide an opportunity for students to self-select and to learn independently. Students can be encouraged to consider their interests and ability as criteria to choose a particular learning station. Unlike a learning center, these learning stations are designated as sites to investigate a *single task,* using a collection of predetermined resources. The use of learning stations is an instructional strategy facilitating both the assimilation of content and mastery of learning-to-learn skills.

Unit Sequence   *Teacher Reflections*

Introduce the learning stations to students and describe their purpose as an area to conduct research on the principle "Adaptation is necessary for survival." Discuss how each learning station provides a disciplinary perspective on the principle and enables the students to understand the principle across the various disciplines. Share the information students have gathered from the different learning stations to form a retrieval chart.

Adaptation is necessary for survival.			
Science	Literature	Art	Social Studies

Determine if there is sufficient evidence collected from the research at the learning stations to support the principle.

Provide information about a culture students are studying currently or have studied previously to prove that "Adaptation is necessary for survival." Refer to this information to respond to the following statements about cultures:

- All cultures rise and fall.
- All cultures are susceptible to internal as well as external influences.
- The rigidity of a culture could lead to its demise or end.
- Cultures that respond "to the times" have a longer life span.

Introduce the "art of argumentation" to provide students with a background to engage in informal debate. Have students select one of the statements and use it as the basis of formulating their argument to support or negate the selected statement. Have students use the skill of using evidence to structure and prove their argument.

AID. The introduction of additional big ideas in the context of the lesson provides the opportunity to stimulate more depth and complexity of understanding. This is one method for achieving AID. Advanced students should begin to realize that big ideas interact. In some instances, big ideas reinforce each other and, in other instances, one big idea provides insight or clarity to comprehend the other big ideas.

CURRICULUM OF IDENTITY LESSON

Lesson 4: Extend

(3–5 hours, approximately)

Unit Sequence	Teacher Reflections

Concepts. Culture, Environment, Change, Adaptation

G1–10, SD1–6, S1–10

Introduction. Discuss the relevance of timelines and their value for disciplines and disciplinarians as a record of events and chronology of progress. Instruct students on how to create a layered timeline:

Layer 1—Learning about . . .

Layer 2—Learning from . . .

Layer 3—Learning for . . .

Layer 1—Learning About is a chronological accounting of the actual topic under study.

Layer 2—Learning From is a chronological analysis of the value of the knowledge for a societal perspective.

Layer 3—Learning For is a chronological unfolding of one's perception of self as a learner in the process of acquiring and assimilating information to create the layered timeline (Layer 1 and Layer 2).

Learning Activities. Construct for class a layered timeline using Layer 1 to learn about a culture, Layer 2 to learn from the culture how it has affected *today's* society, and Layer 3 to learn about detailing what the class experienced as a collective group of students or learners.

Provide students with a list of areas from which to select a topic of study to chronicle for their layered timeline:

The major goal of the layered timeline is for students to correlate *what* is learned with *who* is learning. This is another strategy that promotes reflection as a valued practice for cognitive and affective development. Like many journals, the layered timeline is interactive. However, here, the important aspect is Layer 3—Learning For, which stresses an examination of self as a learner in the process of learning.

Unit Sequence	*Teacher Reflections*

- Contributions of Margaret Mead, the anthropologist
- Development of a custom or tradition: from one culture to the world
- Advancement of technology: from wheel to space rocket
- Development of communication: from cave to software company

Introduce the concept of sharing corners or the idea that students are each allocated a corner of the room on a predetermined schedule to share Layer 1 and 2 of their layered timeline.

Grouping Strategies. Since the traditional process of sharing usually does not allow all students to participate, the strategy of sharing corners is used to provide time for every student to share and also to enable sharing to occur in a smaller and more intimate venue.

Instruct students to review Layer 3 of their timeline to extrapolate insights into the self as a learner. Have them note examples of insights that could characterize their patterns, such as

- expenditure of time;
- organizational behaviors;
- planning; and
- dealing with problems that thwart progress.

Discuss how patterns or habits can enhance or negate one's abilities as a learner, scholar, academician, expert, or disciplinarian. Discuss the subtle, but important, nuances of differences among the students' patterns. Relate the statement "History repeats itself" to world events. Define the alternative meaning of *history* as the "yesterdays of one's life." Ask students to apply the statement "History repeats itself" to their personal behaviors as learners.

Define the relationship between attributes that identify an artifact and traits that identify the self as a learner. Review the statement "Culture is a reflection of environments." Discuss the statement "Learners are a reflection of their environments." Compare the meanings and interactions between these two big ideas.

(Continued)

(Continued)

Unit Sequence	*Teacher Reflections*

Look again at the unit principles. Ask students to point out changes in their thinking about and understanding of the big ideas they have been investigating.

Optional Assessment. Provide individuals or groups of students with a set of artifacts from an unnamed culture. Ask them to examine the artifacts and respond to a set of questions similar to those addressed in class lessons. Be sure students are required to do the following in their investigation and reporting:

- Use the skills and practices of practitioners and scholars.
- Point out how their conclusions about the artifacts reflect an understanding of one or more disciplines of study.
- Make connections between the artifacts of the new culture and those found in other cultures.
- Reflect on ways in which their work fits or does not fit their personality and interests.

Demonstrate an understanding of the unit big ideas by relating those ideas to their speculations about the artifacts.

Open Your Eyes

A Parallel of Practice Unit on Visual Art History and Artistry for Middle School Students

Meg Easom Hines

BACKGROUND FOR THE UNIT

This unit on art history and art appreciation provides opportunities for students to work as historical researchers and problem solvers. Its main focus is on the relationship of the visual arts to the history and culture of the artist—thus, the emphasis on the macroconcept of culture. Students study culture through art history by gaining a deeper understanding of time and place through visual art.

This unit emphasizes the Curriculum of Practice. In lessons, students develop a sense of historical time and chronology of events in eight major periods of Western art history (prehistoric, Egyptian, Greek and Roman, medieval, Renaissance, Baroque, late nineteenth- and early twentieth-century Impressionism, and modern). They analyze and "do" historical inquiry through developing a knowledge base in the organization of art history and how it is studied and shared. The knowledge students build helps prepare them to think as an art historian, develop terminology, analyze artwork, respond when answers are not readily available, as well as share the knowledge they have uncovered. Having developed an introductory knowledge for art history through various activities, students then become detectives of history by examining resources and facts that lead to a greater understanding of various pieces of artwork and the culture from which those pieces come.

As a learner in school, I wasn't always able to grasp the intricacies and understand historical happenings in full detail. Although I did well on assessments of facts and skills, I did not really develop a deep understanding of the important concepts related to the study of history. I was, however, extraordinarily drawn to the arts and their integration into content studies. Now armed with knowledge and understanding of constructivist theories of learning, I have come to realize the significance of studying history and culture through the visual arts, not only for students like me but for all students.

Understanding the history of visual arts was a perfect avenue for helping students develop an idea about how time, place, and people are connected. I decided that the best way to develop this sense of time and chronology was to focus on culture, because I felt that it would be a concept that students at this level had studied to some degree but could be developed at a deeper level. The "big ideas" in this unit involve connecting time, place, and the visual arts, leading students to the idea that their own cultures are influenced by the time and place in which they live.

CONTENT FRAMEWORK

Organizing Features

Discipline-Specific Concepts. Communication, Interpretation
Macroconcept. Culture

Principles and Generalizations

G1 Art is a way of communicating meaning and expressing ideas.
G2 Time and place influence visual characteristics and give meaning and value to a work of art.
G3 Using the structures and functions of art improves the communication of ideas.
G4 Art is an extension of the self through expression of ideas, information, experiences, stories, and feelings.
G5 Art is interpreted differently by various individuals based upon their experiences.

National Standards for Visual Arts

SD1 Understanding the visual arts in relation to history and cultures
SD2 Reflecting upon and assessing the characteristics and merits of the work of others
SD3 Choosing and evaluating a range of subject matter, symbols, and ideas
SD4 Using their knowledge of media, techniques, processes, structures, and functions to interpret and evaluate art

Skills

S1 Describe how history, culture, and the visual arts can influence each other.
S2 Identify subject matter, symbols, and ideas to communicate meaning in artworks.
S3 Identify media, techniques, and processes to communicate ideas, experiences, and stories.
S4 Distinguish among multiple purposes for creating works of art.
S5 Describe and analyze using art vocabulary the use of elements and principles of design in the composition of artworks.

MAKING SURE THE CURRICULUM OF PRACTICE REMAINS CENTRAL IN TEACHING AND LEARNING

Curriculum Component	Component Descriptions and Rationale
Content	Students examine the relationship between history and art and the macroconcept of culture through utilizing the methodologies of an art historian. They focus on the habits of mind that professionals in the field use, such as observation, reflection, interpretation, and expression. By using culture as a way of studying art history, the lessons designed in this unit help students develop the skills of communicating meaning, expressing ideas, and interpreting works of art.
Assessments	The teacher observes and documents students' conceptual understanding through rubrics, conferencing, and discussion. Proficiency of skills and evidence of personal growth are demonstrated as students are asked to work as practicing art historians through simulation and presentation. The major tasks of the unit require students to work with the macroconcept of culture through research, presentation, creation, and reflection.
Introductory activities	The opening activities engage the students with the major ideas of the unit: culture, communication, and interpretation. By building a capacity for careful personal observation and analysis, students immediately connect to the life and skills of art historians and see how art reflects culture through discussion. The initial lesson helps the teacher assess prior knowledge and motivate and familiarize students with the unit.
Teaching methods	Teaching strategies challenge and support students in their cognitive engagement with the concepts, facts, and skills of the unit. Whole-group strategies such as discussions are used to introduce and process the "big ideas" of the unit. Small-group and individual projects and assignments ask students to practice and reflect as disciplinarians in the areas of art. Key to the Practice parallel are the skills of art historians, used in student-led teaching and simulation activities.
Learning activities	Students perform tasks that help them analyze and critique works of art. These activities are designed to be aligned with content goals and provide for students' individual learning needs. Students utilize the methodologies of the art historians in a simulation as well as practice other important job-related responsibilities, such as researching, teaching, and disseminating information. In addition, they use primary, secondary, and technology resources for research.

(Continued)

(Continued)

Curriculum Component	Component Descriptions and Rationale
Grouping strategies	Students receive whole-group instruction for the introduction and conclusion portions of most lessons. Several lessons group students in pairs based on their interests (e.g., the Time Period Project) or readiness levels (e.g., the simulation). Just as many professional historians must work in unison with others to uncover the historical past through consultation, deliberation, and teaching, so too will the participants in this unit.
Products	Products and presentations should demonstrate the attainment of content knowledge and growth in the understandings of the unit. Through various strategies and activities, students create products similar to those of practicing professionals.
Resources	Resources are selected to support students' thinking and communication processes for the activities of the unit. Students use methodological tools to collect data as historians of art through primary and secondary resources and work with community experts in both art history and the visual arts.
Extension activities	Extension activities that emerge from the guiding questions and understandings of the unit have been designed to explore areas of student interest while incorporating the Curriculum of Practice. Students scan various art history materials, critique and research famous pieces of art, are exposed through Web adventures to many different issues and ideas related to art and art history, and study eminent people in the field.
Modifications for learner need, including Ascending Intellectual Demand (AID)	Students work in different areas of interest and readiness through the teacher's and students' chosen projects. Efforts to meet students' level of sophistication and thinking have been synthesized into the teaching strategies and learning activities designed for the unit. These modifications accommodate students' levels of challenge and should increase levels of achievement in the concepts and principles of the unit. Students who show evidence of needing AID are able to guide their own inquiries, develop skills of professionals, and transfer their learning through an array of materials and activity levels.

UNIT SEQUENCE, DESCRIPTION, AND TEACHER REFLECTIONS

Lesson 1: Unit Introduction and Preassessment

(1–2 hours, approximately)

Unit Sequence	Teacher Reflections
Concepts. Culture, Communication G1–2, G4, SD1–2, S1–2, S4 **Guiding Questions.** How does art shape a culture? How does culture shape art? How does an art historian interpret subject matter, symbols, and ideas in art?	This unit was originally designed for an enrichment pull-out program, in which students would have several hours a week of experiences with the unit. However, this unit can be modified for various time allotments and ages. It can also be incorporated into the entire year's curriculum, in smaller time segments, as a means to provide arts integration into the regular classroom.
Preparation. Before beginning the unit, provide students with a notebook or folder for unit materials and create a timeline of art periods in the classroom.	A three-ring binder works well because students can easily add pages and take out assignments on an ongoing basis. I place a visual timeline across a long bulletin board in the room for reference and to stimulate student interest in the unit. It includes major periods, labels, dates, and many art images. The images I try to include are those that are both familiar to students (e.g., da Vinci's *Mona Lisa*) as well as unfamiliar, such as images that we might discuss or focus on during the unit.
Preassessment. Begin the unit by having students create a list of words related to art and art history. Then have them create a web or concept map that organizes their ideas and words about art. Next, ask students to share their personal webs and create a class web or graphic organizer that will be posted in the room for the duration of the unit.	To help students get started on their web or concept map after brainstorming art words, we have an informal discussion of what types of categories might evolve from the center of their web or how they might represent their ideas about art graphically. A concept map such as this encourages students to organize information into conceptual groupings. The class web will serve as a visual for students to compare old and new learning. Provide each student with a copy of this class web. They will make additions to it during the end of the unit assessment. I also use this preassessment information to shape the questioning, discussion, and focus of the various lessons in the unit. It lets me know what kind of art training students have had in the past, their ideas about art,

(Continued)

(Continued)

Unit Sequence	Teacher Reflections
	and what gaps exist in their knowledge and understanding.
Introduction. To introduce the major concepts of culture, communication, interpretation, and expression, I have students walk through an artwork. I use the worksheet titled **Walk Through an Artwork: Image Discussions Using VITAL—Visual Impact in Teaching and Learning**, which is a discussion strategy on a piece of artwork that clearly demonstrates a relationship between culture and history.	Walk Through an Artwork is the title for the thoughtful, planned discussions that students engage in as they are exposed to various pieces of artwork by observing and developing a vocabulary in interpreting art. In other words, students create the kinds of vocabulary and thought processes that are used by art historians in their work. Students learn to identify key features and indications of historical time and place, at first with the teacher's assistance and then on their own as they increase in comfort level with viewing art.
This discussion should highlight the idea of viewing versus looking at art and how art is a tool to communicate and a way to look at the past historically.	I usually use Diego Velasquez's *Las Meninas* to begin the VITAL discussions because it is has many things that can be highlighted about the history and culture of the time. VITAL discussions must be thoughtfully planned.
After viewing the piece of artwork, discuss with students what they think the role of an art historian might be in interpreting the work. Through the discussion of the image, prompt students to come up with a definition of culture and to notice how artwork gives us clues about the history of that time.	You will have to gain some knowledge about the artwork and its historical time period in order to help students discover the cultural clues of the time. Many art history books do this for you. For example, students can discover that Velasquez was a court painter to King Phillip IV of Spain and that the painting was both a portrait of the Princess Margarita and a self-portrait of the artist himself. Viewers of this piece are invited into the life of royalty and, thus, the culture of that time. Along with the ideas of portraiture and history, students will notice the use of light and color in the artwork, all indicators of the Baroque period in art. If culture is the way in which a group of people lives, this painting might suggest what life was like in Spain at that time.
	Teacher questioning to students using the VITAL process should respond to the readiness of the student in observing the piece of artwork. Some students may be

Unit Sequence	*Teacher Reflections*
	more observant or thoughtful or have the ability to see more abstract meanings, whereas other students may simply observe the piece at face value. The teacher will be able during this first Walk Through an Artwork to see where students are in viewing artwork and pose questions according to readiness (see supplemental explanation of **Walk Through an Artwork: Image Discussions Using VITAL**).
In closing your discussions, talk about how culture can shape artwork and how art can shape culture. Incorporate the students' own observations and ideas into this discussion.	Three important messages (viewing vs. looking, art as a way to communicate, and the history/art connection) are essential to this discussion. They will be the basis for many discussions and activities throughout the unit.
Unit Overview. Share the **Unit Concept Map** with students. This map highlights the guiding questions we will uncover, the concepts we will study, and the activities we will participate in.	I find that informing students of where we are going with the unit focuses them on what it is we will learn and what they should be thinking as we move through the course of the unit. I usually make a poster copy of this concept map to hang in the room to reference. I make a colored copy for student notebooks to be kept in the front of their binders, and I send a copy home to parents to share what we will be studying during the unit. Having the guiding questions front and center helps reinforce major concepts and principles of the unit.

Lesson 2: Prehistoric Art and Introduction of Time Period Project

(3–8 or more hours)

Unit Sequence	Teacher Reflections

Concepts. Culture, Communication, Interpretation
G1–2, SD1–2, SD4, S1–4

Guiding Questions. How does art shape a culture? How does culture shape art? How does an art historian interpret subject matter, symbols, and ideas in art?

Walk Through an Artwork. Use the Walk Through an Artwork VITAL strategy to view several images of prehistoric art, described in Walk Through an Artwork: Lauscaux Cave Paintings (Prehistoric Art Lesson Script). See Part 1: Background Information on this worksheet to help prepare for a Walk Through discussion with students. In addition to the historical data uncovered about each image and its artist, and depending on the particular artwork selected, various principles, features, techniques, or media used in the artwork can be highlighted.

Use this Walk Through activity on prehistoric art to reinforce what was studied in the first lesson about the relationship between art and culture; that is, art reflects the culture of the time and culture dictates the art. During the discussion phase, I find it again important to get some of the important vocabulary terms and ideas into the discussion, such as subject matter (i.e., what is represented in the artwork), interpreting (i.e., why the cave artists created art), and symbols (i.e., what the artwork means). These artistic observations are indicators of the culture and help solidify the connection between art and culture. This process also allows students to continue developing their method of observation by recognizing clues and elements in the art that tell about the time in which it was created.

Using the second portion of the **Walk Through an Artwork: Lauscaux Cave Paintings** worksheet, **Part 2: Prehistoric Art Lesson Script**, as your reference, ask students to discuss the historical information about the art as well as look at media and techniques used by the prehistoric artists.

Next, distribute copies of **Part 1: Background Information** of the **Walk Through an Artwork** worksheet to each student. This worksheet provides facts to give to students *after* the discussion as an example of work an art historian might compile on a piece or series of artwork.

Modification for Learner Need. VITAL discussion sessions lend themselves to facilitating and posing questions that can best suit various students at the levels they are able to observe and interpret the artwork. It also gives the teacher insight into preferences and abilities for future assignments at various levels of AID.

Unit Sequence	*Teacher Reflections*

Students can use this as an example for the write-up they prepare about their simulation pieces in Lesson 5.

Introduction of Time Period Project. Talk with students about how art historians go to school for many years studying their discipline. In the beginning of their studies, they begin to build a basic knowledge of artwork and, over time, as they grow as historians, their knowledge and research become more focused. Explain to students that before they are able to do some art history work, they need to build their own basic knowledge of art history. Share with them that they will do this through the Time Period Project.

Show students a teacher-created sample Time Period Project on prehistoric art (based on the supplemental sheet titled **Requirements: Time Period Project**). Discuss the research process utilized for the presentation. For example, share the various kinds of resources used, what types of information were sought out, and how decisions were made about the important information needed in the presentation. After viewing the presentation and discussing its formulation, have students summarize for you what they think prehistoric culture was like based on what they learned from your presentation.

Showing an example of a PowerPoint (or other presentation software) presentation allows students to see how research can be represented in a visually stimulating, technology-oriented product. Basically, by completing the Walk Through and viewing a model presentation on prehistoric art, students are immersed in that particular time period. Through the discussion of your research process and presentation conclusions, students will understand the process of researching and studying pieces of artwork to share with others as practicing historians.

Explain to students that just as you have shared with them information about prehistoric art, so too do art historians share information they have learned through their research with various audiences. Tell students that the purpose of the Time Period Project is to help all class members get a general sense of the chronology of art history through the teaching of their fellow classmates. Tell them that their ultimate goal is to help the class understand their time period's connection between culture and art.

(Continued)

(Continued)

Unit Sequence	Teacher Reflections
Poll students for interests in various time periods. Using that information, along with your knowledge about their levels of ability in thinking about historical art, assign them to dyads and small groups for the project. Students will then research and develop a presentation on a period in art history.	Because I have already covered prehistoric art thoroughly with students as an example, I assign Egyptian, Greek and Roman, medieval, Renaissance, Baroque, late nineteenth-century Impressionism, and modern periods of art. However, many more movements and styles exist along the time period spectrum. The choice is really up to the teacher and is usually based on the number of students involved in the project. The only stipulation I have is that all major time periods are covered and none is repeated. Therefore, after the presentations, students have a sense of chronology in art history.

Modifications for Learner Need. Using your observations of student performance in the Walk Throughs, a student who is able to point out that the prehistoric art represented the daily life and focus of the cave people has demonstrated the ability to connect the art with the culture. However, students who make more literal and basic observations of the cave art might be better suited to work on a time period that requires less sophisticated analysis. Based on the research materials you have and the particular time period basics, different time periods might require varied levels of interpretation. Make use of the Novice to Expert Continuum (see Figure 5.3 on Ascending Intellectual Demand in Book 1) to help you determine the kind of supports students need to move to higher levels of expertise. |
| Review the sheet called **Requirements: Time Period Project**, as well as the grading **Rubric: Time Period Project.** The requirements ask students to give a general overview of their time period through documenting its history, culture, and geography and synthesizing those areas through the art connections. Students also highlight important artists and particular techniques used during this time period. | I find that having an area on this rubric for both earned points and comments allows students to receive not only a grade (school requirement for report cards) but also comments on the strengths and weaknesses of the presentation. The rubric differentiates levels of the presentation product from novice to exemplary levels. The Time Period Project represents an opportunity for students to act as art historians by researching the past to build a |

Unit Sequence	Teacher Reflections

Explain to students that they will become practicing art historians as they uncover and find information about their assigned time period by immersing themselves in the artwork of their time. As experts in their area, they will be able to share the major ideas, discoveries, and art of their time period in their class presentation. Just as art historians prepare to share their own findings about art, students will research, synthesize information, and prepare their presentation. Through this process, they will discover that they are working much like art historians, who utilize multiple resources to gather information about various pieces of artwork.

basic working knowledge of the artwork of a certain period. Art historians are researchers, analyzers, and interpreters of the past and can work as art critics, curators, restorers, or teachers. In this particular project, students will become experts in the art of their time period and share this knowledge with the rest of the class. Although students will not be able to study all historical movements in art history in depth, by becoming experts on one particular time period, they are able to provide classmates with an overview of their researched period and learn and use the tools used by art historians when investigating any culture or time period.

Research and Presentation Work Time. Students will use primary and secondary resources to acquire information to complete the content requirements for their presentation projects. Provide students who need it with the **Graphic Organizer: Time Period Project** to help them keep track of their growing knowledge of the culture of the time period and to help them focus on drawing conclusions about the ideals and values of the unit macroconcept.

Modifications for Learner Need (Research). Students are able to work at various levels of intellectual demand during this project in both the research and presentation portions of the project. For research, provide art and art history resources with varying levels of difficulty. I have art history books for the young and for introductory and advanced levels. I have a collection of books on artists, particular time periods, and special movements within a period. I also have developed a drop file of articles from magazines, newspapers, and other sources that help students in their research. In addition, students are reminded that they have access to local museums, communication via e-mail with art historians and artists, and the Internet for information on their time period. To avoid students becoming "lost" while surfing the Net for information, I created a hot list of links to assist them in gathering research and images (see www.kn.pacbell.com/wired/fil/pages/listtimeperme.html).

PowerPoint Tutorial. Based on student familiarity and facility with PowerPoint, assign each to an appropriate level of a PowerPoint Tutorial. Tutorials should be

Generally, by the time I use this unit during the year, students have participated in a variety of technology lessons and activities and have demonstrated their level of ability

(Continued)

(Continued)

Unit Sequence	Teacher Reflections
designed based on the level of experience students have had with the presentation software and familiarity with technology in general. The Time Period Project is designed with the idea that teachers have access to a computer lab. However, this project could be carried out over several weeks using classroom computers as a learning station.	with technology tasks. I use this information in suggesting levels of activity within the tiered tutorial on PowerPoint. These self-guided tutorials vary according to student interest and readiness with presentation software. For example, I provide a lesson that charts students through the basic options in PowerPoint, such as slide insertion, text production, Internet picture transferring, transitions, and effects. I also provide a midlevel lesson that goes a step beyond the basics involving options such as sound effects, word art, and varying background options. The most advanced tutorial involves more difficult options, such as music clips, video, digital camera pictures, and timed presentations. If your comfort level with technology does not allow you to design your own PowerPoint Tutorial lesson, several online tutorials can be used and modified for various levels of intellectual demand (see www.actden.com/pp/index .htm or www.electricteacher.com/tutorial3 .htm). The self-directed nature of the tutorial allows me to move about the lab answering questions and assisting students as needed. By collecting and organizing information about works of art, students are able to use methodologies art historians might use when they have to analyze many pieces of information in their research. They are able to ask the following questions: What are the most important things I have uncovered in my historical research? How can I best communicate this? By using the various options in presentation software, students are able to expose classmates to the art and culture of their time period, not only through their research but also through other visual information as well. Art historians constantly face the challenge of disseminating information in various ways. Becoming adept at several methods of sharing their work only makes for a better art historian. Art historians, much like

Unit Sequence	*Teacher Reflections*

artists, have to figure out the best ways to communicate their thoughts and ideas with different people. Although PowerPoint is only one method of delivery that art historians may utilize in their work, this activity is an opportunity to encourage students to stretch their skills in using the tools of presentation software as well.

Designing the PowerPoint Presentation. After students conduct their research, they must take time to design their PowerPoint product. Remind students not to be so eager to get to the computer that they rush through this portion of the project. They should create a "storyboard" of the various slides they will use in their presentations, planning out text, images, titles, and so on. Point out that the storyboard is a requirement in the final grade because planning is an important step in creating a product. They will also need to plan time for editing and practicing the delivery of their presentation.

The time students need for designing and constructing their presentations varies greatly. Calling on a fellow technology specialist or parent with PowerPoint background helps during this portion of the project. There just does not seem to be enough of me to go around in many cases, especially for the more skilled students tackling more advanced presentation software techniques.

Presentations and Timelines. Schedule time for students to deliver their presentations to the class. Audience members will listen and make notes on the **Note-Taking Organizer: Time Period Project**, which asks them to make notes on the history, culture, and geography of each time period. When the presentations are concluded, review each time period briefly for the relationship between art and culture as presented in the art connections portion of the projects and re-pose the questions to the students: How does art shape a culture? How does culture shape art? What evidence of these two principles have we seen in these presentations? How does art communicate meaning and ideas related to the culture and time period of the artist?

Optional Extensions. Students work at various skill levels in PowerPoint and bring their products to a close at different times. I provide the **Extension Activities: Open Your Eyes Unit** sheet for students to work on in the computer lab after they have finished and practiced their presentations. The online Web adventures are particularly appropriate in this situation since students have access to the Internet in the lab. A variety of Web adventures are featured on various key concepts in the unit. For example, A. Pintura is a mystery adventure where the player is a detective with a degree in art history who has to examine paintings to solve the crime (see Educational Web Adventures, www.eduweb.com/).

Lesson 3: Walks Through Artwork

(simultaneous with the Time Period Project)

Unit Sequence	Teacher Reflections
Concepts. Culture, Communication, Interpretation G1–4, SD1–4, S1–4 **Guiding Questions.** How does art shape a culture? How does culture shape art? What are and how do you use the structures and functions of art? How do you interpret subject matter, symbols, and ideas in art? **Continue the Walks Through Artwork.** Throughout the unit, open each class session with a VITAL discussion on historical pieces of art from various time periods and artists. Like previous VITAL discussions, these walk-throughs will provide students with additional insight into the culture and history of various time periods and also further their art history vocabulary, which can be used in the art history simulation later on. Be sure to constantly reinforce unit principles concerning the relationship between culture and art. Use the walk-throughs as opportunities for pointing out factual and skill-related information of the unit, such as the structures and functions of art.	As I select pieces of artwork for Walks Through Artwork, I make sure that I select a variety of techniques, media, and artists to expose students to the plethora of historical information that can demonstrate the idea of culture and its connection with art. I try to make sure I do a VITAL discussion with each time period we study in class. This allows students to gain artistic information on the structures of art, such as elements and principles. These discussions help firm up their ideas about composing and creating artwork and make them more careful observers of information contained within a piece of artwork. They also continue to develop their ideas about culture by studying artwork, inquiring about available resources, and questioning as practicing art historians. Through these discussions, they are building a foundation about history and culture through the art, while utilizing the cognitive skills of interpretation that art historians must use in their work.

Lesson 4: Field Experience and Interview

(5–6 hours)

Unit Sequence	Teacher Reflections
Concepts. Culture, Communication, Interpretation G1–5, SD1–4, S1–4 **Guiding Questions.** What are the strategies that art historians use in identifying and classifying art? How do you interpret subject matter, symbols, and ideas in art? **Preparing for the Interview.** Prepare for a visit to a local art museum by brainstorming questions for an interview session with one of the art historians working there. Ask students to brainstorm ideas about what	After students have begun developing their knowledge base about art history, it is important to expose them to the methodologies that art historians use to do their work. Having the opportunity to meet an expert within the field of art history allows them to hear, firsthand, the skills, methods, and activities of the practicing professional. The knowledge and methods of the art historian that they learn here will culminate in Lesson 5, where they are asked to study, find the artist, and provide motivation for a series of paintings.

Unit Sequence	Teacher Reflections

they believe art historians' work is all about. Brief students on appropriate interviewing protocol and question formulation to ensure rich information from the interviewee. For example, a good question might be "What do you do daily as an art historian?" rather than "Do you like being an art historian?"

After brainstorming, evaluate and select a series of questions that investigate the role, responsibilities, and methodologies of an art historian. Tell students that they will each be responsible for posing a question to the historian and recording it while on the visit. If a local art historian is not available, try to locate an art historian in the greater community, an artist with a background in art history, or an art historian whom the class can contact via e-mail, teleconferencing, or phone.

This is also a good place for honing in on the other skills and methodologies of art historians. Prompt students to ask questions that help them understand the problems faced in this field, the strategies art historians use in various situations, how they make guesses and draw conclusions, what personalities work well with this practice, or what makes one successful in this area.

Field Experience. Take students on a tour of a local museum and interview an art historian. Ask museum personnel to highlight *historical* and *cultural* issues related to the artwork featured at the museum. As local museums generally feature work from the area, students may also get a sense of their region's art history and culture.

Having students view real artwork is integral to this unit. It also allows students to continue to develop the observation and interpretation skills that art historians use in their work. I feel that being in a place with local, authentic art bridges the connection between culture and art for the students. I generally request a special tour that highlights various historical and local pieces within the museum. I suggest contacting the educational representative at the museum and setting this up. I have used several museums in the past and have always had a warm response to special requests. Art educators are thrilled at the idea of students studying art history and want to help any way they can.

I request docents who are not only familiar with the pieces of art we will view but also experienced with working with students. I talk with the docent ahead of time to explain the various levels of student work so that they might be better prepared to go beyond the normal viewing of artwork or answer any questions on the tour.

(Continued)

(Continued)

Unit Sequence	Teacher Reflections
Writing Prompt. Upon returning to class after the field experience, have students reflect on the museum tour experience by writing a response to the following:	These prompts start students thinking about the connection between culture and individuals, something that will be reinforced in subsequent lessons.
• How are art and culture related? Give examples. • What do the artwork and information I experienced at the museum have to do with me? • Did I recognize myself or elements of my culture in any of the artwork? Explain.	Collect student responses to review for evidence of understanding of major unit concepts so far and to get a preview of students' ability to connect art to their own experience.

Lesson 5: Art Historian Simulation

(2–3 hours)

Unit Sequence	Teacher Reflections
Concepts. Communication, Interpretation G2–4, SD1–4, S1, S2–3, S5	
Guiding Questions. What are the strategies art historians use to identify and classify art? How does an art historian interpret subject matter, symbols, and ideas in art? How do you?	
Interview Debriefing. Upon returning from the field experience, students will debrief the interview with the art historian to create a flowchart or graphic representation of the methodology and processes that art historians use to date and study a piece of artwork (see **Flowchart: Art Historian Interview**). Tell students that they will be using these same processes in an upcoming simulation.	I find this discussion useful in helping students synthesize the data they received in interviewing the art historian. By formulating a flowchart or organizer, students are able to see how the methods of an art historian could be reused or modified in a new situation. It also gives them a working process for the simulation that follows.
Simulation/Performance Assessment. Students will participate in a simulation whereby they take on the role of an art historian at a local museum. *Assignment*: As an art historian at your local museum, you are responsible for studying, dating, and teaching patrons and visitors about the artwork in your museum. Recently the museum acquired some	Art historians use many sources of information in their research, such as records, newspapers and other periodicals, photographs, interviews, films, and unpublished manuscripts, such as personal diaries and letters. I utilize examples (either historical fiction I created or real items) that can be used to uncover the simulation. In the past, I have used items such as partial newspaper clippings, pseudo-certificates of

Unit Sequence	Teacher Reflections

paintings from the late Ms. Welhemina Pennington, town philanthropist and lover of the arts. Ms. Pennington's art collection has been dispersed and sent to museums across the country. However, she did not forget her own hometown museum and has left several pieces to your collection. There are three pieces of art and several documents in the package that were delivered to the museum. Because of the extensive and valuable collection Ms. Pennington kept, we are sure that these are valuable pieces of art. However, there is one problem: There is no indication of when the art was created or by whom. Your job is to study and date the artwork so that you will be able to document, display, and teach museum visitors about the pieces, the artist, and the motivations for creating the art.

authenticity (on which the names and dates of artists have been "faded away"), a journal or diary entry of the artist, excerpts from the artist's sketchbook, and so on. Really there are no right answers for what to include in these packets—just be creative. For example, the following is an excerpt from an essay written by Romare Bearden, who was an early twentieth-century African American artist. Transposed as an entry into the memoirs of his life, it helps students grasp some pieces of information that help them decipher the artist and his work.

Memoirs of an Artist

When I first started trying to make pictures, I was particularly interested in using art as an instrument of social change. As far as I was concerned at the time, which was in the mid-1930s, aesthetic technique was simply the means that enabled the artist to communicate his or her message—which as I saw it then was always essentially social, if not political.

Students will also need access to art researching materials, such as the Internet and historical books, to begin the process of comparing and contrasting the cultural and aesthetic elements found in the artwork.

Modifications for Learner Needs, Including AID. Because I know that there are differences among my students' prior knowledge and ability, I usually have them work in dyads of similar levels for this assignment. I pair students of like ability because the packages for the simulation are designed for various levels of thinking, interpretation, and sophistication. These packages include artwork and artist profiles and contain resources that are at various levels of sophistication and abstraction. Students who are already functioning at the practitioner level of AID may be given resources that include distracting or conflicting information to help them refine their skills in analysis and generalization even further.

(Continued)

(Continued)

Unit Sequence	Teacher Reflections
Students should use the flowchart they created during the debriefing to help them process through materials to solve the simulation problem.	This simulation allows students to work through the process that art historians use when doing their job. Students work on expertlike problems as well as test methodologies used in dating a piece of artwork.
Tell students they will need to keep a process log that will track their thinking by answering the following questions:	The process log questions make use of the focusing questions from the Curriculum of Practice.

- What structures and functions in the artwork or materials help you solve your simulation problem?
- What clues about the culture of the artist or artwork help you solve your simulation problem?
- How do people who do art history think and work?
- What do you think about the processes they use and in what ways do you function like an art historian? How and when?

Students should also prepare a summary of their findings that includes the historical background and other important information uncovered about the series.

When the simulation is completed, reveal the artist, dates, and messages of the simulation packets. Pull together all students to compare and contrast the process they used in the simulation with what they know about what art historians do. Have them share portions of their process logs that highlight the work of an art historian. Be sure to ask students how they felt about the simulation: What did you learn? Was it easy or difficult for you to do this kind of work? Did you like being involved with this kind of work? What are the strengths you have with art history? With the work of an art historian? How might these strengths transfer to other life or career situations?

Unit Assessment. Students should then complete the **Unit Assessment: Open Your Eyes**, in which they reflect and discuss the major concepts, principles, and guiding questions of the unit. This assessment incorporates the class concept map or web, which students created in the preassessment (Lesson 1).

Walk Through an Artwork: Image Discussions
Using VITAL—Visual Impact in Teaching and Learning

> *The process of teaching thinking skills requires more than just teaching a process.*
> *It requires repeated long-term practice.*
> —Dewey, Khun, and Glaser, as cited in Earhart, 2001 p. 11

Walk Through an Artwork is the title for the thoughtful, planned discussions that students will engage in as they are exposed to various pieces of artwork by observing and developing vocabulary about interpreting art. In other words, students will be creating a method of practice that would be used by an art historian in beginning to date and interpret art. As students practice the skills used in these activities, they will begin to develop a common process of inquiry that promotes flexible thinking, drawing on past knowledge and applying questioning; problem asking; risk taking; a sense of humor; the use of the senses; originality; insightfulness; creativity; a sense of wonder; inquisitiveness; curiosity; and efficacy as a thinker. This process uses visual images to teach students to think better by teaching them how to do so (Presseisen, 1987). Because this unit asks students to do Walk Throughs on an ongoing basis throughout the unit, students will continue to develop their ideas about the concepts of artist communication, expression, and audience interpretation.

This process is gleaned from three philosophies by Bloom, Roland, and Housen, which combine "big ideas" with higher-order, open-ended questions to empower students to discover and test the validity of their hypothesis about visual images (Earhart, 2001). In this process, students must have personal interaction and internalization with the information that the artwork presents through a facilitated discussion using probing questions.

The VITAL discussion process follows an active listening strategy for teachers and facilitators. It involves optimizing the environment, beginning with an open question, verifying the observation, and adding closure. A typical Walk Through an Artwork should include the following:

Start	Facilitators want to create a space for observation and discussion to occur by eliminating distractions. Facilitators will also need to position themselves both in and out of the level of the students by playing the dual roles of facilitator and participant.
Look	Facilitators present an open question to the group that avoids any particular point of entry into the piece. They allow a good bit of time (i.e., viewing takes time), acknowledge the speaker's comments, repeat or restate others' responses, and use appropriate vocabulary.
Listen	Facilitators carefully listen to participants and probe for more information that might invite them to discover new things about the artwork. They focus the viewers on what can be observed in the art and encourage students to explain where they found their information.
Learn/Respond	Facilitators close the discussion by paraphrasing what observers said by asking questions that lead viewers to even more ideas presented in the artwork.

Other important items also help boost the impact of the VITAL process:

1. Using a teaching vocabulary that helps reinforce the language of visual arts in various situations

2. Using an "up-front why" approach encourages transference into new inquiry situations by presenting students with the reason why the question is asked before asking the question itself

3. Using a "seg-way" (i.e., segment + pathway) process to provide transitions and clarify learning that helps students follow a technique for discussion

Resources

Bloom, B. (1956). *Taxonomy of educational objectives: Handbook 1. The cognitive domain.* New York: David McKay.

Dewey, J. (1933). *How we think.* Boston: D.C. Heath.

Earhart, S. (2001). *VITAL: Visual impact in teaching and learning.* Charleston, SC: Carolina Art Association.

Glaser, R. (1984). Education and thinking: The role of knowledge. *American Psychologist, 39*(2), 93–104.

Housen, A. (1979). *A review of studies in aesthetic education.* Unpublished manuscript. Cambridge, MA: Harvard Graduate School of Education.

Khun, D. (1986). Education for thinking. *Teachers College Record, 87*(4), 495–512.

Presseisen, B. Z. (1987). *Thinking skills throughout the curriculum.* Bloomington, IN: Pi Lambda Theta.

Roland, C. (n.d.). The @rtroom. Retrieved December 5, 2004, from www.arts.ufl.edu/art/rt_room/ index.html

Unit Concept Map

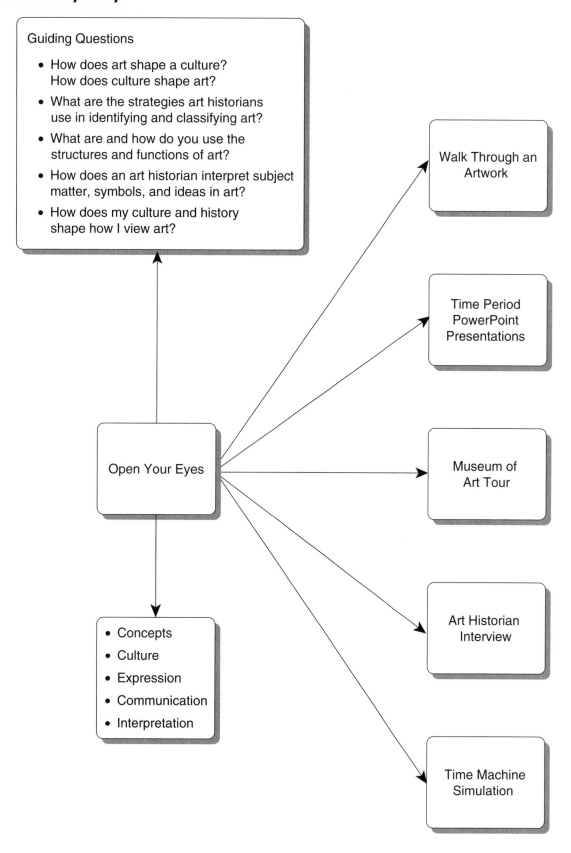

Guiding Questions

- How does art shape a culture?
  How does culture shape art?
- What are the strategies art historians
  use in identifying and classifying art?
- What are and how do you use the
  structures and functions of art?
- How does an art historian interpret subject
  matter, symbols, and ideas in art?
- How does my culture and history
  shape how I view art?

Open Your Eyes

- Concepts
- Culture
- Expression
- Communication
- Interpretation

Walk Through an
Artwork

Time Period
PowerPoint
Presentations

Museum of
Art Tour

Art Historian
Interview

Time Machine
Simulation

Walk Through an Artwork: Lauscaux Cave Paintings

Part 1. Background Information

The Artists—Historical Facts
Lauscaux, France
(approximately 15,000 B.C.)

Much of what we know about prehistoric cave art we have discovered through the findings of the ancient cave paintings in Europe. Finding this artwork has provided evidence for historians and scientists about what these people were like, how they lived, and much more. We have gleaned some of this information from the Lauscaux paintings, which were created by prehistoric people some 17,000 years ago.

Before this artwork was painted, we are pretty sure that humans had limited technical progress. Up to this point, people had learned the importance of hunting in small groups and forming communities, whereby they could share their daily tasks and make life easier. *Homo habilis* during this time discovered clever instruments and processes for hunting, creating shelter, and preparing food. Later these people evolved into *Homo erectus* and learned that they could begin inhabiting other places on Earth by traveling. We know that these people developed greater intelligence and probably had some form of language communication. Eventually as *Homo erectus* disappeared, a form of *Homo sapiens* evolved—a people we call the Neanderthal. The people who lived in the area of the Lauscaux caves are called Cro-Magnon and were similar in some ways to the Neanderthal but were taller. Both of these groups of people were skilled hunters and lived in small communities.

We know through evidence of fossils that reindeer provided food. Through the drawings that have been discovered, we also know that these people were interested in art, creating both symbols and animals. Another important historical fact to note is that through the development of the fat-burning lamp, cave dwellers were able to move farther into the caves to create their artwork with a means of illumination.

Read the story "Cave Paintings," from *Art in Story: Teaching Art History to Elementary School Children*, by Marianne Saccardi. This story records the discovery of the cave paintings in Europe.

The Artwork

Media

Many and varied various materials were used to create prehistoric cave art. Artists who engraved used sharp tools such as flint points. For applying paintings, artists used fingers, pads of animal fur, or brushes made from animal hair and crushed twigs. Pigments and colors seen in cave art included earth tones such as red, yellow, brown, and black. These colors were collected from minerals that could be ground into powder or turned into a crayon. Scientists have learned that ochres were burned to make cooler and darker shades. Black was made from manganese or charcoal, and reds were made from rock haematite. What did the artists mix with these pigments to make paint? Scientists carrying out many experiments finally discovered that water was the liquid used to make these paints.

Creating the Cave Art

Ancient artists would gather their art materials, food, and fuel for lamps to enter into the caves for several days. Inside the caves, artists would cross lakes and work their way through stalagmites and stalactites to reach their destination for painting. They painted on ceilings and high walls as well as surfaces that could be reached easily. To get higher into the caves, they probably had to build a series of ladders or scaffolding to create their artwork.

Cave paintings most often depicted hunters and scenes from the hunt. Animals that were most often represented, in detail, were horses and bison. There are also many pictures of wild cattle, deer, goats, and mammoths. Some bears and lions appear, and there are rare pictures of the rhinoceros, musk-ox, donkey, wolf, fox, and hyena. Plants are also rare, although they were important foods. Not all the animals in the paintings were a part of the hunting ritual; some were merely depicted in the artwork. Few human figures appear in the artwork except for the stencils and prints of hands, and much of the artwork includes markings such as dots, circles, rectangles, zigzags, grids, and other signs. No one is sure what the markings represent.

What this art may tell us is really up to our own interpretations. Scientists, art historians, and anthropologists speculate that these paintings were not ways of decorating but ways of recording hunting magic, beliefs of these early people, explanations of their surroundings, a way to aid prehistoric peoples' memory, or places where ceremonies were held. There is probably some truth in all of these ideas, although no one idea is certain.

Resources

Crystal Productions, Cave Art Prints, Teacher's Guide, ISBN 1-56290-165-6.
Lauber, Patricia. (1998). *Painters of the caves*. Washington, DC: National Geographic Society.

Part 2. Prehistoric Art Lesson Script

Big Idea About Art
Artists seek out and use media, tools, and techniques that are available to them for creating artwork.

Big Ideas About Connection to History and Culture
Artists use subject matter that is pertinent to their space, time, and history.

Start	**Instruct students.** I would like everyone to gather over here with me around this collection of artwork. Today we are going to begin observing, discussing, and making predictions about this art. I like to call this a Walk Through an Artwork. We will weave our way through a discussion of the artwork and look at many things. I want you to be careful observers, looking at the things that the artists do in the painting. I also want you to think about how what is in the painting is meaningful. We all have the ability to contribute to this discussion, so please put your thinking and listening skills to work.
Look	**Introduce Lauscaux cave painting series.** Today we are looking at a series of paintings created by prehistoric people about 17,000 years ago. People call this artwork cave art, prehistoric art, or stone age art. All of these names describe a time period that occurred many thousands of years ago (direct students to timeline displayed in room).
	Media describes what the art is made of. Look carefully and begin to imagine what tools and items these prehistoric people might have used to complete their artwork. Subject matter is what we actually see within the artwork. Look carefully at what subject matter is present in this series of cave paintings. Artists during this time also utilized subject matter from their own lives to record and create the artwork.
Listen	**Ask students** what they see happening in these pieces of artwork.
Focus	**Allow student responses**, probing them for depth and encouraging students to add detail to their observations and ideas. Restate their responses, adding vocabulary and information that may assist their thinking.
	Say to students, "I heard you say animals . . . Tell me more about the types of animals or what they are doing" or "Jared mentioned colors of brown, red, and black. . . . What conclusion can you make about the choices these artists had?"
Learn/Respond	**Allow students' ideas to stretch further.** Instead of praising observations, reflect ideas or observations back to students with a question that might have them think a bit further about what they've shared. For example:

"Are you saying that only animals seem to appear in these artworks because their role in the lives of the cave people is significant?"

Clarify and add information

This reflection and questioning process assists students in thinking further about the art and gives them a chance to extend or add to their previous statement about the artwork.

Probe

Encourage more thinking through probing questions:

What do you observe in the artworks besides animals?

Imagining the time that these artists worked, what kinds of tools do you think they used?

What materials did they use for paint, and how do you think they discovered them?

What is significant about the symbols and designs you observe in this series?

Why do you believe these artists painted and why in deep caves?

Media, technique, and subject matter

Instruct students. Artwork from this time period dates back so long ago that we don't necessarily have proven facts about what the artists used to create the artwork or why they created them. At best, we have some scientific knowledge that helps us make predictions about what the artists used, and we have some ideas about why they decided to create the artwork.

The medium that cave artists used to create the paintings was paint collected and ground from materials readily available to the artists. Scientists speculate that minerals such as ochre, manganese, and haematite were ground into fine powders, mixed with water, and used in the artwork. That is why we only see earth-tone colors in the artwork—the paints came from the earth. We also have some evidence that the instruments the painters used included pads of animal fur that could be used like sponges, brushes made from twigs, and animal fur, and they probably also used their hands.

Why did these ancient people create paintings in caves? That is an even bigger question. Our educated guesses include that this (1) was a means of recording their history or life events, (2) was a part of a special ritual or belief system, or (3) was an explanation of their surroundings. What we do know is that this artwork tells us about the time, history, and place in which these people lived. We know what was important to them and what they held sacred. Artwork has the ability to tell us the cultural influence an artist was under and where that artist would take his or her culture through artwork.

Show next artwork (Ancient Egyptian)

Our next Walk Through an Artwork will focus on ancient Egyptian art. Look at this photograph of the sarcophagus of King Tutankhamen. We'll look at the materials artists might have used to construct this artwork as well as the reasons it was created.

Requirements: Time Period Project

Name: _____   **Partner/Team Members:** _____

Date: _____   **Time Period Assigned:** _____

Art historians are researchers, analyzers, and interpreters of the past and generally work as art critics, curators, restorers, or teachers. In this particular project, you will become an expert on a particular time period in art history and share with the rest of the class what you find. Although you will not be able to know everything about your time period, by becoming experts on one particular time period, you will be able to share your knowledge with the rest of the class by using the methodological skill of teaching.

Your team will create a PowerPoint presentation that will synthesize important information about your time period. The minimum number of slides is seven. Please see the Time Period Project Rubric for grading procedures. The requirements are as follows:

Research Outline   **10 points**

　Research information

Storyboard   **10 points**

　Plan/Design of presentation

PowerPoint Presentation   **50 points**

Description of Time Period

Tell me about the geography (where), historical happenings (major events, discoveries, etc.), and culture (daily life, rituals, significant people/places/things) of this time period. "Set the stage" for us. This should include the who, what, when, where, and why of your time period. Your information should capture and document the traditions, interests, and experiences of your time period. Highlight the history and heritage of the time you are studying.

History, Culture, and Art Connections

Summarize your research in the section above. How does art shape the culture? How does the culture shape the art? How did the history, geography, and culture of this time period affect the art and artists of that time? Or how did artists make their mark on the culture and history of that time? What are the ideals and values of your time period?

Techniques and Medium

What types of artwork surfaced during this time period? How did artists work, and what media were used during this time period? Define. Why did these particular techniques evolve, and how were the media discovered? Why are the techniques and media of your time period different from the other time periods?

Artist Slides

Briefly tell about two artists from your time period. What are their birth and death dates? What were their contributions to art? What does that say to you? Did they employ a special style or begin a movement? How did that affect the world they lived in, and how does that affect you? What were some of their famous pieces? Do you know other interesting facts about the artists?

What I Learned . . .

This statement should be composed by all group members and reflect what you have all learned about your time period and what is most important to convey in sharing this time period with the class. Use a word to describe this time in your statement.

Creativity and Aesthetics   **20 points**

This section highlights the creativity and design of your presentation product. Refer to the Rubric: Time Period Project and tutorial presentation to help you understand the logistics of the program and what you can do in your PowerPoint presentation. In addition, make sure to have at least seven images in your presentation and use creativity by adding something "new and different."

Team Contribution/Work Ethic   **10 points**

Group members must share work equally. Each member should work efficiently and productively during all phases of the project. Solve problems and divide responsibilities on your own.

Rubric: Time Period Project

Activity	Work in Progress	Dabbler	Apprentice	Master	Comments
Research and note taking 10 points	0–2 points Organizer shows that members recorded minimal information from two or fewer sources. Important information is left out or incomplete.	3–5 points Organizer shows that members misinterpreted research information and used only one to two sources.	5–8 points Organizer shows that members recorded relevant information from two to three sources by synthesizing information into their own words.	8–10 points Organizer indicates that members accurately researched information from three or more sources. They recorded and interpreted statements using their own words and even questioned and evaluated different points of view.	
Storyboard 10 points	0–2 points Storyboard does not provide enough overview of the presentation or is missing.	3–5 points Storyboard sketches are not logical or sequential and have incomplete information.	5–8 points Storyboard sketches only include titles, text, and image location. The slides are in a logical order and are complete.	8–10 points Storyboard illustrates the entire slide presentation structure with indications of titles, text, background color, placement of images, hyperlinks, headings, and so on.	
Content 50 points	0–20 points The content lacks a clear point of view and logical sequence. Missing a good bit of the required information. There is no evidence that the connection between culture and history is high-lighted in the presentation.	20–30 points The content is vague in conveying information and does not create a strong sense of purpose. Includes some of the required information, but some information seems not to fit. The idea of the connection between culture and art is mostly missing.	30–40 points The content includes all project assignment requirements but only briefly features the idea of the connection between culture and art. The presentation does not flow in a logical manner. Required content information is complete but disjointed and/or confusing.	40–50 points The content includes all information highlighted in the Time Period Project assignment, clearly featuring the idea of the connection between culture and art. Content information is accurate, current, and insightful.	

(Continued)

Activity	Work in Progress	Dabbler	Apprentice	Master	Comments
	No citations are given, and errors in spelling, capitalization, punctuation usage, and grammar repeatedly distract the audience. Major editing and revision is required.	Includes few citations of the information, and grammar, punctuation, capitalization, and spelling errors are distracting.	Includes some citations, and there is little editing required for grammar, punctuation, capitalization, and spelling.	Includes citations, and there are no errors in grammar, punctuation, capitalization, and spelling.	
Creativity and aesthetics 20 points	0–5 points	5–10 points	10–15 points	15–20 points	
	The text is extremely difficult to read with long blocks and small-sized fonts. Some inappropriate contrasting colors and poor use of headings are used.	Overall readability is difficult, with lengthy paragraphs, too many different fonts, dark or busy background, or overuse of bold, italics, and underlined phrases.	Fonts are easy to read most of the time but are occasionally distracting or busy.	Fonts are easy to read, point size varies appropriately, text is the appropriate length, and the background enhances the text.	
	The layout is cluttered and confusing, and spacing is not used correctly. The number of images is below requirement and distracts from the presentation.	The layout shows some structure but appears cluttered and busy with distracting gaps of space. The number of images is minimal.	The layout uses horizontal and vertical space appropriately. The number of images required is exceeded but does not enhance the presentation.	The layout is pleasing and contributes to the overall message of the presentation. The number of images exceeds the requirement and enhances the presentation.	
	Only basic PowerPoint design and technical skills are used.	Few to no advanced PowerPoint skills are utilized in the presentation.	Students have utilized some advanced PowerPoint skills.	Students have utilized and gone "above and beyond" their technical skills using	

Activity	Work in Progress	Dabbler	Apprentice	Master	Comments
	No evidence of an attempt to be creative.	Little evidence of creativity through the use of originality, elaboration, or flexibility.	Some evidence of originality, elaboration, and flexibility in the presentation.	PowerPoint, including items such as sound, digital pictures, custom animation, and diagrams. The use of originality, elaboration, and flexibility is apparent in the images, text, and layout of the presentation.	
Teamwork 10 points	0–2 points The group required teacher assistance in dividing tasks and resolving differences.	3–5 points The group members occasionally helped one another but occasionally required teacher assistance to resolve differences.	5–8 points Group members document how members divided tasks, shared the workload, and managed problems.	8–10 points Group members are able to document how they each contributed to the project—that is, who assumed what role (brainstormer, editor, researcher, designer, etc.) and solved what problems.	
	Few people contributed to their fair share of the work.	Some of the students were able to document that they did the work. But some members did not contribute their fair share.	It is evident most of the time that this was a group effort.	There is evidence that members helped one another, shared ideas, and worked toward the presentation project. The project is clearly a group effort.	

SOURCE: Adapted and used with permission from Joan M. Vandervelde. Available from www.uwstout.edu/soe/profdev/pptrubric.html

Graphic Organizer: Time Period Project

History	Culture	Geography

Art Connection

Artist:	Techniques and Media Artist:	Geography:

What I learned . . .

_____

_____

_____

_____

_____

_____

_____

_____

_____

_____

_____

Extension Activities: Open Your Eyes Unit

As in most situations with a group of students, there are those who finish at super speed with accuracy and thoughtfulness as well as those who move through the activity with more detail or challenge. Given this situation, extension activities are used that support the concepts, principles, generalizations, and guiding questions of the unit. These activities can be used to give more accelerated students an opportunity to work in their area of interest or talent while the teacher is focusing on some other students' needs.

Suggested Activities:

1. Students are able to become scholarly inquirers of information when exposed to the various resources used by cultural and art historians. In this extension activity, students will have time to explore text materials located in the classroom library. I always display a class library of art books that I have collected over the years. These can be used for research in the Time Period Project. However, I find that because of the limited time in most enrichment programs and the project at hand, students do not always have the time they would like to spend reading, looking at, and filtering through research materials. The art collection includes books on art history, time periods, artists, images, art techniques, and how-to art at different levels of expertise. I find that students are especially intrigued with the books on the lives of artists and on the how-to art books. Having time to explore the materials helps students develop a deeper understanding of time period culture and preferences for art.

2. Students will critique a piece of artwork that represents a particular culture or historical event. Critiquing a piece of artwork is an essential skill that allows students not only to identify but also to evaluate and interpret various pieces of artwork. A graphic organizer or process sheet should be developed that has students identify the subject matter, line, shape, balance, and focal point of the piece. Next, the students should be able to note the purpose of the piece and use words to describe and formulate a personal reaction to the artwork. These observations and notes should culminate in a short written reflection or critique. Make sure to provide various pieces to select from so that students may choose artwork based on their interest. By critiquing pieces of art from the past, students continue to build knowledge of art history as well as begin to uncover the essential elements they must use when creating artwork of their own.

3. As you share with students some information about the life situations, artistic journeys, problem-solving experiences, and events of famous artists, they are better able to situate themselves and reflect on their own ideas about art. Students will use Devine Entertainment's (www.devine-ent.com/) video series to examine more closely the lives of several famous artists. This series highlights the history, geography, and culture of the artist's time by telling

the stories of his or her family, motivation for art, and lifetime influences. Students should complete an ongoing log, comparing and contrasting the lives of different artists.

Videos include the following:

Mary Cassatt: *American Impressionist*

Degas: *Degas and the Dancer*

Monet: *Shadow and Light*

Goya: *Awakened in a Dream*

Rembrandt: *Father and Sons*

Homer: *An American Original*

4. Students will utilize Web adventures to explore art history and self-awareness in art. These online, interactive activities provide deeper exploration and familiarity with most of the guiding questions of the unit. Students can explore art history, art techniques, art structures, artists, and the thinking of an artist. See the following brief descriptions of some activities. Note: Educational Web Adventure's site provides process sheets; Sanford's site does not. However, teachers can easily create graphic organizers or Web browsers that highlight important information for students to note while working through the activities.

Educational Web Adventures

A. Pintura, Art Detective
www.eduweb.com/pintura
- art history mystery through comparison and contrast

The Artist's Toolkit
www.artsconnected.org/toolkit/
- historical look and self-exploration with visual elements and principles

Surrounded by Beauty: Arts of Native Americans
www.artsmia.org/surrounded-by-beauty/
- informative comparison of Native American and European art

Sanford Art of Crime Detection
www.sanford-artedventures.com/play/crimedetection/index.html
- exploration of the role of left and right brain thinking in art

Go West, Young Artist
www.sanford-artedventures.com/play/gowest/index.html
- American art history through landscapes

Leonardo's Workshop
www.sanford-artedventures.com/play/leonardo/index.html
- time machine to da Vinci's workshop to study line and shape

Color Theory Versus Dr. Gray and His Dechromatizer
www.sanford-artedventures.com/play/color2/a1.html
- color theory

Portraits From the Past
www.sanford-artedventures.com/play/portrait2/a1.html
- role of art historian by dating and gathering information on various pieces

Note-Taking Organizer: Time Period Project

Use the line below to identify the seven time periods and their dates.

|——————————————————————————|——————————————————————————|

0

Ideals and values that summarize each time period

Information that tells us about the geography, history, and culture of the time

Geography	History	Culture

Flowchart: Art Historian Interview

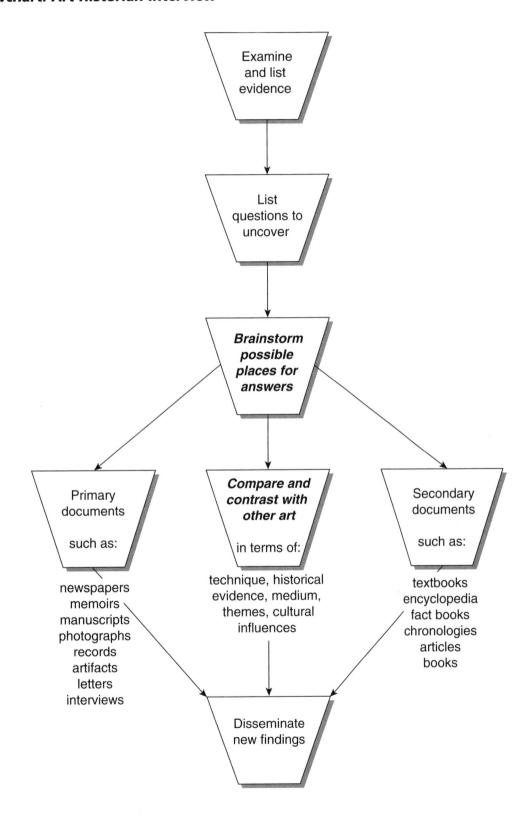

UNIT ASSESSMENT: OPEN YOUR EYES

Word Web

1. Take a look at the copy of our class web on the back and make any additions we made to our study of art history and appreciation.

Short Response

1. What are the purposes or functions of art? In other words, why do we create art?

   _____

   _____

2. What is the difference between looking at art and viewing art?

   _____

   _____

3. Think about one time period discussed in class. Explain how the history and culture of that time period relates to the art of that time (art connections).

   _____

   _____

4. Explain the methods art historians use in dating artwork. What other routine skills must they use in their work? How do art historians think and work?

   _____

   _____

5. What do you feel is your greatest strength and greatest weakness as an art historian? What is surprising or intriguing to you about the work of the art historian?

   _____

   _____

Essay

Explain in a paragraph your definition of *culture*. Also explain what you have learned about this concept in our unit this semester. What have you learned about yourself?

Historical Sleuthing

A Parallel of Practice Unit for Middle School Students

Carol Horn and Janice Strauss

BACKGROUND FOR UNIT

The further I go in my studies, the more amazed I am. What a war!

Everything we are or will be goes right back to that period.

It decided for once and for all which way we were going, and we've gone.

—*Shelby Foote to Walker Percy, November 29, 1956,*
in C. S. Chapman, Shelby Foote: A Writer's Life

Historical Sleuthing is designed to provide learners with an understanding of the tools, methods, knowledge, and skills needed by historians as they delve into the past to make meaning for the present. By engaging in the intellectual struggles of historians, students are able to explore and make sense of the past through systematic intellectual inquiry.

Comprehension, interpretation, issue analysis, and decision making, as understood and practiced by historians, are integral to each learning experience. Through the discipline of history and the practice of historical writing, students incorporate the high standards of historical thinking into lessons and activities. This process requires them to assume attitudes and behaviors of the scholar-practitioner, such as critically examining evidence. They also use discovery and revision to extend and deepen their vision of the place and importance of history in our democratic society. The role of scholar-practitioner thus allows students to uncover the complex interrelationship among knowledge, concepts, and skills within the discipline and leads to their own development as historians.

Throughout this concept-based unit, a study of the Civil War is the arena in which students will progress toward expertise. This topic is a vehicle to establish, clarify, and refine Ascending Intellectual Demand (AID) as described in The Parallel Curriculum (Tomlinson et al., 2002). The unit activities can be continuously adjusted in response to students' readiness level. Each component incorporates understanding and meaning in a unique and dynamic way that guides the students' journey from novice to expert.

Last, this unit leads students to a deeper and richer understanding of the struggles, conflicts, and issues of the Civil War. Barbara Fields, a historian, wrote,

> For me, the picture of the Civil War as a historic phenomenon is not on the battlefield. It's not about weapons; it's not about soldiers, except to the extent that weapons and soldiers, at that crucial moment, joined in the discussion about something higher—about humanity, about human dignity, about human freedom. (From www.regent.edu/acad/schcom/rojc/melton.html, retrieved November 5, 2004)

The activities in the unit are designed to catalyze such a discussion, giving students a real-world pathway to issues of significance that historians are bound to encounter.

CONTENT FRAMEWORK

Organizing Concepts

Discipline-Specific Concepts. Historical Evidence
Macroconcepts. Discovery, Revision

Principles and Generalizations

G1 Discovery is driven by inquiry.
G2 Discovery challenges known information and leads to new understandings.
G3 Discovery provides understanding yet initiates further inquiry.
G4 Discovery is built on previous knowledge by an individual's curiosity, open-mindedness, active investigation, sound judgment, and ability to communicate effectively.
G5 Revision is the attitude and behavior of relooking, rethinking, and reseeing.
G6 Revision uncovers and communicates deeper understandings that result in new insights.
G7 Revision is a product of reflection and inquiry.
G8 Historical evidence is constantly being uncovered and interrogated.
G9 Historical evidence is the basis for sound historical interpretation.

Standards for History

SD1 Develop an understanding of the work of a historian.
SD2 Apply and revise varied writing skills through historical narrative that examines and interprets historical evidence.
SD3 Refine and strengthen metacognitive skills through journal reflections in order to clarify student thinking and understanding of the historian's work and its connection to the wider world.

SD4 Refine the connection between social studies and writing through an integration of the two disciplines.

SD5 Research, analyze, and interpret historical documents created during the Civil War time period.

Skills

S1   Distinguish between past, present, and future

S2   Reconstruct patterns of historical continuity and change

S3   Use appropriate strategies to locate, identify, and evaluate historical evidence

S4   Practice the habits and thinking of historical scholar-practitioners

S5   Analyze and interpret historical print and nonprint resources

S6   Consider multiple perspectives in interpreting past issues, events, and people

S7   Research and describe historical figures to include the depth and complexity of the issues, time, and events that influenced their lives

S8   Formulate historical questions

S9   Reflect on the concepts and principles as they relate to the cause and character of the Civil War

S10 Assume and defend a position on a controversial issue that relates to the Civil War and consequences in the present

S11 Apply the methods used by historians to generate questions and new knowledge and to solve problems

S12 Employ assessments that incorporate indicators of quality used by scholar-practitioners

MAKING SURE THE PARALLEL OF PRACTICE REMAINS CENTRAL IN TEACHING AND LEARNING

Curriculum Component	Component Descriptions and Rationale
Content	Students work with the discipline-specific concept of evidence and the macroconcepts of discovery and revision to organize and make meaning of their work. Key principles relate to all three concepts. Social studies standards guide the instructional content and activities.
	The "big ideas" of evidence, discovery, and revision provide organization, clarity, and power for the teacher and students as they read, discuss, and arrive at sound historical interpretations of past events. By focusing on the big ideas rather than skills alone, students are more likely to find relevance in their work and develop a deeper understanding of and appreciation for the work of a historian.

(Continued)

(Continued)

Curriculum Component	Component Descriptions and Rationale
Assessments	Assessments focus on the concepts and principles of the unit and on the knowledge and skills needed by a historian in the field. A culminating complex performance assessment challenges students to apply the methods, knowledge, skills, and expertise of a historian.
Introductory activities	The concepts of historical evidence, discovery, and revision provide the framework for both the unit and the introductory activity. The learning experience connects directly to the students' personal lives. Students think about primary and secondary sources of historical evidence and how these sources are analyzed and interpreted.
Teaching strategies	In both whole-class and small-group instruction, students learn and practice the methods and skills used by historians as they uncover and interpret the past. Whole-class teaching strategies help students develop background knowledge that is necessary to make meaning of the unit's concepts and principles and to apply the unit's key skills. Small-group and individual instructional strategies focus on helping students develop skills of historical analysis and historical interpretation.
Learning activities	The unit's learning activities are designed primarily to help students come to understand and apply the knowledge, ideas, and skills designated as most important to the work of a historian. Through the guiding questions that open each lesson, and the journal prompts at each lesson's closing, students are asked to revisit and reapply the unit's key concepts and principles as they apply to the work of a historical scholar-practitioner.
Grouping strategies	Grouping is used to ensure that all students work with the unit's big ideas and important skills while still receiving instruction important for individual growth and development in the skills of a historical scholar-practitioner. Groups will be both heterogeneous and homogeneous throughout the unit.
Products	The interim and culminating products, as well as the accompanying appendices that help assess these products, are focused on the unit's key concepts and principles as they apply to the work of a historical scholar-practitioner. Student products are varied and provide multiple opportunities for students to apply new knowledge, skills, and understandings through study that replicates and approaches the work of a historical scholar-practitioner.

Curriculum Component	Component Descriptions and Rationale
Resources	A variety of resources, including primary and secondary sources of historical evidence, guide the students' focus on the knowledge, understanding, and skills essential to the unit. In addition, they allow students time to work at their own skill level and to pursue personal interests.
Extension activities	Journal reflections at the end of each lesson, follow-up activities, and independent research allow students to practice and reflect on the work of a historian at appropriate levels of challenge.
Modifications for learner need, including Ascending Intellectual Demand (AID)	Throughout the unit, instruction, materials, tasks, assessment, and criteria for success are modified in response to learner readiness and interest. AID for advanced learners asks them to work at more expertlike levels of historical analysis and interpretation, to use more advanced resource and research materials, and to focus on key AID questions for the Practice parallel.

UNIT SEQUENCE, DESCRIPTION, AND TEACHER REFLECTIONS

Lesson 1: Preassessment and Introduction

(60 minutes)

Unit Sequence	Teacher Reflections
Concepts. Evidence, Discovery, Revision G1-2, G7, SD1, SD3, S3-5, S11	
Guiding Questions. At the beginning of the lesson, pose the following guiding questions to focus student thinking. • How do we discover information about the past? • What do we mean by evidence, and how do we know that something we read is true? • How does discovery of the past revise our thinking about it and the present?	Guiding questions are posed at the beginning of each lesson to assess students' understanding of the unit concepts and the work of a historian. These questions are reexamined at the end of each lesson to assess evolving understandings of the content and to identify personal goals for growth. This first set of guiding questions is used as a preassessment to determine students' understanding of the work of a historian, as defined by **Lesson 1 Rubric: Student as Historian** and **Lesson 4 Rubric: Final Project.** Therefore, there are few teacher-provided supports (i.e., artifacts or texts) to assist the students in formulating their answers.

(Continued)

(Continued)

Unit Sequence	Teacher Reflections
	The guiding questions focus the students' attention on the concepts, strategies, problems, tools, and methodologies of a historian. In the introductory and subsequent lessons, students distinguish between meaningful evidence versus less significant information in their efforts to replicate the role and practice of a historian (see **Lesson 1 Worksheet: A Historian's Approach to History— Advice to Young Historical Sleuths From a Historian**).
	The guiding questions also provide the complementary benefit of attuning students to personality traits that support productivity within the field of historical writing, a clear link to the Curriculum of Identity. The questions deal with the concepts of discovery or revision to organize students' thinking and to uncover generalizations about people, periods, and issues as they occur in varied situations. Students' responses are one tool to use in deciding which unit activities are appropriate.
Learning Activities. Students work in think-pair-share groups to discuss, then write responses to the guiding questions. Record responses on a graphic organizer represented by pillars and an arch. Label the pillars as "evidence" and the arch as "validity." On the pillars, list sources of evidence. Be sure to discuss the difference between primary and secondary sources and how that may affect their usefulness to historians. On the arch, generate reasons why the evidence provides valid information that could be used by a historian. Take time to discuss this graphic organizer as a visual example of reasons (evidence) that support a conclusion (validity) and how the two are linked.	The think-pair-share strategy was chosen because it can establish a climate of trust and risk taking for reluctant or quiet students.

In this introductory activity, students attempt to identify reasons and draw conclusions about historical data. It is a process similar to analyzing (finding the reasons or proof) and evaluating arguments (drawing conclusions or bringing about the results). The pillar and arch serve as a main idea graphic organizer and should remain posted in the room for future additions, modifications, or deletions. |
| Conduct a whole-class discussion of the concepts of discovery and revision and how these concepts relate to a historian's work. | Throughout the unit, the teacher works with the students to further their understanding of the concepts of discovery |

Unit Sequence	*Teacher Reflections*
Have the class begin to construct generalizations that link these concepts to the work of a historian. Students should note their generalizations in a personal reflection journal.	and revision and how these concepts lead to a deeper understanding of a historian's work. As students explore various tasks within the Civil War unit, they will record their own conceptual and historical understandings in a personal reflection journal.
Tiered Journal Prompts. Use the **Lesson 1 Rubric: Student as Historian** as a guideline to assign journal prompts to individual students. If there is not enough time to assess the placement level of students within the rubric, use prior knowledge about the student and/or student observation during the think-pair-share activity. Assign the appropriate journal prompt (from less to more expertlike):	Journal prompts, similar to the guiding questions posed at the beginning of each lesson, are provided at the end of each lesson to promote student reflection on historical understandings and students' self-knowledge of their practice as a historian. These journal prompts prepare the students to reflect on historical problems, skills, methods, and solutions. As this is the beginning of a new unit, it is important for the teacher to closely monitor students' understanding. The rubric is suggested as a guideline, but other measures may also be needed (e.g., prior knowledge, readiness level) to ensure the appropriate students have access to AID activities in the unit opening.
• How would you share your past with someone who does not know you? What evidence would be considered valid and reliable? • Think of an important event in your own past that has been challenged by your friends, relatives, or others who may question what you said and did. What evidence would you collect, and how would you present it to defend your thinking and behavior? • Describe a time that you have believed when others have doubted or doubted when others believed. How did you resolve the conflict to yourself and others? What evidence did you use and what did you do?	Students enter these daily reflections in a personal journal. Collect the journals periodically for formative assessment and provide feedback to the students. Your feedback provides opportunities for ongoing clarification and supports evolving understandings of the criteria in unit rubrics. Frequent and continuous written reflection about their own thinking about problems within the field enables students to discover and revise their viewpoints in the rigorous process of building knowledge and deepening understandings as they engage in the work of historical scholar-practitioners. It also helps you spot those students who are moving ahead on the Student as Historian rubric in order to provide them with AID opportunities.

Lesson 2: Examining Primary Sources

(90 minutes)

Unit Sequence	*Teacher Reflections*
Concepts. Evidence, Discovery, Revision G1–3, G8, SD1, SD3, SD5, S3–5, S9	Lessons 2, 3, and 4 follow a similar sequence as students become familiar with the role of a historical scholar-practitioner.
Guiding Questions. At the beginning of the lesson, pose the following guiding questions to all students to focus their thinking: • How does the examination of primary sources of information lead to the discovery of new knowledge and insights? • What does *interpretation* mean, and how might historical evidence be influenced and revised by the historian?	Throughout the unit, the guiding questions may take on a different format to retain novelty and student interest. For example, individual response or dyad, triad, or quad organizational patterns may become the basis for a group response. Likewise, oral and written reflection may be emphasized as needed. By contrast, retaining the same format for the guiding questions will underscore the features of routine inquiry practiced by a disciplined historian. Student responses should be routinely shared and discussed during whole-group class discussions.
Group Investigations. Share a compilation of documents, photographs, and other evidence from the Civil War. The evidence could include letters, news articles, photographs, and other documents that might be used by a historian to uncover and interpret the Civil War.	Group investigations promote inquiry, investigation, and student interest as the entire class grapples with challenging material. In this process, students self-select an area, topic, issue, or interest. Multiple **Unit Resources** are listed at the end of the unit for easy access to Web and multimedia titles and sites.
Have students work together in small heterogeneous groups of three to four students. They will examine and discuss the evidence about a Civil War event to discover information about this time period.	During the group investigations sessions, you may wish to offer mini-lessons on the skills of conflict resolution, planning, decision making, organization, and so on as needed to enhance group functioning. Open the mini-lessons to all students, but invite those students you have noted as needing work on a particular skill.
Students complete the **Study Guide: Primary Sources—Connections to the Past** during the group investigations task.	
Once students have finished the small-group activity, meet as a whole class to discuss how each piece of evidence about a significant event could match up to the validity conclusions on the graphic organizer presented in Lesson 1. Add	

Unit Sequence	*Teacher Reflections*

new conclusions about validity to the graphic organizer as students share their evidence.

Review the many statements that had been generated about evidence and validity in these two lessons. The students' next step will be to formulate generalizations about the process of discovery (evidence, reasons, or proof) and revision (or drawing conclusions about the validity of one's evidence or arguments) to deepen their understanding of the work of a historian. Record the student responses on chart paper to provide a chronology of evolving understanding.

The charts should remain visible within the classroom during the duration of the unit.

AID. A common problem associated with generalizations is the tendency to lead oneself and others astray with limited or unfounded information. Various forms of bias also evolve from faulty generalizations. These are features of routine problems and ethical issues and standards that historians face in their attempts to interpret the past. If student curiosity and skill development are evident in some or all students, use personal letters and journals to stimulate a discussion about bias and its effect on historical interpretation.

Tell students that as they explore various tasks within the Civil War unit, they will continue to discover and revise their own conceptual and historical understandings, just as historians do in their work to understand people and events in history.

Jigsaw Strategy. After students have completed the study guide and reached consensus on the information that the evidence provides, re-form into new groups composed of at least one person from each of the original groups. This is called a jigsaw strategy. Students will then share the information that they discovered from their evidence and discuss the understandings that it reveals about the Civil War.

Similar to group investigations, the jigsaw strategy provides diverse students with the opportunity to contribute to a group understanding of chronological thinking, sources of historical evidence, and criteria for evaluation.

Students should remain in these groups to begin a chronological timeline of the events of the Civil War. Show the students examples of different types of timelines and ask them to create one of their own design.

The timeline could take the form of a large classroom display. Like the discovery and revision charts, make the timeline available for refinement and additions throughout the study.

(Continued)

(Continued)

Unit Sequence	Teacher Reflections
Be sure to highlight the connection among the overarching concepts, guiding questions, and lesson activities. Encourage students to continually revise the class list of generalizations in their journals. Amend the classroom chart as needed.	
Tiered Journal Prompt. Assign an appropriate journal prompt from the following questions: • What type of evidence did you find to be the most believable? Why? • What biases might be present in a journal, letter, or other document written by an individual? How would you overcome this bias? • How does a historian identify gaps in available records to discover information about the interests, time period, and place in which an individual lived or an event occurred?	Continually assess where you feel students fall on the unit rubrics in order to determine the appropriate journal prompt to assign to each student. Students' evolving understanding of biases and prejudice as well as meaningful evidence versus less important information determines prompt assignment. In your written feedback to students, highlight specific connections students make and possible gaps of conceptual understanding. The journal prompts throughout the unit, along with the lesson activities, are another vehicle for student investigation of ethical issues and standards of credible performance, theories that govern historical interpretation, and personality traits displayed by writers of history.

Lesson 3: Historical Inquiry

(90 minutes)

Unit Sequence	Teacher Reflections
Concepts. Evidence, Discovery, Revision G1-4, G7-9, SD1, SD3, S1, S3-6, S8, S11 **Guiding Questions.** At the beginning of the lesson, pose the following guiding questions to focus student thinking: • What do we mean by revision? • How does the revision process challenge our thinking and historical interpretation? **Group Interaction.** Return students to their original group investigation teams. Instruct each group to elaborate upon one of the "What" questions on the **Study Guide: Primary**	Students need multiple opportunities to consider various viewpoints, challenge each other's thinking, and work together to arrive at a tentative consensus as they begin to learn and apply the thinking and skills of a historian. To understand multiple interpretations of events, students make assumptions about the strategies, tools, and methods of historians as they formulate new questions, generate new knowledge, solve problems, and practice the written expression of their thinking and understanding.

Unit Sequence	*Teacher Reflections*

Sources—Connections to the Past.
They must use evidence to support the narratives. Students self-select another team to review their narrative against the evidence and validity guidelines organizer developed in earlier lessons. Use the variety of narratives generated by the evidence to initiate a discussion of the impact of choice, viewpoint, bias, and author's style on the historical narrative. Encourage students to challenge each other's claims and revise their writings in response to the feedback they receive. Adjust the discovery and revision charts as the groups deem necessary.

Tiered Journal Prompts. Assign an appropriate journal prompt from the following:

- How did your thinking change as you listened to and shared your ideas with others?
- How do multiple perspectives affect your own emerging viewpoint?
- How do choice, viewpoint, bias, and author's style help you revise old ideas and discover new understandings?

The journal prompts invite students to think about the tentative nature of historical interpretations. As arguments are challenged by new information, the student is confronted with the variance between historical judgment and historical documentation or narrative.

Encourage students to self-assess using the unit rubrics. In response to their self-assessments, offer them the opportunity to self-select their journal prompt.

Homework. Assign the individual research project, as outlined in **Lesson 3 Worksheet: A Historical Inquiry**. Students research their own past or the past of a family member through evidence collected from their families and friends. Provide a reasonable due date. You may wish to provide check-in points along the way for those who need them.

Individual research gives students an opportunity to apply the work of a historian to their own lives through an assignment that connects to student background and interests. It requires the students to distinguish between relevant and substantive versus appealing yet insignificant evidence to establish a balanced profile of the individual. This assignment takes into account students' readiness levels, interests, and learning profiles.

Lesson 4: The Issue of Slavery

(90–180 minutes)

Unit Sequence	Teacher Reflections

Concepts. Evidence, Discovery, Revision
G2–3, G5–6, GP9, SD2–5, S4–7, S11–12

Guiding Questions. At the beginning of the lesson, pose the following guiding questions to focus student thinking:

- What do we discover through the process of relooking at, rethinking, and reseeing the Civil War?
- How does a consideration of multiple perspectives provide a deeper understanding of the Civil War?
- What prompts historians to continue to inquire and rethink what they thought they knew about the Civil War?

Socratic Seminar. Introduce the historical document "Slavery Denounced," by Frederick Douglass, as a read-aloud to accommodate a variety of readiness levels. Engage in a Socratic dialogue about its meaning and significance. Encourage students to generate open-ended questions about the reading that engage their minds and challenge their thinking. Students then take turns sharing their questions by writing them on a chart or chalkboard. As questions are shared, the class should revise them until they agree that they have questions that will lead to deeper understandings of the text.

This speech was originally published as a pamphlet. It can be located in James M. Gregory's *Frederick Douglass, the Orator* (1893, pp. 103–106). It is also available on several Web sites, for example, at http://docsouth.unc.edu/neh/gregory/menu.html.

The Socratic seminar is a powerful teaching and learning strategy that improves comprehension and challenges students to think and apply knowledge on increasingly higher levels. As a thoughtful dialogue that fosters reflective and critical thinking, the seminar is a catalyst for lively discussions leading to a deeper understanding of issues, themes, and ideas in a climate of shared respect. Information on using the Socratic seminar as an instructional strategy may be found in the following sources:

Use this set of questions to conduct a group discussion of the text.

Terry Roberts and Laura Billings, *The Paideia Classroom: Teaching for Understanding* (Larchmont, NY: Eye on Education, 1998).

Michael Strong and Douglas M. Strong, *The Habit of Thought: From Socratic Seminars to Socratic Practice* (Tonowanda, NY: New View Publications, 1997).

Unit Sequence	Teacher Reflections
Seminar Follow-up. From teacher observation and anecdotal records of student responses, assign appropriate seminar follow-up for an oral class reading: *Novice:* Write a speech for a present-day "Fourth of July" observance. Persuade your audience of the importance of observing this event and the ideals that it represents. Cite evidence from history to support your ideas. *Apprentice:* Write a letter to the editor of a newspaper in which Frederick Douglass's speech appeared. Tell why you agree or disagree with his viewpoint. *Proficient:* Write a persuasive speech from the viewpoint of a contemporary group that may or may not believe that the ideals that the Fourth of July represents are practiced today. Cite evidence to support your viewpoint and beliefs. Speeches may be worked on during class time or for homework. Students may share their speeches with the class orally or publish them in a class magazine.	The follow-up provides an important opportunity for students to apply new insights and understandings that they have gained through the seminar discussion as they make the connections between past and present issues, people, and events. Use unit rubrics to assign tasks. Note that for this rubric we have determined a category beyond "expert," called "innovator." You may choose to add additional assignments for expert and innovator if there are students who are beginning to approach these advanced levels.
Tiered Journal Prompts. Assign the appropriate journal prompts to each student (from easier to more difficult): • What did you discover about Frederick Douglass by reading his speech? Do you agree or disagree with his viewpoint? Why? • Identify the weaknesses in Frederick Douglass's argument. Provide suggestions for improving or revising his speech. • How might the points that Frederick Douglass posed in his speech have impacted those who opposed slavery? Those who supported slavery? Those who were indifferent?	The journal prompts require students to expand their understanding of historical figures and events as they obtain and interrogate historical data. With an opportunity to elaborate upon the evidence, the students must be mindful of the difficulties of constructing a sound historical interpretation from documents and records of the past. Students who struggle with writing may be permitted to keep an audio or video journal with bulleted annotations of the content of the entry.
Culminating Project. Introduce the culminating project (see the following) to all students. Clarify any misconceptions, review the schedule, and explain the **Lesson 4 Rubric: Final Project**.	By informing the students of the unit's purpose, the required and optional aspects of the performance tasks, and the criteria by which the work will be judged, they will become better equipped to sense whether they are effective scholar-practitioners.

(Continued)

(Continued)

Unit Sequence	Teacher Reflections

Project Directions. You may want to do the following:

- Compare the capital and human resources of the Union and the Confederacy prior to and during the course of the Civil War.
- Identify the innovations in military technology and explain their impact on people and property in the North versus the South during the war.
- Evaluate how political and military leadership affected the course and outcome of the war.
- Describe the position of the major Native American nations during the Civil War and explain their involvement in the war and the effects of the war on those nations.
- Compare the motives for fighting and the daily life experiences of white and African American Union soldiers with those of Confederate soldiers.
- Evaluate the significance of slavery in the South and the importance of the "free labor" ideology in the North.
- Add additional ideas of your own that you formulate and present to the teacher for approval.

Your documentary may be a visual, written, or multimedia presentation, performance, or other product of your own design that employs the rigor and methods used by historians. Based on the standards of excellence for a scholar-practitioner, each product or presentation is submitted for a self, peer, and scholar-practitioner review and evaluated according to the **Lesson 4 Rubric: Final Project**. It is most important that the documentary reveals your understanding of the main concepts of discovery and revision uncovered through the lesson activities and personal research.

You will probably need to revise your product multiple times. Frequent sessions with the teacher and continual review of the final project rubric will keep you heading in the right direction.

These authentic tasks engage students in the work of a historian who interrogates historical evidence to proffer sound historical interpretation. By devoting a portion of each class session to actively investigating the cause, course, or character of the Civil War, the students apply sound judgment and then reflect upon the evidence to revise previously held beliefs. The culminating project challenges students to organize their knowledge and skills as a historical scholar-practitioner. Evidence of their understanding of the major concepts of discovery and revision is judged against standards employed by a historical scholar-practitioner. You may wish to post a chart listing suggested research steps to help those students who are less comfortable with the research process.

Although much of the work on this project is completed outside the school setting, a portion of each class should be reserved for clarification and refinement of work as need dictates. Individual learning contracts may be used to accommodate student differences and provide an ongoing record of their progress. Schedule student conferences each week to assess student progress, guide student thinking through questions that promote critical thinking, and help with any questions or concerns that may arise.

Encourage students to choose from a variety of product options using the mode of expression(s) that best suits their individual learning preferences, interests, and readiness. An examination of authentic methodologies and products of historians (e.g., debates, essays, photo journals, editorials) should be conducted with students as they learn to replicate the approaches and methods of a historian.

It is also necessary to teach production and presentation skills to achieve high-quality products. A caveat: Less is more. Show exemplars of a limited and focused documentary that reveal high quality and successful achievement. A close examination of the rubric delineates levels of quality performance in content, process, and product areas.

Lesson 5: The Course and Character of the Civil War

(90–180 minutes)

Unit Sequence	Teacher Reflections
Concepts. Evidence, Discovery, Revision G1–2, G4, G6, G8–9, SD1–5, S1, S3–5, S7–8, S10–11	Lessons 5, 6, 7, and 8 provide for AID along a continuum from novice to proficient to innovator and are designed to challenge and engage a diverse group of learners in a heterogeneous class. Students gain firsthand experience of the key elements that drive the work of practitioners in the field.
Guiding Questions. At the beginning of the lesson, pose the following guiding questions to focus student thinking: • How does your thinking change as you discover new information about people and events in the past? • How did the issue of slavery lead to conflicting viewpoints among leaders and citizens during the Civil War period?	
Study of People. Instruct students to examine various profiles of familiar Civil War leaders who vigorously promoted or rejected slavery. Provide profiles that include information about individuals' background, their political and social views, and the impact and influence of their thinking on the time. Engage the class in a discussion of the importance of varied sources and the influence of conflicting perspectives upon understanding a controversial issue.	Each student chooses a leader to research, based on interest. Make resources of varied levels available in the classroom, library, and computer (via bookmarked Web sites). A study of key people through a variety of sources allows the students to reconcile conflicting perspectives that impact a historian's work. Throughout the unit, students are confronted with ethical issues that are value-laden and worthy of focused analysis. This is a particularly challenging aspect of the historical writer's quest to provide a balanced interpretation to contentious social issues. By investigating the people of the time period, students not only gain a clearer understanding of the issues and events but also discover the humanity of the individuals involved (e.g., motives, hopes, and fears). **Optional Extension.** By asking students to compare their own motives, hopes, and fears with those of their research subject, you incorporate an aspect of the Curriculum of Identity into this unit. To enhance this connection, ask students questions such as the following (derived from the focusing questions for the Curriculum of Identity): • What does your leader think about this issue?

(Continued)

(Continued)

Unit Sequence	Teacher Reflections
	• What do you think? • What are the problems and issues on which this leader spends his or her life? • To what degree is this familiar, surprising, and/or intriguing to you? • What difficulties did your leader encounter? • How did he or she cope with the difficulties? • How do you think you would cope with them? • What do you learn about yourself by studying this leader? • How did this leader handle ambiguity, uncertainty, persistence, failure, success, collaboration, and compromise? • How do you handle those things?
Group Research. Invite students to assemble into groups based on their choice of a Civil War leader who supported or opposed slavery (Harriet Beecher Stowe, William Lloyd Garrison, Jefferson Davis, John C. Calhoun, or others). Remind students that the objective is to act like a historian as they use biographies, historical narratives, newspaper editorials, political cartoons, diaries, and other primary documents in their research. As students gain proficiency in the research process, instruct them to include information about the individual's background, political and social views, and the impact of his or her influence on the thinking of the time. They should avoid "present-mindedness" by taking into account the historical context in which events unfold. An essential behavior of a historian is the nonjudgmental depiction of evidence of the past. Review elements of persuasive writing before the groups write a brief editorial explaining their viewpoints. The groups then exchange their writings with those of an opposing position.	Group research is used to give students an opportunity to collaborate with someone who has investigated slavery from a similar viewpoint. This activity engages students as they develop historical perspective. It is a key ability for historians to describe the past in its own terms and not by present-day norms and values. Awareness of the historical context in which events occurred is the basis for historical theory and argument. **AID.** Expert historical analysis and interpretation requires the investigation of competing sets of views and documentation to sort out relevant and less significant information. Some students may choose to collaborate with someone who has researched a historical figure of an opposing position. Students should work together to incorporate both viewpoints into a product that reveals the struggles, dilemmas, aspirations, and visions of the figures in conflict. To hypothesize and draw conclusions, students must balance their explanations of the past with the limitations and opportunities of available evidence. Product suggestions might include a point-counterpoint exchange between the two leaders, a diary entry of the person's struggles with the issue of slavery, a letter to the editor of a local newspaper written by the individual, or a similar product of one's own choosing.

Unit Sequence	*Teacher Reflections*
Tiered Journal Prompts. Assign an appropriate journal prompt to each student (listed from easier to more difficult):	Continually refer to unit rubrics to assess each student's performance level and to identify when students are ready to transition to a higher level of expertise.

- Why is it important to read and compare competing accounts of the Civil War?
- How do historians consider competing accounts of events and people of the Civil War and then decide what to use to explain what happened?
- How do historians incorporate new information into their understanding of the Civil War and then transfer this understanding to current events and leaders?

Culminating Project. Return to the section under the culminating project in Lesson 4. Provide opportunities for students to work on their final projects as time and need dictate. Remind students to remain focused on the assignment and assessment by posing questions, such as the following: How will you establish your big ideas or theory of the cause, course, or character of the Civil War? Will it reflect what historians have understood about the conflict? How will you organize your information? What forms of research will you use? Are they the tools a historian would use? On what basis will you draw conclusions? Have you considered important historical evidence and not just information that was easy to find? How will you know? What standards would you offer as proof? How will you determine if you are being fair and just in your examination of historical figures, events, and issues? How can you be sure your historical narrative is written through the eyes and understanding of the times? How will you incorporate your understanding of the concepts of discovery and revision as they apply to a historian's work?

It is important for students to have access and opportunity to explore the big ideas of their topics in order to become equipped with the theories, concepts, skills, and knowledge of a historian.

By reserving a portion of each class period to reflect on the culminating project, students will become better equipped for expertlike production.

LESSON 6: CAUSES OF THE CIVIL WAR

(90–180 minutes)

Unit Sequence	Teacher Reflections
Concepts. Evidence, Discovery, Revision G1–9, SD1–5, S1–5, S8–9, S11–12	
Guiding Questions. At the beginning of the lesson, pose the following guiding questions to focus student thinking: • Is revision an end or a beginning? • How can revision and discovery reform your opinions, values, and interpretation about the causes of the Civil War?	The major concepts of discovery and revision are revisited through ongoing questioning and probing.
Introduction to Independent Study. Walk students through an independent study of one critical event leading up to the Civil War. Help students analyze the Missouri Compromise of 1820 to investigate why and how the Compromise was created. The background, interests, and points of view of slave and free state politicians must be considered to evaluate the political consequences of the compromise. After interpreting the research data, assign students to heterogeneous groups where they compose a historical argument supporting or opposing the Missouri Compromise of 1820.	A whole-group practice activity allows the teacher to model the components of historical research. By engaging in nonfictional research, students will view historical narratives as arguable, tentative, and continued inquiry.
Individual Research. A suggested list of topics for student investigation and discovery include the following: Amistad uprising, Dred Scott decision, Compromise of 1850, publication of *Uncle Tom's Cabin*, the Kansas-Nebraska Act, Lincoln-Douglas debates, John Brown's raid, Lincoln's presidential election, secession of Confederate states, and the Emancipation Proclamation. Encourage students to choose events	This is an opportunity for the students to engage in the methods used by practitioners and contributors to generate new knowledge and to solve problems through the eyes of a historian. Through the work of a historian, the learner becomes an eager respondent grappling with unresolved problems and ethical issues in the field of historical research. This activity is intended to develop a practical clarity about the key concepts of

Unit Sequence	*Teacher Reflections*

for their own inquiry that they find of particular interest.

discovery and revision as they relate to the discipline of history.

Novice Students: Read from extensive and varied sources, then write an argument supporting or opposing the significance of a critical event from the list of suggested topics. Recount the meaning of the event, what led up to it, and the outcomes that followed to construct an evolving historical understanding of the causes of the Civil War. Work like a historian, citing details and incorporating appropriate language to relate one's evolving historical understandings. Submit an article for publication in a classroom magazine focused on the Civil War.

Proficient Students: Use varied sources and materials to conduct a broad exploration of a critical event from the list of suggested topics in the introductory activity. Work as a historian to explain the significance of the event, its underlying causes, the immediate and long-term consequences, and interests and beliefs of individuals or groups involved. Then write a factual and unbiased explanation of the critical event that will be submitted for publication in the classroom magazine.

Innovator Students: Work like a historian to investigate one of the critical events from the list of suggested topics in the introductory activity. After wide, varied, and rich reading, identify a relevant concept, such as conflict, that is transferable to other times and locations. Explain your information and ideas through relevant connections, compared and contrasted to events in other times and locations, and posed as unanswered questions requiring further discovery and revision. Submit the final revision for publication in the classroom magazine.

(Continued)

(Continued)

Unit Sequence	Teacher Reflections

Tiered Journal Prompts. Assign the appropriate journal prompt:

- Reflect on your research of one particular event. What surprised you? What was pointed out to you? What are you still wondering about?
- The Civil War was a period of controversy and intense debate. How did the event that you researched challenge our nation's ability to continue the ideals of liberty, equality, justice, and human dignity upon which it was founded?
- What metaphor could you develop that captures the essence and controversy of the issues surrounding the event that you researched (e.g., federal versus state rights; slavery for some versus freedom for all; Southern versus Northern; economic, social, and cultural differences).

Culminating Project. Return to the culminating project section in Lesson 4. Provide opportunities for students to work on their final projects as time and need dictate. Encourage students to review project guidelines and assessment tools. Remind students to remain focused on the assignment and assessment. They should consistently rethink the work they have accumulated so far by considering the following questions:

- Is your evidence credible, accurate, and precise? Is it valid and reliable?
- Are you using the research tools and methods of a historian?
- Are you continuing to ask yourself questions about your findings?

Are you remembering that an open and deliberate attitude toward research is as important as the knowledge you gather and interpret?

Scheduled lesson time for the culminating project establishes an atmosphere of trust and challenge between the teacher and student. By guiding the students to establish their own goals for personal growth and achievement, the teacher encourages them to not only think like historians but also practice the processes of issue analysis and decision making.

LESSON 7: EFFECTS OF THE CIVIL WAR

(90–180 minutes)

Unit Sequence	Teacher Reflections
Concepts. Evidence, Discovery, Revision G4, G6–9, SD1, SD3, SD5, S2–6, S8–9, S11	In this lesson, the students' inquiry into the past through an ongoing narrative study provides opportunities to see the events that led up to the Civil War in a larger context. For example, the issue of civil and human rights has been debated in many eras in U.S. history. This does not mean that students should abandon a respect for the past as it unfolded. What it does imply is the need for an examination of historical problems and consequences as relevant or different from contemporary issues.
Guiding Questions. At the beginning of the lesson, pose the following guiding questions to focus student thinking:	
• Does a varied collection of humans' work inform and revise our thinking about the past? Its meaning to the present?	
• What do documents and artifacts of the Civil War period reveal about the driving forces of the time?	
• Does an understanding of these forces have any relevance today? Explain.	
Group Analysis of Documents. Supply varied examples of Civil War oral histories, letters, music, and photography to investigate the impact of the conflict on various segments of the population during this time period.	This learning activity demands learning tasks that have been thoughtfully organized by the teacher and then by each group. Primary and secondary documents are collected from electronic and print sources gathered by students and/or provided by the teacher. The groups, balanced for student strengths, use relevant, reliable, and valid historical data to construct an interpretation of the powerful circumstances of the times.
	The Unit Resources listed at the end of the unit provide varied examples of Civil War material that may be used to engage student interest. Excerpts from Ken Burns's video series would work well in this lesson to introduce students to oral histories, letters, music, and photography as evidence of the impact of the war on people during this time period.
Form heterogeneous teams of four or five students. Assign each team a particular segment of the civilian or military population (e.g., women and children on the home front, soldiers on the battlefield, men who did not serve). Instruct	Create groups that incorporate individual students' strengths to maximize learning. This helps build a sense of camaraderie within a heterogeneous learning community, where students value and appreciate each other's strengths. Discuss

(Continued)

(Continued)

Unit Sequence	Teacher Reflections
teams to examine, interpret, and reach consensus about the meaning of diary and journal entries, accounts of oral history, field dispatches, letters sent home, music, photography, crafts, and artwork of the Civil War period through the eyes of their assigned population. Tell students to use the tools and methodologies of historians as they analyze various types of documents and artifacts to explain the driving forces of a period in history in order to see its relevance to life today.	the importance of group cooperation and individual responsibility. Provide direct instruction in these skills if necessary. This activity occurs at this point in the unit in the hope that the teacher has had time to teach the skills that are needed by a historical scholar-practitioner and to observe and document students' strengths.
Assign each student a role of facilitator, materials manager, recorder, or time monitor. Each group must submit a written work plan with timeline, group conference times, and presentation criteria for peer assessment.	
Review the production skills that were discussed in Lesson 4. Suggest ways students may reveal their findings through authentic narrative, visual, and/or performance examples. Examples of performances are structured interview, a day in the life, panel discussion, video commentary, multimedia performance, or interactive museum. This is also the time to remind students of the "less is more" aphorism.	
Schedule a rehearsal presentation to another group for feedback and questions. Point out how this type of rehearsal might be authentic to historians' work. After they make revisions based on the rehearsal experience, meet with each group to discuss its work, using unit rubrics as a guideline for feedback.	
Tiered Journal Prompts. Assign an appropriate journal prompt to each student: • How did your research and your examination of historical data and artifacts replicate the work of a historian? What did you discover about the responsibilities and	Student journals also provide the teacher with an excellent opportunity to reference other parallels of the Parallel Curriculum Model (PCM). For example, the students are asked to reflect on the work of a historian and how the work connects to their own strengths, interests, and lives, one aspect of the Curriculum of Identity.

Unit Sequence	*Teacher Reflections*
problems historians face as they provide historical interpretations of the past and their application and relevance for the present? • What did you learn in your research that you did not learn in your textbook? About the past? And today? • Explain this statement: A good historian is interested not in manipulation or indoctrination but in acting as an honest messenger from the past.	Questions that suggest the importance of self-reflection and assessment are critical to continued student learning at high levels of personal demand and professional standards of quality. By comparing and contrasting their own approaches to discipline-based problems with those of professionals, students engage in authentic, expertlike work.
Culminating Project. Schedule time for a final revising and refining of student products. Remind students to remain focused on the assignment and assessment by asking these questions: • Have you identified any gaps in your research or knowledge of the topic? If so, what have you done to correct them? • Are you comfortable defending, displaying, or demonstrating your position? • Have you measured your position or product or presentation against the standards set in the rubrics? • Did you model the work of a historian scholar-practitioner throughout the design, creation, and production stages of your project? • Point out to the students that throughout the unit, they have been challenged to rethink their understanding of the work of a historian. They have examined historical evidence through the lens of the concepts of revision and discovery.	Basically, this is the time to conduct a complete review of the project before the final demonstration, display, or assessment. The concepts of discovery and revision are the central pillars to a sound, yet imaginative, historical narrative.

LESSON 8: DEBATING THE CAUSES OF THE CIVIL WAR

(90–180 minutes)

Unit Sequence	*Teacher Reflections*
Concepts. Evidence, Discovery, Revision G2–6, G8–9, SD1–5, S3–6, S8, S10–11 **Guiding Questions.** At the beginning of the lesson, pose the following guiding questions to focus student thinking: • How does historical interpretation help us discover and revise an understanding of the past as well as the present? • How was an understanding of state versus federal rights contested and debated throughout our nation's history? Introduce students to the nature of debate through video excerpts of current or past historical debates.	Students identify problems in the past and analyze them for relevance to contemporary debates and challenges. It is the singular responsibility of a historian to recognize historical antecedents that play a part in the decision making facing leaders and prominent figures today through the dual expectations of responsibility and accountability. For example, students can briefly discuss the presidential election of 2004 and the need for historians to make probing, intelligent analyses of partisan positions. The guiding questions function as a primer for the more formal debate activity of the lesson.
Debate. Assign students to the appropriate-level activity: *Novice:* Research the principle of state versus federal rights as it was understood and challenged during the Civil War. Create arguments for both sides in a point-counterpoint debate. Cite historical evidence in your arguments. *Proficient:* Research how the issue of state and federal rights was challenged during the Civil War. Study one particular aspect of this issue. Develop a proposition that clearly and convincingly states your position. *Innovator:* Engage in a debate on state and federal rights contested during another time in our nation's history. Debate either side of the issue after a thorough investigation of the evidence. Present your viewpoint to a historian or a U.S. history expert for feedback and review. Revise as needed.	As always, student assignments are based on their current readiness level as determined by guidelines in unit rubrics. Lessons 5, 6, and 7 have prepared students for participation in a more formal debate process. The debate allows students to experience the value of historical evidence that is credible, authoritative, authentic, and complete. They also learn the importance of evidence to construction and support of a sound historical interpretation. Advancing in their journey, students develop an ability to describe the past on its own terms. Avoiding "present-mindedness," by taking into account the historical context in which events unfold, demands a critical, analytic aloofness. An essential behavior of a historian, the nonjudgmental depiction of evidence of the past, fosters an intellectual independence. Question formation, development of interpretations, explanations, and

Unit Sequence	*Teacher Reflections*
Tiered Journal Prompt. Assign an appropriate journal prompt to each student: • What did you discover about the roles of the state and federal governments? How is power distributed between them (cite specific examples to support your ideas)? • What did you discover about the resiliency of our government? Its leaders? What were the underlying forces that caused individuals or groups of people to act the way they did? • Reflect on the distribution of power between the state and federal governments during two different time periods. Evaluate the ethical dimensions of the decisions that were made; the position, power, and priority of each stakeholder; and the cost and benefits of the final outcome from more than one perspective. Engage students in a final discussion of the unit. Within an informal, whole-group setting, ask the following questions to provoke interaction: • How has your thinking about and working with historical evidence helped you understand the role of a historian? • How has the unit's emphasis on discovery and revision changed your understanding of the tools and methods used by historians? • How has your work shown you have grown in understanding the cause, course, and character of the Civil War? In what ways has the unit inspired you to question for further inquiry?	solutions to issues, problems, and dilemmas of the past are inescapable to all historians. The final set of journal prompts focuses on the major concepts, understandings, and skills of historical writing. Through the Curriculum of Practice, the scholar-practitioner has participated in the democratic process of discussion, debate, and compromise. Through a critical examination of evidence, a process of discovery and revision extends and deepens the student's vision of the place and importance of history in our democratic society. You may wish to invite a college professor or local historian to visit your class, discuss the work that he or she is doing and any similarities to the students' work, and answer student questions about their practice.

(Continued)

(Continued)

Unit Sequence	Teacher Reflections
Culminating Project. Return to the culminating project that was introduced in Lesson 4. Provide a final opportunity for students to reflect and revise before their work is presented and assessed. Culminating projects should be presented and evaluated at a specific time that is determined by the class schedule and the availability of local historians. Have students conduct a self-assessment prior to their presentation. Choose at random a group of up to five students to peer assess each of the other presentations. Every student should get the opportunity to assess at least one other presentation. The teacher and historians (if available) also assess each presentation. Use the **Lesson 4 Rubric: Final Project** for all assessment reviews.	The culminating project will give students an exhibition arena to reveal their understanding of the role and responsibilities of a historian. It may also provide a springboard for further inquiry as well as temporal closure to a challenging unit.

Lesson 1 Rubric: Student as Historian

Novice Scholar-Practitioner to	→ → → → → →	Expert Scholar-Practitioner
Knowledge		
Student is exposed to historical writing and different viewpoints and audiences through a range of quality resources.	Student is open to and aware of varied sources of historical writing, multiple viewpoints and audiences, and a range of quality resources.	Student self-initiates topic of interest and enjoys self-directed pursuit of knowledge and understanding through an evolving personal style.	Student's written expression synthesizes diverse values and perspectives of historical people, places, and events with applications for current and future times.
Performance		
Student begins to employ the writing process to explore conceptual understandings within historical documents.	Student incorporates conceptual understandings into his or her written interpretations of the content within historical documents.	Student's written expression clarifies, extends, and synthesizes conceptual understandings through a critical examination of historical documents.	Student's refined and revised written expression reveals deep understandings of historical content and implications for current and future thinking.	Student recounts, encapsulates, and evaluates historical content through written expression that is designed to impact and enlighten others.
Scholar		
Student has awareness of exemplars, rules, and conventions of historical writing.	Student follows strict adherence to exemplars, rules, and conventions of historians in his or her writing.	Student's written reflection considers the purpose, values, styles, and methods of historians.	Student's written reflection takes into consideration multiple perspectives that uncover a complex understanding of the issues, people, or events.	Student's written expression employs a critical and objective interpretation of historical topics that transcends temporal, social, and emotional constraints.
Practitioner		
Student becomes aware of the standards of quality used by a historian and begins to set goals for personal growth.	Student reveals an evolving sense of historical writing that leads to self-fulfillment and provides enjoyment for others.	Student interprets and communicates an understanding of historical issues, people, and events that impacts self and others.	Student shares insightful understandings through artful expression that informs and influences an audience.	Student interprets the values, perspectives, and visions of historians as they attempt to understand, advance, and enhance the human condition.

Lesson 1 Worksheet: A Historian's Approach to History

Advice to Young Historical Sleuths From a Historian

SOURCE: Rebecca Hayes, PhD, University of Mary Washington.

1. Think of past events and people as a puzzle.

2. Look for clues about events and people from the past. Broad context clues include time, place, and culture. Also note specific clues related to the events and people.

3. Review possible sources of information (evidence). Start with secondary sources and read general information written about the time and place in which the event occurred or the person lived. Next search for primary sources of information and read documents from the time period that provide first-hand accounts or information about the events or people.

4. Plan the investigation of the puzzle. Develop key questions to guide your search. Make sure you collect information (evidence) from a variety of sources. Plan the time you will spend on your investigation so you can balance your coverage of all important issues.

5. Evaluate the clues. How reliable (i.e., accurate, trustworthy, credible) is your information? How important is each piece of information to the whole picture of the person or event?

6. Draw conclusions. Fit the puzzle pieces together. Think about what they mean. Make informed statements about the events or people and the connections among them.

Study Guide: Primary Sources—Connections to the Past

Historians study the written record (documents and images) in order to understand and interpret events and people of the past. Using this study guide, you will be studying and analyzing historical documents collected from the Civil War. Working together with your group, discuss the evidence and complete the study guide. Each person will need to complete his or her own guide so he or she will be prepared to share this information with others.

Name of Person/Place/Event:

Type of Source:

When and Where was it written or produced?

What does this source tell you about the Civil War?

If this is a written document, how did the author get this information? How well could the author see the event or person that he/she describes? How may the author's background and status influence the reader?

Why was this document written or created, and who was the intended audience? What possible biases might the author have that may have affected what he/she recorded?

Do you think this source tells you everything you need to know about the person? What other questions would you like to have answered? What other perspectives should be considered?

What other sources of information would be helpful?

Meet with a new group that includes students who have reviewed other evidence about this person. Share information from your study guide and record additional information that you learned about this person from their investigations. Be sure to include the source of information as you collect it.

Lesson 3 Worksheet: A Historical Inquiry

Choose a person (may be a family member) that you know and would like to learn more about. Learn about the person using multiple sources of evidence (e.g., interviews, news articles, family albums, letters, and others).

- Set up an interview with the individual. Conduct the interview either in person or on the telephone. Prepare your questions ahead of time and record what you learned and what you thought about the information in your journal. A copy of the interview questions, the name of the interviewee, and the date of your interview should be placed in the pocket of your research folder.
- If you are not interviewing a family member, a computer may help you access information about the person online through e-mail, a Web site, or a search engine.
- Plan a site visitation to a place where the person lives or works. Record what you learn and add a response in your research journal. Include photographs, postcards, or drawings of what you saw and learned. Often a site visit can be combined with a personal interview.

Choose one aspect of this person's life that you find especially interesting (e.g., childhood experiences, schooling, family event, personal success and struggle, unusual interest and pursuits) and write a short historical narrative for our class newspaper based on the evidence that you have collected. Examine the evidence and review the rules of validity as you make your choices.

Journal prompts:

- Were there any ideas that were revised after you reviewed your findings that might initiate further inquiry and lead to new discoveries?
- How might your own biases have influenced your understanding of this person's life?

Lesson 4 Rubric: Final Project

In the realm of the scholar-practitioner, learning becomes more complex, sophisticated, and refined through the progressive development of knowledge and performance. Learning becomes an ongoing journey for the student, revealing the present and future self, as one progresses from novice to apprentice to proficient to expert and ultimately to innovator. We delineated all levels to accommodate the academic diversity that may be realized through a challenging curriculum that sets no limits.

Novice	Apprentice	Proficient	Expert	Innovator
Content				
Student demonstrates accurate knowledge and understandings of the main ideas within the historical documents.	Student effectively incorporates accurate knowledge and understandings in his or her interpretation of the historical documents in order to make sense of issues, people, and events.	Student clarifies, extends, and synthesizes knowledge, understandings, and interpretation of historical issues, people, and/or events through a critical examination of primary and secondary resources.	Student refines and revises thinking, writing, and presenting in order to promote and defend evolving understandings of historical issues, people, and events and their implications for current and future thinking.	Student recounts, encapsulates, and evaluates historical persons, issues, and/or events through authentic work that is designed to impact and enlighten others.
Process				
Student follows rules and conventions of historical interpretation.	Student aptly employs rules and guidelines of historians in his or her interpretation of historical issues, people, and events.	Student's interpretation of historical issues, people, and events reflects values, knowledge, and methods of historians.	Student has an understanding of the depth and complexity of historical issues, people, and events through an objective consideration of multiple perspectives.	Student analyzes historical problems, people, and/or events and discovers new insights that lead to a deeper understanding of contemporary issues and dilemmas.
Product				
Student product/ presentation reveals an awareness of the standards of quality used by a historian.	Student interprets and communicates an understanding of historical issues, people, and events through a product/presentation that impacts self and others.	Student reveals an evolving sense of historical interpretation through a product/presentation that leads to self-fulfillment and provides enjoyment and knowledge for others.	Student's accomplished product/presentation shows insightful understandings that reveal personal insights and inform and engage the audience.	Student's sophisticated product/presentation reveals an understanding of the complexity of the human condition and the role of self and others as decision makers and problem solvers.

UNIT RESOURCES

Because this unit may be used in varied settings with multiple resources, only a few of numerous Internet sites are suggested for reference.

The American Historical Association
www.theaha.org/

Biography.com
www.biography.com/search

Biography Dictionary
www.s9.com/biography

Booknotes
www.booknotes.org

Civil War.com
www.civilwar.com/

The Civil War
www.pbs.org/civilwar/

History Alive! Teachers Curriculum Institute
www.teachtci.com/default.asp

History Channel
www.historychannel.com

Library of Congress
American Memory: Historical Collection for the National Digital Library
http://lcweb2.loc.gov/ammem/ammemhome.html

National Center for History in the Schools
www.sscnet.ucla.edu/nchs

National Council for History Education
www.history.org/nche

National Council for the Social Studies
www.ncss.org

The Power of Exponents

A Middle or High School Math Unit Incorporating All Four Parallels

Kristen Wogman Baron

BACKGROUND FOR UNIT

The topic of exponents and exponential functions is an important part of any Algebra I course. Students need to be able to multiply and divide exponential expressions, use scientific notation, and solve and graph simple exponential functions. This unit puts these initial concepts into a context to which students can relate and for which they can see a purpose.

Students act as mathematicians in this unit as they discover the rules of exponents and the common characteristics of exponential function graphs. They also learn to use graphing calculator technology as a tool to aid them in computations. They act as scientists as they explore scientific notation of large and small numbers in the context of astronomy and microbiology. They act as financial planners as they learn to invest money for maximum profit.

There are several options for assessment at the end of the unit. These options relate to the different fields of study we cover in the unit. Students choose an assessment based on their interest in a field area. This allows them to work in areas of interest to share their knowledge of the subject.

CONTENT FRAMEWORK

Organizing Concepts

Discipline-Specific Concepts

Multiplication properties of exponents

Zero exponents

Negative exponents

Division properties of exponents

Exponential functions

Graphs of exponential functions

Scientific notation

Exponential growth model

Exponential decay model

Compound interest

Depreciation

Principles and Generalizations

G1 Multiplication and division of exponential expressions follow specific rules called properties.

G2 Powers can be used to model real-life problems.

G3 Zero and negative exponents can be defined and simplified in exponential expressions.

G4 Graphs of exponential functions share certain characteristics just like other groups of functions.

G5 Scientific notation can be used to simplify real-life problems involving very large and very small numbers.

G6 The exponential growth/decay model can be used to represent real-life situations.

G7 Graphs of exponential growth/decay can provide a visual display of a real-life situation.

Guiding Questions for Each Parallel

Core Curriculum

How are the properties of exponents used in mathematics?

What are zero exponents and negative exponents, and why do we need them?

How are exponential expressions simplified?

How are exponential functions graphed?

What are the characteristics of an exponential function graph?

How is the TI-83 Plus graphing calculator used to simplify and graph exponential expressions and functions?

How are scientific notation expressions simplified?

What are exponential growth and decay models, and how do they work?

Curriculum of Practice

How do mathematicians form and test hypotheses?

When is a mathematician sure that a hypothesis is proven?

How important is scientific notation in the work of astronomers and biologists?

How do financial planners use exponential mathematics to aid their clients?

Curriculum of Connections

How are exponential function graphs similar to other groups of graphs?

What are the common characteristics of the graphs studied this year?

Curriculum of Identity

How do people in the "real world" use exponents and exponential functions? How might I?

How can mathematics be used to support and defend a position?

National Mathematics Standards

SD1	Students will understand numbers, ways of representing numbers, relationships among numbers, and number systems
SD2	Students will understand meanings of operations and how they relate to one another
SD3	Students will compute fluently and make reasonable estimates
SD4	Students will understand patterns, relations, and functions
SD5	Students will represent and analyze mathematical situations and structures using algebraic symbols
SD6	Students will use mathematical models to represent and understand quantitative relationships
SD7	Students will analyze change in various contexts
SD8	Students will apply appropriate techniques, tools, and formulas to determine measurements
SD9	Students will formulate questions that can be addressed with data and collect, organize, and display relevant data to answer them
SD10	Students will develop and evaluate inferences and predictions that are based on data

SD11   Students will build new mathematical knowledge through problem solving

SD12   Students will solve problems that arise in mathematics and in other contexts

SD13   Students will make and investigate mathematical conjectures

SD14   Students will organize and consolidate their mathematical thinking through communication

SD15   Students will communicate their mathematical thinking coherently and clearly to peers, teachers, and others

SD16   Students will analyze and evaluate the mathematical thinking and strategies of others

SD17   Students will use the language of mathematics to express mathematical ideas precisely

SD18   Students will recognize and use connections among mathematical ideas

SD19   Students will understand how mathematical ideas interconnect and build on one another to produce a coherent whole

SD20   Student will recognize and apply mathematics in contexts outside of mathematics

SD21   Students will create and use representations to organize, record, and communicate mathematical ideas

SD22   Students will select, apply, and translate among mathematical representations to solve problems

SD23   Students will use representations to model and interpret physical, social, and mathematical phenomena

Skills

S1   Use the properties of exponents to simplify exponential expressions.

S2   Graph exponential functions by sketching and on the graphing calculator.

S3   Identify common characteristics of exponential function graphs, and then relate to other groups of graphs.

S4   Multiply and divide with scientific notation by hand and on the graphing calculator.

S5   Solve real-life problems involving scientific notation.

S6   Define and set up exponential growth and decay models.

S7   Use the exponential growth model to find compound interest.

S8   Use the exponential decay model to find depreciation.

S9   Use the exponential growth/decay models in other real-life situations.

MAKING SURE THE PARALLELS REMAIN CENTRAL IN TEACHING AND LEARNING

Curriculum Component	*Component Descriptions and Rationale*
Content	Students will act as mathematicians to discover the important properties of exponents and exponential functions, look at how these concepts fit into the field of mathematics, and find connections to other areas of interest.
	Core Curriculum: The focus of this parallel is to establish the properties needed to multiply and divide exponential expressions, work with negative and zero exponents, simplify scientific notation expressions, and calculate using the exponential growth/decay model.
	Curriculum of Connections: Students will use their knowledge of simplifying scientific notation expressions to look at the use of this number notation in the field of astronomy. Students will also look at graphs of exponential functions and connect this family of functions to earlier knowledge about linear functions.
	Curriculum of Practice: The focus of this parallel is to allow students to conduct experiments and collect data as a scientist or mathematician would. Students will then analyze their data and draw conclusions based on their data and knowledge of exponents.
	Curriculum of Identity: This parallel allows students to select an area of personal interest and discover how exponents affect this area.
Assessments	The primary tool used for assessment in this unit is the lab notebook that all students will keep. This notebook can be collected and reviewed as often as the teacher wishes, with the goal of students becoming able to self-assess their progress by the end of the unit. Other assessments involve written work in the forms of persuasive essays/letters and lab reports in the curricula of Connections, Practice, and Identity.
Introductory activities	The introductory activities in this unit focus on drawing in the student and creating an initial high-interest level.
	Core Curriculum: The Mission Impossible activity is designed to allow the teacher to informally preassess students' knowledge of exponents. It also provides students with an opportunity to interact with each other in a fun activity.
	Curriculum of Connections: The "Heebie-Jeebies" activity is mainly an introductory activity to help students understand the "power" of exponential functions. The subject matter is appealing to students, and the persuasive essay format is familiar to them.
	Curriculum of Practice: The counting pennies activity provides an opportunity for the teacher to provide a fairly structured experiment to familiarize students with the important elements needed to conduct research.
	Curriculum of Identity: The introduction of the interest-based activity and the choosing of topics serve as introductory activities for this parallel.
Teaching strategies	The role of the teacher in this unit is to act as guide and mentor to students. The teacher needs to be clear in introducing each activity and modeling

(Continued)

(Continued)

Curriculum Component	Component Descriptions and Rationale
	expectations, if necessary. Many of the activities employ discovery, and the teacher may sometimes need to ask guiding questions to assist students in coming to valid conclusions. Other teaching strategies include Socratic questioning, problem solving, cooperative learning, and demonstration. It is important for the teacher to give prompt and constructive feedback to students throughout the unit.
Learning activities	The goal of the learning activities in this unit is to provide students with the skills needed to become more independent thinkers. By using the teaching strategy of discovery, students can become better problem solvers and learn how to deal with an ambiguous situation. Students will learn how to develop a conjecture, collect data, and draw conclusions about the initial assumption. Students will also learn how to organize data, keep a lab notebook, and write a mathematical paper or lab report.
Grouping strategies	Students are grouped in a variety of ways in this unit. Heterogeneous grouping is used when a variety of viewpoints may be needed. This is also used when introducing a new activity or concept. Students are homogeneously grouped when advanced students are ready to move ahead independently and other students may require more assistance. This way the teacher can focus time with certain groups of students. Students will sometimes work independently to further develop ideas at their own levels. Finally, whole-class discussions are used to share knowledge and build on each other's ideas.
Products	The lab notebook is the primary product in this unit. It is the main way a mathematician organizes his or her data, and students will work in the same way. Other written assignments and discussion with the teacher provide more evidence of understanding.
Resources	Many of the resources are provided as worksheets with the unit. In addition, the unit makes use of various Web sites. Teachers may wish to supplement the provided resources with additional practice from their own curricular materials.
Extension activities	There are several opportunities for extension activities provided in the Teacher Reflections for each of the parallels.
Modifications for learner need, including Ascending Intellectual Demand (AID)	Students will inevitably come to this unit with various backgrounds and experiences with exponents. Some students may know *how* to manipulate expressions with exponents, but they may not know *why*. It is therefore important not to immediately test students out of the material. It may be more reasonable to move some students at a faster pace through the material.
	Students will differ in the quality of the written work; there really is no ceiling to what they can do. Advanced students should see more complex connections and be able to better relate these concepts to the bigger picture of mathematics. AID is also provided through opportunities to tackle more sophisticated applications of unit concepts and principles and to focus on disparate areas of such applications.

UNIT SEQUENCE, DESCRIPTION, AND TEACHER REFLECTIONS

Preassessment: Mission Impossible?

(45–100 minutes)

Unit Sequence	Teacher Reflections
Hand out copies of **Preassessment: Mission Impossible?** to all students and read through the directions with the group.	This preassessment activity should allow students a glimpse into what is coming in the unit and also give you a feel for where students may need more assistance and which areas might be shortened. The goals of the unit are for students to learn the properties of exponents and to learn how to apply them to real-life situations.
Place students into heterogeneous groups of three to four to work on the activity. Allow students to "grapple" with the material, offering guiding questions only if needed. Circulate among groups to note students who have particular strengths and weaknesses in grappling with the task.	**Grouping Strategies.** Grouping the students heterogeneously for the first activity should help students come up with a strategy for working out the problem. This type of problem can be worked out with a shortcut or can be done by calculating each day for the month.
Debriefing. Once all groups have completed the activity, lead a discussion about student findings. Students should come to the conclusion that the first payment option is the best. Facilitate this discussion with some of the following questions: • Which option should you take to make the most money? How much money can you make? • How did you figure out Option 1? Did you find any shortcuts in the process? • At what point did Option 1 surpass Option 2? • What do you think 10 million dollars looks like in pennies? • How do you think this activity is related to exponents?	Discussing the students' findings and then the extent of prior knowledge about exponents as a whole class will help you get a feel for the pace of the students. You need to develop a sense of how much time to take for each lesson in the sequence to keep it challenging yet manageable for students. Also, students can be assessing what they know in comparison to each other and may decide that they need extra help to keep up with the group. You can also start to figure out which students are ahead of the group and may need curricular modifications at some points in the unit.
Once this activity has been fully debriefed, it is time to discuss what students know about exponents. This can be a great webbing activity with "exponents" as the starting point. The following questions may be used as starting-off points:	You may wish to have individual students complete this webbing activity in order to get a better sense of individual knowledge and competencies.

(Continued)

(Continued)

Unit Sequence	Teacher Reflections
• What rules do you know about exponents? • What do you know about scientific notation? • What real-life situations do you know of that involve exponents? • What are some professions that might use exponents? Once this web has been generated, it can be displayed somewhere in the classroom, and as students learn more in the unit, they may add to it or make modifications of their original ideas.	

CORE CURRICULUM LESSONS

Lesson 1: Properties of Exponents

(three class periods)

Unit Sequence	Teacher Reflections
Concepts. Multiplication/Division Properties of Exponents, Zero Exponents, Negative Exponents G1–3, SD1–5, SD9–10, SD12–13, SD15, SD19, S1	The activities incorporated into this lesson use a discovery method to guide students through the process of understanding the properties of exponents in multiplication and division and why they work as they do. Also, students should be looking for exceptions to the rules and why certain numbers would not work. There is also homework each night to reinforce the day's activity. There are three sections in this lesson. Each one should take about one 40- to 50-minute class period to complete. There are accompanying homework assignments for each section to allow students to practice the concepts learned each day.
Lab Notebooks. All students should have some kind of lab notebook to use throughout the unit. An actual science lab notebook is the best, as it has space to write on one side and graph lines on the other. If this notebook is cost prohibitive, a regular	You may need to discuss the lab notebook with students and how it should be set up. The purpose of the notebook is to get students to act as mathematicians and scientists by collecting data in the same way. It is therefore important that students

Unit Sequence	*Teacher Reflections*

notebook can also be used, or students can make their own lab notebooks.

Introduction. Spend a few minutes discussing the previous day's activity with students. Have them respond to the following questions:

- What did you find interesting about the results of the **Preassessment: Mission Impossible?** activity?
- Have you thought of any more information about exponents we might want to add to our exponent web? Any more uses or professions?

Explain to students that over the next few days they will be working in groups to try to find out how and why the properties of exponents work. Encourage students to work as a team to look for patterns and develop conjectures about exponents.

A short demonstration for students about what a conjecture is could go as follows:

A conjecture is a statement about something that is believed to be true but is not necessarily proven. You will be writing conjectures based on the observations of patterns you see developing as you work through different examples. Keep track of your conjectures in your lab notebook so you can track your thinking throughout the unit. Here is an example of a conjecture: I take five different numbers, say 1, 7, −3, −2.5, and 5, and multiply them all by −1. I observe that each time I do this I get the opposite of the number I started with. I then try to multiply 0 by −1, and I observe that this seems to be the only number where I don't get the opposite. I also know that 0 does not have an opposite. I make the following conjecture: If I multiply any number, except 0, by −1, I will always get its opposite. This can be put into algebraic form:

$$a \times -1 = -a, a \neq 0.$$

Students should be ready to start the activity after this discussion.

collect and present data in an organized way and that they construct neat and orderly graphs. Also, students need to lay out their work so it is not all crammed onto one page. It may be useful to show students an example of what a page should look like.

The activities for each day are designed to guide students through a discovery process, giving more structure in the beginning and moving toward more of a choice of how to organize data at the end. You may need to spend a few minutes the first day discussing what a conjecture is and how to make one.

(Continued)

(Continued)

Unit Sequence	Teacher Reflections

Learning Activities. On Day 1, put students into heterogeneous groups and give them copies of the **Lesson 1 (Day 1) Worksheet: Multiplication Properties of Exponents**. Review the instructions on the worksheet and then allow students to work in groups to complete the activity. Move among the groups, encouraging students to work together and asking guiding questions if needed. If students seem to be heading in the wrong direction, question them about their ideas and try to get them back on track. Some potential questions to ask are the following:

- What do all of your answers have in common? What is different?
- Do you think that pattern will work in all cases? What about for _____? (Fill in a number that may not work.)
- Can you write the conjecture in an algebraic form so a person could fill in any numbers?
- How can you test your conjecture further?

When the groups are finished with the activities, facilitate a discussion with the whole class on the findings. Have representatives from three of the groups come up and share their conjectures on the board or on an overhead. The class should come to a consensus about the multiplication properties of exponents and should record the final properties into their lab notebooks for future reference.

Here are the properties that students should come up with for multiplication. Keep in mind that each class may come up with different variables—encourage them to use their own, as it gives the students ownership of the property.

$$a \times a^n = a^{m+n}$$

$$(a^m)^n = a^{mn}$$

$$(ab)^n = a^n b^n$$

Grouping Strategies. An important part of the daily activities is teamwork. Stress to students the importance of validating each other's work. It should be pointed out that scientists and mathematicians often duplicate each other's experiments in order to check for validity. They are working as a team and their answers reflect on one another.

It is important in the class discussion to have students come up and explain their conjectures. Try to encourage different students to participate each time. This will help improve the confidence of students in putting their ideas "out there" for others to critique. It is not necessary for students to duplicate each table in front of the class just to explain how they arrived at their conjecture based on the table's results.

Unit Sequence	*Teacher Reflections*

Write unit principles 1–3 on the board and discuss how the day's class activities helped students to understand these important principles. Point out that these principles will continue to be addressed on Days 2 and 3. Suggest that students copy these principles into their lab notebooks.

Assign **Lesson 1 (Day 1) Worksheet: Multiplication Properties of Exponents** for students to complete that night.

Days 2 and 3 follow a similar format as the **Lesson 1 (Day 2) Worksheet: Zero and Negative Exponents** and the **Lesson 1 (Day 3) Worksheet: Division Properties of Exponents** and the corresponding **Homework** assignments for each worksheet. Have students work in groups and then discuss results as a class. Teachers need to always point out and/or ask students how the work they did reinforces the unit principles. Encourage students to record their growing understanding of unit principles in their lab notebooks. Review the previous night's **Homework** before starting each new activity to ensure that the students understand the material.

Properties for Days 2 and 3 follow:

The homework assignments are very important for students to gain mastery of the skills. Each assignment begins with questions on the lesson to check student understanding of the concept. These are followed with some practice in using the properties. Finally, word problems give students practice in applying their knowledge to something real.

It is important to assess student understanding through the homework assignments and to adjust accordingly. One way to do this is to collect papers after students have corrected them and check to see which problems students are getting wrong. If there is a consistent area of incorrect answers, go back and review that concept.

$$a^0 = 1 \quad \frac{a^m}{a^n} = a^{m-n}$$

$$a^{-n} = \frac{1}{a^n} \quad \left(\frac{a}{b}\right)^n = \frac{a^n}{b^n}$$

Lesson 2: Scientific Notation

(One class period)

Unit Sequence	Teacher Reflections
Concept. Scientific Notation G5, SD1–3, SD8, SD12, SD16, SD18, SD20, S4–5	In this lesson, students learn how to multiply and divide with scientific notation. This concept will not be a difficult one for advanced students to grasp and master. If they understand the multiplication and division properties of exponents, they should have no trouble applying it to the concept of scientific notation.
Preassessment. Conduct an informal or formal preassessment of this concept to see what previous knowledge students have. Most students at this point know how to convert from standard notation to scientific notation and vice versa. This lesson does not include conversion, so if students have not mastered this concept, you may wish to spend an additional day covering that material.	
Learning Activity. Introduce unit principle 5. Tell students that their work today will help them to evaluate the truth of this principle. Have them copy the principle into their lab notebooks. Distribute **Lesson 2 Worksheet: Scientific Notation**. Group students in pairs for this activity by readiness so that students work at their own pace and level. This activity may be modified to increase the complexity of the problems.	Because a math classroom, even when more homogeneously grouped than other classrooms, has such a wide array of knowledge levels, some students may need more support on this lesson. Therefore, if students are paired with others of similar background knowledge and skill in this lesson, they can work at their own pace and get appropriate help from the teacher. The hope is that students will have a good understanding of the concept upon completing the activity and the homework, regardless of how much time was spent or how much assistance was given.
Debriefing. At the close of this lesson, ask students to respond orally to some of the questions below to provide you with insight into their understandings. If you prefer, you may assign one or more of these questions to be answered in the lab notebooks or as an exit card prompt.	The role of the teacher is to facilitate the pairs as they try the two methods of simplifying multiplication and division with scientific notation. If students are grouped by readiness, you can focus on the groups that need more assistance and allow advanced groups to learn more independently. If groups finish early and have the correct answers, they should be allowed to begin the homework assignment.
• How is the associative property important in the multiplication and division of numbers in scientific notation? • Which properties of exponents are you using in the multiplication and division of numbers in scientific notation? • How do you know a number is in proper scientific notation?	It is left to you to decide how much the calculator should be used. Students

Unit Sequence	Teacher Reflections
• What are some advantages to using Method 2 over Method 1? • Which method is better if you do not have access to a calculator? • How does an understanding of scientific notation help us simplify real-life problems involving very large and very small numbers?	should gain an understanding of how to multiply and divide with scientific notation by hand, but it is also important to know how to use the calculator correctly to work with scientific notation. Some time in the lesson should be devoted to discussing the use of the calculator and how to interpret calculator answers. **Modifications for Learner Need.** The worksheet may be modified to increase the complexity of the examples students work through. This may be done by adding more negative exponents, putting in more examples where the answer is not in proper scientific notation, or putting in zero exponents.

CURRICULUM OF CONNECTIONS LESSONS

Lesson 3: Scientific Notation and Astronomy, Part 1

(one to two class periods)

Unit Sequence	Teacher Reflections
Concepts. Scientific Notation G5, SD8–9, SD12, SD15, SD18, SD20, S4–5	The purpose of this lesson is to connect to the field of astronomy. This is a topic often covered in middle school science classes, so students should have some background knowledge of the planets and their characteristics.
Introduction. Begin by reviewing the process of multiplication and division of numbers in scientific notation. This can be done in a variety of ways, including the following: • Have a student come to the board to explain. • Give students a problem to try and then compare answers with each other. • Have students, in groups of four, do a round-robin format, in which they each have a different problem to write down and then pass it to the right. The next person does a step and then passes to the right again. The last person checks the answer.	If you prefer, you may administer a brief preassessment of this skill and group students accordingly.

(Continued)

Unit Sequence	Teacher Reflections

Learning Activity. Introduce the activity by telling students the following:

Today we will be looking at the connection between scientific notation and astronomy. Why do you think astronomers might use scientific notation? (Students' answers should include something about the large distances between planets, or the large size of planets.) All of the information that is available about the planets is based on mathematical formulas, because astronauts, for example, have not been able to use the spaceship's odometer to calculate distance. Also, you'd need a really big scale to weigh the Earth! Amazingly, a lot of this information has been known for centuries because of mathematics. Before average people had ever seen pictures of the different planets, astronomers knew how far away they were and how large they were.

Today you will have the opportunity to find some of this information and use it to create questions for your classmates. Carefully follow the directions on your **Lesson 3 Worksheet: The Cow Jumped Over the Moon? How Far?** Please look it over and make sure you have completed each piece as instructed. You will also need to fill out the sheet called **Lesson 3 Rubric: Student Assessment—Experience With Spreadsheet Questions.** You will be evaluating your classmates' questions, which are considered in your grade for this activity. Be creative with your questions and have fun!

The Cow Jumped Over the Moon? How Far? activity asks students to research the distance to the sun and the weight of an assigned planet, along with other factual information of their choosing. Students work on this activity with a partner who has a similar skill level so that they can work together at an appropriate pace. They will need to use the Internet or teacher-supplied reference materials to find the information, create a spreadsheet containing all their information, and then

The teacher's role in this activity is to assist students with any problems they might be having. Potential problems may be in finding information on the Internet, setting up the spreadsheet, coming up with workable questions, and so on. In terms of finding information and setting up a spreadsheet, you may need to scaffold processes depending on the students' experiences with these tools.

Modifications for Learner Need. There are several modifications you may need to make depending on the resources available. In researching, the ideal situation would be for each student to have a computer with Internet access available, or at least one computer per pair. If this is possible, you may want to research Internet sites and provide students with a page of links to get them started. Some possible links follow:

- www.eps.mcgill.ca/wtp/planets/index .html
- www.solarviews.com//eng/data2.htm
- http://janus.astro.umd.edu/ introastro.html
- www.Iasalle.edu/~smithsc/ Astronomy/Units/astro_units.html
- www.kidscosmos.org/kid-stuff.html

If Internet access is not possible, provide students with books, encyclopedias, almanacs, and so on to make the information available.

Students may have varying levels of experience in using a spreadsheet. Ideally, students will be able to organize their data on their own in a way that is logical to them. If you need to scaffold this process, a template may be set up ahead of time where students can simply fill in the information, or you may need to spend a day teaching students about spreadsheets.

Modifications for Learner Need. Students can adapt this activity themselves by the depth of information they look for and the challenge of the questions they create.

Unit Sequence	Teacher Reflections

create five questions involving multiplication and/or division of numbers in scientific notation for another group to answer.

As groups finish, have them exchange spreadsheets and questions with each other to try the problems. Once a group completes its set of problems, the students should fill out the evaluation form.

Debriefing. Take a few minutes at the end of the activity to ensure that students made some connections to the field of astronomy. If you prefer, you may assign one or more of the following questions to be answered in the lab notebooks or as an exit card prompt.

- What key concepts and principles have you learned today?
- In what other contexts might you be able to use what you have learned?
- How can you use this information to solve other problems?
- How does looking at astronomy with scientific notation help you understand another area?
- What connections do you see between what we studied today and your own life and times?

You may want to preview student questions before allowing them to exchange. It is important that the questions be clear to the reader and also that they include any formulas students may need to plug into.

Optional Extension. If students need additional challenge or show interest in the field of astronomy, an independent study can be set up for them to research the history of astronomy from a mathematical perspective. Also, the book *Go Figure!* (Brookhart, 1998) has some great information on astronomy that students could read and use to perform more difficult calculations.

Lesson 4: Scientific Notation and Astronomy, Part 2

(one to two class periods)

Unit Sequence	Teacher Reflections

Concepts. Exponential Functions, Graphs of Exponential Functions, Exponential Growth Model, Exponential Decay Model G4, G7, SD2, SD4, SD6, SD10, SD13, SD14–15, SD19–21, SD23, S2–3

Introduction. This class, ideally, should be held in the computer lab. Put students into pairs randomly. If you prefer, you might pair students with more knowledge of

There are two connections being made in this lesson. The first connection is an opportunity to connect with disease control. Many television shows and movies use spread of a disease as a topic or theme, so Heebie-Jeebies should initially draw students in. The second connection is to a previously studied concept. Earlier in the year, students would have studied the family of linear functions. This is a great

(Continued)

Unit Sequence	Teacher Reflections
spreadsheets with novices. Demonstrate how the spreadsheet will be set up on an overhead or computer projector, if possible.	opportunity to reinforce a previous concept and build on student knowledge.

Modifications for Learner Need. There are several places in this lesson where some scaffolding or preteaching of concepts may need to occur. It is assumed that students have experience in creating spreadsheets. This lesson and the previous one provide opportunities for students to learn to use this software, and you may wish to spend a day teaching some simple skills on creating spreadsheets. This is time well spent!

Learning Activities. Introduce principles 4 and 7. Have students copy them into their lab notebooks. Tell students that the next activities will help them investigate the merits of these principles. Distribute the **Lesson 4 Worksheet: Who's Got the** Heebie-Jeebies?

In the Heebie-Jeebies activity, the role of the teacher after the opening discussion will be to assist students who have difficulty with the spreadsheet. Circulate about the room and make sure students are able to complete the activity.

The conversation with students could go as follows:

> Have you ever heard of the "Heebie-Jeebies"?
> Let's brainstorm together a list of what things come to mind when you hear this expression. (Brainstorm list with students.)

We are going to use mathematics to prove once and for all if Heebie-Jeebies really exist. There are several assumptions upon which we will have to agree to build our evidence:

1. The Heebie-Jeebies starts with one person.
2. That person spreads the Heebie-Jeebies to one person per week.
3. Once a person has the Heebie-Jeebies, he or she will pass it on in the same manner as in #2.

We are going to set up a spreadsheet to organize our numbers. You will need to title three columns:

- Week
- Number of People Infected
- Total Number of Heebie-Jeebie Cases

Unit Sequence	*Teacher Reflections*

We will start with Week 0, in which no people were infected and there is one case of the Heebie-Jeebies. In the first week, that person will infect one person, making the total number of infected people two. In Week 2, each person with the Heebie-Jeebies infects one more person (two people total), making four contaminated people. You will need to fill in through Week 8 with your partner! Work in pairs to complete the activity.

Debriefing. Spend a few minutes debriefing this activity with students at the conclusion of the lesson. Some questions for discussion are listed:

- In what other contexts can you use what you learned about the spread of the Heebie-Jeebies? About population growth in general?
- Who might need to look at the ways population grows? How may this relate to you and your life?
- Is population growth important to you? Why or why not?
- How does looking at the spread of a disease help you understand other areas of exponential growth?

We Are Family. The second activity in this lesson involves an investigation by students in groups. Student groups should be of mixed ability so that students may benefit from varied perspectives. Begin the class with a discussion of families of functions. Tell the students the following:

Let's think back to the unit on linear functions. Do you remember graphing lines? Remember when we discussed families of functions, and that linear functions form a family? Families of people usually share certain characteristics that make their family unique. Think about the characteristics of your family.

We developed characteristics of the family of linear functions that helped us sketch a quick graph from a linear equation. Let's review the characteristics we found (take input from students).

Optional Extension. For a rubric on Mathematical Representations in Problem Solving, see the one by the Northwest Regional Educational Laboratory Mathematics and Science Education Center at www.nwrel.org/msec/mpm/scoregrid.html. Review the evaluation process with students and encourage them to be objective and fair in their grading process.

This rubric needs to be revised slightly to reflect that you are evaluating students' spreadsheets and their questions. Student input will be especially helpful when completing the Communication and Execution section.

In the second activity, students work on a discovery activity to find common characteristics of exponential functions. The teacher leads a discussion in the beginning and then brings students to a consensus at the end. The role of the teacher during the activity is to answer student questions and give students a guiding question if needed.

It may be worth the time to look at some graphs of linear functions and have students develop the list of characteristics themselves, if they have not done so previously.

(Continued)

(Continued)

Unit Sequence	*Teacher Reflections*

Unit Sequence

Answers should include the following:

- All straight lines
- No exponents
- Slope—rate of change
- Positive slope—increasing
- Negative slope—decreasing
- Slope—less than 1 is flat line
- Slope—greater than 1 is steep
- Y-intercept is where point crosses y-axis
- Horizontal/Vertical lines—special cases

Families of exponential functions also have certain characteristics that make them unique. These features can be used to draw quick sketches of the graphs. Keep in mind as you work through the activity that you are looking for these characteristics. Make notes in your lab notebook for anything you observe. We will come together at the end of the activity to see what everyone has found!

Distribute the **Lesson 4 Worksheet: We Are Family**. Students work on their activity in groups. Groups can record their characteristics on giant newsprint paper to put up around the room. When all groups are finished, a representative from each group can share the group's findings with the class. Facilitate a discussion to lead to the final list of characteristics, which students should record in their notebooks.

Debriefing. After a list of observations has been generated, a final discussion should take place to reinforce the connections made during the lesson. If you prefer, you may assign one or more of these questions to be answered in the lab notebooks or as an exit card prompt.

Here are some starting questions:

- What did we learn about exponential equations and graphs?
- How did generating this list help reinforce what you know about linear functions? Did it cause you to change some of your earlier beliefs?

Teacher Reflections

Modifications for Learner Need, Including Ascending Intellectual Demand (AID). Students who are able to easily complete the family of functions activity should be urged to explore other exponential functions. They should test different possibilities and try to come up with more characteristics. Some possibilities include putting a negative or a number in front of the a^x *term* (the a^x *term* must be in parentheses).

Unit Sequence	Teacher Reflections

- How did you adjust your way of thinking and working when you encountered the new equations?
- How did you know if your adjustments were effective?
- How does looking at exponential functions help you understand functions in general?

Here are the observations students should find:

- Increasing a ($a > 1$) makes the graph steeper.
- Using a proper fraction causes the graph to decrease (reflection over the y-axis).
- Adding/Subtracting a number to/from x shifts the graph left/right, respectively.
- Adding/Subtracting a number to/from a^x shifts the graph up/down, respectively.
- Putting a negative sign outside parentheses (around a^x) reflects the graph over the x-axis.
- Putting a number outside parentheses (around a^x) shifts the graph so that the number is the y-intercept.

Lesson 5: Exponential Growth Model

(two class periods)

Unit Sequence	Teacher Reflections
Concept. Exponential Growth Model, Compound Interest G6, SD3–8, SD10–12, SD16, SD19, S6–7, S9 **Group Investigation.** Place students in heterogeneous groups to learn about the Exponential Growth Model through an example on compound interest. Students should already be familiar with simple interest, so begin by asking a student to explain how to compute simple interest. Write the formula for simple interest	This lesson may be broken into two days, depending on how fast students work. The last two examples in the activity may be worked on in the second day. If the lesson is broken into two days, the **homework** can also be divided. Students should be able to complete Numbers 1 and 2 after the first day.

(Continued)

(Continued)

Unit Sequence	Teacher Reflections

(I = Prt) on the board and discuss with students what each variable represents (I = interest, P = principal, r = rate, t = time). Explain to students that most financial institutions use something called compound interest instead of simple interest, and today students will learn what the formula is and how it works. Explain that in compound interest you get interest on your interest as well as the principal each year. Ask students, "Would this be better than simple interest? For whom?"

Introduce Principle 6. Have students copy the principle into their lab notebooks. Give students the **Lesson 5 Worksheet: Exponential Growth Model**, and read through the directions together. Take the amounts given in the example, and have students calculate the simple interest earned based on $500 at 4 percent for six years. Leave that information on the board to come back to at the end of class.

Move between the groups, asking guiding questions if needed. Some questions are as follows:

- What is the difference between "growth factor" and "growth rate"?
- In Number 3, did you use your balance after one year or the initial deposit?
- Look back at your answers to Numbers 2, 3, and 4. What did you do each time to get the next answer?
- Did you plug the correct information in for each variable?

Students may have some difficulty with Method 1, as there are many calculations to be completed along the way to the answer. Students should be allowed to use calculators for this activity.

Hold a discussion when groups have completed the two methods of finding compound interest. Discuss the advantages of using the model. Be sure to point out the possible errors students may have made in

It is important that students make the connection between Method 1 and Method 2. If students make this connection, they will be able to derive the formula for the model whenever they need it, rather than merely memorizing the model.

Another important concept is time period. Students need to pay attention to the number of times per year that the compounding takes place.

A third important piece of this lesson is for students to understand the difference between growth rate and growth factor. This knowledge is assessed in the two additional examples in the activity and in the homework.

The students' ability to complete the homework assignment will be a good indicator as to whether they have gained mastery of how and when to use this model. It will also give students the opportunity to start to see some additional uses for exponential growth.

Unit Sequence	Teacher Reflections
using the model (i.e., watch the time periods and growth rate versus growth factor). Come back to the simple interest calculated at the beginning of class and discuss with students the advantages and disadvantages to each type of interest. Possible answers include the following: • You earn more with compound interest. • You pay more with compound interest. • Simple interest is easier to calculate. **Debriefing.** Ask students to refer to Principle 6 and give examples that support the truth of this principle.	**Optional Extension.** A nice extension to this lesson, if time allows, is to invite a bank manager to come in and talk to students about what methods of interest are available at the bank and how compound interest is handled. A variation on this might be assigned to students ready for more of a challenge. They could research methods of interest calculation and report back to the class. This reporting could be done in a PowerPoint presentation or a spreadsheet table. The students could also look at their own savings and "shop around" the local banks to see if their earning potential is being maximized.

CURRICULUM OF PRACTICE LESSONS

Lesson 6: Counting Pennies

(one class period)

Unit Sequence	Teacher Reflections
Concepts. Exponential Decay Model G6–7, SD4, SD6–10, SD12–15, SD17–18, SD21–23, S2, S6, S8, S9	In this lesson, students act as scientists to collect data and develop conjectures. Earlier in the unit, students had the opportunity to do this in more structured activities anchored in the Core Curriculum. It is important in the Curriculum of Practice that students truly feel that they are in the role of a real scientist. Students should continue to use their science lab notebooks. Students who show a facility for this type of thinking and working should be given increasingly less direction in this activity, allowing them to make their own decisions about how to collect and format their data.
Learning Activity. Begin with a discussion. Tell students the following: Today you will act as scientists to collect and analyze data from an experiment. You will be given some initial directions about the activity, but it will be up to you and your partner to decide how to collect and display your data in your lab notebook.	For this first activity, you will need 100 pennies in a cup for each pair of students. Depending on the maturity of students, a discussion may need to take place about appropriate use of the pennies. This activity will be somewhat loud, with pennies being tossed about, but students should remain fairly focused on the task at

(Continued)

Unit Sequence	Teacher Reflections
You should use the graphing calculator to help analyze your data, but make sure you sketch your graph(s) in your notebook. Use the questions on your worksheet as a guide to help you come to some final conclusions. Record your conclusions in your lab notebook. Place students in random pairs for this activity. Distribute the **Lesson 6 Worksheet: Counting Pennies**. Circulate among the groups and offer guiding questions to pairs who need assistance. Questions could include the following: • How did you collect data in previous activities? Do you think that method will work here? • What labels should you use on your tables and/or graphs? • How do you input information into the graphing calculator? • What do you notice about the change between trials? **Debriefing.** When students have completed the activity, bring the class back together to debrief. If there was a group you observed that really did an excellent job in collecting and displaying its data, ask those students to come up and explain their methods. Collect student notebooks at the end of the session and review them. Give students feedback on how to improve their scientific data collection and analysis. Discuss how today's activity helps us understand the principles we have studied so far in this unit. Return notebooks at the next class and discuss with students the improvements they should make in recording their work and thoughts about their work.	hand. It is not meant to be a graded activity. It is a warm-up activity for the next day's Bouncing Balls activity as well as an opportunity for you to spot developing talents and skills. Therefore, it is important that you give students good feedback on this activity. At the end of the session, collect student lab notebooks and give detailed feedback to students. It may also be helpful to photocopy some students' work to give to others as an example of the correct method. Try not to focus on only one method, because students may collect and display data in many different ways. The important thing is that the work be organized, neat, and easy to interpret.

Lesson 7: Bouncing Balls

(one or more class periods)

Unit Sequence	*Teacher Reflections*

Concepts. Exponential Decay Model G6–7, SD4, SD6–10, SD12–15, SD17–18, SD21–23, S2, S6, S8–9

This activity requires a bit of advanced planning. There needs to be a fairly large area for students to conduct their experiment. You will need to collect the following materials for each group:

Introduction. Start with an introduction to the activity by telling students the following:

Today you will work in teams of four to conduct an experiment to see what pattern develops between the maximum height of a ball on successive bounces (the rebound height) and the number of bounces. You will be collecting motion data using the CBL units and a sonic motion detector. You will then analyze the data and use the graphing calculator to see if the Exponential Decay Model is a good fit for the relationship.

Each member of your group will need to participate in the activity in order to be successful. One person needs to hold the motion detector still, one person needs to drop the ball, one person needs to work the calculator and CBL unit, and one person needs to collect data. You may need to perform the experiment several times to get consistent data.

Remember to use the feedback you received on the last activity to improve your collection and reporting methods. You will be graded on the mathematics **Lesson 7 Worksheet: Bouncing Balls.**

Learning Activity. Students should begin the activity. Encourage them to complete the collection of data the first day. If groups are not sure if their data collection is consistent, have them "check in" before moving forward. When groups finish, they should review the directions to be sure they have fulfilled the requirements, and then turn in their work.

- 1 TI-83 Plus graphing calculator with cables
- 1 CBL unit
- 1 Vernier CBL motion detector
- 1 ball (racquetball or basketball)
- CBL program: BALL

Students work in groups of four for this activity. Groups should be of mixed ability, but it may be helpful to put in each group at least one student who feels very comfortable using the graphing calculator and the CBL (calculator-based laboratory) unit.

Modifications for Learner Need. It will be important to scaffold this activity to the experience of your students with the CBL unit and the TI-83 graphing calculator. If your students have not used the features they are asked to use in this activity, you will need to spend a day training students in the proper use. You could also put together a step-by-step guide for how to complete the activity. Another option is to see if college students may be available to come in to assist groups in using the calculators.

It is important to get a good bounce from the ball, and an uncarpeted surface will work better. If possible, use a science lab in your building for the first day.

This activity may be difficult for some groups as it can be hard to collect the data if the ball is not dropped in the center of the group. A basketball may be easier to use than some balls because it is larger. Also, the motion detector needs to remain

(Continued)

Unit Sequence	*Teacher Reflections*
	still to collect accurate data. Some science labs may have equipment to mount the detector, so talk to the science teacher.
If time remains, students may begin work on the **Lesson 7 Worksheet: The Field of Pharmacology** application. This should be finished for homework to reinforce the use of the Exponential Decay Model.	Try to allow students to work independently on this activity. Students have enough practice in collecting data at this point and have also had the opportunity for feedback on the previous activity. If students ask for assistance, try to pose questions to the group.
Debriefing. When all groups have completed this activity, spend a few minutes debriefing the lesson with students. If you prefer, you may assign one or more of these questions to be answered in the lab notebooks or as an exit card prompt:	**Optional Extension.** Students who are ready for a higher level can do some research in the field of pharmacology. You may also bring in a pharmacologist to speak to a group of students, and then have students research different medications to look at concentrations and dosages. See the **Lesson 7 Worksheet: The Field of Pharmacology.** Students can also look into what other factors may be involved in determining proper dosages.

- How do scientists organize their knowledge and skills when experimenting and researching?
- What are the common elements you noticed among the activities of the past few days? Differences?
- How does a scientist know which skills to use under given circumstances?
- What tools does a scientist use in his or her work?
- What constitutes meaningful evidence versus less significant information in scientific research?
- What drives the work of scientists in this field?
- What are the ethical issues and standards in scientific research?
- How does today's activity illustrate unit principles 6 and 7?
- What other professions or applications can you think of that might use the tools we have been working with?

CURRICULUM OF IDENTITY LESSONS

Lesson 8: Exponential Experts

(three to four class periods)

Unit Sequence	Teacher Reflections
Concepts. Exponential Growth and Decay Models, Applications G2, G6–7, SD6–7, SD9, SD12, SD14–15, SD20–21, SD23, S2, S6, S9	The purpose of this lesson in the Curriculum of Identity is to allow students the opportunity to select an area of interest and explore in depth how exponentials impact that area. Students are required to research their area and look for examples of how exponentials are used. They then need to compile all of their information into an organized format and put together a presentation to share with the class. They also complete reflection questions independently to explore their own interests in relation to the area investigated. Students will need to use teamwork skills, research skills, analysis, problem solving, organizational skills, and creativity to complete this project. This lesson's activity and rubric were adapted from the Web and Flow Web site and are a compilation of three Webquests from the following teachers: • Doug Raylman, draylman@srsd.org, Webquest at www.srsd.org/~kcornelius/raylman/webquest.htm • Ellen Plumley, eplumley@srsd.org, Webquest at www.web-and-flow.com/members/eplumley/exponentials/webquest.htm • Kathleen Haines Cornelius, kcornelius@srsd.org, Webquest at www.web-and-flow.com/members/khaines/exponents/webquest.htm
Introduction. Begin by grouping students in fours according to interest. Distribute the **Lesson 8 Worksheet: The Exponential Experts.** Then introduce the activity by telling students the following:	The activity requires students to be grouped together by interest. This can be accomplished in a number of ways. If there is time, it would be useful for students to complete an interest survey to determine

(Continued)

(Continued)

Unit Sequence	*Teacher Reflections*

Over the past few weeks, we have been studying the properties of exponents, exponential graphs, scientific notation, and growth and decay models. We have also made connections to several different occupations and fields of study that use exponential information. We have practiced as scientists to complete experiments and make conclusions based on exponential data.

Now it is time for you to explore how exponents affect our world and, potentially, you. As you complete this activity, try to put yourself in the role of a person who works in this area. Think about what this person thinks about, how he or she works, and what problems or issues this person works on. Can you see how this profession "fits" your interests and preferred ways of working?

Read through the introduction, the question, and the individual roles of the **Lesson 8 Worksheet: The Exponential Experts** with the students and answer any questions they may have. Then read through the group synthesis and conclusion.

Be sure to spend some time discussing presentation options. You may want to have students brainstorm some other options as a class. Review the **Lesson 8 Rubric: Web and Flow** with students and encourage them to review it periodically in the process.

Students will probably need about two class periods to collect data from the Internet and then at least two class periods to synthesize and organize their data into a presentation. Encourage or require students to do some of this work at home as homework.

The teacher's role in this activity is facilitator. Move between groups and encourage students to analyze data carefully and look for meaningful

an area of interest. In some schools, the guidance department works with students on this kind of thing, and you may be able to get this information from that office. If these methods are not possible, list subject areas (based on those of the activity) and have students sign up for something of interest. Then group students into fours based on level of interest.

The best way to set up this activity is as a Web page. That way, students can hyperlink directly to the Web sites and not waste time typing in the addresses. Another option is to set up the computers with the Word document. Students can still hyperlink to each site.

Encourage students to use their creativity in coming up with presentation formats. For example, the Greenpeace activists may want to hold a "demonstration" (peaceful, of course), or the population controllers may want to do a simulation of population out of control. On the presentation day, you may wish to incorporate students' own creativity and dress up like the president. All of these things will make the presentations more fun and interesting, and students will remember the experience.

Modifications for Learner Need, Including AID. This activity lends itself to individual levels. Some students will use the Web sites given, and other students will conduct more research. Encourage advanced students to work with actual professionals in the field they have chosen, when possible. These students would benefit from having professionals evaluate and/or comment on their presentations. Higher-level materials may be provided to students with stronger math ability. Students who express a strong interest in an area may be candidates for a mentorship of some kind.

Unit Sequence	*Teacher Reflections*

connections. Encourage students to take risks and be creative.

When groups have finished the activity, additional time will be needed for students to present their work. Since the activity centers around persuading the president to spend money on a particular cause, someone will need to decide which group was the most persuasive. You may do this yourself, have the class vote, or invite in a panel of judges (teachers, administrators, parents, etc.).

Conclusion. Once the activity has been completed, be sure that students have worked on the questions from the **Lesson 8 Worksheet: Self-Reflection**. Initiate a group discussion concerning the effectiveness of the entire unit. If you prefer, you may assign one or more of these questions to be answered in the lab notebooks or as an exit card prompt:

- What are some of the interesting things you learned about exponential functions in this unit?
- What have you learned about yourself during this unit? What were some of the strengths you reinforced or refined during the unit activities? What new strengths do you see in yourself? How do your strengths compare with those of a mathematician?
- What new understandings do you now have about the role of mathematics in real life? What is still confusing? How can you find the answers?
- Did you enjoy being involved in this type of work? Why or why not?
- What did you find most interesting about your area of study? About the areas of study presented by other students? What areas of study might you be interested in learning more about?
- Look again at the unit principles. What other principles can you infer that relate to what we have been studying in this unit? This year?

(Continued)

Final Reflection Lesson

(two class periods)

Unit Sequence	Teacher Reflections
Begin by commending students for the good work they have done with the unit. Then assign students to groups according to their performance throughout the unit.	This lesson provides a final closure for the unit. Its purpose is to provide students with a wrap-up of the unit's activities. It is an opportunity for students to reflect on the activities in the unit and to make sure they can answer the questions given at the beginning of the unit.
Pass out a copy of the **Final Reflection Worksheet: The Power of Exponents** to each student and assign one set of questions to each group. Review the instructions with students. Provide one class period for students to answer the questions. It may be good for students to produce a visual display of their answers, or they may wish to type responses into a handout to give to other students.	The more concrete thinkers in the class should answer the Core Curriculum questions, while the most abstract thinkers can answer the Curriculum of Identity questions. It is OK that the curricula have different numbers of questions, because the Curricula of Connections and Identity questions require more in-depth answers. The teacher's role in this activity is to facilitate discussion in the groups. Some groups may need assistance in answering some of the questions.
In the next class period, have each group present its findings to the rest of the class. You may wish to allow other students in the class to add ideas following each presentation. Provide a final wrap-up of the session by summarizing each group's main points and providing positive feedback to the class regarding the group's performance in the unit.	An important part of this activity is that students be able to support their ideas with evidence from the unit. Students should be able to name specific activities that they feel help them answer the question, and they should explain why they see a connection.

Preassessment: Mission Impossible?

The teacher's edition of the Algebra I book has been stolen from your fantastic teacher! The U.S. government deems this book to be extremely valuable and would like to hire your class to retrieve it from the thieves (and then, of course, you will return it to your teacher!).

The U.S. government is prepared to pay you for thirty days of work (this mission may be a dangerous one!). Should you choose to accept this mission, you will have your choice of two payment options:

1. One cent on the first day, two cents on the second day, and double your salary every day thereafter for the thirty days.

2. Exactly one MILLION dollars.

Before you begin your mission, you will need to decide which payment option you will take. Work in groups of three to four to calculate the first option (please show your work) and then compare the two options to maximize your earnings.

❖   ❖   ❖

Lesson 1 (Day 1) Worksheet: Multiplication Properties of Exponents

1. Copy and complete the table in your lab notebook. Use a calculator as needed.

Product of Powers	Simplify With Order of Operations	Expanded Product	Number of Factors	Product as a Power	Simplified Answer
$4^2 \cdot 4^3$	1,024	$(4 \cdot 4)(4 \cdot 4 \cdot 4)$	5	4^5	1,024
$3^3 \cdot 3^2$					
$2^4 \cdot 2^5$					
$x^3 \cdot x^6$					

What pattern do you notice? Develop and write down a conjecture based on your findings.

2. Copy and complete the table in your lab notebook. Use a calculator as needed.

Power of a Power	Simplified With Order of Operations	Expanded Product	Expanded Product	Product as a Power	Simplified Answer
$(2^2)^4$	256	$(2^2) \cdot (2^2) \cdot (2^2) \cdot (2^2)$	$(2 \cdot 2)(2 \cdot 2)(2 \cdot 2)(2 \cdot 2)$	2^8	256
$(5^2)^3$					
$[(-3)^2]^2$					
$(x^2)^5$					

What pattern do you notice? Develop and write down a conjecture based on your findings.

3. Allison says that $(ab)^n = a^n b^n$. Jeff says that $(ab)^n = ab^n$. Decide which person you believe and develop a conjecture based on that person's statement. Then test your conjecture in your lab notebook with several numerical and algebraic examples. Convey your findings in an organized format.

Lesson 1 (Day 1) Homework: Multiplication Properties of Exponents

1. How are the expressions $x^7 x^3$ and $(x^7)^3$ different? Explain your answer.

2. Can $a^3 b^4$ be simplified? Explain your answer.

Simplify, if possible. Write your answer as a power or as a product of powers.

3. $4^2 4^6 =$

4. $(2^3)^4 =$

5. $x^5 x =$

6. $(3x)^3 =$

7. $(-3x^4 y^3)^2 =$

8. $[(-2x^2 y)^2]^5$

9. $[(4x + 5)^2]^3 =$

12. $(-x)^5(-x)^4(-x)^3 =$

10. $(-2x)^3(5x)^2 =$

13. $(a^2bc^3)^4(a^2b)^2 =$

11. $(-3xy)^3(-x^2) =$

Solve each of the following problems.

14. The formula for the volume of a sphere is $V = \frac{4}{3}\pi r^3$, where r is the radius. What is the volume of a sphere with radius 2a in terms of a?

15. The formula for the volume of a cone is $V = \frac{1}{3}\pi r^2 h$, where r is the radius of the base and h is the height. What is the volume of a cone with radius $2b^2$ and height 12 in terms of b?

16. Part A of a test has 10 true-false questions. Part B has 10 multiple choice questions. Each of the multiple choice questions has 4 possible answers.

   a. How many ways are there to answer all 20 questions?

   b. If you guess the answer to each question, what is the probability that you will get them all right?

Bonus question: Should you study?

Lesson 1 (Day 2) Worksheet: Zero and Negative Exponents

1. Copy the table in your lab notebook. Then discuss any patterns you see with your group. Use the patterns to complete the table. If needed, use fractions instead of decimals. Try not to use calculators for this activity.

Exponent, n	3	2	1	0	−1	−2	−3
Power, 2^n	8	4	2				
Power, 3^n	27	9	3				
Power, 4^n	64	16	4				
Power, a^n	a^3	a^2	a^1				

2. What appears to be the value of a^0 for any number a? Are there any numbers this will not work for?

3. Develop a conjecture about a^0.

4. How can you evaluate an expression in the form a^{-n}? Are there any numbers this will not work for?

5. Develop a conjecture about a^{-n}.

Lesson 1 (Day 2) Homework: Zero and Negative Exponents

1. Eve Aluate made an error on this problem. Can you find and fix it?

$$5x^{-3} = \frac{1}{5x^3}$$

2. Tell whether the following statement is true.

If **a** is positive, then **a**$^{-n}$ is positive.

Evaluate the exponential expression. Write fractions in simplest form.

3. $5^{-2} =$

4. $\left(\frac{1}{4}\right)^{-1} =$

5. $3(3^{-4}) =$

6. $-5^0 \left(\frac{1}{4^{-2}}\right) =$

7. $10^4 0^{-1} =$

8. $7^5 7^{-5} =$

9. $(4^{-2})^3 =$

Simplify each expression with positive exponents.

10. $x^{-3} =$

11. $\frac{1}{4x^{-6}} =$

12. $x^{-3}y^{-5} =$

13. $\frac{1}{4x^{-2}y^{-4}} =$

14. $(-4)^0 x^6 =$

15. $[(-12x^4 y^7)^3]^0 =$

16. $(5x^{-6})^3 =$

17. $\frac{1}{(2x^2)^{-3}} =$

❖   ❖   ❖

Lesson 1(Day 3) Worksheet: Division Properties of Exponents

1. Copy and complete the table in your lab notebook. Use the y^x key or the $\wedge$ key on your calculator, if needed.

a	m	n	$\dfrac{a^m}{a^n}$	$a^{(m-n)}$
2	7	4		
3	9	5		
4	3	1		

2. Compare the values in the fourth and fifth columns for each row. What conclusion can you make? Test your conclusion by adding several more rows of values for a, m, and n and calculating.

3. Develop a conjecture about the following quotient and test it by plugging in different values. Convey your findings in an organized format.

$$\left(\frac{a}{b}\right)^n = ?$$

❖ ❖ ❖

Lesson 1 (Day 3) Homework: Division Properties of Exponents

1. Can you simplify $\frac{x^5}{x^7}$ with the quotient of powers property? If so, what would the answer look like? (Remember to always simplify using positive exponents.)

2. Can $\frac{x^8}{y^4}$ be simplified? Explain.

Evaluate the expression. Write fractions in simplest form.

3. $\dfrac{7^4}{7^1} =$

4. $\dfrac{(-8)^5}{(-8)^5} =$

5. $\left(-\dfrac{4}{5}\right)^3 =$

6. $\left(\dfrac{8}{6}\right)^{-1} =$

Simplify the expression. The simplified expression should have no negative exponents.

7. $\dfrac{x^3}{x^8} =$

8. $\left(\dfrac{x^5}{x^2}\right)^{-1} =$

9. $\left(\dfrac{-8x^3y^2}{2xy^4}\right)^3 =$

10. $\dfrac{35x^5y}{xy^3} \cdot \left(\dfrac{7}{xy}\right)^{-1} =$

11. $\dfrac{4x^{-3}y^2}{xy^{-5}} \cdot \dfrac{(2x^2y)^{-2}}{x^2y^3} =$

12. $\left(\dfrac{2x^2y^{-3}y^5}{3x^{-3}y}\right)^{-2} \cdot \left(\dfrac{4x^3y}{2x^{-2}y^{-4}}\right)^2 =$

13. The formula for the volume of a sphere is $V = \frac{4}{3}\pi r^3$, where r is the radius of a sphere. Assuming that the radius of the moon is ¼ the radius of Earth, find the ratio of the volume of Earth to the volume of the moon. Let r represent the radius of Earth.

14. You memorize the definitions of all the words in the Algebra I book glossary—all 215 of them (yes, I counted). Unfortunately, each week you will forget 1/6 of the words you knew the previous week. The number of words W you remember after n weeks can be approximated by the following equation:

$$W = 215 \left(\frac{5}{6}\right)^n$$

Complete the following table.

Weeks, n	0	1	2	3	4	5	6
Words, W							

About how many weeks does it take to forget all the words? Explain.

Lesson 2 Worksheet: Scientific Notation

Today you will work with two different methods for multiplying and dividing numbers in scientific notation. Try to identify where the multiplication and division properties of exponents are being used. Please do all of your work in your lab notebook, and feel free to jot down observations you make along the way!

Multiplication

Method 1

Convert the following expressions into standard notation and multiply. Then convert your answer back into scientific notation. Do not use a calculator!

$$(1.2 \times 10^8)(2.3 \times 10^3) = \underline{\hspace{2cm}}$$

Method 2

What property allows us to do the following? _____

$$(1.2 \times 10^8)(2.3 \times 10^3) = (1.2 \times 2.3)(10^8 \times 10^3)$$

Multiply the first product (1.2×2.3) by hand, and then multiply the 2nd product $(10^8 \times 10^3)$ using the properties of exponents.

Answer: _____

Is your answer in scientific notation? _____

Compare the answer in Method 1 with the answer in Method 2. Which method is more efficient?

_____

Multiply the following using Method 2.

$$(1.4 \times 10^4)(7.6 \times 10^3) = \underline{\hspace{2.5cm}}$$

Is your answer in scientific notation? If no, how can you fix it?

What is your final answer? _____

Division

Method 1

Convert the following expressions into standard notation and divide. Then convert your answer back into scientific notation. Do not use a calculator!

$(1.82 \times 10^{-1}) \div (1.4 \times 10^{-3}) = $ _____

Method 2

This problem has been rewritten in fraction format. Rewrite the quotient as a product of two quotients.

$$\frac{1.82 \times 10^{-1}}{1.4 \times 10^{-3}} = \underline{\hspace{1cm}} \times \underline{\hspace{1cm}}$$

Divide the first quotient by hand and then multiply the second quotient using the division properties of exponents.

Answer: _____

Is your answer in scientific notation? _____

Compare the answer in Method 1 with the answer in Method 2. Which method is more efficient?

_____

Divide the following using Method 2.

$(1.2 \times 10^{-1})(4.8 \times 10^{-4}) = $ _____

Is your answer in scientific notation? If no, how can you fix it?

What is your final answer? _____

Lesson 2 Homework: Scientific Notation

1. Is the expression 13.75×10^3 in scientific notation? Explain.

Evaluate each expression without using a calculator. Write the result in scientific notation.

2. $(3 \times 10^{-6})(5 \times 10^3) =$

3. $(1.75 \times 10^5)(9.8 \times 10^{16}) =$

4. $(2.5 \times 10^{-6})(4 \times 10^{-12}) =$

5. $\dfrac{6 \times 10^5}{3 \times 10^{-2}} =$

6. $\dfrac{4.2 \times 10^{-3}}{5 \times 10^5} =$

7. $\dfrac{5 \times 10^6}{8 \times 10^{20}} =$

8. $(4 \times 10^{-6})^3 =$

9. California has an area of approximately 1.56×10^5 square miles. In 2001, the population of California was about 2.98×10^7. How many people were there per square mile? Express your answer in scientific *and* standard notation.

10. Figure out about how many seconds you have been alive. Round your answer to the nearest million. Then convert your answer into scientific notation.

Lesson 3 Worksheet: The Cow Jumped Over the Moon? How Far?

1. Today you will be working with your partner to research your assigned planet on the Internet. You are looking for information about the distance of the planet from the sun and/or to other planets, the size of the planet, and any other information that involves large numbers (the sky's the limit, so to speak!).

2. Once you have your research, you will need to compile your data into a spreadsheet. Organize your information so that others can understand and interpret the data.

3. Now you need to use your data to create five questions involving scientific notation. At least three of the questions must involve multiplication/division. Make sure your questions are clear and concise. If you use an unusual formula, you should include it in your question. Try to include questions at a variety of difficulty levels, and don't be afraid to be creative!

Here are some additional numbers you may want to use:

Speed of light: 186,000 miles per second, or 5.87×10^{12} miles per year (called a light yr), or 3×10^8 meters per second

Speed of sound: 7.42×10^2 miles per hour (in air)

$$\text{Density} = \frac{\text{Mass}}{\text{Volume}}$$

1 AU (Astronomical Unit) = 150 million km = 1.5×10^8 km

Lesson 3 Rubric: Student Assessment—
Experience With Spreadsheet Questions

Please put a check mark in the box that best describes your experience with your classmates' questions. Answer the other questions.

1. Were you easily able to understand what the question was asking, or did you need to make inferences and guesses about what you were asked to do?

I couldn't follow the thinking—I needed to make guesses as to what to do.	The question was hard to follow in places, and I had to guess sometimes.	I understood what I was supposed to do. There was a logical sequence.	The questions were very clear and well worded.

2. Were you easily able to understand the spreadsheet you were given, or did you have to find additional information to answer the questions?

I couldn't understand the spreadsheet. There were few or no labels, and I had to guess what the numbers meant.	The spreadsheet seemed disorganized in places. I had to hunt sometimes for the information I wanted.	The spreadsheet was labeled, and I was able to find the information I needed.	The spreadsheet was completely organized, and numbers were easy to find.

3. Did you feel that there was a range of difficulty levels in the questions you were given?

There was no range of questions (they were either all easy or all difficult).	There was a small range of difficulty (they were mostly easy or difficult).	There was a moderate range of difficulty (they were on the easy/ difficult side).	There was a wide range of difficulty (there were a few easy and a few difficult).

4. Were you able to answer all the questions?

Lesson 4 Worksheet: Who's Got the Heebie-Jeebies?

Have you ever had the Heebie-Jeebies? To quote the *Oxford English Dictionary*, the "heebie-jeebies" are "a feeling of discomfort, apprehension, or depression." I heard that a bad case of the Heebie-Jeebies is going around, but I'm not sure if it's something we should worry about or not. Today, we will use mathematics to help us investigate the situation. There are several assumptions we will have to agree to in order to build our evidence.

1. The Heebie-Jeebies starts with one person.

2. That person spreads the Heebie-Jeebies to one person per week.

3. Once a person has the Heebie-Jeebies, he or she will pass it on in the same manner as in #2.

Using the spreadsheet started in class, complete the following steps to build your case.

1. Fill in the spreadsheet through Week 8. How many infected people do you end up with at the end of the eighth week?

2. Now it's time to graph your data. Follow the steps below and ask for help, if needed.
   a. Select your data in Column C, go to Insert, and choose Chart. Using Chart Wizard, select a type of chart that shows data over time. Click Finish.
   b. Move your chart to the right side of your worksheet so you can look at it side by side with your data. What kind of trend does your data show? Where might the pattern go from here?
   c. Print out your data sheet and your chart to have on hand for the next step.

3. Look again at your statistics through Week 8. In math terms, what is the relationship between the number of people with the Heebie-Jeebies at the end of one week and the number of new cases the next week?

4. With your partner, create a formula for Columns B and C in Week 9 that will extend the pattern of Weeks 0–8.

5. Now you can use Excel's AutoFill feature to complete your worksheet. For Column A, highlight cells A9 and A10, point to the "handle" in the lower right corner of A10, and drag it through A37.

6. Now fill in Column B by using AutoFill to drag the formula through Week 35 (cell B37). Fill Column C by dragging the formula in C10 down through C37.

7. You may wish to format your Heebie-Jeebie statistics by selecting Columns B and C, going to Format, choosing Cells, and Selecting Numbers on the list. Type in 0 decimal places, and select Use 1000 Separator. Save your work.

8. How many people have the Heebie-Jeebies at the end of Week 35? If your formulas are correct, you should show 34,359,738,368. That's a lot of Heebie-Jeebies! Should we be worried?

9. So how does your Heebie-Jeebie census match up against the actual world population? Let's find out! Go to the Web site http://www.census.gov/cgi-bin/ipc/popclockw. This site gives up-to-the-second projected count of the world's human population, based on actual numbers plus estimated births and deaths. Record the current population on your spreadsheet.

10. You are now ready to construct a "proof by contradiction." Look at your data and summarize your findings in a one-page persuasive essay. Decide if we should be worried about the spread of the Heebie-Jeebies or not. Take a stand, using mathematics to support your conclusion.

Lesson 4 Worksheet: We Are Family

Today we will look at a new family of functions: $y = a^x$. You will need to use your lab notebooks to sketch graphs and record your observations.

1. Use a table of values to find five points on the graph of the function $y = 2^x$. Graph the function carefully.

2. Graph each of the following functions on the TI-83 and sketch the graphs in your notebooks.

$y = 3^x$
$y = 5^x$

3. Develop a conjecture about the relationship between $y = 2^x$ and the two sketched graphs. Think about what shortcuts you could use to sketch a graph quickly.

4. Follow the same process on the next two sets of functions.

$$y = \left(\frac{1}{2}\right)^x \qquad\qquad y = 2^{(x+5)}$$

$$y = \left(\frac{1}{5}\right)^x \qquad\qquad y = 2^x + 5$$

5. Think about the family of linear functions that we discussed earlier. Exponential graphs form another family. In your group, see if you can come up with the characteristics of the family of exponential functions. Record this information in your lab notebook.

Lesson 5 Worksheet: Exponential Growth Model

Today you will look at a formula often used to calculate exponential growth. You will find the answer to the following problem in two different ways, and then decide which way you think might be more efficient. Please complete all work in your lab notebook.

You deposit $500 in an account that pays 4% annual interest compounded yearly. What is the account balance after 6 years?

Method 1—Solve a simpler problem

1. The *growth factor* is the percentage rate (*growth rate*) plus 100%, put into decimal form. Find the growth factor in this problem.

2. In order to find the new balance after 1 year, multiply your initial investment ($500) by the growth factor you just found.

    Balance after 1 year _____

3. Use your answer from #2 to find the balance after 2 years. _____

4. Find the balance after 3 years. _____

5. What process are you following each time? _____

6. Find the balance after 6 years. _____

Method 2—Use a formula

Exponential Growth Model $y = C(1 + r)^t$

y = new balance
C = initial amount
r = growth rate
t = time period

7. Plug in the correct information for each variable, and find the balance after 6 years.

8. Compare the answers in Methods 1 and 2. Which method do you prefer and why?

9. What does the "1 + r" in the model represent?

10. A population of 20 mice is released into a wildlife region. The population triples each year for 5 years.
    a. What is the percent of increase each year?
    b. What is the population after 5 years?

Lesson 5 Homework: Exponential Growth Model

1. A principal of $350 is deposited in an account that pays 2.5% interest compounded yearly. Find the account balance after 3 years.

2. How much must you deposit in an account that pays 5% interest compounded yearly to have a balance of at least $1,000 after 8 years?

Write an exponential growth model for each problem and then solve.

3. A computer software company had a $50,000 profit in 1995. Then the profit increased by 20% per year for the next 8 years. What is the profit in 2003?

4. A population of 30 rabbits is released in a wildlife region. The population doubles each year for 4 years. What is the population after 4 years?

Lesson 6 Worksheet: Counting Pennies

Question: Can an exponential decay model show a decreasing amount?

The exponential decay model is similar to the exponential growth model. It is defined as the following:

$$y = C(1 - r)^t$$

C = initial amount
r = decay rate
$1 - r$ = decay factor
t = time

Today you will work with a partner to conduct an experiment to look for evidence of an exponential decay model. Be sure to collect data carefully and display your information accurately and neatly. Record all of your information and findings in your lab notebook.

Explore the Concept

1. Make a table to record your results.

2. Place the pennies in the cup. Shake the pennies in the cup and then spill them onto a flat surface. Remove all of the pennies that land face up. Count and record the number of pennies remaining.

3. Repeat Step 2 until there are no pennies left in the cup.

4. Make a scatter plot of the data you have collected.

Drawing Conclusions

1. Describe any patterns suggested by the scatter plot.

2. Write the theoretical exponential equation to model this situation. Then use the TI-83 to calculate the exponential regression equation. Compare your answers. Which one seems more realistic? Which one seems more accurate?

3. Compare your equation and graph with another group. Describe any similarities you see.

Lesson 7 Worksheet: Bouncing Balls

Bouncy Balls and *The Best Bounce* are two competing manufacturers of various types of balls. They both claim that their balls have the highest rebound height (the maximum height attained by the ball on a given bounce) in relation to the number of bounces since the ball was released. These companies have competed for years! *Bouncy Balls'* slogan states:

"Bounce for bounce, our ball bounces higher than our competition!"

The Best Bounce counters:

"Don't mess with the Best, 'cause the Best don't rest!"

The Consummate Consumer magazine has decided to settle the debate once and for all. They have come to your team of ball-bouncing scientists for an objective decision on which company should get the magazine's top rating.

Each team will be testing either two racquetballs or two basketballs from each company. The instructions below will help guide you through the process of collecting and interpreting your data. You will need to present your data and findings, plus answer the given questions, in a final lab report for *The Consummate Consumer* editors.

Instructions

1. You will collect data using the CBL unit and the BALL program. Set up your unit with the TI-83 graphing calculator and the Vernier CBL motion detector. The detector should be five to six feet above the floor, parallel to it. Do not let anything obstruct the path between the motion detector and the ball while data are being collected. Follow the instructions on the TI-83 screen to complete the activity.

2. Collect data on both companies' balls. If you have fewer than five consecutive bounces, you will need to perform another trial. In this case, start with a smaller initial height. Be sure to sketch a plot of your distance versus time data in your lab notebook.

3. *The Consummate Consumer* would like to see a table of the Bounce Number (0 starting height through fifth bounce) versus Rebound Height. Record this in your lab notebook for later reference.

4. Enter this data into your TI-83 lists and plot the scatter plot. Then use the calculator to find the Exponential Regression information for the data. Record all of this information and sketch the graph. Repeat for second ball.

5. Report all of your data and findings into a neat and organized final lab report. Be sure to include all the information you gathered and calculated in your lab notebook. Make your final conclusion and recommendation to *The Consummate Consumer* and then be sure to answer the questions below.

Questions to Answer

1. According to your data, which ball has the higher rebound, bounce for bounce? Explain how you know this.

2. Use your equation to figure out which ball will bounce the longest. Include your calculations.

3. Use your models for each ball to determine the smallest number of bounces required for the rebound height to be less than 10 percent of its starting height. Remember that the number of bounces must be an integer value.

4. Compare your results with another group that tested the same types of balls. Did you come to the same conclusions? If yes, do you think that *The Consummate Consumer* can be confident in reporting your conclusions? Why or why not? If no, what variables may have caused groups to reach different conclusions? What should *The Consummate Consumer* do next to reach a satisfactory conclusion?

Lesson 7 Worksheet: The Field of Pharmacology

Pharmacists must understand the use, composition, and effects of a large variety of drugs. Go to the following Web site to read about what pharmacists do and what it takes to be a pharmacist: www.classzone.com/books/algebra_1/ and click on Chapter 8, then Careers & Applications, and then Pharmacist. Is this a career you have some interest in? Why or why not?

An important part of being a pharmacist is calculating the correct dosage for a given patient. A mistake in this task could prove life threatening for the person taking the medication. Each medication has its own mathematical equation, which takes into account the dosage, the amount of time that has passed, and the decay factor of the medication. Putting this information into the Exponential Decay Model can tell the pharmacist the concentration of medication left in the person's bloodstream at any given time. From this information, the pharmacist can let the patient know how often to take a medication for optimal results.

The concentration of aspirin in a person's bloodstream can be modeled by the equation $y = A(0.8)^t$, where y represents the concentration of aspirin in a person's bloodstream in milligrams (mg), A represents the amount of aspirin taken, and t represents the number of hours since the medication was taken. Find the amount of aspirin remaining in a person's bloodstream at the given dosage.

1. Dosage: 250 mg
   Time: after 2 hours

2. Dosage: 500 mg
   Time: after 3.5 hours

3. Dosage: 750 mg
   Time: after 5 hours

4. The concentration of an allergy medication in a person's bloodstream in nanograms per milliliter (ng/mL) can be modeled by the equation $y = 263(0.92)^t$, where t represents the number of hours since the medication was taken.

   a. What is the concentration of medication remaining in the person's bloodstream after 4 hours?

   b. What does the "263" in the equation represent?

Lesson 8 Worksheet: The Exponential Experts

Introduction

What's the truth and who says so? In the old days (say just before you were born), people could read books, study, and feel pretty sure they knew what was going on. Then things started changing. We realized everyone had an opinion, and if we listened, we could learn something. We also found that a lot of topics weren't separate, but connected to each other. So thinking in little boxes didn't work so well. Then along came the Web. Uh-oh. . . . Because anyone can publish a Web page, and passionate people tend to want to get their ideas out there, almost any interest, concern, or issue has its online community.

As a group, you're going to explore the topic of Exponentials. Each member of your team will become an expert in one part of the topic. Then you'll have to come back together to answer a question that gets to the heart of "What's the truth, and who says so?" Please read the evaluation rubric at the end of this material so that you understand what is expected.

The Question

The main question you will be asked to find an answer for is the following:

I am the president of the United States and have some money to spend. Your job is to research an area that affects society and demonstrates some form of exponential growth or decay. You will need to persuade me to spend the money on your interest area and show me the math that the American public needs to understand.

Individual Roles

Questions this big and important are better answered when a few people are working on it at one time. Things work even better when a group decides to look at the question from different points of view. This way group members can become experts on an aspect of the question and then come together to demonstrate their learning. This is where teamwork pays off. The links given with each area are merely starting points—you may need to do some additional research. Also, some of the links may be outdated (this happens from time to time). You may also use other sources besides the Internet (an almanac, video, live people in the field, etc.). Are you ready to go out and gather information to successfully lobby for your cause?

Population Controller

Use the links below to learn more about your role. Specifically, look for information about the following:

- Is the world overpopulated?
- What dangers do we face in an overpopulated world?
- What can we do to help the situation?
- What role do exponents play in understanding these issues?

World population numbers

www.col-ed.org/cur/math/math51.txt

Zero population growth

www.zpg.org/

World population graph

www.starch.dk/isi/energy/population.htm

World population clock

http://metalab.unc.edu/lunarbin/worldpop

Greenpeace Activist

Use the links below to learn more about your role. Specifically, look for information about the following:

- How is radioactive waste dealt with?
- How long will this stuff be around?
- What harm can it cause?
- What role do exponents play in understanding these issues?

Civilian nuclear waste management

http://usgovinfo.about.com/culture/govpolitics/usgovinfo/library/weekly/aa012398.htm?COB=home&terms=radioactivity&PM=112_300_T

Decay calculator

www.geocities.com/SiliconValley/7116/jv_nuke.html

Radioactive elements

http://van.hep.uiuc.edu/van/qa/section/Everything_Else/Hard_to_Categorize/20030223104346.htm

How hot are you?

www.seattletimes.com/trinity/supplement/radiate.html

Nuclear tourist

www.nucleartourist.com

Uranium production

www.ncf.ca/~cz725/cnf.htm#k

Financial Advisor

Use the links below to learn more about your role. Specifically, look for information about the following:

- What is the national debt?
- How is it growing?
- How does this affect the average person?
- What role do exponents play in understanding these issues?

Investment calculator

www.bankrate.com/brm/calc/math_smm.asp

Savings bonds calculator

www.publicdebt.treas.gov/sav/sav.htm

Debt clock

http://math2.org/math/general/interest.htm

National debt

www.house.gov/istook/debt.htm

FAQ national debt

www.ustreas.gov/opc/opc0037.html#quest8

Spread of a Disease

I have given you some links for general information but also for several specific diseases. Select one of the diseases given or investigate a different disease using additional Web sites.

- What are the public concerns of this disease?
- Is there an accurate detecting test? A vaccine, a cure?
- What are the public and health costs of this disease? Why would money spent on this issue save money in the long run? Justify your argument.
- Is this disease a serious future public concern?
- What role do exponents play in understanding these issues?

Plant disease—an introduction to plant disease epidemiology

www.apsnet.org/education/AdvancedPlantPath/Topics/Epidemiology/Disease Progress.htm

SARS epidemic

www.squeak.org/us/ted/sars-graph.html

General information

www.who.int/en/

Look up the disease you are interested in through the index at www.cdc.gov/az.do

AIDS—transmission/prevention

http://pomo.kn.pacbell.com/wired/fil/pages/samhivandm.html

Bacteria Growth

Use the links below to learn more about your role. Specifically, look for answers to the following questions:

- Where are bacteria in our everyday life?
- How fast does it grow?
- Should this be a public concern (sickness, fatalities)? Pick one type that is and discuss it. You may choose different bacteria other than the ones found in the following links. If so, be prepared to do some surfing at home, as class time on this task is limited.
- What measures can the public take to minimize its spread?
- What are the health costs of the spreading? Is there a major future concern?
- How can government spending help this issue?
- What role do exponents play in understanding these issues?

Bacteria growing problem

www.physics.uoguelph.ca/tutorials/exp/probs.html

Bacteria growth chart refrigeration

www.bmil.com/bally/nwnotwi.htm

Food safety

www.foodsafety.gov/

Laws for safe cooking

www.sbcphd.org/ehs/meat.htm

Time and temperature

http://ag.arizona.edu/pubs/health/foodsafety/az1086.html

Earthquaker

You need to convince the president to spend more money educating the public about earthquakes and helping people be prepared. Here are just some of the many questions you could keep in the back of your head to guide your presentation:

- How do scientists come up with the numbers on the Richter scale?
- Do you think we are "due" for another large earthquake?
- What are some of the hazards of quakes?
- What could the government do to help prepare for a large earthquake?
- Compare the intensity of some U.S. earthquakes from various areas of the Richter scale and investigate the damage of each.
- What role do exponents play in understanding these issues?

Geology lab on virtual earthquake—work through the lab online to determine the Richter scale for your choice of earthquakes and compare your result with the actual one

http://vcourseware3.calstatela.edu/VirtualEarthquake/VQuakeExecute.html

Recent earthquakes with preparedness and hazard plans—some good stats with probabilities and frequencies

http://quake.wr.usgs.gov/

Modified Mercalli Scale of Intensity—from the Federal Emergency Management Agency (FEMA), a good picture of how far out an earthquake reaches from its epicenter

www.seismo.unr.edu/ftp/pub/louie/class/100/mercalli.html

U.S. list of earthquakes

www.fema.gov/hazards/earthquakes/eq_usa.shtm

Forest Protector

Your job is to convince the president to spend more money protecting the environment, specifically our forests. Here are some of the many questions you could use to guide your presentation:

- How have gypsy moths affected our forests?
- Are these moths on the rise or declining?
- Do they impact just our trees?
- What can we learn from Canada?
- What role do exponents play in understanding these issues?

Forestry

www.fs.fed.us/

Defoliation bar graph—great bar graph on recent outbreaks

www.mda.state.mi.us/hot/gypsymoth/defoliation.html

Gypsy moths in North America

www.fs.fed.us/ne/morgantown/4557/gmoth/

Forest insects of Canada—look at the graphs of insects on this site

http://nfdp.ccfm.org/compendium/insects/index_e.php

Sustainable forest management—The Sierra Club of Canada is devoted to forest preservation

www.sierraclub.ca/national/programs/biodiversity/forests/index.shtml

Gypsy moth insecticide spray—stats and glossary on amount of spray and danger to humans

http://infoventures.com/e-hlth/pestcide/gypchek.html

Gypsy moth page for Pennsylvania

www.dep.state.pa.us/dep/PA_Env-Her/history_1681_1945/gypsymoth.htm

Internet Controller

Your job is to convince the president to spend more money to ensure that the Internet is a safe and happy place. There is some good information in charts on the growth of the Internet, and you could use your graphing calculator to analyze these. Here are some of the many questions you could use to guide your presentation:

- Is the Internet growing too rapidly?
- Should we limit it?
- What is currently going on in Congress to regulate the Internet?
- What role do exponents play in understanding these issues?

Internet stats on growth—great site but data only through 1996

www.mit.edu/people/mkgray/net/web-growth-summary.html

Internet Development Act

www.house.gov/boucher/docs/inetpage.htm

Internet growth charts—this site contains graphed data on growth

http://navigators.com/stats.html

Internet timeline

www.zakon.org/robert/internet/timeline/

Group Synthesis

Congratulations! Your team is now full of expertise. Each person on your team has become an expert on the topic of Exponentials. You've all gathered a lot of information. But gathering useful information isn't the same as truly understanding a topic. What experts in the field of learning suggest is that you now use that information in a new and challenging way. Then you'll really know about this topic.

So with your team members, carefully read and try to answer the main question for this activity. Use the information, pictures, movies, facts, opinions, and so on that you explored to convince your classmates that your viewpoint is important and should receive the presidential funding. You may present your case in whatever way your group feels will be the most powerful. Options include (but are not limited to) the following: oral presentation with visuals, PowerPoint presentation, video presentation, Web site, or a simulation. Be sure you make clear how an understanding of exponents is important to understanding the issues involved in your topic. Before you begin, check out the rubric and the self-reflection questions you will answer upon completion of the activity.

Conclusion

You deserve a lot of praise for all the work you've done. And so does your brain. You've sure put that gray stuff to the test. You gained background information, developed expertise in one particular area, and got into some pretty expert analysis. At times, you must have felt confused with ideas spinning every which way. That's normal when you're building new mental connections. How will you use these ideas and strategies as you continue to grow and learn? It's all up to you. Good luck.

This activity and rubric were adapted from the Web and Flow Web site and are a compilation of three Webquests from Doug Raylman, Ellen Plumley, and Kathleen Haines.

Doug Raylman, draylman@srsd.org, Webquest at www.srsd.org/~kcornelius/raylman/webquest.htm

Ellen Plumley, eplumley@srsd.org, Webquest at www.web-and-flow.com/members/eplumley/exponentials/webquest.htm

Kathleen Haines Cornelius, kcornelius@srsd.org, Webquest at www.web-and-flow.com/members/khaines/exponents/webquest.htm

Lesson 8 Rubric: Web and Flow

Rubric	Beginning	Medium	Expert
Individual expertise	Little more was done than to copy and paste from Web pages. Not too much seemed to get into the brain.	Clear learning on the topic has taken place. There's an ability to discuss the topic using examples or evidence.	New information has been firmly connected to previous related knowledge. An easy use of evidence shows a sound understanding.
Group synthesis	The group's decision seems more a mixing than a blending. Ideas are thrown together, not necessarily thought through.	The group decision is based on clear understanding of key issues and work to balance them. Some weak spots may still exist.	This group decision is soundly reasoned and addresses key issues that make the topic a challenge to come to terms with.
Final outcome	The final work seems rushed or incomplete. Careless errors may confuse the audience.	Care has been taken to create a finished product. Few errors exist, and these wouldn't be confusing.	Care and creativity make this an interesting and polished final work. The quality of the ideas is reflected in the product.

Lesson 8 Worksheet: Self-Reflection

Please answer the following questions about the activity you just completed individually.

1. What do practitioners and contributors in the area you just researched think about?

2. To what degree is this familiar, surprising, and/or intriguing to you?

3. How do people in this area think and work?

4. In what ways do those processes seem familiar, surprising, and/or intriguing to you?

5. What are the problems and issues that practitioners and contributors in this area spend their lives working on?

6. To what degree are these problems and issues intriguing to you?

7. What is the range of vocational and avocational possibilities in this area? Do you see yourself pursuing any of these options? Why or why not?

Is there anything else you would like to add? Please use the space below.

❖   ❖   ❖

Final Reflection Worksheet: The Power of Exponents

Congratulations! You have all done a wonderful job with this unit. It is time now to reflect back on the activities we have completed together and connect this information to the guiding questions we set out to answer. Each group will be assigned one set of the following questions to review. Work with your group to brainstorm answers to each question by looking back through your lab notebook. Please provide evidence to support your answer by citing specific activities from the unit. Be prepared to present your answers and evidence to the class. Each group will have 15 minutes to present its work.

In addition to answering your assigned questions, please write a brief (no more than a total of one page) response to the following questions:

How has using a lab notebook in this unit helped you stay organized and focused on the activities?

Do you feel that it is useful in math class to use a lab notebook? Why or why not?

Do you think this notebook will help you in the future with related material? Explain.

Core Curriculum Questions

How are the properties of exponents used in mathematics?

What are zero exponents and negative exponents, and why do we need them?

How are exponential expressions simplified?

How are exponential functions graphed?

What are the characteristics of an exponential function graph?

How is the TI-83 Plus graphing calculator used to simplify and graph exponential expressions and functions?

How are scientific notation expressions simplified?

What are exponential growth and decay models, and how do they work?

Curriculum of Practice

How do mathematicians form and test hypotheses?

When is a mathematician sure that a hypothesis is proven?

How important is scientific notation in the work of astronomers and biologists?

How do financial planners use exponential mathematics to aid their clients?

Curriculum of Connections

How are exponential function graphs similar to other groups of graphs?

What are the common characteristics of the graphs studied this year?

Curriculum of Identity

How do people in the "real world" use exponents and exponential functions?

How can mathematics be used to support and defend a position?

With Liberty and Justice for All

A U.S. Government Unit Based on the Core and Identity Parallels for Middle or High School Students

Cindy A. Strickland

BACKGROUND FOR UNIT

This six-week unit introduces and examines the ideals associated with the founding of the United States, reviews the basic structure and function of the government and the Constitution that guides it, and provides an in-depth look at the justice system with respect to the Supreme Court. The unit is closely aligned with the National Council for the Social Studies Standards for Civics and Government. While rooted in the Core Parallel, this introductory module also provides students the opportunity to work in the Curriculum of Identity. Students learn how studying the ideals and working habits of the founding fathers as well as the current guardians of the Constitution can help them begin an examination of their own ideals and ways of working.

The unit is designed for high school students, but middle school students would also enjoy and benefit from unit activities, particularly the emphasis on exploring and understanding the parallels between the ideals and identity of the American people and those of the adolescent. The lessons are set up to fit classes that are conducted on the block schedule, but could easily be adapted to shorter class periods.

CONTENT FRAMEWORK

Organizing Concepts

Discipline-Specific. Ideals, Identity, Liberty, Justice, Rights
Macroconcept. Government

Principles and Generalizations

G1 Government is an institution or system that provides services to people.

G2 Enduring ideals are the basis of Americans' political identity and culture.

G3 Ideals are important to society and to individuals because they serve to guide actions and decisions.

G4 Specific documents in American History set forth shared values, principles, and beliefs.

G5 The structure and services of government affect the lives of its citizens both directly and indirectly.

National Standards for Civics and Government
(National Council for the Social Studies, www.ncss.org)

SD1 Civic life, politics, and government

SD2 Foundations of the American political system

SD3 Purposes, values, and principles of American democracy

SD4 Roles of the citizen in American democracy

Skills

S1 Use a variety of texts and other resources to build understanding.

S2 Use appropriate strategies to comprehend, interpret, evaluate, and appreciate a variety of resources.

S3 Participate in discussions as knowledgeable, thoughtful contributors.

S4 Analyze personal goals, traits, and choices.

S5 Adjust written and visual language for particular purposes.

S6 Describe personal goals, traits, and choices.

MAKING SURE THE CORE AND IDENTITY PARALLELS REMAIN CENTRAL IN TEACHING AND LEARNING

Curriculum Component	*Component Descriptions and Rationale*
Content	All lessons are designed not only to help students learn key information and practice key skills but also to further their understanding of unit concepts. These concepts are drawn from national standards. Lessons typically end with a discussion or writing prompt designed to firmly reinforce unit concepts and principles.
	Unit activities help students become aware of the concepts, principles, skills, methodologies, and dispositions of practicing professionals. Students relate key concepts and skills to their own lives. Unit content is used as a vehicle to reveal students' own ideals, thoughts, and preferred ways of working.

Curriculum Component	Component Descriptions and Rationale
Assessments	Preassessments help the teacher discover student learning gaps as well as advanced knowledge and understanding of Core unit concepts and principles and to identify students for Ascending Intellectual Demand (AID) activities. Journal prompts and group discussions serve as a means of ongoing assessment for both the Core and Identity curricula. Quizzes and performance tasks are used to assess students' end knowledge and understanding of unit concepts and principles. An assessment tool to determine student comfort with skills of self-expression and self-disclosure is incorporated into the unit.
Introductory activities	An introductory lesson firmly roots the unit in concepts and principles and helps students begin the task of relating these concepts and principles to their own lives and ways of thinking and working.
Teaching activities	A variety of teaching strategies are used throughout the unit to respond to student variance and encourage focus on Core concepts and principles. These strategies include direct instruction, concept attainment, writing prompts, small- and large-group discussions, simulations, and demonstrations. All lessons in the unit incorporate questions for students' written and oral reflection about unit concepts as well as the knowledge, skills, and dispositions of professionals in the field. Students are encouraged to reflect on past, current, and future selves.
Learning activities	A variety of learning activities are used to respond to student variance and encourage focus on Core concepts and principles. These strategies include small- and large-group discussion to analyze and refine unit concepts and principles and identify patterns and categories, writing prompts to promote reflection on these concepts and principles, and performance tasks requiring research. Learning activities help students develop the skills of introspection and the ability to compare their own personal characteristics and goals with those of practicing professionals.
Grouping strategies	The unit offers a variety of grouping strategies. In addition to large-group and individual work, students work in small homogeneous and heterogeneous groups assigned according to background knowledge of subject matter and unit concepts and principles. Students are given choices that respond to preferred modes of learning and particular interests.
Resources	Students make use of biographical information about historical and contemporary players in the field. Journals and graphic organizers help students reflect on this information and support cognitive and methodological skill acquisition. Text and Web resources provide students with access to information about current professionals in the field and a variety of products created by those professionals.

(Continued)

(Continued)

Curriculum Component	Component Descriptions and Rationale
Products	Students are consistently asked to make connections between unit activities and experiences and unit concepts and principles through reflective inquiry and analysis. Authentic products are central to the final project and are evaluated by rubrics.
	Reflective journals require students to write down their thoughts and questions in a systematic manner.
Extension activities	Extension activities encourage students to expand their knowledge and understanding of unit concepts and principles. These activities are suggested at appropriate points in the lessons.
	A menu of options is provided to support and extend the learning of students who have particular talents and/or interests in the subject matter.
Modifications for learner need, including Ascending Intellectual Demand (AID)	The unit offers several opportunities for independent or small-group activities, varied scaffolding, readings, and other resources. Students who are in need of AID are encouraged to move from Apprentice to Practitioner in terms of expert-level skills.
	Teachers are reminded that students may be at varied levels of development with respect to introspection and communication of thoughts and feelings. Ongoing assessment helps spot emerging talent and identify students who are moving ahead on the Novice-Expert continuum.

UNIT SEQUENCE, DESCRIPTION, AND TEACHER REFLECTIONS

Preparation and Preassessment

(one-half block)

Unit Sequence	Teacher Reflections
A few days before the beginning of the unit, ask students to bring or make a blank reflective journal to use throughout the unit.	Teachers will need a journal as well. Prepare your own answer to the Lesson 1 journal prompt or "Question of the Day" and place on a transparency.
Administer the preassessment.	Use the questions on the **Unit Preassessment: Instructor Sample** as a starting point for designing a pretest. Depending on the text series you use and what you intend to emphasize during the unit, you may need to add, subtract, or adjust some questions.
	The pretest should solicit information about students' general and specific knowledge about the U.S. government as well as their understanding of the unit concepts.
	You should also have or seek out information about students' reading levels, need for organizational scaffolding, ability to think abstractly, and facility with advanced discussion skills.

Lesson 1: Introduction to Ideals

(one-half block)

Unit Sequence	*Teacher Reflections*

Concepts. Liberty, Justice, Ideals

G2–3, SD2–3, S3–4, S6

Question of the Day. Write the Question of the Day on the board or overhead:

> What beliefs, ideas, or thoughts are most important to you? If you had to summarize these beliefs or ideas in one or two words, what would they be?

The Question of the Day is a strategy that focuses students' attention on unit topics from the moment they enter the classroom. Do this every day and train your students to start thinking and/or journaling on these questions as soon as they are seated.

Tell students they will have five minutes to write, diagram, or draw their response to these questions in their journal. Remind students that if they draw or diagram their image, it must be clear enough that a reader can understand what they are communicating.

You may want to provide an example and a nonexample of what you mean by *clear*.

While students are writing in their journals, write the words *liberty* and *justice* on two large pieces of poster board or butcher block and hang them on the board.

The activities in this part of the unit center on these two words. You may also wish to devote a classroom bulletin board to each. Each period's definitions and conclusions about these words could be written on different colored paper and displayed and then adapted throughout the unit. Another idea is to have a word wall on which you display concepts and other important words and phrases related to the unit as they come up.

Share your own response to the Question of the Day. When students have finished their journal entries, ask if anyone would be willing to share a response. Talk about how the things we believe in and value most highly are said to be our *ideals*.

Don't insist that all students share their ideas on such personal questions. The more comfortable the classroom atmosphere, the more likely students are to discuss personal feelings. Even so, some students will prefer not to open themselves up to others to the extent required by these questions. They should still be asked to consider these questions, but don't force them to share their answers with the whole class.

Tell students that some political scientists (people who study politics) believe that the words *liberty* and *justice* represent important American ideals. Ask students to think-pair-share (random pairs) on "What

You might suggest that students consult various dictionaries for ideas and comparisons.

(Continued)

(Continued)

Unit Sequence	Teacher Reflections
is an ideal?" Ask them to agree upon a definition and write it down. After each group has shared its answer, come up with a written definition that the class can agree on. Have students copy these definitions into their reflective journal.	
Hand out three to five sticky notes in two contrasting colors to each student. Tell them which color is for *liberty* and which is for *justice*. Ask students to write words or phrases on the sticky notes that define one of the words or give an example of what is meant by one of the words, or that is something they associate with one of the words. When they are finished, they should stick the notes to the bulletin board section dedicated to the appropriate word.	This kind of activity not only lets students know that you care about their ideas and opinions but also gets the adolescent up and moving for a minute or two! It will help if you have a new set of poster board or chart paper or different sections of the bulletin board devoted to each period's work, as students will return to this activity the next day. Otherwise, collect the sticky notes and save them in a folder labeled with the appropriate period.
Tell students that they will be wrestling with the meaning and significance of these two words (concepts) throughout the unit, both as a way to understand the thinking and vision of the founding fathers and the ideals and beliefs of today's Americans and as a catalyst for examining and clarifying their own thinking and personal vision.	
Journal Prompts. Additional journal prompts may be given. For example, "What other ideals do you associate with the United States? Explain."	Journal prompts are designed to help students focus on unit concepts as well as make a personal connection to lesson material. By responding periodically to student journals, you show them that you care about who they are and who they are becoming.

Lesson 2: The Importance of Ideals

(one block)

Unit Sequence	Teacher Reflections
Concepts. Ideals, Liberty, Justice G2–3, SD2–3, S1, S3	You may find that some students are able to finish class work more rapidly or that there is occasionally extra time left at the end of a class period. The **Extension Activities Menu** provides options appealing to varied student interest and learning profiles. You might require that all students do a certain number of the activities by the end of the unit or offer extra credit for completed activities.
Question of the Day. Post the Question of the Day on the board. Remind students to begin writing a response as soon as they enter the classroom.	
What do the words *liberty* and *justice* mean to *you*? What do you think they meant to the founding fathers of our nation?	
While students are responding to the Question of the Day, post the sticky notes from the introductory lesson on the board. When students are finished writing, share your response to the Question of the Day and ask for volunteers to share their answers too.	
Learning Activities. Divide the class into homogeneous groups of four, based on their facility for abstract thought and their capacity for sophisticated expression. To facilitate direction giving, place the directions for each task on different colored cards to hand to each group. The tasks are listed from simplest to most complex.	**Modifications for Learner Need.** Things you might look for to determine where to place students: • Amount of detail and concrete examples they require when presented with new information • Level of sophistication of their comments in class • Number and variety of ideas during brainstorming • Whether or not and to what extent they combine ideas from disparate sources to make something new
	AID. Use Figure 5.6. Expertise in History, the AID history continuum (see Book 1, Chapter 5), for a good tool to help identify students who are ready for activities calling for AID.
Task 1. Tell students the following: Work together to organize the previous day's sticky notes related to *liberty* and those related to *justice* into categories. Once you have organized the sticky notes to your satisfaction, write a	Groups working below grade level and who need concrete examples of things are assigned Task 1. These might also be students who would benefit from practice sorting and classifying. Highly tactile students would also enjoy this activity.

(Continued)

(Continued)

Unit Sequence	Teacher Reflections
statement for each category that summarizes how the words in each category work together to help us make sense of the meaning and importance of the unit concepts *liberty* and *justice*. Remember, there is no right or wrong way to group the notes, but be ready to tell why you ended up grouping them the way you did. Discuss and be ready to comment on the question "What connections do you see between your categories and American ideals?" Appoint a spokesperson for your group.	If you have large numbers of students assigned to this task, have one group work on the word *liberty* and the other on *justice*. It is vital that students complete the final step in which they come up with a statement summarizing or synthesizing their categories. If not, the sorting and classifying could just turn into a fun (or tedious!) activity with little connection to unit concepts and principles.
Task 2. Ask students to appoint a scribe to take notes on their group's discussion. Students should appoint a discussion leader to ask the following questions: What ideals do you think of when you think of the United States of America or Americans? How do the ideals we have today compare with the ideals of early America? How might our ideals change in the future? Are some ideals "better" than others? Remind students that both the scribe and the discussion leader must participate in the discussion.	Assign Task 2 to students working roughly at grade level. Scaffolding for the scribe in tasks two and three might include a graphic organizer with a table or grid with each student's name and columns in which to jot main ideas expressed by each.
Task 3. Ask students to appoint a scribe to take notes on their group's discussion. They are to discuss whether or not they agree with the following statements: • Enduring ideals are the basis of a people's political identity and culture. • Some ideals are "better" than others. When groups are finished, ask students from each group to summarize their group's work or share two to three interesting points brought up in their discussions. Ask questions (or encourage students to ask questions) that clarify and extend each group's thinking.	Groups working above grade level, who are strong abstract thinkers with strong vocabulary and skills of expression, should be assigned to Task 3. **AID.** Task 3 is also appropriate for students at the Apprentice level described in Figure 5.6, who are ready to extend this discussion to countries beyond the United States and to speculate on the possible universality of this statement. Discussions such as these help students refine their skills and push them toward the Practitioner level. While students are working in groups, circulate among the groups and jot down interesting ideas you overhear that would be worth exploring in the whole-group sharing activity to follow.

Unit Sequence	Teacher Reflections
Debriefing. Reveal the second unit principle: Enduring ideals are the basis of Americans' political identity and culture. Discuss what students think this means. Ask them if their ideas about liberty and justice have changed after hearing the ideas of their classmates. **Journal Prompt.** Ask students to write whether or not they agree with the following statement and why: The ideals of *liberty* and *justice* are the basis of Americans' political identity.	It is important to consistently return to the big ideas and essential questions of the unit if we want to ensure a focus on concepts and principles rather than on facts and figures alone. This is a key requirement for a Core Curriculum unit. Remember, you should respond to the journal prompt too. You may wish to make your own journal available to struggling students as a model.

Lesson 3: What Is a Government?

(one to two blocks)

Unit Sequence	Teacher Reflections
Concepts. Government, Rights G1, SD1, S1–3 **Question of the Day.** Post the Question of the Day, "What is a government? Do people need a government? Why or why not?"	
Introduction. Provide an introductory reading or direct instruction on the definition and functions of government to those students whose pretest indicated a need for this material.	**Optional Extension.** Students who already have expertise in the meaning and function of government may be assigned a more advanced reading or the following extension (AID):
Discussion. Follow this instruction with a class discussion. Suggested discussion points include the following: • A government is an institution through which a society makes and enforces its public rules and policies. • Every country has a form of government, and there are different forms of government in different countries. • The form of government a country has is determined by one, some, or its entire population. • Every system of government has positives and negatives, advantages and disadvantages.	Students work in pairs. Distribute the reading selection titled "Does This Seem Right to You?" in Lesson 18, "What Democracy Is . . . and Is Not," from the *Comparative Lessons for Democracy* notebook (available at cost from the Center for Civic Education, 5146 Douglas Fir Road, Calabasas, CA 91302-1467; see www.civiced.org). Have students work together to discuss the scenarios on the worksheet. Next, student pairs should fill out the **Graphic Organizer: What Is a Democracy?** Assign one student to read "What Democracy Is" and the other to read "What Democracy Is Not" from the *Comparative*

(Continued)

Unit Sequence	Teacher Reflections
Invite students working on AID activities to join the rest of the class in a discussion of the following: • What does the following statement mean? "Governments are usually a work in progress." • In what ways does the form of government in a country relate to the ideals of its people (e.g., certain forms of government do not fit with the ideals of freedom of speech)? What happens if ideals change over time (e.g., government may need to respond; people may rebel)? Provide examples. **Group Brainstorming Session.** Return to whole-group instruction and have students participate in a group brainstorm. What are some good things government can do for citizens? Some bad things? What specific things do people appreciate about our government? Complain about in our government? Make a class list of student answers to these questions on the board. Introduce the first unit principle: Government is an institution or system that provides services to people. Ask students, "How does this principle change or reinforce our thinking about the answers we gave to the Question of the Day?" Solicit ideas about what a country needs to function effectively. **Debriefing.** Ask students to add to their journal by choosing one of the following: • Draw a picture or chart that shows how you are governed in your personal and/or school life. What are the advantages and disadvantages of this "governing"? • Find a creative way (poem, sketch, symbol, brief essay, etc.) to express how *you* are a work in progress. • Today we talked about what a country needs to function effectively. What does an *adolescent* need to function effectively?	*Lessons for Democracy* notebook. (Note that the first reading is a bit easier than the second.) Pairs should then meet to compare what they read and then add or change information on their original organizer as needed. **AID.** The *Comparative Lessons for Democracy* notebook has additional resources that are appropriate for students who are ready for AID. **Modifications for Learner Need.** Today's journal prompts make an effort to respond to students' preference for self-expression (drawing or other visual, poetry, etc.). It is important to provide timely and ongoing feedback to student journal entries. Collect journals from time to time and respond to student work. You do not have to look at every student's journal every day, but try to provide each student with feedback at least once a week. This feedback can consist of comments on their entries, questions to further their thinking, and/or personal notes about their work in class. You may wish to share particularly good entries with the class (with student permission).

Lesson 4: The Constitution of the United States

(two to three blocks)

Unit Sequence	Teacher Reflections
Concepts. Ideals, Identity, Liberty, Justice G1–5, SD1–3, S6	Students should routinely be given the option to do a concept map or other visual representation of their thinking in answer to the Question of the Day. Be sure they know that they must be able to explain how the visual representation answers the questions posed.
Question of the Day. Present the Question of the Day to students: What clues do historical documents such as the Declaration of Independence, the Constitution, and the Bill of Rights give us about American ideals? Are there any documents that give clues about *your* ideals? Explain.	For lessons that span more than one block, you will need to prepare additional Questions of the Day. Here are some ideas to consider:
	• Why do you think our government was called "the great experiment" or "a bundle of compromises"?
	• Read the following quote by Benjamin Franklin at http://sln.fi.edu/franklin/statsman/statsman.html: "I now take up a resolution to do for the future all that lies in my way for the service of my countrymen." What does this quote tell you about Franklin's ideals?
Pair Work. Have students pair up with someone they did not work with yesterday to share answers. After they have shared their answers with each other, ask random students for their partners' opinions on each question.	Asking for partners' responses, instead of their own, encourages students to really listen to what is said. Warn students that this is coming!
	Optional Extensions. These extensions are designed based on Robert Sternberg's (1985) theory of triarchic intelligences (see also Sternberg & Grigorenko, 2000):
	• (Analytic) Provide students with access to learning centers that contain art with a patriotic theme, books or folders of patriotic song lyrics, poetry, and so forth. Encourage students to browse the materials at each center. They should then choose examples from one or more centers and compare the works in a brief essay addressing how these works communicate American ideals and/or exemplify the second unit principle: Enduring ideals are the basis of Americans' political identity and culture.

(Continued)

(Continued)

Unit Sequence	Teacher Reflections
	• (Creative) Ask students to compose or design their own artistic work expressing what they perceive American ideals to be. They must compose an exhibit card to go along with the work that explains the connection between their work and the ideals they chose. • (Practical) Ask students to create and set up a road map for their own new or restyled system of American government. What does the government look like? How does this system of government reflect American ideals? Their personal ideals?
Introduction to the Constitution. Be sure students understand that the Constitution describes the basic structure of the U.S. government. Discuss the following: • Who were the key players in the writing of the Constitution? Who are the key players in *your* life? • What led our forefathers to write the Constitution? What factors influenced them? What texts inspired them? What were the most important issues for them? • What did the role of writer of the Constitution involve? What kind of person would take on that kind of role? Are *you* that kind of person? Could you be?	This discussion starts students thinking about the kind of people who were involved in setting up our government, leading them to compare the characteristics of these historical figures with their characteristics, a direct link to the Curriculum of Identity.
Direct Instruction. Based on results of the unit preassessment, determine which students need instruction on the format and importance of the Constitution. Students with little or no working knowledge of this document, its historical context, and its importance to the foundations of our government will need to receive direct instruction or appropriate readings on those topics. The amount of time you need to devote to this instruction depends on your students' previous exposure to these documents.	**AID.** For students who have a mastery of the history leading up to the establishment of the Constitution and/or have advanced abilities in the area of political analysis, use the **Discussion Guide: How Democratic Is the American Constitution?** Assign the reading from this source by Robert A. Dahl (2002, pp. 1–4, 15–20). This selection stimulates discussion about the relevance of the Constitution to our country today and raises questions about what the author sees as possible shortcomings of the document. Provide students with a discussion guide

Unit Sequence	Teacher Reflections
Learning Activities. Discussion points and questions include the following: • What were the goals of the U.S. Constitution (short-term and long-term goals)? In what ways have these goals changed? Remained the same? • What are the powers granted by the Constitution, and to whom are they granted? • What are the branches of government? How do they relate to one another? • What are the major attributes of the U.S. system of government? • What is *balance of power*?	based on the reading. A similar text may be substituted as long as it pushes students to move to the Practitioner or Expert levels of competency (see Figure 5.6. Expertise in History in Book 1, Chapter 5). This assignment may also be provided as a learning center or optional extension activity.
Discussion. Assign students to small heterogeneous discussion groups, being sure to mix students from the direct instruction and the AID groups. Assign some or all of the following discussion questions to each group: • What powers are granted to you? To others in your life? Do *you* grant powers to anyone? • Is there the equivalent of a legislative, executive, and judicial branch in your life? Describe. • In what way(s) does your life at home or at school reflect the idea of a separation or balance of powers? • How does the idea of a separation of powers reflect those ideals we classified as American in earlier lessons? Could these ideals survive in another form of government? • What is the relationship between structure and power? How might the structure and powers of a government impact citizens' perceptions of *liberty* and *justice*?	As you listen to the student discussion, you will likely notice that students differ in their ability to self-reflect. Some of these questions are easier in that they directly connect to students' lives and personal opinions. Others require students to look at unit activities from a more distant and abstract perspective. Their answers to these questions will provide you with information about their level of comfort and/or expertise in this type of thinking. It is important throughout a unit to watch for indicators that students are ready to move ahead on the Novice to Expert continuum. Use answers to these and other questions to judge student skill at analysis, extrapolation, and metaphorical thinking. Students who show strengths in these areas may be ready for AID activities.
Debriefing. Talk to students about their reactions to those questions that require skills of self-reflection. Ask them why you ask them to think about and discuss such questions.	
Journal. Post the student portion of the **Self-Reflection Continuum (Students and Teacher)** on the overhead or on a bulletin	Use the teacher portion of this continuum to help you determine where students are in these skills. Because the unit stresses

(Continued)

(Continued)

Unit Sequence	Teacher Reflections
board. Ask students to write in their journals, using this scale to self-assess their comfort level with the bulleted skills or with other reflective skills you feel are emphasized in this unit.	personal reflection throughout, it will be interesting to reassess students at the end of the unit to see if there has been any change in their comfort and skill levels

Lesson 5: Constitutional Rights and Responsibilities

(two to three blocks)

Unit Sequence	Teacher Reflections
Concepts. Rights, Responsibilities G1, G4–5, SD1–4, S1–4, S6	
Question of the Day. Address the Question of the Day: Of the rights you have, which *one right* is most important to you? Why? Discuss the students' answers and your own.	Remember to share your own answer as well. Students will feel more comfortable sharing who they are with you if you are willing to share who you are with them. Suggested additional Question of the Day for the next class meeting: With *rights* come *responsibilities*. Do you agree or disagree with this statement?

Small-Group Discussion. Place students in heterogeneous discussion groups of no more than four. Be sure each group assigns a recorder. Provide large chart paper for note taking.
 	
  • What are your rights at school or at home? What rights do you have as a teenager that you did not have when you were younger? What rights do you not have now but hope to have when you get older?
  • Who protects your rights at home? At school? What happens at home or at school when rights conflict?
  • Look back at your list of rights at home and at school. Are their any limits placed on these rights? Is this fair? Why or why not?
  • What responsibilities come along with your rights at school and at home? Which are stated? Which are implied? How did you learn about the implied responsibilities?
	This discussion provides another opportunity for personalization of content and foreshadows many of the big ideas related to *rights* and *justice* at the national level.

Unit Sequence	*Teacher Reflections*

Ask each group to share its answers to one question. Segue into a brief presentation that answers or inspires discussion of the questions below:

- What rights do Americans have? How do we get these rights? Who protects our rights?
- Why are there limits on the rights granted to us in the Constitution? Is this fair?
- What happens when the rights of individuals or groups conflict?
- According to the Constitution, what stated responsibilities go along with rights? Implied?

Based on the results of the unit preassessment, divide students into two groups: those students with little knowledge of Constitutional rights should get a basic reading introducing the Bill of Rights. Follow the reading with oral (or written) questions to be sure students have understood the material. See sample questions below.

1. What is an amendment?
2. How do we amend our Constitution?
3. Why do we amend our Constitution?
4. Why have there been so few amendments to the Constitution?
5. What is the Bill or Rights?
6. What is its function?
7. What amendments make up the Bill of Rights?

Debriefing. Place students in heterogeneous groups of three to four for a ten-minute discussion. Tell them that the amendments in the Bill of Rights are often grouped together in the following manner:

- Citizen rights: religion, speech, press, assembly, petition (Amendment 1)
- Police and court (Amendments 4–8)
- States' rights (Amendments 9–10)
- Military protection and rights (Amendments 2–3)

Modifications for Learner Need. Those students who appear to have a pretty good knowledge of the rights granted to us by the Constitution may do an alternate reading on the amendments not ratified by the states, available at www.law.emory.edu/FEDERAL/usconst/notamend.html

Ask them to be prepared to give a brief summary of what they read to the rest of the class. Push all of the students to speculate on why the amendments did not pass. Do they think these or similar amendments would pass today? What other ideas for amendments do students have?

(Continued)

(Continued)

Unit Sequence	Teacher Reflections

They should discuss the following:

- In your opinion, which group of amendments is most important? Defend your opinion.
- Are any of these categories of amendments more or less intimately related to the ideals of liberty and/or justice? Why do you say so?

Invite groups to share their thoughts with the whole class. Focus on how the rights outlined in the Constitution reflect and shape American ideals.

Journal Prompt. Ask students to choose one of the discussion questions and briefly state their opinion in their journal.	Here is another opportunity to see which students choose to answer the more abstract second question. If you prefer, you may assign students the prompt you think is most appropriate.

Lesson 6: When Rights Conflict

(one block)

Unit Sequence	Teacher Reflections

Concepts. Rights, Justice

G1, G5, SD1–2, SD4, S1–5

Question of the Day. The following scenario leads to the Question of the Day:	This activity may be found at http://kancrn.kckps.k12.ks.us/Harmon/breighm/zog.html.

Another day in the contentious kingdom of Zog, and you, the mighty F'bob, are required to rule on yet another matter in the Court of Justice. But this case is different from the normal, run-of-the-mill robberies, traffic violations, and civil suits. Today the problem is one of balance. The issue is simple. Half your kingdom is, by virtue of a strange malady, unable to learn to read. These citizens are relegated to menial jobs and are a drain on welfare funds. A device has just been invented that will enable them to read and thereby help them to become full members of society,

Unit Sequence	*Teacher Reflections*

but equipping all these unfortunate citizens means taxing the upper half of the kingdom a third of their income. There is no way to avoid making the decision. You are the judge, and your ruling cannot be appealed. Question of the Day: Is it fair to take money away from those who have freely and legitimately earned it? Or do you feel that it is worse to allow those who are terminally deprived to remain that way even though a cure now exists for their condition?

Discussion. Discuss student responses to the scenario. Relate this scenario to the previous day's discussion about rights and responsibilities of citizens and lawmakers.

Direct Instruction. Depending on student background, provide direct instruction on the purpose and function of laws. Suggested discussion points include the following:

Optional Extension. Look at various seminal laws as a whole group, in small groups, or individually. Students should discuss how the laws exemplify the discussion points from the lecture.

- Laws are written for the common good and are designed to help us navigate and negotiate the varied perspectives of our nation.
- The exercising of *rights* may create conflict. Therefore, consider the following:

  o Whether or not you think something is just may depend on your perspective.
  o What happens when conflict occurs?
  o How can conflict be solved? Escalated? Terminated?
  o How does the law settle conflicts (negotiation, mediation, arbitration, and litigation)?

Journal Prompt. Ask students to write in their journal their response to the question "How do I approach, think about, and/or solve conflict?"

This question is drawn from the focusing questions of the Curriculum of Identity (see Book 1, Chapter 2, Figure 2.7).

Lesson 7: Supreme Court Cases

(one to two blocks)

Unit Sequence	*Teacher Reflections*

Concepts. Justice, Rights

G1, G4–5, SD2–3, S1–3

Question of the Day. Ask students, "What is fairness? Who should decide?"

Discuss this Question of the Day and then ask, "Who decides what is fair in *your* life? Home? School? Town? State? Country?"

Introduction to the Supreme Court. Introduce the fifth unit principle having to do with the structure and services of the government. In exploring how the Supreme Court plays a vital role in our system of justice, discuss the following questions:

- What are the various layers of justice available to people in the United States?
- How did these layers come about?
- Why do we have so many layers to our justice system?
- Who are the justices? How are they chosen? How long do they serve?

Learning Activity. Go on a virtual tour to www.oyez.org/oyez/tour/. Tour the Supreme Court and meet the current justices.

Exit Card. Ask students to do the following on an index card or half sheet of paper: List three interesting things you saw in the virtual tour. List two new questions you have about the Supreme Court or the justices.

Collect the cards immediately or as students leave the classroom. Use the information on these exit cards to help you plan the next day's instruction.

Modifications for Learner Need. Remind students that if they prefer, they may journal via bullets or visual representations with explanatory annotations.

If enough computers are available, students could do this activity alone or in pairs.

Check other helpful Web sites:

- www.oyez.org/oyez/frontpage—Here you can find a summary of decisions by entering the name of one of the parties to the lawsuit. It is in difficult language, however.
- http://supct.law.cornell.edu/supct/ cases/name.htm—Find historic cases searchable by party name.
- www.aclu.org/StudentsRights/ StudentsRightsMain.cfm—This Web site is by the ACLU and concerns students' rights issues.
- www.landmarkcases.org—Find excellent resources for teachers, including links to landmark cases.

Unit Sequence	*Teacher Reflections*
Introduction to Court Cases. As a whole class, look at the following Web site, where you will find a sample case concerning school newspaper censorship: http://kancrn.kckps.k12.ks.us/Harmon/breighm/case.html. Go through the case together so students can see how a case is set up. Be sure to point out that all the cases follow a similar format. Link the issues in the case to the ideals of liberty and justice (as well as any other ideals identified by the class in Lesson 1). Was the ruling in this case consistent with these ideals? Why or why not? What other factors besides ideals must come into play in deciding a Supreme Court case? **Exit Card.** Have students rank their interest in studying the following topics in more depth. Tell them you will use this information to assign case study groups for the next final project. • Freedom of speech (Amendment 1) • Freedom of religion (Amendment 1) • Freedom of the press (Amendment 1) • Right to bear arms (Amendment 2) • Protection from unlawful search and seizure (Amendment 4) • Civil rights (Amendment 14) • Prohibition (Amendment 18) • Women's suffrage (Amendment 19) • Other idea? _____	Some students might benefit from having a copy of the case in front of them as you discuss it. Highlighting the important phrases in the document would help students with written language difficulties. The site also provides a case analysis form that would be a helpful organizational tool for those students who need it.

Lesson 8: Introduction to Long-Term Research Project

(four or more blocks)

Unit Sequence	Teacher Reflections

Concepts. Liberty, Justice, Rights, Ideals, Identity

G1–5, SD1–4, S1–5

Question of the Day. Ask, "How is the Supreme Court like an umpire?"

After students share their answers, ask them to generate other metaphors for the Supreme Court.

The group tasks and instructions reflect the thinking and recommendations of the Complex Instruction model developed by Elizabeth Cohen (see, e.g., http://cgi .stanford/group/pci/cgi-bin/site.cgi)

This Question of the Day activity promotes creative and critical thinking in its emphasis on metaphorical thinking.

Case Study. Assign students to case study groups based on information from the previous day's final exit card. During the next several blocks or as an ongoing research project, students will work to complete the tasks set out in directions for the **Long-Term Research Project: Liberty and Justice for All**. Carefully go over these directions with students. Be sure to take time also to go over the **Rubric: Long-Term Project (Groups and Individuals)**. Point out that students will be evaluated not only as part of a group but also in terms of their individual work. Remind students daily to refer to these rubrics to help them monitor and revise their work.

As best you can, try to group students together who have diverse talents, as sections of the assignment call for different skills. Be sure you do not put three or four students who will struggle with research into the same group.

You do not need to have groups interested in every topic. Try to go with student interest as much as possible, yet balance group sizes. Groups of three to four students are best, but consider the needs and abilities of the students when deciding on exact group size. Try to have exactly nine groups so that each of the justices can be studied by a different group. (This part of the task would work well as an interdisciplinary connection to a Language Arts study of biography, research, search for bias, and writing. Perhaps you can convince the Language Arts teacher to work with you!

Complex Instruction Journal. Introduce the **Complex Instruction Journal Prompts**. Be sure students understand that they need to choose one of these prompts for each day they work on their long-term project in class. You may decide to have all students complete the journal at a specific time during the class period or you may let them do the journal whenever they wish. Just make sure they don't forget!

Unit Sequence	*Teacher Reflections*
Your role during the project work is to check on the progress of the groups' work, ask questions concerning their findings (see project instructions), design and conduct mini-lessons on how to do research (e.g., finding appropriate Web sources), writing skills (e.g., use of formal language in writing of briefs, oral presentation skills, persuasive argument), and/or group interaction skills (e.g., conflict management).	Some groups will likely need a closer watch on their progress than others. If necessary to meet the group needs, you may eliminate or modify one or more of the tasks. Be sure to provide a space in the classroom for students to keep their work in progress. This will help avoid problems related to student absences and forgotten or "lost" material.
Debriefing. End each day with a discussion of what interesting things the students came across, new ways to think about things, problems they ran into, ways to get over being stuck, and so on. Ask what their work has taught them about the important role of the Supreme Court, about American ideals, and/or about themselves?	**Optional Extension.** Using case summaries from *You Decide: Applying the Bill of Rights to Real Cases* (see **Unit References**) or from other sources, set up a learning center in which students read a case summary and try to identify which amendment might be used in arguing for or against the case. Provide an answer key so students can self-check. Prepare two levels: Level 1 should have case descriptions that are paraphrased, and Level 2 should have the actual case "syllabus" for those with more advanced reading skills. Place the materials for each level in a different colored folder or crate. You can have students choose which level they would like to try or you can assign students to the appropriate colored folder.
	AID. Obtain basic-level case law textbooks with sample cases that beginning law students analyze. They are very interesting to read, and students get to decide how they would rule based on the evidence and the laws. They are particularly interesting because they are real-life cases. Students can then read about how the courts decided the matters.

Lesson 9: Presentations

(one block)

Unit Sequence	Teacher Reflections

Concepts. Liberty, Justice, Rights, Ideals, Identity

G1–5, SD1–4, S1–5

Question of the Day. Ask the Question of the Day: The issue of governing is the most difficult issue facing a society. Explain what this statement means. Do you agree or disagree?

Group Presentations. Ask groups to present *one* of their tasks. Ask them to assess their work on tasks 1–4 and on group dynamics. Individual group members should self-assess on the **Rubric: Long-Term Project (Individual).** Collect these assessments along with the students' final products, as described in the **Long-Term Research Project: Liberty and Justice for All.**

If possible, try to have at least one presentation on each of the required and optional tasks described in the long-term research project.

Use the information from these assessments to conference about and/or record students' growth over the course of the unit.

After each presentation, ask the listeners what the product reveals about the unit concepts of *liberty* and *justice* and/or *American ideals*.

Debrief. How have your ideas about these principles changed over the course of the unit? What new questions do you have about American ideas, our government, and our justice system? What has an examination of American ideals revealed about your own ideals? How has your knowledge and understanding of yourself changed over the course of this unit?

Encourage students to reevaluate their reflective skills on the student portion of the **Self-Reflection Continuum.**

Remember that the Core Curriculum requires a continual emphasis on unit concepts and principles. This type of discussion helps bring students full circle in their study of the unit concepts.

Unit Preassessment: Instructor Sample

Identifications: Please identity the following. You do not have to write complete sentences.

1. Balance of power

2. Bill of Rights

3. Civil rights

4. Constitution

5. Declaration of Independence

6. Democracy

7. Government

8. Ideals

9. Separation of powers

Short Answer: Answer the following. Give as much detail as you can in your answers.

1. **Who** wrote each of these documents? **Why** were they written?

Declaration of Independence	Constitution	Bill of Rights
WHO		
WHY		

2. Why should we learn about the Declaration of Independence, the Constitution, and the Bill of Rights?

3. What do these documents have to do with *your* life?

4. What is a government? Why do we have one?

5. How is the U.S. government structured? Give as much detail as possible. You may write or diagram your answer.

6. What is the role of the Supreme Court? Its importance to U.S. citizens?

7. Fill in the chart below with as much information and as many details as you can:

Meaning—What does it mean to have rights? Inalienable rights?	Importance—Why do Americans care so much about rights?
Examples—Rights granted to us by the U.S. Constitution	Nonexamples—Rights not granted to us by the U.S. Constitution
What happens in the United States when a person's rights are violated? What *should* happen? Why do you say so?	

Extension Activities Menu

You may wish to assign one or more of these activities to students who are able to finish class work more rapidly than others or when there is extra time left at the end of a class period. You may also decide to require that all students do a certain number of the activities by the end of the unit. If they exceed this number, you could offer extra credit for additional activities.

Compose your own version of a pledge that represents your vision of America, what it stands for, and what it means to you personally.	Write or diagram how American ideals have changed over time and how they might change in the future. Provide evidence for your opinions in the body of your writing or as annotations to your diagram.	Find a current newspaper, magazine article, song, or artwork that exemplifies the ideas of liberty or justice. Tell how your exemplar relates to unit principles.
Go to the learning center and read *The Children's Story* (Clavell, 1989). Answer the questions on one of the colored **Extension Activity: Conversation Cubes** or modernize the fable.	If you could create and set up your own system of government, what would it look like? Make a visual that would explain the basics of your government structure.	Read and comment on each of the scenarios in "Does This Seem Right to You?" (see Lesson 3). Use evidence from the U.S. Constitution to support your commentary.
Read "What a Democracy Is" and "What a Democracy Is Not" (see Lesson 3). Make a graphic organizer that clearly shows the differences between a democracy and a nondemocracy.	Find one to two partners and play the **Power Grab Game.**	Investigate and report on how the rights we enjoy here compare with rights of people in other countries. Is there such a thing as universal rights? How might universal rights be enforced?
Play "You Decide: Applying the Bill of Rights to Real Cases" (see Lesson 8). If you have already played Level 1, you may repeat this game with Level 2.	Write this statement in your own words: Responsible citizenship depends on informed perspective, recognition of difficulty of governing effectively, and realizing it is important to try. Do you agree or disagree? Why?	Investigate these questions: What is judicial activism? Is it a good idea, or is judicial restraint a better idea?

Extension Activity: Conversation Cubes

The Children's Story
(Clavell, 1989)

Cube directions: Cut out each figure and glue or tape into a cube shape. Students roll the cube and answer the question on top. They continue to roll until all questions are answered. Students may work alone or in small groups, taking turns rolling the cube.

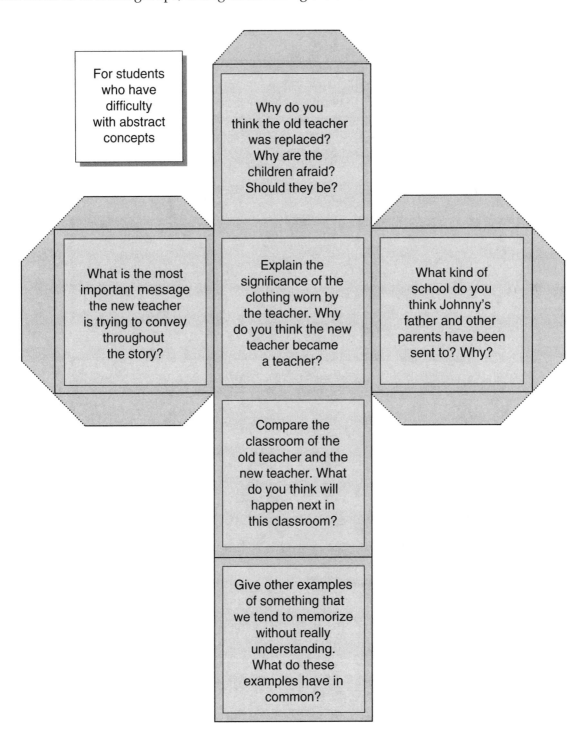

For students who have difficulty with abstract concepts

Why do you think the old teacher was replaced? Why are the children afraid? Should they be?

What is the most important message the new teacher is trying to convey throughout the story?

Explain the significance of the clothing worn by the teacher. Why do you think the new teacher became a teacher?

What kind of school do you think Johnny's father and other parents have been sent to? Why?

Compare the classroom of the old teacher and the new teacher. What do you think will happen next in this classroom?

Give other examples of something that we tend to memorize without really understanding. What do these examples have in common?

For students skilled in dealing with abstraction

Why do you think the new teacher tries to win over Johnny and not some other child? What if she had not done so?

What other societal institutions are likely to be targeted right away by "them"? Why?

What is the significance of the story's brief time frame?

Why did the new teacher cut up the flag? Discuss this action both at face value significance and at a deeper, more hidden level.

What is freedom? Why is it so hard to explain?

Give other examples of something that we tend to memorize without really understanding. What do these examples have in common?

For students fairly comfortable with abstraction

Why do you think the old teacher was crying? What kinds of emotions and thoughts were probably running through the new teacher's mind?

Who are "they"? Why have "they" come to school? Why doesn't the author give "them" a name?

Explain the significance of the candy incident. Why is this included? What implications does it have for the characters' future?

Why is the title of this book *The Children's Story . . . , but Not Just for Children*? What exactly do you think this means?

Give other examples of something that we tend to memorize without really understanding. What do these examples have in common?

Could a group of adults be as easily swayed as the children in this story could? Explain.

Extension Activity: The Power Grab Game

SOURCE: Adapted from a lesson by Don M. Carlson, Columbia River High School, Vancouver, WA; available at http://score.rims.k12.ca.us/score_lessons/power_grab_game/)

1. Place each of the "power grabs" on a separate piece of paper (see below). You may wish to color code the paper so that one color corresponds to a presidential grab for power, one for a congressional grab for power, and one for a judicial grab for power.

2. Have students work in their project teams (made up of one student who did each of the different readings). Provide each student with a copy of the U.S. Constitution.

3. You (or a student you assign) should draw one slip of paper at a time and read the attempt to "power grab." (You might read from the list at random if you prefer.)

4. Groups have two minutes (or a reasonable amount of time) to find proof in the U.S. Constitution (amendments included), by article, section, and clause, as to why the power grab is unconstitutional.

5. When a group thinks it has found the appropriate check of the power grab, the students yell "check." They must be prepared to immediately identify the corresponding article, section, and clause. If correct, the group receives ten points. If wrong, other groups have one more minute (adjust as needed) to try to earn the points. If no one finds the constitutional check in time, the teacher earns the points. The team with the most points in the winner. (A good prize would be pocket-sized copies of the U.S. Constitution, available in bulk at https://secure.freedom.org/eco/buy-const.dyn, or pocket-sized cards of the Bill of Rights, available at www.BillofRightsInstitute.org)

Power Grabs

President—A serious economic crisis takes place in the United States. The president decides to run for a third term.

President—The president declares war on China.

President—The president appoints John Doe to Senator Smith's seat when he resigns due to a personal scandal.

President—To fight terrorism, anyone found guilty of hijacking will be punished by having his or her fingernails ripped off.

President—The president decides that Congress will meet in regular session on December 15 of each year.

President—The president orders that a mass murderer be sent back to Washington State from Oregon.

President—A famous movie star comes to town and cuts off the heads of all parking meters. The president pardons him.

President—The president orders that since all citizens over 18 want to vote for the president, they may do so by popular vote.

President—The president, concerned about drug violations in the state of North Dakota, allows the governor and the attorney general to suspend democracy for a period of one month.

President—Your land is in the way of a federal highway, so the president takes your land without compensation.

Congress—Congress passes a law that allows it to take 10 percent on lumber being exported.

Congress—Congress passes a law stating that people from New Hampshire may not drive cars in New York because of pollution.

Congress—Congress decides that beards are illegal; anyone who wore one in the last year must pay a $100 fine.

Congress—Congress decides to impeach the president with the president pro-temp of the Senate presiding.

Congress—A House member dies; the House takes four days off to mourn, but the Senate says they can have only two days off.

Congress—Congress passes a law naming 15 university students guilty of crimes against the government and orders them expelled from school.

Congress—Congress passes a law that says you can sue your state in federal court.

Congress—Congress decides, because of the contributions of Pete Rose in baseball, they will honor him with the title, "Sir Pete Rose."

Congress—Congress decides to change the Constitution to allow the president to be elected to one term of six years.

Courts—Since Washington, D.C., is not in any state, residents there may not vote in national elections.

Courts—The Supreme Court rules that because of our large national debt, the United States can no longer borrow money.

Courts—The Supreme Court decides that religion and politics don't mix; therefore no government official is required to take an oath of office.

Courts—The U.S. ambassador to Spain is brought home and tried in a New York court for crimes.

Courts—The Supreme Court rules that the heads of departments may no longer make appointments of inferior officers—only the president of the United States can.

Courts—A male teacher sues over sexual discrimination by taking the case directly to the Supreme Court.

Courts—The Supreme Court rules that income tax is illegal, and you don't have to pay.

Key

President—A serious economic crisis takes place in the United States. The president decides to run for a third term. (Amendment 22)

President—The president declares war on China. (Article I, Section 8, Paragraph 11)

President—The president appoints John Doe to Senator Smith's seat when he resigns due to a personal scandal. (Article I, Section 3, Paragraph 2)

President—To fight terrorism, anyone found guilty of hijacking will be punished by having his or her fingernails ripped off. (Amendment 8)

President—The president decides that Congress will meet in regular session on December 15 of each year. (Amendment 20, Section 2)

President—The president orders that a mass murderer be sent back to Washington from Oregon. (Article IV, Section 2, Paragraph 2)

President—A famous movie star comes to town and cuts off the heads of all parking meters. The president pardons him. (Article II, Section 2, Paragraph 1)

President—The president orders that since all citizens over 18 want to vote for the president, they may do so by popular vote. (Amendment 26)

President—The president, concerned about drug violations in the state of North Dakota, allows the governor and the attorney general to suspend democracy for a period of one month. (Article IV, Section 4)

President—Your land is in the way of a federal highway, so the president takes your land without compensation. (Amendment 5)

Congress—Congress passes a law that allows it to take 10 percent on lumber being exported. (Article I, Section 9, Paragraph 5)

Congress—Congress passes a law stating that people from New Hampshire may not drive cars in New York because of pollution. (Article IV, Section 2, Paragraph 1)

Congress—Congress decides that beards are illegal; anyone who wore one in the last year must pay a $100 fine. (Article I, Section 9, Paragraph 3)

Congress—Congress decides to impeach the president with the president pro-temp of the Senate presiding. (Article I, Section 3, Paragraph 6)

Congress—A House member dies; the House takes four days off to mourn, but the Senate says they can have only two days off. (Article I, Section 5, Paragraph 4)

Congress—Congress passes a law naming 15 university students guilty of crimes against the government and orders them expelled from school. (Article I, Section 9, Paragraph 3)

Congress—Congress passes a law that says you can sue your state in federal court. (Amendment 11)

Congress—Congress decides, because of the contributions of Pete Rose in baseball, they will honor him with the title, "Sir Pete Rose." (Article I, Section 10, Paragraph 1)

Congress—Congress decides to change the Constitution to allow the president to be elected to one term of six years. (Article IV or Amendment 22)

Courts—Since Washington, D.C., is not in any state, residents there may not vote in national elections. (Amendment 23)

Courts—The Supreme Court rules that because of our large national debt, the United States can no longer borrow money. (Article I, Section 8, Paragraph 2)

Courts—The Supreme Court decides that religion and politics don't mix; therefore no government official is required to take an oath of office. (Article II, Section 1, Paragraph 8 or Article VI, Section 3)

Courts—The U.S. ambassador to Spain is brought home and tried in a New York court for crimes. (Article III, Section 2, Paragraph 1)

Courts—The Supreme Court rules that the heads of departments may no longer make appointments of inferior officers—only the president of the United States can. (Article II, Section 2, Paragraph 2)

Courts—A male teacher sues over sexual discrimination by taking the case directly to the Supreme Court. (Article III, Section 2, Paragraph 2)

Courts—The Supreme Court rules that income tax is illegal, and you don't have to pay. (Amendment 16)

Graphic Organizer: What Is a Democracy?

Features of a democracy:	Features that make something *not* a democracy:

Our definition of *democracy*:

Discussion Guide: How Democratic Is the American Constitution?

How Democratic Is the American Constitution? (2002) by Robert A. Dahl. New Haven, CT: Yale University Press.

1. Read the "Introduction: Fundamental Questions," beginning on page 1 and ending in the middle of page 4.

2. Choose one of the following and journal your thoughts or discuss them with a partner or small group:
   - Should Americans be *allowed* to question the U.S. Constitution? Why or why not?
   - Should Americans be *encouraged* to question the U.S. Constitution? Why or why not?

3. Now read the section titled "Undemocratic Elements in the Framers' Constitution," beginning at the bottom of page 15 and ending near the bottom of page 20.

4. As you read, you may wish to fill out the accompanying graphic organizer to help you keep track of what you read.

5. Meet with your group to discuss the following question:
   - From the perspective of a citizen of the late eighteenth century, which of the elements in the graphic organizer posed the greatest threat to the success of the union? Defend your response.

Undemocratic Element	Problem	Implications
Slavery		
Suffrage		
Election of the president		
Choosing senators		
Equal representation in the Senate		
Judicial power		
Congressional power		

Self-Reflection Continuum

SOURCE: Adapted from Strickland and Hench (2003).

For the Student:

Place a check mark where you feel you fall on the continuum below with respect to the statements or questions your teacher posts. Use a different color or different symbol for each item or subitem.

I can't do this. I don't
want to do this.

This is hard, but I kind
of like doing it.

This is no problem for
me! I love doing this!

Sample skills to assess:

- Thinking about myself
  o Talking to others about myself

- Examining my own beliefs, ideals, and values
  o Sharing this information with others

- Evaluating my strengths and weaknesses
  o Sharing this information with others

- Setting goals
  o Sticking to my goals

For the Teacher:

Place a mark where you feel individual students fall on the continuum below with respect to the bulleted items. You might use a different color or different symbol for each item.

Student struggled
and gave up.

Student struggled
but persevered.

Student seemed
comfortable with
the task.

Student relished
the task.

Sample student characteristics to assess:

- Brainstorms numerous or varied possibilities
- Examines ideas from multiple perspectives
- Projects self into the future
- Demonstrates self-knowledge or self-understanding
- Has a balanced view of strengths and weaknesses
- Accepting of self
- Shares thoughts and/or feelings with others

Long-Term Research Project: Liberty and Justice for All

You will have approximately ___ blocks to complete the following four tasks. Expect to do some work at home as well. To accomplish this, you will need to divide up the work among team members. Think about what various group members are good at and the kinds of things that interest them. Try to assign tasks so that you take as much advantage of these factors as possible. Remember, everyone will probably have to do something they would prefer not to! Divide up the work any way you want, but be fair about it! It is perfectly OK to work together on some of the tasks, but keep track of your time so you are able to finish all the tasks on time.

In addition to completing those individual tasks assigned by the group, each group member will be responsible for being familiar with other group members' work at all times. Meet briefly every day to bring each other up to speed on what you have accomplished and what you have learned. It is my right to ask you at any time for an update on each of your group members' work. If you can do so successfully, you will earn extra points for you and for your group. Use each other as a resource. Help each other out. Review and critique each other's work. Your motto should be "All for one and one for all!"

Required Tasks

Task 1: What's Up, Docket?

Find out what kinds of cases are being considered this year. A good Web site to visit is http://journalism.medill.northwestern.edu/docket/

Another good source of information is www.aclu.org/StudentsRights/Students RightsMain.cfm—This site has a section devoted to current issues of concern to students in particular.

www.billofrightsinstitute.org/index.php—This site has a section called Bill of Rights in the News that deals with current cases concerning Bill of Rights issues.

Browse through the current or previous season's cases to get a broad view of what is of interest to the current court. Take brief notes on the cases you find particularly interesting.

Product. Make a graphic organizer showing the categories of issues you found. Choose one of these categories and prepare a cover and a table of contents for the next issue of "The Journal of Contemporary Court Concerns."

Task 2: This Court Rules!

Your job is to find out what exactly goes on in the courtroom and leading up to the court process. How do lawyers and clients get the Supreme Court to consider their case? What happens if the case is not accepted? What if it is? Then what? How do lawyers write and file a brief? How do others show their support for or against the case? What are the guidelines lawyers must follow when appearing before the court? What happens if they don't follow the rules?

www.supremecourtus.gov/oral_arguments/guideforcounsel.pdf—This is a guide for lawyers appearing before the Court.

www.supremecourtus.gov/visiting/visitorsguidetooralargument.pdf—Visit this site for a visitors' guide to what happens during oral arguments.

www.oyez.org/oyez/tour/—Take a virtual tour of the Supreme Court here.

Product. Prepare a silent movie or a photo-essay in which you show what goes on in the Supreme Court during oral arguments. You will need to prepare text to accompany your movie, just like they used to in the olden days, or captions for your photos. Be sure your product shows all you know about court procedures.

Task 3: Land Ho!

Choose a landmark case to study in depth. You will find a listing of some of these cases at www.billofrightsinstitute.org/pdf/landmark-cases.pdf.

Pick a case that is interesting to your group. You will probably decide to study a case in the interest area that brought you together (speech, religion, arms, etc.), but it is OK to change topics if your group finds something more intriguing.

You can find the actual case you choose at http://supct.law.cornell.edu/supct/cases/name.htm.

Read the entire brief (whew!). Refer to our class example about newspaper censorship to help you with this.

Product. Prepare and perform an oral argument that might have been used by a lawyer arguing this case. Be sure you follow the rules for proper Court procedures. Be sure to include a reference to the importance of upholding one or more of the ideals we have identified as American.

Choice of Tasks

You will choose or be assigned one or more of the following:

Task 4: Who's Who?

You will be assigned one of the current Supreme Court justices. Your job is to find out as much as possible about that justice concerning his or her personal, professional, and political life. An excellent place to begin is www.oyez.org/oyez/portlet/ justices/, but do not stop there! If possible, find out what the justice was like at your age. Find an opinion for the majority written by your justice and read it. Do you agree or disagree? Find dissenting opinions written by this justice as well. What do they tell you about the justice? What do they tell you about the ideals this justice holds most dear?

Product. Make a collage representing this justice and his or her life. Use pictures and symbols to represent important ideas and themes. Be sure you can explain why you chose the components you did for the collage. Before you glue anything down, play with the pictures to find the most aesthetically pleasing and/or most powerful arrangement. Compose an exhibit card to accompany the collage.

Task 5: Find the Dirt! (AID)

Do some digging to find out what current scholars and political analysts are discussing in terms of the Supreme Court. What do they think about the Supreme

Court and how it works? Are there any problems with the current system? What are the controversies concerning the role of the Supreme Court justices? How and why has the Court changed over time? Is this a good or a bad thing? What changes are predicted for the future?

Product. Write a persuasive essay in which you argue for a change in policy concerning the Supreme Court. Include references to one or more of the ideals we have identified as American.

Task 6: Did You Ever Know That You're My Hero?

Read a chapter from Peter Irons's *The Courage of Their Convictions* (1990). Outline the issues involved in this case. What else can you find out about this person and/or this case? Profile the key player: What is he or she like? Why was this issue important to this person? How did being involved in this case affect his or her life? What do you find admirable about this person and his or her actions? Not so admirable? Compare this person with yourself. How are you like and not like this person? Could you have done what he or she did?

Product. Think of a problem that you or someone close to you has encountered in your life. Write and illustrate a children's storybook about a similar situation, but make the person you read about the main character in this new story. How would he or she have dealt with the problem? Be sure your story illustrates one or more of the ideals we have identified as American.

Task 7: Your Idea

If you have an idea for an investigation and a resulting product that would further your knowledge and understanding of the American justice system, please discuss it with me as soon as possible.

Scoring Guidelines

- You will receive a more detailed rubric for each of the product options outlined above. Each task is worth up to 25 points.
- Up to 25 additional points will be awarded according to the ability of your group to function well together.
- Successful "quizzes" on what group members are up to at any particular point will be worth 5 points each to both the individual and the group.

Your group grade will be calculated as follows:

120+ points	A+
110–119	A
100–109 points	B
85–99 points	C
75–84 points	D
Below 75 points	F

Complex Instruction Journal Prompts

Your class journal should include all of the research notes and product drafts you make while completing the group project as well as a log of what you accomplish each day.

You should also plan to set aside at least five minutes a day in which you respond to one of the following journal prompts. I will be collecting your journals at random during this time to check and respond to your entries.

DATE	*PROMPT*
	What do Supreme Court justices think about? How do they work? To what degree are these things familiar, surprising, and/or intriguing to me?
	When I am intrigued by an idea, what do I gain from that and give as a result of that, and what difference does it make to me and others? (Give an example.)
	What are the problems and issues on which Supreme Court Justices spend their lives? How do Supreme Court Justices handle these and other problems associated with their position?
	How do I handle problems and issues in my life? (Give specific examples.) What are my strengths and weaknesses in this area?
	What kinds of cases does the Court seem particularly drawn to? Why do I think this is so? What principles or ideals are at the core of these cases?
	Should the Supreme Court be allowed to refuse to hear a particular case? Why or why not?
	How does it happen that the Supreme Court has reversed itself numerous times? What are the implications of this? Should this be allowed?
	What happens when I change my opinion about something concerning my ideals and/or beliefs or those of my family? (Give an example.)
	What paradoxes are evident in the set-up or actions of the Supreme Court? How does the Court handle these? How do I handle paradoxes? (Give an example.)
	What changes do I foresee for the Supreme Court in the next two hundred years? (Justify your predictions.)
	What kind of a person appeals a case to the Supreme Court? Am I that kind of person? Explain.
	Who are the heroes when a case goes to the Supreme Court? Who are the villains? Who are my heroes? Why?
	What makes a good Supreme Court justice? Could I be that kind of person?
	How does learning about the Supreme Court help me understand the ideals America was founded upon? How does learning about the Supreme Court help me understand myself better?
	What do I like and dislike about working in groups? What kind of a group member am I? What are my strengths? Weaknesses?

Rubric: Long-Term Project

Group Rubric

(Possible Points)	Novice (15–17)	Emerging (18–21)	Competent (22–24)	Expert (25)
Tasks	Product does not show evidence that the instructions leading up to the product or the product requirements were seriously considered.	Project shows attention to task instructions leading up to product and to product requirements, although some parts seem to have received less attention than others.	Project demonstrates clear and consistent attention to task instructions leading up to product and all product requirements are met.	Project demonstrates attention to task and product requirements that go beyond what is asked (research, discussion, contemplation).
	Product contains inaccurate or misleading information.	Product information is accurate with the exception of minor details or omissions that do not detract from the overall impact.	Product contains accurate information.	Product content is accurate and insightful, fresh, and/or surprising to the viewer.
	Errors in mechanics (spelling, grammar, etc.) or aesthetics (balance, contrast, emphasis, etc.) distract the viewer.	Errors in mechanics (spelling, grammar, etc.) or aesthetics (balance, contrast, emphasis, etc.) are noticeable, but do not distract from overall impact of product.	There are no mechanical errors and/or project is aesthetically pleasing.	Use of mechanics and/or impact of elements of design are what you would expect from a professional in the field.
Group dynamics	Not all group members contribute to the final product; work is divided up unfairly.	Each group member contributes to the final product, although some group members do more than others.	Work is divided fairly.	Work is divided fairly.
	Group members do not seem to be aware of what others are doing and/or accomplishing.	Group members have a general sense of what others are doing and/or accomplishing.	Group members review and critique each others' work on a regular basis.	Group members consistently and carefully review and critique each others' work.
	Conflicts are not resolved.	Conflicts that arise require teacher intervention.	Conflict is handled appropriately with assistance of the teacher when necessary.	Conflict is handled quickly and fairly with no intervention by the teacher.
	Tasks are divvied up with no regard to individual strengths or interests.	Group members appear aware of individual strengths and interests although these strengths are not clearly exploited.	Tasks are divvied up according to individual strengths and interests where possible.	Group takes clear and consistent advantage of individual strengths and interests of members in division of labor.

Individual Rubric

	Novice (15–17)	Emerging (18–21)	Competent (22–24)	Expert (25)
Group progress checkpoints	Individual is unable to provide updates on other group members' progress.	Individual is able to provide general updates on other group members' progress.	Individual is able to provide consistent and accurate updates on other group members' progress.	Individual is in constant contact with group members about progress of self and others and helps others keep up to speed as well.
Journal— Project log	Entries do not allow reader to track project progress.	Entries, while not daily, do appear to track project progress.	Daily entries note project progress.	Daily, detailed entries concern all phases of project progress.
Journal— Personal reflections	Responses to daily prompts are incomplete. Personal prompts, when completed, are nonreflective in nature.	Responses to daily prompts are consistent overall and reflective in nature as appropriate. Writing reflects progress toward self-understanding.	Responses to daily prompts are thorough and reflective when appropriate. Writing reflects accurate knowledge of self.	Daily, detailed entries are insightful and highly reflective when appropriate. Writing demonstrates a thorough understanding of self.

UNIT RESOURCES

Print Sources

Agel, J. B. (1997). *We, the people: Great documents of the American nation.* New York: Barnes & Noble.

A resource book of two hundred documents, writings, speeches, and patriotic song lyrics. Includes the Constitution and Federalist Papers.

Alesi, G. (2000). *How to prepare for the U.S. citizenship test.* Hauppauge, NY: Barron's.

Guide to citizenship application process. May be useful as learning center activities or as source of basic inforFmation on documents and governmental structures.

Center for Civic Education. (1998). *Foundations of democracy: Authority, privacy, responsibility, and justice* (Teacher's Guide). Calabasas, CA: Author.

High school level workbook designed to promote effective citizenship. Use of essential questions helps teachers maintain conceptual focus. Includes complete lessons plus general teaching strategies. Would be useful in setting up learning centers and as a background resource for the teacher.

Center for Civic Education & the National Conference of State Legislatures. (1996). *We the people . . . Project citizen* (Teacher's Guide). Calabasas, CA: Center for Civic Education.

Teacher's guide to a competition sponsored by the Center for Civic Education. Tips, procedures, sample checklists, and rubrics are included. The rubrics and lists of requirements may be helpful in planning for and evaluating the final projects.

Clavell, J. (1989). *The children's story . . . But not just for children.* New York: Dell.

Short novel about how patriotism can be easily warped by the right techniques. The story was inspired by a conversation the author had with his daughter about the meaning of the Pledge of Allegiance.

Dahl, R. A. (2002). *How democratic is the American Constitution?* New Haven, CT: Yale University.

Fascinating analysis of issues concerning democracy and the Constitution. The author wants to change the way readers think about the Constitution. Written for an adult audience, but excerpts could be used with advanced secondary students.

Friendly, F. W., & Elliott, M. J. (1984). *The Constitution: That delicate balance. Landmark cases that shaped the Constitution.* New York: Random House.

Seminal Supreme Court cases are profiled in a storylike style from the initial issue to the conclusion of the court case. Includes analysis of both. Appropriate reading level for upper-middle school students and beyond.

Garraty, J. A. (Ed.). (1966). *Quarrels that have shaped the Constitution.* New York: Harper & Row.

Collection of essays on seminal Supreme Court decisions. Includes background, analysis, and results. High school or beyond reading level.

History of a free nation: Supreme Court case studies. (1996). New York: Glencoe.

A companion workbook to *The History of a Free Nation* textbook series. Cases are summarized with follow-up questions for the reader.

Irons, P. H. (1990). *The courage of their convictions: Sixteen Americans who fought their way to the Supreme Court.* New York: Penguin Books.

Engaging stories about the people behind the cases.

Jaffe, C. S., & Roberts, B. T. (1987). *We the people: Exploring the U.S. Constitution.* Hawthorne, NJ: Educational Impressions.

Succinct summaries of key concepts and documents along with teaching and learning activities. May be useful source of material to adapt for struggling learners, but be careful of a somewhat more simplistic approach than most middle school students need.

Monk, L. R. (2000). *The Bill of Rights: A user's guide.* Alexandria, VA: Close Up Foundation.

Tells the story of the birth and development of the Bill of Rights. Each of the ten amendments is profiled in a separate chapter. Short summaries of court cases that relate to each of the amendments are included along with profiles or writings by key players. Good source for cartoons for questions of the day. Appropriate reading level for upper middle school students.

Patterson, T. E. (2002). *We the people: A concise introduction to American politics* (4th ed.). New York: McGraw-Hill.

Comprehensive teacher resource that could also prove useful to advanced students. Organized around key concepts, it moves beyond the time of the birth of the Constitution to present day issues.

Shinew, D. M., & Fischer, J. M. (Eds.). (1997). *Comparative lessons for democracy: A collaborative effort of educators from the Czech Republic, Hungary, Latvia, Poland, Russia, and the United States.* Calabasas, CA: Center for Civic Education in cooperation with Ohio State University.

Awesome resource for teachers and advanced students. Includes lesson plans, readings, documents, and handouts related to the state of democracy in the United States and other countries. Funded by a U.S. Department of Education grant, it is available at cost from www.civitas.org. Excellent source for learning centers.

Smith, G. B., & Smith, A. L. (1992). *You decide: Applying the Bill of Rights to real cases.* Pacific Grove, CA, Critical Thinking Press & Software.

Organized by amendment, this workbook provides brief summaries of cases related to each amendment in the Bill of Rights. There are student questions and activities throughout, but they tend to be rather low-level in nature. Might be a good resource for identifying important cases and for an easy introduction to the meaning of each amendment.

Social Science Education Consortium. (2000). *Teaching the social sciences and history in secondary schools: A methods book.* Prospect Heights, IL: Waveland.

Excellent teaching methods book on background of social studies education, important themes in social studies education, and classroom-tested strategies for use in the social studies classroom. Lots of resources for the teacher.

Stockard, J. W. (2001). *Methods and resources for elementary and middle-school social studies.* Prospect Heights, IL: Waveland.

Another excellent teaching methods book designed for elementary and middle school classroom teachers.

Electronic Sources

General

www.billofrightsinstitute.org
Premier source of information on the Bill or Rights. Articles, teaching resources, lesson plans, Bill of Rights in the News, etc.

www.billofrightsinstitute.org/sections.php?op=viewarticle&artid=13
To get an online monthly newsletter about the Bill of Rights.

www.billofrightsinstitute.org/pdf/borcardsorderform.pdf
Source for pocket-sized Bill of Rights cards—good for prizes!

www.civiced.org
Invaluable resource. Lesson plans, resource lists, information on teaching civics at all grade levels.

www.crfc.org
Nonprofit, nonpartisan site to promote responsible civic action in schoolchildren. Online lessons, annotated Web resource lists, articles, current events, etc.

www.aclu.org/StudentsRights/StudentsRightsMain.cfm
Web site by the American Civil Liberties Union (ACLU) concerning students' rights issues.

http://kancrn.kckps.k12.ks.us/Harmon/breighm/zog.html
Kingdom of Zog simulation

www.usconstitution.net/const.html
Web site teaching about branches of government, elementary–middle school.

www.cccoe.net/govern/webquestintro.html
Web site teaching about branches of government, elementary–middle school.

Constitution

http://usconstitution.net
U.S. Constitution online. Includes articles discussing numerous issues and interpreting the text of the Constitution.

www.usconstitution.net/consttop_sepp.html
Article about separation of powers.

www.megalaw.com/top/constitutional.php
Links to state constitutions.

https://secure.freedom.org/eco/buy-const.dyn
Pocket-sized copies of the Constitution, available in bulk.

http://score.rims.k12.ca.us/score_lessons/power_grab_game/
Source of Power Grab game.

Amendments never ratified for the Constitution

www.law.emory.edu/FEDERAL/usconst/notamend.html
www.usconstitution.net/constamfail.html

Supreme Court

www.supremecourtus.gov/index.html
Supreme Court Web site. Lots of good stuff—spend some time exploring here; encourage students to do so as well.

www.law.cornell.edu/rules/supct/overview.html
Current rules of the Supreme Court.

Supreme Court cases

www.oyez.org/oyez/frontpage
Supreme Court cases searchable by subject—past and current cases.

www.billofrightsinstitute.org/pdf/landmark-cases.pdf
Landmark cases.

www.landmarkcases.org/
Excellent resources for teachers, including links to landmark cases.

www.crf-usa.org/bria/bria18_3.htm
Solid descriptions of cases related to the Bill of Rights in language appropriate for middle school students. Cases are divided by subject area and are followed by critical thinking questions.

http://supct.law.cornell.edu/supct/cases/name.htm
Historic cases searchable by party name.

www.aclu.org/StudentsRights/StudentsRightsMain.cfm
This site has a section devoted to current issues of concern to students, in particular.

http://docket.medill.northwestern.edu/
Find out what kind of cases are being considered this year.

http://kancrn.kckps.k12.ks.us/Harmon/breighm/case.html
Sample case concerning school newspaper censorship.

www.access.gpo.gov/congress/senate/constitution/bright.html
Listing of Supreme Court cases according to related amendments.

www.citadel.edu/citadel/otherserv/psci/courses/kuzenski/cases.htm
List of cases according to subject.

www.nationalmocktrial.org/
Will send you sample fictitious cases used in Mock Trial competitions.

Using Biography and Autobiography to Understand Challenge, Choice, and Chance

A Unit for High School Students Incorporating All Four Parallels

Jann H. Leppien and Curt Bobbitt

BACKGROUND FOR UNIT

Biography and autobiography reveal to us "the human heart of history" and provide a way for students to explore human behavior and agency. In this way, they can come to grips with specific characters and interrelate with their specific times. The four parallels of the Parallel Curriculum Model (PCM) provide students with an increasingly complex view of how biographies and autobiographies are organized, structured, and written; how biographies reveal the ways in which an individual in the past faced obstacles, brought about social change, questioned existing boundaries, and endured and persevered through time; and how biographies, through investigation, can contribute to self-understanding and identity.

The unit requires high school students to learn how to read biographies and understand how biographies are constructed. At times in the unit, they become the social scientists, historians, and writers in order to understand and appreciate a biography in all its complexity. As scholars, students are asked to identify recurring traits and characteristics and other patterns of behavior to reach consensus on whether a set of universals can be applied to the lives of the individuals they read about and perhaps themselves. In the final phase of the unit, students look inward to apply what they have learned about the lives they have read about to discover what they have learned about themselves. Several project options will be offered in this last stage of the unit, in which students explore their own conception of the life they have

293

lived by sharing their triumphs and tragedies, to develop action plans that explore personal challenges, to profile someone meaningful in their lives, or to conduct actions to solve a problem. With these goals in mind, all four parallels are used to create this unit of study.

CONTENT FRAMEWORK

Organizing Concepts

Chronology

Challenges, Chance, or Choice

Identity

Patterns

Change

Principles and Generalizations

G1 Through various literary and artistic forms, biography and autobiography illustrate the value of individual lives.

G2 Internal and external factors shape the progress and generativity or disruption of lives.

G3 Biography and autobiography firmly place a life in several universal contexts (temporal time, psychological, cultural, political, spiritual, gender, social, economic, political, and technological), taking into account how these contexts shape a life and how a life shapes them.

G4 Responsible biography does not romanticize individuals but holds them responsible for their acts within a historical context.

G5 Biographies and autobiographies rely on a variety of credible sources to construct a life story.

G6 Biographers use a set of tools and methods in their research to profile and chronicle the lives of people.

G7 Universal traits and environmental factors exist to explain why people create and make contributions to others.

G8 Our identity is shaped by the actions we take, the traits that help define who we are, and the choices that we make.

Reading/Language Arts Performance Standards

Adapted from standards of the International Reading Association (IRA) and the National Council of Teachers of English (www.readwritethink.org/standards/)

SD1 Students read a wide range of print and nonprint texts.

SD2 Students enjoy a wide range of strategies as they write and use different writing process elements appropriately to communicate with different audiences for a variety of purposes.

SD3   Students apply knowledge of language structure, language conventions (e.g., spelling and punctuation), media techniques, figurative language, and genre to create, critique, and discuss print and nonprint texts.

SD4   Students conduct research on issues and interests by generating ideas and questions and by posing problems. They gather, evaluate, and synthesize data from a variety of sources (e.g., print and nonprint texts, artifacts, people) to communicate their discoveries in ways that suit their purpose and audience (for biography only).

SD5   Students use a variety of technological and informational resources (e.g., libraries, databases, computer networks, video) to gather and synthesize information and to create and communicate knowledge.

SD6   Students develop an understanding of and respect for diversity in language use, patterns, dialects across cultures, ethnic groups, geographic regions, and social roles.

SD7   Students use spoken, written, and visual language to accomplish their own purposes (e.g., for learning, enjoyment, persuasion, and the exchange of the information).

Social Studies Performance Standards

From the National Council for the Social Studies (NCSS; www.socialstudies.org/standards/strands/)

SD8   People, places, and environments
        Students study the lives of people, the places in which they live, and the environment that surrounds them.

SD9   Individual development and identity
        Students study how personal identity is shaped by one's culture, by groups, and by institutional influences.

National History Standards

From the National Center for History in the Schools (NCHS; http://nchs.ucla.edu/standards/)

SD10   Distinguish among past, present, and future time.

SD11   Establish temporal order in constructing [one's] own historical narratives: working forward from some beginning through its development to some end or outcome; working backward from some issue, problem, or event to explain its origins and its development over time.

SD12   Read historical narratives imaginatively, taking into account (a) the historical context in which the event unfolded—the values, outlook, crises, options, and contingencies of that time and place—and (b) what the narrative reveals of the humanity of the individuals involved—their probable motives, hopes, fears, strengths, and weaknesses.

SD13   Formulate questions to focus their inquiry and analysis.

SD14   Compare and contrast differing sets of ideas, values, personalities, behaviors, and institutions by identifying likenesses and differences.

SD15 Distinguish fact and fiction by comparing documentary sources on historical figures and events with the fictional characters and events included in the story and its illustrations.

SD16 Explain causes in analyzing historical actions, including (a) the importance of the individual in history, human will, intellect, and character; (b) the influence of ideas, human interests, and beliefs; and (c) the role of chance, the accidental, and the irrational.

SD17 Obtain historical data from a variety of sources, including library and museum collections, historic sites, historical photos, journals, diaries, eyewitness accounts, newspapers, documentary films, and so on.

SD18 Interrogate historical data by determining by whom and when it was created; testing the data source for its credibility, authority, and authenticity; and detecting and evaluating bias, distortion, and propaganda by omission, suppression, or invention of facts.

Technology Standards

From the Technology Foundation Standards for Students (http://cnets.iste.org/students/s_stands.html)

SD19 Students will use technology tools to enhance learning, increase productivity, and promote creativity.

SD20 Students will use technology tools to collaborate, publish, and interact with peers, experts, and other audiences using a variety of media and formats to effectively communicate information and ideas to multiple audiences.

SD21 Students will use technology to locate, evaluate, and collect information from a variety of sources.

Skills

S1 Conducting literary and historical analysis

S2 Summarizing and analyzing biographical and historical evidence

S3 Critiquing primary documents

S4 Making comparisons to identify trends or patterns of behavior

S5 Learning how to interview and conduct oral histories

S6 Using multiple resources to gather reliable and accurate data

S7 Checking for facts against reputable sources

S8 Judging the credibility of a source

S9 Combining image, sound, and text for final products

S10 Applying the use of a research protocol to guide investigation

S11 Applying spoken, written, and visual language to accomplish a variety of purposes (e.g., for learning, enjoyment, persuasion, and the exchange of the information)

S12 Deciding on, planning, and implementing a self-selected project

MAKING SURE THE PARALLELS REMAIN CENTRAL IN TEACHING AND LEARNING

Curriculum Component	Component Description and Rationale
Content	Students work within the discipline-specific field of biography and autobiography and the concepts of choice, challenge, chronology, patterns, change, and identity to organize and make meaning out of their work in each of the parallels.
	Core Curriculum. Focus is on how the basic structure, organization, forms, and purposes of biographies and autobiographies reveal the foundational knowledge and skills for using biography as a way to identify the internal and external factors that shape and influence life stories.
	Curriculum of Practice. Students assume the role of biographers to understand how evidence is gathered through the use of multiple sources; how to critique the quality and credibility of sources; and to apply these new skills as they analyze an aspect of the biography that is personally intriguing to them.
	Curriculum of Connections. Students collectively compare the traits and chronologies of lives across gender, culture, and time to reveal the similarities and differences in how various factors shaped these lives and how these traits reveal patterns to why people create.
	Curriculum of Identity. Students discover the power of biography and autobiography in helping them to understand their own lives and lives of others in their community.
Assessments	To ensure a steady focus on the concepts of the unit, the teacher will design many assessments to focus on key concepts and principles rather than focusing solely on facts and skills. The assessment techniques will vary in each of the parallels and move students toward self-assessment as they approach the Curriculum of Identity.
Introductory activities	Introductory activities focus on a series of question prompts that build an understanding of the principles and key concepts.
	Core Curriculum. The introductory activity focuses on the importance of chronicling a life and how the genre is structured to reveal the chronology of a life.
	Curriculum of Practice. The introductory activity engages students in understanding the type of detective work that takes place when trying to study a life.
	Curriculum of Connections. The introductory activities help students identify the traits and environmental factors that are common among all the lives that are studied and how these traits help us to understand the connectivity among the lives of those who create.

(Continued)

(Continued)

Curriculum Component	Component Description and Rationale
	Curriculum of Identity. The activities are designed to ask students to consider how their lives parallel the lives of those that they have read about by "trying on" the traits and characteristics of these individuals in carrying out a self-designed project.
Teaching strategies	In both whole-class and small-group instruction, the teacher will emphasize the unit's key concepts and principles that are identified in each parallel. Each parallel deepens the knowledge behind each principle and concept so that as the students approach the Curriculum of Identity, these concepts become interrelated to form a large generalization. The teaching strategies are varied to move students from a concrete look at someone else's life to an application of these principles and concepts in the formation of their own identity.
Learning activities	The unit's learning activities are designed primarily to help students come to understand and apply the knowledge, ideas, and skills designated as most important in achieving the goals and purposes of each parallel. The learning activities have been created to have students grapple with the questions that have been generated for each parallel. In addition, small-group learning activities include a focus on extending students' individual skills of literacy (reading, text analysis, writing, use of multiple sources) and historical comprehension, interpretation, analysis, and application.
	Core Curriculum. Students identify the types of choices and chances that occur in life and that influence an individual's life journey. They identify how biographies reveal to us a sense of the past by describing how individuals solved problems, dealt with issues, made creative contributions, experienced challenges, and promoted change.
	Curriculum of Practice. Using the tools and methodologies of a biographer, students locate and analyze biographical data; research the social context by identifying the factors that shape and influence these lives; assess the quality of the information; choose the most relevant findings to apply toward the writing of a biography; and learn how one human being (the biographer) resurrects another on the basis of human records, memories, and dreams. Students retell the biography using the data gathered from the research activities completed in the Core Curriculum and the Curriculum of Practice, paying attention to the past as viewed through the eyes of the subject.
	Curriculum of Connections. Students identify how they depart from or fit within their research findings to identify personal connections between their lives and those they are reading about.

Curriculum Component	Component Description and Rationale
	Curriculum of Identity. Students will identify choices and challenges they have personally faced, the issues that "haunt" them and that they are waiting to solve or resolve, and the actions that might right a wrong, illuminate an issue, or develop a solution to a problem.
Grouping strategies	Grouping is used to ensure that all students work with the unit's big ideas and important skills while still receiving instruction necessary for individual growth and development in skills of reading and writing. During the Core Curriculum lessons, students are asked to select texts based on their interests and academic readiness. As students move into the Curriculum of Practice lessons, the analysis becomes individual. In the Curriculum of Connections, students work in groups that focus on individual, group, and whole-class analyses. During the Curriculum of Identity, students can group themselves by interest or select to conduct the project by themselves.
Products	Ongoing products and planned student reflections are organized around students demonstrating and providing evidence of understanding the key principles and concepts.
Resources	Resources guide the students' focus on the knowledge, understandings, and skills essential to the unit. In addition, they allow students to work at their own level of need much of the time and to pursue personal interests as well. Key resources in each parallel provide students with the necessary materials they can use to construct understanding of the key concepts and principles. These resources vary according to each parallel. Resources and Web addresses have been written into the unit to ensure that students and teachers have the available resources to complete the unit.
Extension activities	Extension activities, included in the teacher's reflections, allow students to explore the unit's big ideas in areas of particular interest to individuals and to work at appropriate challenge levels while doing so.
Modifications for learner need, including Ascending Intellectual Demand (AID)	Students vary in their ability to interpret text and analyze text and in the degree to which they can connect to the idea that lives are shaped by numerous factors, traits, and environmental conditions. A biography offers more to us in understanding human behavior and, when analyzed accordingly, can yield new ideas about others and ourselves. To assist all students in acquiring these understandings, the unit provides strategies

(Continued)

(Continued)

Curriculum Component	Component Description and Rationale
	(e.g., reading texts that match their reading levels, providing alternative note-taking strategies, answering more concrete questions that can be scaffolded by the teacher, and project options that best meet student interest, styles of learning, and readiness).
	AID for advanced learners asks them to work at more expertlike levels of text analysis and writing production, to use more advanced resource and research materials, and to focus on key AID questions generated for each parallel.

UNIT SEQUENCE, DESCRIPTION, AND TEACHER REFLECTIONS

Preassessment of Biography

(30 minutes)

Unit Sequence	Teacher Reflections
Before starting the unit, preassess current understanding of the purposes of and experiences with biographies. The following questions provide a starting point for this assessment: (1) Name any biographies you have read or watched on TV or video in the past year. (2) What is the purpose of a biography? (3) What types of information are revealed in biographies and autobiographies? (4) How does a biographer gather this information? What tools and methods are used to write a credible biography and autobiography? (5) How do reading biographies and autobiographies affect a reader? (6) What thinking skills do biographers use in their work?	This preassessment provides evidence of the depth of content understanding and skill acquisition students have previously mastered. It is important to acknowledge what students have already learned about this genre and the degree to which they understand the transformational power that biography and autobiographies hold for a reader.

CORE CURRICULUM LESSONS

Lesson 1: The Purposes of Biography and Autobiography

(one to two class periods)

Unit Sequence	Teacher Reflections
Concepts. Chronology, Challenge, Choices G1, SD1, SD3, SD5–6, SD12, S1, S4, S11	The Core Curriculum serves as the foundational curriculum that establishes a rich framework of knowledge, understanding, and skills. These lessons are the starting point or root system for all of the other parallels in this model.
Introduction. Hold a brainstorming session on the importance of chronicling a life. Begin by asking, "Why are the lives of others interesting to read about? What is it about a life that is so compelling to readers? Why do people have their heroes? How is a hero's life created?"	The lessons have been created to have students understand how biographies and autobiographies are structured in a format that helps reveal how a life is lived as interpreted, in some cases, from an outside source (biographer and autobiographer). After completing the lessons in this parallel, students will be able to move into a more rigorous study of how biographers tell the stories of these lives and the skills and methods they use to construct the stories. Therefore, this unit moves in stages from the Core Curriculum to the Curriculum of Practice to the Curriculum of Connections and finally to the Curriculum of Identity.
Learning Activity. To explore this idea further, arrange students in heterogeneous or random groups of six to read a simple biography, which you have provided at each table. (Select elementary biographies and autobiographies with illustrations that enhance the reading.) The students can select a reader at their table to read this biography aloud to the group. Ask them to read this biography or autobiography, keeping in mind the same questions that were posed earlier in the discussion.	**Grouping Strategies.** This type of grouping was arranged to allow students to work together in heterogeneous groups. Since this is a beginning activity, teachers can use this session as a way to gather more information about what their students know and understand about this genre.
Once they have completed the reading, begin the brainstorming activity by placing a cube in the center of each table. The questions on the cube will be used to	The questions posed on the cubes vary in complexity, some yielding more concrete responses and others revealing abstract ideas about the use, intent, and purpose of

(Continued)

(Continued)

Unit Sequence	Teacher Reflections
generate some unusual ideas about biographies and their purposes. They must work as a group to apply the questions to the biography they just read. The following questions are listed on the faces of the cube: (1) What would be an unusual purpose for this biography/autobiography? How could this biography/autobiography be applied or used in an unusual way? (2) When would it be wrong to use this biography/autobiography? When would it be misapplied or out of place? (3) Brainstorm at least four ways to change this biography to make it better, more interesting, or more effective. What recommendations would you make? (4) What are the main purposes of this biography/autobiography, and for whom does it seem to be written? What are the most important things it is supposed to do or be used for? (5) How well does the biography/autobiography work? List two questions you wish the biographer had answered. (6) Identify two examples of this biography/autobiography in action. Think of situations, instances, or places in which people could use or apply the use of this biography/autobiography. If possible, have the students record their ideas on computers so all responses can be compiled for discussion. If computers are not available, then place all responses on the overhead. **Debriefing.** The group will discuss the purposes and uses of biographies and autobiographies. Conclude the lesson by asking students to share their responses generated from the question cubes. Pose	this genre. Questions 1, 3, and 4 are perhaps more familiar and concrete to students. Questions 2, 5, and 6 will appeal to those who are ready for a more complex view of biographies/autobiographies. The questions offer multiple entries into the discussion, where the intent is to explore other uses and purposes of biography/autobiography that the students would not have thought about until the questions were posed to them. The responses to these questions prompt parallel instructional activities that appear later in the unit and foreshow the instructional session in which students explore how audience, purpose, and style dictate the types of writing and evidence collecting a biographer uses when creating text. Students can also discuss parts of the biographies that explicitly appeal to males or females, African Americans or other groups, or to general audiences. Another format to use with this activity requires handing out six colored index cards to the whole group. Have group members record their ideas on a specific color-coded card that has been assigned a question number. After all responses have been recorded, collect the cards by color, then redistribute them to the groups and ask them to summarize all the responses on one chart or overhead for group discussion. Cards sorted by color (or electronically sorted responses on a computer) can later help students generate ideas for their project work in the Curriculum of Practice. The discussion should result in students understanding that biographies reveal to their readers the making of a life, a travelogue of interesting events, descriptions of triumphs over adversity,

Unit Sequence	Teacher Reflections
the following questions as summary to the lesson: • Do biography and autobiography have a purpose? • Do the biographies seem to have a structure? • What similarities do all biographies and autobiographies share in common? • Who would study them? What would their messages reveal to a reader? • If it is believed that biographies and autobiographies can be transformational, what qualities and characteristics do biographers reveal about their subjects? How would the reader know if the information is credible? • Would the purpose of biography and autobiography differ by age group? • Do biographies ever affect our personal lives? • Where can you find biographies in places other than a library or bookstore?	the stories of the mighty who have met a tragic fate, or the inside story of a type of life few of us could ever imagine living. In essence, the biography becomes a story and, if chosen carefully, one that can assist its readers in understanding their own lives. If necessary, to encourage discussion, the teacher can read comments from the group responses and ask for elaboration.
Record all responses on a piece of chart paper for future use.	These lists will be revisited in the unit as students acquire more knowledge, understanding, and skill. Keep this list in a safe place so other responses can be added.

Lesson 2: Selecting an Appropriate Biography for Study

(one to two class periods)

Unit Sequence	Teacher Reflections
Concepts. Chronology, Challenge, Choices G1, G5, SD1–7, S8, S11 **Introduction.** Hand out the following sheets: **Lesson 2 Worksheets: Through the Eyes of an Author** and the excerpt from **The Rambler**. Have the students read these texts independently or with a partner sitting next to them.	Selecting an appropriate biography to read during this unit depends not only on finding biographies that the students can read but also on assisting young people in selecting those biographies that are challenging and contain the appropriate character development, factual accuracy, and worthiness of the subject that you

(Continued)

(Continued)

Unit Sequence	Teacher Reflections
	would prefer that they consider. In setting up this activity, we want students to make their selection based on valid decisions after they read what other writers say about the purpose of biography and what potential it has for shaping lives. This activity requires students to consider the merits of their selection based on sound reasoning.
As they read the selections, ask them to identify what Jean Fritz and Samuel Johnson have to say about the writing of a biography: • What reasons do they give for writing biographies? • What do they say about the challenges biographers face and how they face these challenges? • How does what they have to say differ from our ideas regarding biographies?	The essays by Jean Fritz and Samuel Johnson vary in density of text and sentence structure. This was intentional to accommodate the varying levels of reading expertise within the classroom. **AID.** An advanced class or a student with a high level of expertise can be asked to read Johnson's entire essay for more background. The teacher should mention that Johnson established his early career based on biographies of poets of the generation preceding his.
Have the students record their responses on the **Lesson 2 Worksheet: Reflections on Jean Fritz's and Samuel Johnson's Words**, which will ask them to consider the authors' ideas and extend their thinking as they identify how these ideas would shape the kind of biography to select for this unit of study and the recommendations that they can infer about how to read the biography.	Other sources of biographers' perspectives on biographies can be found in sources such as *Bartlett's Familiar Quotations* and other indexes of quotations. (Some of these are quite specialized and can be used by the students in their upcoming research.) Web sites can be accessed to collect online essays and quotations that describe the varying perspectives of the use of biography and how the stories are revealed. We encourage teachers also to consider how artistic portraits are a form of biography used to reveal stories of lives long ago. For example, Oliver Cromwell's comment to his portrait painter, Lely ("I desire you would use all your skill to paint my picture truly like me, and not flatter me at all; but remark all these roughnesses, pimples, warts, and everything as you see me"), highlights the question about whether to include negative details in biographies and provides an opportunity

Unit Sequence	*Teacher Reflections*
	to pose some humorous questions to students, including these:
	• Why would it be important to write a biography that exposes all the pimples, warts, and everything you see in the individual?
	• Do you feel that biographers struggle with this idea? Why or why not?
	• Can a biographer take this idea too far? (Return to Samuel Johnson's cautionary note about the responsibility biographers face in seeking balance in their research and portrayal of their subjects.)
Discussion. Discuss the selection of an appropriate text after students have completed the worksheet. Have them generate criteria that can guide the selection of a biography. As they think about the words of the essayists, have the students consider what these words might mean when selecting a text. Also consider adding the criteria below to the students' generated list of criteria. Place all the criteria on the board to guide student selection of a biography that will be read and analyzed during this unit:	We chose to have the students generate their own criteria for the selection of a biography, hoping that they would select biographies that were personally relevant to their own interests. It is difficult to read this genre when students do not have some type of vested interest in the person or topic.
(1) Is the biography one that I can read?	
(2) Is the subject of the biography worth reading about? In other words, does the subject of the biography have a significant history?	
(3) Is the biography written by a reputable biographer?	
(4) Does the writing style appeal to me?	
(5) Does the biography include photographs, quotations, and other documents that increase the credibility of the text?	
(6) Does the biographer use primary sources when conducting research for the text, including positive and negative details?	
(7) Is this a life that is personally interesting to me?	

(Continued)

(Continued)

Unit Sequence	Teacher Reflections
Also discuss with students that it is important to select a person or time period in which they have the most interest. Is there a writer, historian, poet, artist, photographer, scientist, mathematician, and so on that students have come in contact with in other classes that seems appealing or unusual in character and whose life they would like to explore?	A teacher has a choice here to group the students by disciplines or time periods. If a history teacher is using this unit, he or she may find it useful to select those biographies and autobiographies that represent a specific time in history to uncover how these individuals shaped history and how history shaped these lives. A teacher of literature might have students choose a poet's biography to explore commonalities in artistic temperament.

Modifications for Learner Need. Students with similar interests in people can also work with partners to conduct the research, preferably using two different biographies of the same person. Partners with different reading-skill levels could select their books accordingly with the teacher's guidance. |
| Take students to the library and assist them in their decision-making process. Knowing the background of your students, you may be able to guide students toward a selection that is an appropriate match to their interest and reading level. Instead of going to the library, you can place biographies in boxes or tubs marked by discipline, event, or issue. This might narrow the selection process down for some of the students. | Advanced teacher preparation may lead to having several additional biographies in the school library prior to this assignment, perhaps borrowed from another library or museum or from your colleagues' personal collections. |
| Sharing personal recollections for some of these biographies or even your personal favorites may provide enough intrigue to encourage a selection when none of the selections looks interesting to a student. | We believe that teachers can influence students' decisions by sharing their love of biography with students. In a learning community, a teacher who models this interest can help motivate those who have become turned off by the process of enjoying good literature. It might be important to share powerful biographies or autobiographies with the students, such as Elie Wiesel's *Night*, Michael L. Berry's *Georgia O'Keefe: Painter*, or Russell Freedman's biography, *Lincoln: A Photobiography*. |

Lesson 3: The Anatomy of a Biography or an Autobiography

(four to five class periods)

Unit Sequence	*Teacher Reflections*
Concepts. Chronology, Challenge, Choices, Chance, Identity G1–3, G8, SD1–12, S1–2, S4, S9, S11, SD14–16	
Introduction. Tell students that in this lesson they will begin to understand the history and anatomy of a biography. (To accompany this portion of the lesson, download visual art images from the Internet into a PowerPoint [or other presentation software] presentation to enhance the following information, or supply reference materials from art history books so students can see the visual images discussed in the background information.)	When discussing the visual images with the students, there is certainly a great deal to be gained when we can insert humor in the presentation. Ask students to consider in what ways individuals, groups, or even society today still use some of these techniques (mentioned in the slideshow) as a form of communicating human accomplishment. For example, a teacher (with the assistance of the technology specialist, a student, or a parent) can use digital imaging technology to place students' images on vases, portraits, and coins. Then intersperse these images throughout the slide presentation to engage students in the historical lesson. Teachers can play with this technology capacity to bring the visual side of biography to life, and the idea serves as a humorous outlet during a historical presentation. (Wouldn't we have all loved this presentation during our Introduction to Art History course in college?)
Historical Background Information. Share the following with students: For thousands of years, humans have been fascinated by both the sharing of the stories of their own lives and reading about the lives of others. Some of the earliest autobiographies were the drawings on walls produced by prehistoric people. Over the centuries, heroic adventures were related in drawings on the sides of vases or placed on signage and coins to tell of wars won, construction projects or important buildings completed by emperors, or as leadership changed.	
As people became more literate, so did their recordings. These stories were written on scrolls and spoke of important government and religious leaders of the time. Often these stories were accompanied by historic portraits of these individuals and were discussed in a collective biography relating the story behind these men and women. By the 1900s, collective biographies often glorified the lives of the poor who were able to rise to great wealth. The ideal image of the individual revealed a story of those who were able to rise above poverty with a sense of purpose and work ethic.	Be sure students see that this genre has changed over time to reflect a broader range of human endeavors.

(Continued)

(Continued)

Unit Sequence	*Teacher Reflections*

Today, biographies and autobiographies are equally popular and include media other than books. Each month eager readers await publications such as *People, Us, Vanity Fair,* and, yes, even the *National Inquirer.* Several popular films also focus on people's lives: *A Beautiful Mind, Shine, The Pianist.* The biography has the power to reveal hidden truths that have altered the course of history, entertained people, provided invaluable lessons in life, and helped us understand the circumstances that influenced a life whose impact shaped a society at large.

It is important for students to see all the different ways biographies and autobiographies have become part of the popular culture. We feel that it is important to discuss the differences between these popular forms of biographies and those that are based on research. We also feel that it is important for students to understand how to question the authenticity and reliability of the information in these alternative formats.

Research Project Assignment. Use the following directions to introduce students to their biography and autobiography research assignment:

> In this portion of the biography study, you will piece together the life of a subject as told to you by the biographer. You will document the anatomy of your biography by looking closely at the clues the writer provides to you about this person. During times in your reading, you will need to stop and reflect on what the writer is telling you about significant events or episodes in your subject's life. You will also consider what that reveals to you about the types of personal characteristics and dispositions that helped this person face challenges. The fullness of the lives of our heroes and villains makes them fascinating. They come alive in all their human complexity, so you will need to read carefully and "look" for evidence of the emotions, passions and follies, innermost secrets, challenges, and choices that marked their lives.

The format of this research activity has been created to assist students in formulating an understanding of the challenges that individuals face when events or circumstances occur that can encourage or discourage a person. The format also illustrates the choices people make to counter challenges.

In this research, students are actively sifting through evidence in their text that helps them to understand their subjects in all their complexities. In most cases, a life is changed or character or identity is formed as a result of one or more events that occur in that person's life, although the event may be perceived by others or even the subject as inconsequential at the time it occurs. Encourage students to not pass judgment but rather find the connections that are made between the choices (internal decisions) individuals make when faced with challenges—chances in life, obstacles, and adversities (even during childhood)—in relation to these events or perspectives (external factors that influence a life, such as historical, cultural, technological, social, political, spiritual, and economic) during the course of their lifetime. In addressing these issues, students should be able to gain new insight, empathy, and understanding of the challenges that we all face while living our lives. In addition, there are choices and strategies that these individuals employed that may be applied to their own lives.

Unit Sequence	*Teacher Reflections*

Post and discuss the following questions:

- Are we, as human beings, affected, for the better or worse, by the events in our lives?
- Is there a relationship between your subjects' lives and their identities?
- To what degree did the subject's intent shape subsequent public opinion?

Research Notebook. Have each student set up a notebook following the format described in the **Research Recording Format: Three-Column Journal Entry**.

In the first column, students and teachers will generate a set of initial questions to guide the research and analysis. The second column is designated for the recording of notes, references, quotations, and so on that may help address the questions or provide evidence for answering this question. The final column is used to record the inferences that students draw from the notes in Column 2. This three-column format provides a structure that assists students in analyzing the life of the subject they have selected. These elements help students understand how a life is shaped by events, circumstances, challenges, and choices. They also reveal to the students that biographies and autobiographies have a certain literary structure that differs from other genres.

Provide students with small sticky notes that they can use as they read the biography. They can color code or number code the details they find in their texts and then transcribe these references to the chart later.

Mini-Lessons. While students are working on gathering evidence to answer their research questions, offer small-group instruction on such topics as how to take

Teacher Reflections column:

The final question raises the issue of how fickle public reaction can be. Certain accomplishments have broader-ranging results than the originator intended. Mother Teresa did not try to be a celebrity. Sir Arthur Conan Doyle came to hate his creation Sherlock Holmes, who is today far more famous than his creator. Doyle's attempt to kill off Sherlock Holmes failed because of readers' demands (and Doyle's financial straits).

Modifications for Student Need. Depending on the skill level of students, different formats may be easier for some students. The three-column format is for students who have detailed organization skills. The alternate format is highly structured and may be easier for students who have little experience with research. Note that both formats accomplish the same goals.

Using the alternative research format, have each student create a research folder using a file folder, index cards, and an envelope. Students list one question per index card and then color code or mark each card with a symbol for easy reference. These index cards are then taped to the upper left-hand side of the folder. An envelope with the words *Data Cards* is taped to the lower right-hand side of the folder. This envelope holds empty index cards that will serve as the data entry cards.

When students find evidence or clues to the answers, they take out an index card and color code it to match the research question it answers. Students will end up with having many index data entry cards per category of question. Students are to cite the source and list the page number beside each note they record. They will then cite the source on the reference sheet that is stapled to the upper right-hand side of the file folder (see **Alternative Research Recording Format: File Folder Layout**).

(Continued)

(Continued)

Unit Sequence	Teacher Reflections
notes, cite sources, and locate information using the table of contents and indexes listed in the book; how to document evidence; how to select a variety of evidence formats; and how to interpret and make inferences from evidence gathered.	**Modifications for Learner Need.** If students are experiencing difficulty interpreting their text, it may be important to assist students in reading certain chapters. It may be that the references or historical time periods are too difficult for some students to interpret or that the references made are not adequately explained in the text. In some cases, certain students do not have the prior experience necessary to interpret how the issues explored during a certain time period might influence an individual. The teacher should assist these students in gathering enough information about this time period to help establish a connection to their subjects' lives.
Also schedule times for students to share short progress reports with their classmates and/or with you. You might ask them to select interesting details from their journal charts or data envelopes to illustrate how they are responding to the questions.	
The **Recording Charts: Chronology of Events and Relative Importance of Dates** provide students with a visual indicator of how significant events in a biography compare with each other. Tell students to decide on a few details from Column 2 to chart chronologically on the horizontal (x) axis and rate each one in relative importance on the vertical (y) axis.	**AID.** It is of equal importance for a teacher to recognize when students have a great deal of knowledge that they bring to this research process. Meet with these students to pose questions that challenge them and increase their expertise in dealing with complex issues and more rigorous forms of analysis. Students can be asked to generate other research questions that explore the connections between the internal and external factors that shape a life. They can also be encouraged to make multiple and wide-reaching transformational inferences that can be supported by the research.
Debriefing. To conclude this research section of the unit, place students in heterogeneous teams to return to the essential questions that were posed at the beginning of their research. To begin the reflection process, tell students the following about how they will work in a group: Now that you all have completed your initial research, I want your team to reflect on the questions that I posed to you prior to your investigations. Your team's job is to take a position on the questions and defend them by providing examples from the individual biographies that you have read and analyzed. These are the questions that will guide the positions you must construct:	These reflection activities require students to synthesize their research findings. They will address questions that we think move students from understanding the structure of biography to understanding how biographies reveal to us the common sets of choices and challenges people face in relation to their historical context. The team reflection will help illustrate and identify the common themes or set of universalities that these individuals share. Knowing this helps us to understand how history is revealed through an analysis of those who lived during the event being studied.

Unit Sequence	*Teacher Reflections*

- Are we, as human beings, affected, for the better or worse, by the events of our lives?
- Is there a relationship between your subjects' lives and their identities?
- To what degree did the subject's intent shape subsequent public opinion?

You can choose how to chart and communicate these decisions; however, you must back up your position with examples from the research that you collectively gathered in the varied biographies that your team members read. Work as a team to discuss and to reach consensus.

Have students make their presentation to the other teams and note the similarities and differences in the positions that were held by the various groups.

Next, tell students that it is time to *individually* consider the impact of the biography they read. Have them select two of the following questions and respond in their journal:

Is there a relationship between your subject's story and his or her identity?

To what extent is he or she a witness of history or a reflection of the historical context that shaped his or her life?

Have you been affected by the story? How and why has your judgment of your subject changed as a result of reading the biography?

What does this life reveal to you that you had never thought about before?

Distribute the **Lesson 3 Rubric: Biography and Autobiography Research** to guide performance. Explain the categories of the research performance and discuss the indicators chronicling growth in student expertise. Have students chart personal growth during the initial, middle, and ending phases of the research process so they see themselves improving as the research process evolves.

Try to have the students identify a pattern in these varied positions or note the reasons behind the types of similarities that exist between the positions presented.

AID. Adjust and modify these questions for students who find other questions more appealing and personally relevant or if they appear too simplistic for those students who have demonstrated the ability to understand the transformative power that biographies hold for individuals in a society or for themselves.

In addition, questions posed in Lesson 1 can serve as a returning point to expand upon and demonstrate individual student growth that has occurred after participating in these learning activities.

CURRICULUM OF PRACTICE LESSONS

Lesson 4: The Tools and Methods of Biographers

(two class periods)

Unit Sequence	Teacher Reflections
Concepts. Chronology, Challenge, Choices, Change G4–6, SD2–4, SD5, SD7, SD10–12, SD14–15, SD18–19, SD21, S7–8 **Introduction.** Introduce the first lesson in this parallel by asking them the following questions: • Have you ever watched a crime story on TV? • What qualities and traits distinguish the role of the detective? • How do detectives carry out their work? (Record student responses on the overhead and then continue the questioning.) • How would the professional skills, traits, and qualities of a detective compare with those of a biographer? (On the overhead place check marks next to those traits, qualities, and skills that are common to both professionals.) Continue this discussion by giving students the following background information: Like detectives who solve crimes, biographers look for evidence, such as letters, diaries, court documents, and objects used by the people being studied. They may search for buildings where the people lived, for example. Often biographers find poems and memoirs created by people that help them to understand their subjects' emotions, beliefs, attitudes, and perspectives regarding certain historical events or issues. Also photographs, films, drawings, letters, and engravings become tools that biographers may find helpful in understanding the life of the subjects they are researching.	In this parallel, students are introduced and encouraged to apply the tools and methodologies that biographers use to gather and analyze information about their subjects. Since the Core Curriculum had students investigate the text writings (primarily by analyzing and reporting rather than critiquing biographies) to understand that biographies have a basic structure and organizational pattern, the activities created for the Curriculum of Practice are designed to move students toward purposeful evaluation of biographical sources—activities we think more closely approximate the work of biographers. It is important to note that the following lessons are derived from and extend the Core Curriculum by promoting students' expertise as practitioners of the discipline. Students are introduced to specific tools and methods biographers use to judge the quality of their sources.

Unit Sequence	*Teacher Reflections*
Biographers organize their sources into two categories. These sources serve different purposes and can be misused and interpreted incorrectly. The types of sources used by a biographer indicate the extensiveness to which a researcher conducted his or her investigation. The kinds of interpretation and inferences suggested in the biography are used to judge the quality of a published biography.	The activities in this section require students to wrestle with the problems that exist in this field when sources are misused, overgeneralized, and incorrectly interpreted. The field struggles with public perception of what constitutes "truthful" sources and their insatiable thirst for gossip. Therefore, this parallel responds to this concern by helping students understand the difference between an authorized and unauthorized biography, the ethics behind subjecting sources to critical examination, and the skills that will promote critical readers and develop critical minds.

Have students record the following definitions in their journal:

- A *primary source* gives the words of the witnesses or the first recorders of an event. Primary sources include manuscripts, archives, letters, unedited quotations, poems, diaries, tape recordings, transcriptions of interviews, maps, census data, and speeches.
- *Secondary sources* are descriptions of the event derived from and based on primary sources. These might include a newspaper article, magazine articles, a biography, or an autobiography if it is written and synthesized by the biographer and not the subject.

It is important to share with students the many kinds of biographies. An authorized biography is not the same as an autobiography. In authorized biographies, writers interview their subjects exclusively, doing little outside research except to confirm dates or other facts. It is the writer's job to tell the subject's story in his or her own words, using the subject's voice. So the level of interpretation and the reliance of sources that are used vary accordingly.

An unauthorized biography may or may not be written with the aid of subject interviews but might rely on friends, acquaintances, and anyone else a biographer can talk to; therefore, it is possible that an unauthorized biography may be more accurate than an authorized

(Continued)

Unit Sequence	Teacher Reflections

biography because there is no interference on the part of those biased in the subject's favor. An unauthorized biography runs the risk of being completely inaccurate if the subject and his or her acquaintances all refuse to talk to the biographer.

Discussion. Discuss the following questions in large or small groups:

- When does a primary source become a secondary source, and can a secondary source ever become a primary source?
- How would you classify your history textbook? Is it a primary or secondary source? Why?
- Does a textbook ever include primary sources? What categories of sources would be included?
- What would happen if a publishing company left out voices from those who actually witnessed a specific event? How would this change the interpretation of a historical account?

The discussion should reveal that people living in the past left many clues about their lives so that we could understand what events they encountered in their lives, how people reacted to these experiences, and what effects the outcomes had in changing their lives. In essence, they unlock the past and allow us to enter a time period that has helped shape our world today.

Video. Tell students they are going to move back in time by watching parts of the video *The Civil War*, by Ken Burns, an award-winning documentarian and filmmaker. Some student may have seen his documentaries on TV. Students should view parts of this film with a critical eye— looking for places where Burns would have used primary sources and secondary sources to tell the Civil War story. They will view short segments of the film, in which they should try to identify how primary and secondary sources might have been used to reveal the story.

There is one video segment we particularly enjoy showing students. While filming *The Civil War*, Burns became very involved in the irony of Abraham Lincoln's death. Burns was struck by the idea that Abraham Lincoln could devote every waking hour to saving his country, yet when he finally felt he had a few moments to spare, he decided to go to the theater. So, while filming the theater scene, Burns and his crew included everything in the audio mix. "We had the tinny orchestral music, the footfalls, the laugher, the Victorian performance," recalls Burns. "Everything but the sound of the

Unit Sequence	Teacher Reflections

As they watch the video clips, they should try to identify these sources so that they can discuss how the different kinds of sources are used to create credible stories.

Have students identify the type of sources used in the video by keeping track of their ideas in their journals.

Discussion. Discuss with students the use of sources in helping the filmmakers construct credible stories. As students identify the sources used, have them predict why the filmmakers would have selected the sources they did. Continue the discussion by asking students to judge the quality of evidence found in the biographies they read in the Core Curriculum section of this unit. Ask them to find examples of primary and secondary sources used in their biography. Have them check the index of their biographies to identify the type and quality of sources (more primary or secondary) used by the biographers.

Homework. Before the class dismisses, distribute the **Homework: Finding Evidence in Your Daily Life** task sheet and emphasize the importance of completing it for the next day's class. Discuss the categories of items that students can bring for the activity.

gunshot. So we went back to put that sound in on the very last day and I just yelled, 'Stop.' And we kept him alive for five minutes—at about 500 bucks a minute running through the next meter. And we were all crying. I just didn't want him to die. I mean, that's the whole idea—to keep these people alive. Inevitably they have to die, to cement our relationship and their importance to us. But it's always painful" (Ammeson, 2002, pp. 38–43).

This excerpt illustrates the power of this genre on the life of a biographer. It also provides teachers an opportunity to discuss how artistic expression can influence the accuracy of what is told to an audience. There is a limit to the artistic expression biographers can use when telling their stories. The field helps moderate the extent to which biographers can change the story. If a story's accuracy extends too far from the story that is told in the original source, then most biographers will be criticized by other people in the field.

This activity was developed as a way to demonstrate how tempting it is to make inferences from a collection of sources that are haphazardly organized. It also moves students forward in applying the type of critical questioning that each source must be subjected to before a biographer can begin to use it in the writing of a life story.

Teachers may want to have a sample sack of personal evidence as an example. Depending on the culture of the class, some warnings or prohibitions may be practical (e.g., no living creatures or insects, no harmful substances). The structure of this activity is intended to have students personally experience the consequences of having their life told in a story when inferences are incomplete and inconclusive and to understand the danger of making statements that overgeneralize.

(Continued)

(Continued)

Unit Sequence	Teacher Reflections
Pair Work. Introduce this portion of the lesson by telling students the following: Imagine that a biography was going to be written about your life using the artifacts that you leave behind. Today you will be asked to work with one of your classmates to construct these stories by using the items you have brought from home (see **Homework: Finding Evidence in Your Daily Life**). The only difficulty you might experience is that you can't discuss these items with your partner. Each of you will be asked to "uncover" the life of the other and then write a personal profile based on the inferences you make from the contents in the sack. (Team students by randomly selecting names from a hat.) Have students sit in chairs back-to-back and switch sacks. As they pull the items from the sack, students must try to interpret the source, state assertions, and make conclusions about their partner's life during the last week. At this point, don't try to censor the inferences being made by the students. This is part of the lesson and helps demonstrate to students how biographers have to apply questions to prevent bias in their interpretations, determine the authenticity of the sources by verifying them against other sources of information, and seek patterns of repeating themes within the data they are gathering and analyzing. After 15 to 20 minutes, ask students to begin writing a brief account of their partner's life over the past week by using the contents of the sack as evidence. After students have had a chance to write a page or two, have them exchange the "biographies" with their partner. Let the partners "correct" each other's biographies. At this point, the laughter should begin.	A biographer requires a highly analytic mind and a willing disposition to be skeptical and critical of the evidence that he or she gathers. During this part of the lesson, students will probably be so vested in the experience that they will fail to apply these characteristics. This is to be expected, and teachers should not be discouraged. The activity serves as a foreshadowing activity that will enhance student performance in the next activity. Teachers should see students transferring these intellectual qualities of the mind to other activities that are forthcoming. We believe that students should grow both intellectually and emotionally as they progress through the entire unit and that student growth should be celebrated.
Allow at least ten minutes for whole-class discussion, which focuses on the difficulties biographers face when they must work with even a small amount of evidence of a life and turn it into a coherent account.	This is a teaching moment! Students can recommend strategies for preventing this from occurring in similar situations and discuss the ethical implications of faulty thinking, not only in biography but in most other aspects of life as well.

Unit Sequence	*Teacher Reflections*

Debriefing. Pose the following questions to debrief the sack activity:

- How did the stories become so twisted?
- What extra information did you need about the evidence in the sack that would have assisted you in writing a biographical account that is more accurate in detail?
- Which sources were most helpful? Least helpful?

Now let's apply what you just experienced to the work of a biographer.

- What tools, techniques, or methods of thinking would a group of biographers use to prevent themselves from experiencing what you just went through in this activity?
- What types of questions would they use to diminish the possibility of bias in their writing and analyses?

Assessment of Continuing Progress. Place these words on the board:

> source creator
> firsthand knowledge
> opinions and interests
> large audiences
> secondary sources
> primary sources
> persuasion
> bias
> lapse of time

Tell students to look at the words listed on the board. Would any of these words be a part of the speaking vocabulary of a biographer? Ask them to look at the list, consider what the words have to do with a biographer's work, and then quickly turn to the person next to them and share their ideas.

Before students leave the class, ask them to record on an index card three things they learned from today's lesson, two reasons why primary documents are used as forms of evidence of a life, and one question that they still have about the genre of biography or the work of the biographer.

Modifications for Learner Need. The following questions provide slightly different directions for the discussion, yet all of them connect to this class activity and to the work of a biographer. If the class is advanced, students can use these questions to guide their own discussions. Ask students the following:

> Would any of the following questions be of use to biographers? In what ways?

Look at the list, think about it, and then quickly turn to the person next to you and share your ideas:

- Who created the source and why? Was it created through a spur-of-the-moment act, a routine transaction, or a thoughtful, deliberate process?
- Did the recorder have firsthand knowledge of the event? Or did the recorder report what others saw and heard?
- Was the recorder a neutral party, or did the creator have opinions or interests that might have influenced what was recorded?
- Did the recorder produce the source for personal use, for one or more individuals, or for a large audience?
- Was the source meant to be public or private?
- Does the recorder seem to want to inform, entertain, or persuade others?
- How soon after the event itself did the recorder write or talk about it? What verb tense does the recorder use? What other linguistic evidence does the source contain of how much time has passed since the event (dates; modifiers such as "once upon a time," "recently," or "years ago"; references to contemporary historical events)?

This strategy informs teachers about how well a student is processing the information presented in the unit. The feedback received should guide a teacher's instructional plans. If some students are experiencing difficulty with the ideas presented in the unit, meet with them in small groups to provide additional instructional assistance.

Lesson 5: Analyzing Primary Sources and Turning Them Into a Credible Story

(two class periods)

Unit Sequence	Teacher Reflections
Concepts. Chronology, Challenge, Choices, Change, Patterns G3–4, G6, SD1–18, S1–3, S6, S8, S11	The purpose of this lesson is to have students experience the work of a biographer with primary documents. For this activity, they must extract information, select which evidence is most relevant, and decide how to organize the evidence they collect.
Writing a Biographical Sketch. Step One: Tell students that the first step in writing a biographical sketch is to *analyze the evidence* that the teacher will provide. Group students in heterogeneous teams of five. Provide each group with a set of primary documents about an individual at a particular historical or personal turning point (e.g., Nelson Mandela's release from prison and election to president, Clarence Thomas's confirmation hearings, Margaret Sanger's campaign for women's suffrage). Place the collection in an envelope. Be sure the envelope includes five artifacts from the following list: a video clip, audio recording, a letter or diary entry by the subject, a letter or diary entry about the subject, a speech, public record (sales records, licenses), transcript of an interview, and/or a photograph collection. As students enter the room, place these envelopes on team tables to begin the activity. Tell students that the purpose of this activity is to have them analyze this collection in a manner similar to that of a biographer. The analyses then will be used to write a biographical sketch focusing on a specific turning point in that person's life. Tell students the following: Today, you will be working in teams of five (show overhead with team and table assignments). At your tables, you will find an envelope that contains a collection of sources from an episodic event in the life	Selecting a topical person and situation can add to the success of this activity. We chose to structure this activity around an episode, situation, or event, because typically there are multiple issues and perspectives that arise from an episode in an individual life. This idea also accurately simulates the intellectual challenges biographers face when they select an individual to research and to write about. Individuals lead complex lives and face challenges and choices that involve many perspectives as well as other people. This activity also has the flexibility for a teacher to choose an episode about which he or she is more knowledgeable than the students. For example, a literature teacher might focus on a literary event that helped shape the writing of great poets and cause students to raise issues of poetic quality, personal grief, and reputation (e.g., Keats's reaction to the criticism of *Endymion* in his letters and Shelley's "Adonais" after Keats's death, as well as an excerpt of the critical essay that influenced these great writers). History teachers can create a box of collected sources that reveal the significance of a particular era, event, or exploration. We believe that the quality of students' performance will depend on the quality of the primary documents teachers select and the interactions teachers have with their students as they pose questions and help them to analyze the documents.

Unit Sequence	*Teacher Reflections*

of a subject. Each member of your team will be asked to take an object from the collection to analyze and try to find out what part of the subject's story this source reveals. Each of you will use a specific task sheet from the **Lesson 5 Worksheets: Analysis Tasks**. Each sheet includes a series of questions to guide your analysis.

Record your responses to these questions in your journal. You will want to recall all that you have learned from the previous activity and use this knowledge as you try to draw conclusions about the artifact and its relevance to the episode.

You must remember that your primary goal is to analyze and interpret this source so you can bring back information to your team regarding its importance and relevance to the whole story of your subject. You will conduct your analysis with members from the other teams who have been assigned to analyze the same artifact or source. For example, all the people who are analyzing the personal letter will meet at Table 1, all the photograph collection researchers will meet at Table 2, and so on. But remember, your major responsibility will be to help your home team understand the role your source has in telling the story.

Remind students that like any good historian, biographers analyze historical sources in many ways. First, biographers consider when, where, and why a document was created. They consider whether a source was created close to the location and time when the historical event occurred. They also consider the purpose of a source. Was it a personal diary or letter created to be private or public? Was the document created for the public or for private use? Did the composition of the image leave important elements out of the picture that would cause misinterpretation? Some primary

In creating these collections, some assistance can be found in databases found on the Internet. We suggest the Library of Congress (www.loc.gov) as a resource for many kinds of documents. It provides ready electronic access to vast collections of diaries, books, audio recordings, and photographs. History Matters (www .historymatters.gmu.edu) is a site that offers documents with a historical focus and superior guidelines for analyzing various primary sources using historians' tools. Another valuable electronic resource is DoHistory (www.dohistory.org). Also, some commercial packages gather documents for this kind of project, such as the *Civil War Collection* (ISBN: 081182644-9), which contains 24 meticulous reproductions of wartime documents and photographs. And those who love video newsreels can typically purchase many of these from the Internet. In addition, the Web sites can be used by students at a computer station located at the back of the classroom. Students can rotate at the computer stations in small groups to access the information that these sites provide.

The discussions students have while analyzing individual primary documents will reveal how all biographers necessarily bias or shape the information from letters, speeches, news stories, film, or diaries when they contextualize it by combining it with information from other sources. We have suggested questions in the **Lesson 5 Worksheets: Analysis Tasks (for a Letter, Video Clip, Newspaper Article, Diary Entry, Audio Clip, Speech, and Photograph)** to parallel the critical processes biographers must follow.

(Continued)

(Continued)

Unit Sequence	Teacher Reflections

sources may be judged more reliable than others, but every source is biased in some way. As a result, it is important for the biographer to read sources with a skeptical and critical mind.

Step Two: When the analyses are completed, reassemble the students in their original teams. Give them the second set of directions, which is for creating the *biographical episode* (see **Lesson 5 Worksheet: Writing and Research Tasks in the Biographical Episode**).

Now that your analyses are completed, your team is ready to work on your second task. As biographers begin to analyze and interpret the sources, eventually they understand that a story must be told. The time has now come for your team to decide how to create that story from the sources your team members analyzed. Ask yourselves these questions:

- What story will your team tell?
- How will the story be written?
- How will you prevent bias or misinterpretation or prevent overgeneralizing the data that you have gathered from these sources?

Now the challenge begins! Your team must creatively and collectively pool the data and write a biographical sketch of the subject connected to an episode in the subject's life by using the evidence summarized by the individual members of your team.

Debriefing. Allow students to share their biographical episodes. Encourage team members to share the challenges and decisions they encountered when writing the episode and how this might be

The purpose of the written biographical sketch is to have students combine diverse evidence to find meaningful information. Each group's essay will differ in organization and conclusion, leading to possible discussion about "truth." If groups trivialize or overgeneralize the evidence, they may need some guidance about or illustrations of those weaknesses.

Alternative formats can be used to write this biographical episode. The format that we have designed is very structured. Encourage students to suggest alternative formats that best address their learning preferences and that still meet the goals of the lesson. For example, if the class has already studied formal argumentation, the assignment for the biographical sketch could easily require groups to write a thesis statement about the role the subject played in a particular situation.

During the group writing, students should feel free to return to any of the evidence for verification or clarification, supporting it in the subsequent paragraphs. Teachers should circulate among the groups, providing guidance in the writing process.

Note that this activity can also help students learn to distinguish the relative value of multiple or even contradictory sources.

Optional Extension. The debriefing questions require students to compare these simulated experiences with those experienced by biographers. A wonderful follow-up would be to have a biographer,

Unit Sequence	Teacher Reflections
compared with the work of a biographer. Compare the writing formats that were used by the various team biographers. Do these formats parallel any of the formats used in the biographies they have read? Encourage students to share their ideas.	filmologist, archivist, historian, photographer, museum curator, news reporter, and/or journalist (invite a panel) into the classroom to discuss their work. Arrange to have the speakers discuss the varied approaches they use to conduct their research. Have students pose similar questions to these individuals. Compare their responses with those generated by the students.
Reflection. Provide time for students to reflect on the meaningfulness of the activities by addressing at least two of the four following questions: • What have we learned about the tools and methods used by biographers? How has this influenced your work? • What skills are required of the biographers? What challenges do they face when they gather evidence from many sources? What challenges did you face in this activity? • Which sources should be considered when writing a biography? Which sources did your team members find more difficult to use? • Are there certain traits or dispositions that a biographer must have to participate in this type of work? Which of these traits did you experience?	The questions that students are asked to reflect on are written in a parallel structure to encourage them to personalize the learning activities and compare themselves and the work that they have completed with the life and tasks of a biographer. We want students to experience what it is like to be a biographer and to increase their efficacy in using the skills and methods of a biographer. More important, we want to have students "see" that they have grown.

Lesson 6: Student Investigation

(four to five class periods)

Unit Sequence	Teacher Reflections
Concepts. Chronology, Challenge, Choices, Change, Identity, and Patterns G2–6, SD1–2, SD4–7, SD8–19, SD21, S1–4, S6–11 **Applying the Skills and Tools of the Biographer.** Tell students they now have the opportunity to apply the skills and	One of the purposes of the Curriculum of Practice is not only to engage students in the work of the biographer but also to examine the habits, affect, and ethics that permeate the work. This parallel has asked students to define and assume the role as a means of studying the discipline, encouraged students to value and engage

(Continued)

Unit Sequence	Teacher Reflections
tools of a biographer to investigate a question or issue that stems from their personal interaction with the biographies they have read.	in the intellectual struggle of the discipline, and challenged them to consider the implications of the ethical perspectives held by those who value and respect the field.

In some cases, students have become interested in their subject's particular response to an event or situation that caused them to change. Some students might be interested in exploring the historical context in which their subject lived and investigate how this time period shaped who the subject became or a career they pursued. Other students will want to learn more about the relative importance of the field that their subjects spent a lifetime pursuing. They could also expand or alter a hypothesis that they have about their subject, defend or refute conclusions by the biographer, and/or challenge or support information garnered from other documents. It is up to the students (with teacher guidance) to decide the direction for their research.

Once students have selected an issue, event, controversy, and so forth as the focus of study, they must assemble a set of primary and secondary sources that will address their inquiries. Suggest that they use the Internet, school and university libraries, and specialized databases to locate sources that can be used to answer their questions. Provide them with the sheet titled **Thinking Like a Biographer: The Research Protocol**, which guides this process. Tell students that they will use the findings from this research study as well as the research they conducted in the Core Curriculum to help them with their unit product.

Although we recognize that this research could have students become biographers in their community by collecting oral histories and by archiving historical records and photographs, the decision was made to extend and enhance the use of the skills and methodologies that biographers use as they write life stories and to grapple with the issues that biographers face as they conduct their research and begin their writing.

AID. Students who are ready for more challenging work can be encouraged to explore the ethical challenges that biographers face and explore how the field regulates and monitors the ethical behaviors and performances of its members. They can also investigate other challenges in the field by pursuing these questions:

- What are the unspoken truths regarding this genre? Do all literary critics agree that biography should be a genre?
- Historically, why was this genre selected, and has its purpose changed over the years?
- What is the responsibility of a biographer in revealing the "unflattering" parts of a subject's life or personality?
- How do biographers handle situations where they have discovered that their subjects have lied to them?

Lesson 7: Retelling the Stories With a Personal Touch

(three to four class periods)

Unit Sequence	*Teacher Reflections*
Concepts. Chronology, Challenge, Choices, Change, Identity G1–8, SD2–3, SD5–7, SD8–12, SD16, SD19–20, S2, S4, S9, S11 **Product Options.** After students have completed reading their biography and have located evidence to the questions that guided their research, present the following product options as the culminating research performance task. Students will use their findings to complete one of the following products:	The **Lesson 7 Rubric: Evaluating Student Research and Product Development** will help students prepare and assess their work. **Modifications for Learner Need.** The five activities allow students to select the format that best matches their learning preferences and readiness levels. Each activity requires students to identify the significant events or chronology of time in the subject's life, to reveal why this person is noteworthy, and to infuse into the story some of the personal choices and challenges that this individual faced, noting how these two things shaped their identity. In addition, each of the products requires students to use their research findings to contribute to the stories they are to tell. Although these products can be preselected for students, we would prefer to have students select them based on interest or modify them based on their own ideas. We encourage all students to create more meaningful tasks as long as they address the same requirements: choice, challenge, and identity. All five options offer multiple forms of preparation and publication: hard copy, electronic media, and Web sites.
Task 1. Biographical Account 1. Using your research, write a biographical account of the life of your subject for members of a selection team who are looking to nominate individuals to the Hall of Fame. The structure of this account must include an opening paragraph that gives your readers background information as to why this person is noteworthy and should receive this honor. This paragraph should answer the questions "who?" "what?" "when?"	Task 1 is intended for students who may require a more structured product. This product requires students to take the information they gathered and simply retell it for a specific audience.

(Continued)

(Continued)

Unit Sequence	Teacher Reflections

"where?" "why?" and "how?" In addition, you will want to make reference to the choices and challenges that were faced by your subject to show how these events helped shape his or her identity and made him or her worthy of Hall of Fame status.

2. The account then unfolds in paragraphs that retell a series of events, usually in chronological order. Refer to the timeline that you created during your research in the first part of this unit (Core Curriculum). As you tell this story, you must weave your research findings into this nomination.

3. The final paragraph is a type of conclusion with a comment on the contribution this person has made or a summary and evaluation of the person's achievements.

Task 2. Discussion by Your Subject Related to a Contemporary Issue

1. Look through newspapers, *Time* or *Newsweek* magazines, or even *Discover* for a contemporary event, issue, or concern that you think your subject would wish to discuss or would make an effort to influence. Select the contemporary event from a magazine and then divide the article into sections. Glue these sections of the article on the left-hand side of a piece of paper or type the paragraphs into your computer.

2. Running parallel to these sections, create a narrative passage that would reflect your subject's reaction to such an event, issue, or concern. Based on what you know about the challenges and choices your subject faced, and how these things shaped his or her identity, what would he or she say or how would the person react to this issue? Use the research that you found in your study and the evidence that you gathered to create text that would

Task 2 is a more complex task that requires students to make a connection between historical issues in the past and the present. In addition, this project requires students to create a dialogue paralleling that being spoken by their subject. Students who have come to understand their subject well and have empathized with the subject will have an easier time creating realistic dialogue.

Unit Sequence	*Teacher Reflections*

convey your subject's feelings. Try to include dialogue or quotes that sound authentic to the subject.

Task 3. Biography for Younger Readers

1. Knowing that the biography you read is probably too difficult for younger students to read, take a series of events in the life of your subject and create a children's biography that could be beneficial to your readers.

2. Before you begin your writing, first consider several biographies written for young children (e.g., Barbara Cooney's *Elenore* and Ruth Franchere's *Cesar Chavez*). These books share several features. They contain numerous illustrations, and they emphasize positive characteristics and situations. Use these texts to guide your writing. When creating the storyline for young people, consider how you can use the choices and challenges faced by your subject and how these circumstances shaped his or her identity. You will also want to notice how these items weave in the biographical data and how the characters are developed throughout the story. Your story should help young people understand the courageous acts displayed or how the subject's life might parallel an experience that a young person might face. The illustrations that you create should help reveal the story to these young readers.

3. As the story is told, you must also insert some of your research findings into the text or into the illustrations that you create.

Task 4. Illustrated Biography

1. Read *Starry Messenger: Galileo Galilei*, by Peter Sís. This author chose to have readers discover Galileo's search for truth in a world in which the church considered his findings to be dangerous. The author added

Task 3 is created for students who have recognized the personal contributions a subject has made that would be important to retell to young people. Using the books recommended, students who select this project have a model from which to work. They will need to consider the internal and external factors that shape the life they are going to retell, but they are required to retell it only in temporal time.

Task 4 is also complex in the types of decisions that are required of students to creatively weave the internal struggles or issues that the subject revealed in the biography while simultaneously being asked to pay attention to how the story will unfold in a sequential manner for

(Continued)

(Continued)

Unit Sequence	Teacher Reflections
authenticity to the biography by including Galileo's own writings within the text. As you read the text and view the illustrations, search for techniques the author uses to develop an understanding of the historical perspectives and cultural conditions of the time and Galileo's role in helping reshape this time.	young readers. This option requires students to condense a lengthy biography into a few pages. Teachers should carefully monitor documentation of all image sources students use in illustrating the project, even original images by the student.

2. Following a similar format and using your research notes, construct a biography that reveals to the readers not only the significance of the life of your subject and the contribution he or she made to society but also an understanding, through illustration, about his or her beliefs, the choices and challenges he or she faced, and/or the historical context of the time period.

Task 5. Review for Students in Future Classes

1. Think of the students who take this class next year. Your purpose is to tell them whether they would be likely to enjoy the biography you read.

2. Tell your readers what features of the biography would or would not appeal to them. Consider such variables as the level of detail, the writer's style (vocabulary, sentence length and variety, etc.), historical period, relevance to current events, and other features important to you and your friends. Be sure to include your judgment of how well the biography reveals to its readers the subject's reactions to the chances and choices in life and how the subject dealt with challenges.

3. As you write the recommendation, you must creatively use your research findings by including them in the text or in your illustrations.

Task 5 allows students with strong personal opinions a way to communicate them to near-peers, students only one year younger. The literary quality of the biography becomes primary and the content secondary for students who choose this option. Students must still use the content of the biography to support their recommendations.

CURRICULUM OF CONNECTIONS LESSON

Lesson 8: Meeting of the Minds

(two to three class periods)

Unit Sequence	Teacher Reflections
Concepts. Patterns and Identity G2–3, G7–8, SD2–5, SD7, SD14–16, S2, S4, S11 **Introduction.** Introduce the first lesson in this parallel by sharing the following information prior to the student learning activity: As student biographers, you have committed yourself to a distinctive intellectual project by analyzing a life through the recordings of other biographers and by investigating these lives using the tools and methods biographers use to trace a life. For example: • Why might it be important to identify commonalities among these individuals—to identify similar traits, skills, dispositions, and the products and services these individuals share? • What can we learn from these lives that would be helpful to us as individuals, learners, researchers, and someone who may be interested in the career of their selected subject? (Record these responses on a chart and then continue with the teacher talk.) Researchers who analyze biographies often try to reveal factors that influence these individual lives and try to determine if there are patterns or commonalities in their characteristics. They often wonder what it takes to live an accomplished or productive life so that others may follow in their footsteps. Some researchers want to analyze these lives to reveal how leaders are created so that these traits can be used to train others for leadership positions. Others researchers study lives to identify the skills and dispositions that are required to carry out similar types of work that can be replicated in the future.	The lessons in the Curriculum of Connections are designed to have the students use ideas and information from multiple contexts to generate new hypotheses or theories about the lives of individuals who make contributions that positively affect the lives of others. Students have come to understand that the genre of biography helps us understand how individuals make meaning in their lives, how individuals face choices and challenges, and how professional biographers chronicle lives. The purpose of this parallel is to have students consider if there is a set of universal traits that helps explain productivity in the lives of people, across specific disciplines, and among all disciplines. The teacher talk has been created to assist students in understanding that biographical data is often used as a major source of analysis to reveal patterns in behavior. This also reinforces the idea that different disciplines use biographical data to answer different sets of questions. Researchers in psychology, sociology, and history may be interested in the same topic (i.e., individual lives); however, they pursue this topic by looking through a different set of lenses and by asking different sets of questions. We have included in this teacher talk various disciplinary perspectives that should be shared with the students to instill curiosity about the use of biographies in research. This will help students realize that by studying other people, much can be learned about the individuals across time, location, cultures, and gender. There is great similarity in the way we live our lives, and the differences among us help make us unique. Through peeking into the lives of others and identifying recurring traits that help explain behavior,

(Continued)

(Continued)

Unit Sequence	*Teacher Reflections*
Many of the individuals you studied led accomplished lives and made contributions to their families, their communities, and the world at large. The questions then become the following: • Why, in what ways, and for what reasons have these individuals distinguished themselves from the crowd? • Is this need to produce or create a meaningful life driven by money, interest, a sense of purpose, or destiny? In the field of psychology, researchers are always interested in these questions. They may take on a study to learn the habits of mind these individuals possess so that we can understand how they act, how they plan, how they think, and how they behave. By analyzing these traits, we become more knowledgeable about ourselves, and we begin to reflect on our personal lives and how we compare with the lives we admire. The words of others can shape our behavior and change the direction in which we are leading our lives. Researchers in the field of psychology are also interested in finding out how individuals face obstacles and challenges in their lives that might help others understand how varying lives differ in terms of resiliency. Sociologists are interested in studying the effect of culture on individual lives. They ask what types of environments hinder or support a creative life and how belonging to varying cultural groups encourages or discourages a life. Also, these researchers may be interested in analyzing the types of environments certain individuals came from to provide some insight to the type of support received from those environments. It is also common for various disciplines to study the lives of those who have made contributions to a particular discipline or field of study to reveal distinguishing traits	motivation, will, and drive, students can begin to seek identity with some of these individuals. **AID.** Some students will be ready to read the research of scholars who have used biographical data to analyze the lives of others. These students should be introduced to H. Gardner's *Creating Minds: An Anatomy of Creativity Seen Through the Lives of Freud, Einstein, Picasso, Stravinsky, Eliot, Graham, and Gandhi* (1993). This book profiles seven creative individuals who each reinvented an area of human endeavor. Students who are ready for instruction that provides more expertise in understanding how biographical data are used by psychologists can use the profiles from this book to compare and contrast Gardner's findings with their own individual analysis of their subjects. Students can also compare and contrast their research with Dr. Joseph Renzulli's research. He has identified co-cognitive behaviors that are the traits society finds in individuals who have changed the world, such as courage, optimism, romance with a topic or discipline, sensitivity to human concerns, physical and mental energy, vision, and a sense of destiny. His research article can be obtained from the following Web site and can be used to compare and contrast what the students find in their analyses with that found by Renzulli and his colleagues: www.sp.uconn.edu/~nrcgt/sem/expandgt.html. These Curriculum of Connections activities have been purposefully designed to assist students in identifying the underlying traits, dispositions, and so on that may

Unit Sequence	*Teacher Reflections*
or skills or even a lifestyle that all members of the discipline commonly share. From these lives, we can learn how our lives might unfold if we are interested in a particular discipline.	coexist with intelligence in helping explain a productive, creative life. It is often easier to identify these traits in others before we identify them in ourselves. The Curriculum of Connections also provides students with the time to articulate a set of generalizations that can be derived from these lives before asking them to look at their own lives for the application of these ideas. The Curriculum of Identity will then require students to apply some of these traits as they work on a self-selected project.
Introduction to Comparative Analyses. Tell students the following: Now the time has come for you to consider if the lives you have investigated share anything in common. To conduct this analysis, you will first want to look at these lives as individuals, then collectively as members of a disciplinary perspective, and finally across all disciplinary fields of study. You will use the **Comparative Analysis Chart: Round 1—Identifying Distinguishing Traits, Skills, Dispositions, and Products/Services of the Individual** to record your responses to the following questions:	The purpose of the first and second rounds of analysis is to engage students in social science research as they try to search for patterns—for revealing similarities and instructive differences in those that create. The second goal is for the students to generate a set of principles that governs creative human activity and to realize that it is the act of what they do and the challenges they take on in specific fields that contribute to a meaningful life. In these analyses, students are asked a key question: "What connections do you see between the lives you are reading about and your own life and times?"
1. What are the distinguishing *personality* or *environmental traits* that cause some people to use their intellectual, motivational, and creative assets in ways that lead to outstanding creative productivity? 2. What are the *skills* and *dispositions* these individuals use as they carry out their work? 3. What types of products or services did they provide for the good of humanity? What issues, concerns, or perspectives (i.e., economic, political, social, technological, cultural, environmental, etc.) did these individuals reflect in their work?	The analysis was set up for students to collect data, examine these data, identify the traits that individuals possess, categorize group traits that exist within a discipline, and determine the degree to which there is overlap in the traits that these creative individuals share collectively. The Curriculum of Connections bears a strong resemblance to the Core Curriculum in that it examines the concepts and principles within this discipline, but the purpose for making connections in this parallel is to identify macroconcepts (overarching concepts that connect many disciplines and topics), themes, principles, generalizations, processes, or dispositions across disciplines.

(Continued)

Unit Sequence	Teacher Reflections
You will first answer these questions by completing the chart about your individual. The second analysis will be conducted with other members of your class who studied people from a similar discipline. In the third analysis, all of you will come together to see if there is anything that can collectively be identified as the distinguishing traits, skills, dispositions, and products that cut across all of the individual lives you have studied during this biography unit.	As students progress through the three analyses, students take on a detective role. They develop rules about how these individuals work and, in this case, how the lives of the subjects they have read about create. Then they actively search for the ways in which these same characteristics, concepts, processes, dispositions, rules, and principles apply in new contexts. This deductive search for meaningful connections and analogies helps students achieve deeper understanding by drawing conclusions about new and unfamiliar sets of information and about life itself. Although these questions have been generated to guide the analyses, students should be encouraged to add other traits or characteristics they think might be interesting to analyze across disciplines.
Comparative Analyses. Distribute the chart to the students and assist them in completing the first analysis. To accommodate academic student readiness within your class, teachers should meet with students in small groups to encourage and scaffold the analyses. Encourage the students to use a thesaurus to identify adjectives that support the type of personality traits the students consider. You may wish to ask other questions that may prompt the identification of these characteristics and establish a sense of order to the analyses. For example: • How did your individual behave? • What caused him or her to want to pursue this field of study? • When times were difficult, what characteristics did the person reveal through the actions that he or she took?	**Modifications for Learner Need.** It might be helpful to have the students compare and contrast each of the characteristics one at a time, using highlighter pens to record overlaps in the data. Students can also use sticky notes to help locate and note the characteristics that are to be placed on the charts. It may be that the chart format needs to be changed to match a particular learning style. The format is not the major concern for the analyses; the idea behind identifying these traits and seeking understanding of the commonality shared among individual lives is of greatest importance. Encourage students to create other analyses charts they feel will help them complete the project.
For the second analysis, ask students to meet in like discipline groups and to use the **Comparative Analysis Chart: Round 2—Identifying Distinguishing Traits, Skills, Dispositions, and Products/Services of Individuals in a Particular Discipline**. Students should record the commonalities	The second activity focuses on a disciplinary analysis to help students identify how disciplinarians work in their field, the traits that help them to complete their work, and the skills and dispositions required to work in this field of study. You might also want to probe how these traits

Unit Sequence	*Teacher Reflections*

that individuals within a discipline share and note those that do not appear to be universal to those who work in that particular discipline. They can begin this task by using highlighter pens to identify the commonalities that were shared and a second colored marker to denote differences. The students should be encouraged to note patterns that exist between the word choices or phrases that are similar yet different and to identify larger categories or discuss words or phrases that they can agree on and place these in the boxes.

When the chart is completed and the students reach consensus on the traits each group of specific disciplinarians shared, they should select a representative who will speak for their group during the final analysis.

The final analysis should be conducted by having the students compare and contrast their findings across all disciplines. At this stage of analysis, the students will be looking for recurring patterns of behavior, environmental and personality traits, skills, dispositions, and products. They will label these characteristics so that commonalities can be detected.

Discussion. Host an open forum discussion to identify these traits as the students report from various groups. Discuss the selection of group word choices and refine the words or phrases that describe traits of creative producers in all disciplines. Use the **Comparative Analysis Chart: Round 3—Identifying Distinguishing Traits, Skills, Dispositions, and Products/Services of the Individuals Across All Disciplines** to record group responses.

Conclusion and Assessment. After the students have identified the characteristics, distribute an index card and ask students to respond individually to these questions:

are useful to the discipline and what values and perspective each discipline offers humanity in understanding life. Assist students in identifying what connections they see between what they are studying and their own life and times. Help students address the question, "Is there a connection between those who pursue these fields of study and the dispositions and skills that I possess?"

AID. During the final analysis, ask students who need more challenge to identify if and how the perspectives of these individuals were shaped by time, place, cultures, events, and circumstances.

These questions are used to move students into making generalizations about how the act of creating can influence one's identity. These generalizations can be recorded in

(Continued)

(Continued)

Unit Sequence	Teacher Reflections
1. If these traits are those that are shared among individuals, how does this knowledge apply to your life and to the world at large? 2. What do you think is the role of individuals in the evolution of specific disciplines and of the issues embedded in the disciplines? 3. What generalizations can you make about the relationship between these traits and the development of an individual's sense of identity?	journal entries or by having students identify the relationship between these traits and the act of creating. We have posed these questions as a way of intentionally setting up the next parallel, the Curriculum of Identity, in which students will be asked to consider a project that places them in the position of considering how these generalizations and principles that have been identified in this parallel connect to their own lives.

CURRICULUM OF IDENTITY LESSON

Lesson 9: Personal Commitment to a Creative Action

(semester-long project or senior project)

Unit Sequence	Teacher Reflections
Concepts. Challenge, Choices, Chances G1–8, with a focus on G8, SD 2–3, SD5–7, SD13, SD16–17, SD19–21, S1–12 **Introduction.** To set up the Curriculum of Identity lessons and projects, tell students the following: We have spent a great deal of time identifying how individuals face challenges and choices and why and how they make contributions to humanity. We have also discovered the traits and characteristics that helped these individuals live a meaningful life. What would you say if I asked you this question: "What do you do in the course of a day that requires courage, special effort, conquest of self, ingenuity, perseverance, sacrifice, or use of special skills?" Often we take these qualities for granted and don't give ourselves enough credit for some of our accomplishments. Share these accomplishments with a partner or by responding to this question in a personal journal entry. You have found in your study of biographies that individual lives varied in	This parallel stems from the Core Curriculum parallel but also applies the key ideas and skills that were addressed in the Curriculum of Connections and parallels the work found in the Curriculum of Practice. The lessons in the Curriculum of Identity ask students to understand and apply the lessons biographies reveal more fully by connecting them to their lives and experiences; increase awareness of their need for growth; and think about themselves. As stewards of a discipline, they may contribute to that discipline and/or through it by selecting a life filled with meaningful work and using traits conducive to productivity. The Curriculum of Identity lessons ask students to use the curriculum they have experienced in the other parallels as a catalyst for self-definition and self-understanding, with the belief that by looking outward to the discipline, students can find a means of looking inward. The teaching and learning strategies used in this parallel is more project-based to allow students to select a project that is

Unit Sequence	*Teacher Reflections*

the common good that their actions served. You found out that there are commonalities in the traits and environmental factors that helped shape these lives, and the one thing they did share in common was a dream to do something to make the world a better place. The people you studied had concerns about environmental, political, spiritual, social, cultural, and historical issues that helped define the work they pursued. They often risked a great deal either personally or professionally to make contributions to a discipline. At times, they faced challenges and choices that influenced their actions or caused them to continue their quest.

Now the time has come for you to consider how all of this relates to your life and how you can begin to take action based on your concerns, challenges, and choices. We are all affected by the events in our lives. These events challenge our actions and behaviors and help shape who we become.

Products and Services. For your final project, I want you to select some problem, issue, or concern that you wish to pursue, determine a course of action that you will take, and create a product or service that you will share with others. Some of you may choose to take action, chronicle the events, and offer solutions, while others may wish to profile individual lives that have made contributions to your life or to

personally meaningful to them or to a group of students. For some students this project may focus on an issue that deals with personal struggles, challenges, and choices, similar to those lives that they studied. For other students, their projects may address local, state, or national concerns and problems in any discipline. Students can also design service-learning projects to implement based on the identification of a particular problem. Whichever project is chosen, the students are asked to reflect on what they have learned from the previous ideas and skills presented in the other parallels to shape their work in this parallel.

The structure for this project-based approach has been purposefully designed to provide students an opportunity to explore how their lives can impact others and/or how actions can be taken to overcome obstacles and challenges in their own lives. These projects require students to look outward to the key ideas that biographies and/or autobiographies reveal and to look inward to determine how the key ideas apply to their own lives. The teacher must serve as a guide to this process and encourage students to identify projects that they are personally interested in completing. The project serves as an application of all the principles in the unit and, in particular, a focus on the development of personal identity through the actions an individual pursues.

The format used in this Curriculum of Identity parallel helps students to formulate questions that they want to answer, to sequence a series of steps to complete the project, to consider how the project will affect others, and to return full circle in assessing how this project relates to the study of biographies and how personal identity is formed. the lives of our community, state,

(Continued)

(Continued)

Unit Sequence	Teacher Reflections
or nation. Still others will wish to take on a certain cause—one that tries to right a wrong, one that provides awareness, or one that causes you to reflect on a personal event in your life and how you wish for others to learn from your challenges.	Many students do not see themselves as producers or problem solvers. Teachers must guide this process and encourage and support the students. To engender efficacy in completing this project, a teacher can begin to collect stories of students who have implemented plans to solve community problems, stories of young people who have faced challenges and choices and have created a plan for overcoming these obstacles in life, and stories that show how the work of young people has made a difference in the lives of others. Asking students to identify challenges, concerns, or issues that they wish to address moves students toward reflecting on and identifying how their own lives are shaped by an ongoing participation in life's events. At times, their actions will display courage similar to those individuals they studied.

Project Tasks.

1. Your first task is to identify a problem that you feel strongly about and plan a course of actions you will take to address this issue by using your own personal strengths, courage, and perseverance. Then implement these actions, chronicle them, and create a product or provide a service that addresses your problem or concern.

2. The second part of this task requires you to reflect on how your work parallels the lives of biographers and/or the lives of the subjects you read about in your biographies.

3. Finally, explain what your project work revealed to you about your awareness of your own preferences, strengths, interests, and need for growth in this field of study.

You have several options to choose from to complete this project. For example, you can

1. create autobiographical self-portraits, memoirs, or autobiographies that highlight a personal struggle that you faced in your life. You will discuss the factors that shaped how you have faced these challenges and design a plan for future goals;	Students who select Option 1 will acquire new self-knowledge about the relationship between life's events and their personal identity.
2. design a personal plan that is based on your past life and identify an obstacle or problem to research and seek solutions;	Option 2 will help students acquire self-knowledge in learning how to overcome challenges and to learn how resiliency is acquired and used to shape identity.
3. write a biographical sketch of a contemporary local individual who demonstrates some of the traits and Option 4 is for students who wish to	Option 3 asks students to engage in the work of the biographer to chronicle the lives of others and engage in the type of work that biographers offer in understanding a life.

Unit Sequence	Teacher Reflections
take action to solve a problem they identify. characteristics found in the biographies that have read. You will then profile these individuals, using the tools and methodologies of the biographer; or	
4. locate a problem that needs to be solved, one that requires you to stick out your neck and take responsibility for resolving the problem. I have listed some ideas from which you can brainstorm ideas to help you get started on your project. The world needs heroes, people with vision and courage, people who are willing to contribute to the solution of problems. The efforts you take can vary depending on your personal interest, and the products you create should be selected to reflect the best way in which you like to express yourself.	Option 4 is for students who wish to take action to solve a problem they identify. All of the projects place students in the role of creator, and each option provides a potential opportunity for them to gain more insight in understanding the lives of the individuals they studied and the personal traits that helped shape these lives in comparison to their own lives.
To help you gather ideas for this project, I have created several learning centers (see **Taking Action: Interest Development Centers**). Today, I want you to rotate through these centers, look through the materials that I have placed at each center, and read through the various project ideas that others have done to assist you in generating possible ideas for your project. After you read through these profiles and investigate the Web sites listed on the handout, you will complete your own project plan description.	To enhance a student's ability to select a course of action, set up the classroom with interest centers filled with examples of stories, publications, and so on that show various ways to make contributions. The **Taking Action** activity provides examples for students to read about other young people who are engaged in similar types of investigations. Students can use technology to access service learning project examples to spark their interest. Project sites such as What Kids Can Do (www.whatkidscando .org), Welcome to Giraffe Country (www.giraffe.org), or the Montana Heritage Project (www.edheritage.org) are excellent examples of students making contributions to the world in meaningful ways.
	The options on the Taking Action sheet are only a few of the projects possible. While we preferred students to take on individual projects that were of personal interest, you can have students select an area of interest to pursue as a class or in teams.

(Continued)

(Continued)

Unit Sequence	Teacher Reflections
In *planning* the project, tell students the following:	The **Action Planning Guide** was developed to assist students in the planning process. By making thorough plans, students can implement the actions they take in an efficient manner. Teachers will need to schedule time to meet with the various teams to assist them in accomplishing their plans and obtaining the resources that are needed to complete the project. Teachers will find themselves helping students to contact individuals within the community to support their projects. The teacher needs to serve as a coach, facilitator, and managerial and resource assistant to students as they work on these projects.
Now that you have read through the project options, I want you to use the **Action Planning Guide** to help you identify what you will do and the actions you will take to complete the project. You and your teammates will be able to work on this project once a week until the end of the semester (or other appropriate date). The project that you select should be personally meaningful to you and one that demonstrates actions that you take to make a difference.	
As students complete their projects, work to move students toward publication of their work. If, for example, students tackle a community problem that leads to a solution or a change in the actions of others, they could publish their work in the local paper or possibly register it online at the What Kids Can Do Web site. In some cases, the work might be profiled at a local museum or offered as a service publication for some organization. Assist the students in locating an audience for their work and publication opportunities to increase the usefulness of their ideas. In some cases, the project is a very personal account of a challenge. It is important to realize that students who are working on these types of projects may be sensitive to public exposure and their audience may be themselves.	Helping students publish their work can help them feel like professionals. Students should move toward expertise in creating photo-essays or photo biographies, writing editorials, or taking action to solve a problem in a similar fashion to that of the practicing professional. In moving toward publication, students will learn how to identify an audience for their work and begin to apply the skills and methods professionals use to create outstanding products. In some cases, students may need to learn how to use digital photography to create images and learn how to create a layout for their product. Other students will need to learn how to transcribe interviews to complete their project work. If possible, invite community professionals into the classroom to assist students in creating products of high quality.
Assessment. Ask students to reflect on what they have learned about themselves in relation to the study of individuals' lives and to note the evolution of their abilities as they worked on their projects. Have students use the **Lesson 9 Worksheet: Assessing My Project** to self-assess the	The assessment worksheet is simply one way to have students self-assess their growth. It would also be possible to ask a practicing professional to assess the quality of a student's project and provide feedback for continuing growth. For students who are ready for AID, feedback from a

Unit Sequence	Teacher Reflections
completion of their project. The rubrics found in the other parallels in this unit can also be used to guide the quality of student work as the project progresses.	practicing professional would be particularly appropriate.

Debriefing. Close the unit of study by reviewing what students have come to understand. Tell students the following:

We have come full circle in our study. You have read biographies, analyzed these lives to identify qualities that set these individuals apart from the crowd, and acquired knowledge of how biographers conduct their work. In the final phase of this unit, you accepted the challenge to identify a problem and took on some form of action. Your work was profiled by creating a product that you shared with another audience. For our final discussion, I want you to consider these questions and reflect on these in your journal:

1. How would you compare your own personal qualities with those that we read about?	Question 1 is asked to help students reflect on the traits identified in the Curriculum of Connections parallel.
2. Were you affected by any of the actions that you took in your project? How do these actions compare with those of the individual you read about during this unit of study?	Question 2 probes the causal relationships between what we do and the contribution these actions make to our identity.
3. What have you learned about yourself during this unit of study? How does it redirect your efforts and understanding of who you are?	The last two questions are structured to probe a student's reflection of new self-knowledge regarding how he or she has grown both personally and professionally by engaging in the project.
4. How have you changed during this process?	
Celebrating the Work. Students will host a celebration to share their final projects. Invite families, community leaders, and individuals who would be interested in the students' work.	The completion of the projects should be shared with others in the community to let students know how their work can impact the lives of many.

Lesson 2 Worksheet: Through the Eyes of an Author

Jean Fritz

"On Writing Biography"

The reason for writing biography for children is the same as for writing biography for adults: to explore human behavior, to come to grips with specific characters interrelating with their specific times. This is not as obvious as it sounds. It was once a commonly held assumption (one that still persists in some quarters) that biographies written for children should portray idealized heroes and heroines, models held up by the adult world to inspire children to attain virtue and, by implication, its concomitant rewards. Furthermore, according to some educators, the motivation of characters should not be examined, only their deeds.

Such an approach, it seems to me, is dull, unrealistic, and unfair. Children look for clues to life. They want the truth, they need the truth, and they deserve it. So I try to present characters honestly with their paradoxes and their complexities, their strengths and their weaknesses. To do this, I involve myself in as much research as I would if I were writing a biography for adults. Contrary to what I call "old-fashioned" biography for children, I do not invent dialogue. I use dialogue only when I can document it. If the text is meaty enough, I do not think that children need facts dressed up in fictional trimmings. Indeed, children welcome hard, specific facts that bring characters to life—not only the important facts but [also] those small vivid details that have a way of lighting up an event or a personality. Had I been present, for instance, to hear Patrick Henry give his famous "liberty or death" speech, I would certainly have been impressed by his dramatic oratory, but I would also have remembered the man in the balcony who became so excited, he spit a wad of tobacco into the audience below. The trivial and the significant generally travel hand in hand, and indeed I suspect that most people find that memory of trivial-off-the-record detail serves to nail down memory itself. I think of history and biography as *story* and am convinced that the best stories are the true ones.

SOURCE: Norton, Donna E., Norton, Saundra, *Through The Eyes of a Child: An Introduction to Children's Literature*, 6th Edition, (c) 2003. Reprinted by permission of Pearson Education, Inc., Upper Saddle River, NJ.

From "The Rambler," #60 by Samuel Johnson
(originally published October 13, 1750)

I have often thought that there has rarely passed a life of which a judicious and faithful narrative would not be useful; for not only every man has, in the mighty mass of the world, great numbers in the same condition with himself, to whom his mistakes and miscarriages, escapes and expedients, would be of immediate and apparent use; but there is such a uniformity in the state of man, considered apart from adventitious and separable decorations and disguises, that there is scarce any possibility of good or ill but is common to human kind. A great part of the time of those who are placed at the greatest distance by fortune or by temper must unavoidably pass in the same manner; and though, when the claims of nature are satisfied, caprice and vanity and accident begin to produce discriminations and peculiarities, yet the eye is not very heedful or quick which cannot discover the same causes still terminating their influence in the same effect, though sometimes accelerated, sometimes retarded, or perplexed by multiplied combinations. We are all prompted by the same motives, all deceived by the same fallacies, all animated by hope, obstructed by danger, entangled by desire, and seduced by pleasure.

It is frequently objected to relations of particular lives, that they are not distinguished by any striking or wonderful vicissitudes. The scholar who passed his life among his books, the merchant who conducted only his own affairs, the priest whose sphere of action was not extended beyond that of his duty, are considered as no proper objects of public regard, however they might have excelled in their several stations, whatever might have been their learning, integrity, and piety. But this notion arises from false measures of excellence and dignity, and must be eradicated by considering that, in the esteem of uncorrupted reason, what is of most use is of most value.

If the biographer writes from personal knowledge, and makes haste to gratify the public curiosity, there is danger lest his interest, his fear, his gratitude, or his tenderness overpower his fidelity, and tempt him to conceal, if not to invent. There are many who think it an act of piety to hide the faults or failings of their friends, even when they can no longer suffer by their detection; we therefore see whole ranks of characters adorned with uniform panegyric, and not to be known from one another but by extrinsic and casual circumstances. "Let me remember," says Hale, "when I find myself inclined to pity a criminal, that there is likewise a pity due to the country." If we owe regard to the memory of the dead, there is yet more respect to be paid to knowledge, to virtue, and to truth.

SOURCE: Text excerpted from www.samueljohnson.com/ram60.html.

Lesson 2 Worksheet: Reflections on Jean Fritz's and Samuel Johnson's Words

What do the essayists say about writing a biography that you find important to remember?	*How will this information shape the selection of a biography you wish to read during this unit?*	*In what ways can you use this advice to shape your reading? What should you pay attention to when reading a biography? What would be interesting to note about the life of your individual?*

Research Recording Format: Three-Column Journal Entry

Questions	Evidence	Inference
Use these questions to guide your research.	As you read through your text, find quotations, passages, or references that answer the question. Mark each reference with a page number.	Describe the inferences that you are making about your subject.
What significant events or issues did your subject face? For each one you list, indicate whether it results from chance or choice.		
What type of education or training did your subject receive?		
Who are significant people or mentors who helped shape your subject's life?		
In what field or fields is the person known?		
What incident, heroic action, personal experience, or related circumstance has made your subject of national interest?		
What personal internal or emotional challenges did your subject face? How did he or she handle these challenges? Were there times when your subject was at odds with any of the decisions he or she faced?		

Alternative Research Recording Format: File Folder Layout

Research Questions	List of References
Research Question #1	1. _____
	2. _____
	3. _____
Research Question #2	
Research Question #3	
Research Question #4	
Research Question #5	Data Envelope

Recording Charts: Chronology of Events and Relative Importance of Dates

Chronology of Events

Date	Description of Event or Issue Faced (p.)	Why was this a significant event in your subject's life?

Relative Importance of Dates

As you chart these events and judge their relative importance, write an explanation that describes why this event might be considered more significant than other events. Consider the following questions: What did this event lead to? What changes took place in your subject's life that were the direct result of this event? How did your subject respond to the event?

Lesson 3 Rubric: Biography and Autobiography Research

Performances	*Novice*	*Competent*	*Expert*
Evidence gathered	Evidence that is gathered from the text does not address the questions posed for the research and lacks variety.	Evidence is gathered from the text in two or more categories to address the questions posed for the research.	A variety of evidence has been gathered from the text to address the questions posed for the research (quotations, statements, dates, documented events that marked turning points in the subject's life).
Critical lens	Summarizes or uses faulty analysis; little or no evidence used to support the analysis; chart incomplete.	Organizes evidence, assertions, and analysis around central questions that are posed; uses evidence to support the analysis; completes the chart coherently but not in a persuasive manner.	Efficiently organizes evidence, assertions, and analysis around central questions that are posed; uses convincing evidence to support the analysis; completes the chart coherently and persuasively.
Interpretation of evidence	Demonstrates a misinterpretation of the evidence gathered to classify the evidence under the appropriate categorical question; bases inference on hasty or cursory look at only one or two pieces of information; does not consider consequences.	Demonstrates general understanding or interpretation of the evidence gathered in helping classify the evidence under the appropriate categorical question; bases inference on examination of information and some consideration of consequences.	Demonstrates sophisticated and thorough interpretation of the evidence gathered in helping classify the evidence under the appropriate categorical question; bases inference on a thorough examination of the evidence, an exploration of reasonable alternatives, and an evaluation of the consequences.
Connections	Makes inappropriate or incorrect connections between one or more forms of evidence and other issues (historical, genre, contemporary concerns).	Makes appropriate connections (concrete, foundational, and personal) among two or more forms of evidence and other issues (historical, genre, contemporary issues).	Makes insightful connections (abstract, transformational, and societal) among two or more forms of evidence and other issues (historical setting, genre, contemporary concerns).
Conventions	Communication is impaired by errors; little or no use of conventions of quotations and citations.	Some mechanical errors, but communication is not impaired; demonstrates knowledge of accepted conventions of quotations and citations.	Mechanical errors are rare or nonexistent; follows appropriate conventions of quotations and citations.

Homework: Finding Evidence in Your Daily Life

Before class tomorrow, you need to collect physical evidence of your life over the past week. Gather these artifacts from three or four of the suggested categories below and put them in a sack, which will be brought back to class to use in an activity that will help us understand the work of a biographer.

- Evidence You Leave Behind (Did you leave behind any records of your activities, such as a diary entry, a letter to a friend or relative, an e-mail message, a phone call?)
- Evidence Left Behind by Others (Are there traces of your activities that appear in records someone else created, such as a calendar entry, a letter from a friend, notes, a friend's diary?)
- Evidence Left in School Records (Would any evidence appear in school records, employment records, in the school or local newspaper, speeches, in government records or police reports?)
- Testimonials (Are there individuals who could offer testimonial—oral history—about your activities? Who and why? You can include audio or video recordings or written transcripts.)
- Other Sources of Evidence (Are there material objects to locate that you use every day, trash you throw away, items in your room or locker?)

Lesson 5 Worksheets: Analysis Tasks

Analysis Tasks for a Letter

As a biographer, you will analyze historical sources using many intellectual tools. Initially, you must answer the journalist's questions (who, what, when, where, why, and how) as you analyze this source. In addition, consider the proximity of the source's creation to the event described and the stated purpose of the source. You must realize and control your own assumptions and biases and also consider the internal assumptions and biases of each source. In other words, a biographer must examine each source with a skeptical and critical mind.

- Who wrote the letter?
- What is the subject's rhetorical relation to the letter (e.g., writer, recipient, subject)?
- What information about the subject does the letter reveal? (Be sure to include personal opinion, rumor, gossip, and emotion as kinds of information.)
- How reliable would you judge the information to be based on the author of the letter?
- What is the date of the letter? How might that date be significant?
- What might readers learn from the physical condition of the letter? (Determine the quality of the handwriting or typing, stains of tears or blood or food, the kind and size of paper, the color of ink, etc.)
- What is the literary style of the letter, and what does it show us? (Look for sentence structure, nicknames or titles such as *Mr.*, length of sentences, vocabulary, and punctuation.)

Finally, what conclusion might a biographer draw from these responses and include in the biography?

Analysis Tasks for a Video Clip

As a biographer, you will analyze historical sources using many intellectual tools. Initially, you must answer the journalist's questions (who, what, when, where, why, and how) as you analyze this source. In addition, consider the proximity of the source's creation to the event described and the stated purpose of the source. You must realize and control your own assumptions and biases and also consider the internal assumptions and biases of each source. In other words, a biographer must examine each source with a skeptical and critical mind.

- What is the date of the clip?
- Who or what service produced it?
- What is its type: newsreel, documentary, news footage, commercial film, TV commercial, comedy sketch, and so on?
- What information about the subject does the video reveal?
- How reliable would you judge the information to be? What is the basis of your judgment (e.g., What is the camera's point of view? Is editing evident? What is going on in the clip? How realistic is the setting?)?
- How would you label the style of the clip? (Is it comical, intellectual, tragic, impromptu, staged?)

Finally, what conclusions might a biographer draw from these responses and include in the biography?

Analysis Tasks for a Newspaper Article

As a biographer, you will analyze historical sources using many intellectual tools. Initially, you must answer the journalist's questions (who, what, when, where, why, and how) as you analyze this source. In addition, consider the proximity of the source's creation to the event described and the stated purpose of the source. You must realize and control your own assumptions and biases and also consider the internal assumptions and biases of each source. In other words, a biographer must examine each source with a skeptical and critical mind.

- What is the date of the article?
- Who or what newspaper published it? A local newspaper might present an issue differently than a national paper, such as the *New York Times* or the *Wall Street Journal*.
- What is its type: news story, editorial, feature, advertisement?
- Does the writer include eyewitness reports? Was the reporter present?
- What information about the subject does the article reveal?
- Where in the newspaper does the article appear (e.g., front page, back section, entertainment section)?
- How reliable would you judge the information to be? What is the basis of your judgment? What is the reporter's or newspaper's slant? Do pictures or drawings support the article? What emphasis do the pictures or drawings have?
- How would you label the style of the article? (Is it comical, intellectual, tragic, impromptu, staged?)

Finally, what conclusions might a biographer draw from these responses and include in the biography?

Analysis Tasks for a Diary Entry

As a biographer, you will analyze historical sources using many intellectual tools. Initially, you must answer the journalist's questions (who, what, when, where, why, and how) as you analyze this source. In addition, consider the proximity of the source's creation to the event described and the stated purpose of the source. You must realize and control your own assumptions and biases and also consider the internal assumptions and biases of each source. In other words, a biographer must examine each source with a skeptical and critical mind.

- What is the date of the entry?
- Who wrote it?
- What is its type: private, personal?
- If the subject of the biography is not the author of the diary, what information about the subject does the entry reveal?
- How reliable would you judge the information to be? What is the basis of your judgment (e.g., How did the author of the diary know the subject? What professional relationship did they have?)?

- How would you label the style of the entry? (Is it comical, intellectual, tragic, impromptu, angry?)

Finally, what conclusions might a biographer draw from these responses and include in the biography?

Analysis Tasks for an Audio Clip of the Subject Speaking

As a biographer, you will analyze historical sources using many intellectual tools. Initially, you must answer the journalist's questions (who, what, when, where, why, and how) as you analyze this source. In addition, consider the proximity of the source's creation to the event described and the stated purpose of the source. You must realize and control your own assumptions and biases and also consider the internal assumptions and biases of each source. In other words, a biographer must examine each source with a skeptical and critical mind.

- What is the date of the clip?
- Who produced it (e.g., Is it from the personal collection of the subject? Did a radio station or news service record it?)?
- What is its type: speech, interview, song, commentary, reading?
- What information about the subject does the clip reveal? Evaluate the speaker's tone of voice and speech patterns.
- How reliable would you judge the information to be? What is the basis of your judgment?
- How would you label the style of the clip? (Is it comical, intellectual, tragic, impromptu, staged?)

Finally, what conclusions might a biographer draw from these responses and include in the biography?

Analysis Tasks for a Speech

As a biographer, you will analyze historical sources using many intellectual tools. Initially, you must answer the journalist's questions (who, what, when, where, why, and how) as you analyze this source. In addition, consider the proximity of the source's creation to the event described and the stated purpose of the source. You must realize and control your own assumptions and biases and also consider the internal assumptions and biases of each source. In other words, a biographer must examine each source with a skeptical and critical mind.

- What is the date of the speech?
- Who recorded or transcribed the speech?
- What is the type of the speech: personal opinion, public address, address to a special audience, news conference, acceptance of an award, court testimony, endorsement?
- What information about the subject does the speech reveal?
- How reliable would you judge the information to be? What is the basis of your judgment?

- How would you label the style of the speech? (Is it comical, intellectual, tragic, impromptu, staged?)

Finally, what conclusions might a biographer draw from these responses and include in the biography?

Analysis Tasks for a Photograph or Group of Photographs

As a biographer, you will analyze historical sources using many intellectual tools. Initially, you must answer the journalist's questions (who, what, when, where, why, and how) as you analyze this source. In addition, consider the proximity of the source's creation to the event described and the stated purpose of the source. You must realize and control your own assumptions and biases and also consider the internal assumptions and biases of each source. In other words, a biographer must examine each source with a skeptical and critical mind.

- What is the date of the photograph or collection?
- Who or what service produced it?
- What is its type: posed, artistic, individual or group, candid, spontaneous, still from a movie or video?
- What information about the subject does the photograph or collection reveal?
- How reliable would you judge the information to be? What is the basis of your judgment (e.g., What is the camera's point of view? Is editing evident? What is going on in the photograph? How realistic is the setting? How extensive or limited is the photograph?)?
- How does the quality of the photograph or collection influence your judgment? Consider such variables as color, resolution, composition, material, and so on.
- How would you label the style of the photo? (Is it comical, intellectual, tragic, impromptu, staged?)

Finally, what conclusions might a biographer draw from these responses and include in the biography?

Lesson 5 Worksheet: Writing and Research Tasks in the Biographical Episode

Your group will write a biographical sketch about a particular episode in your subject's life based on the evidence individual members gathered from the primary sources. Use at least one detail from each source in the sketch.

Suggestions for Writing

In one paragraph, describe the time in the subject's life you are writing about. Include details such as the month and year, the social or cultural conflict involved, the people involved, and the eventual resolution.

In a second paragraph, explain your subject's role in the episode. Part of the development of this paragraph must come from at least one of the primary sources. In other words, you must paraphrase or cross-reference at least one of the resources.

Write two or three paragraphs about the incidents of and reactions to the conflict. You might organize these with a problem in one paragraph and a solution in the second. Or you might present before and after reflections. Another alternative would be to summarize pro and con viewpoints of an issue central to the conflict. Still another choice would be to describe two issues, sources, or implications of the conflict, one in each paragraph.

Write a concluding paragraph emphasizing your subject's role in the resolution or conclusion of the episode. Include at least one sentence about the subsequent consequences one, ten, or one hundred years later.

Edit your sketch with the following writing skills in mind.

- Introduce each resource with a phrase or clause such as "According to a CBS news broadcast . . ."
- At the end of the sketch, list the primary resources you have quoted or paraphrased.
- Spell the people's names and relevant places correctly.
- Begin each paragraph with a clear transition to the subject or the episode.

Suggestions for Research

1. With your newly found skills as a biographer, you will identify an event, situation, or controversy from the biography you read to conduct a research study. The questions that you wish to investigate should be personally relevant and interesting to you. Were there times when you were reading about your subject's life and you wondered why he or she reacted in a particular manner? Did any of the subject's actions or personality characteristics cause you to be confused, perplexed, or puzzled? Was there an event, situation, or controversy that arose where too little information was provided to help you get an accurate account of what was happening?

2. Using these questions as your guide, your task will be to assemble a set of primary and secondary sources that will answer your questions. You will be required to document these sources and, in some cases, obtain copies so that you can use them when you create your final product.

3. A guide has been created to assist you in this research process. It is called Thinking Like a Biographer: The Research Protocol. As a class we will be spending time in the library assisting one another in locating these sources. At other times, you will be required to complete some of the research activities at home.

4. When your research is complete, you will be asked to apply your findings, coupled with what you already know about your subject, to retell the life of your subject using a new twist. Reading through the product selections prior to conducting your research may influence the type of sources that you wish to add to your collection.

5. To begin your thoughts about this research, I want you to brainstorm at the bottom of this paper any ideas that you have already considered. Use these stem questions to help you generate some questions. It might be interesting to know . . . . How could . . . ? Historically, I wonder how . . . ? What factors . . . ? How might . . . ? Why didn't . . . ?

Thinking Like a Biographer: The Research Protocol

Use this sheet to guide your research. You will go through all the processes several times as you make progress on your research. As you learn new things, you will generate new questions, find other sources of information, and create new ideas for your product.

Define the Research Problem and Generate the Central Question

Why are you doing this? Decide what you want to know. Begin with a problem that is puzzling. A puzzle is not just a lack of information, but a gap in your understanding. Sometimes a primary source that you have read about in your biography will spark your curiosity and drive your research. You need to decide the following: What is it that I am curious about? and Why am I conducting this reseach?

Formulate the Central Question(s)

Explore the sources and reasons that you have for conducting this research and formulate a central question or issue. You will need to ask yourself, "What questions am I interested in answering?" "What issue do I want to further explore?" "Which questions would help me to focus my research?"

Design a Plan

The research you conduct will be applied to your final product, which is to retell the biography you have read. But now it will focus on some of the questions that you have raised as a biographer. You will be asked to creatively weave the findings from your research into the overall design and content of the text that you produce. You will need to decide how to organize your research so that you can use it when the time comes to create your product. Make plans now to figure out a way to systematically record your findings and cite your sources. You need to consider the following: How will I organize my research? How will these findings be used to create my product?

Locate Sources

Track down sources that will provide evidence to help you address your questions. Researchers need to sift through whatever related research exists to see how useful it is for their purpose. You need to ask the following: Where can I find primary and secondary sources that might address my questions? What have other researchers found out that can guide my research? Are the sources credible and reliable? Is there bias in the reporting?

Analzye the Sources

When you locate sources that help you to illuminate the issue you proposed or help support the questions that you posed, you need to carefully analyze the sources for bias, reliability, and credibility. Apply the critical analysis skills that you have used in this unit to interpret, critique, and analyze the quality and integrity of the sources you selected. Ask yourself these questions: Does the evidence support the questions or issues I have raised? Is the source reliable, credible, and free of bias? What interpretation can I make from these sources that will help me address my central questions? What have these sources helped me realize? How does this evidence answer my questions?

Report and Apply the Findings

You will apply your research findings to the product option that you have selected. The purpose of the findings should help you to construct the text and to creatively combine it with other information that you have previously gathered during your initial research. You need to consider the following: What is the significance of my research? How can I best use my findings in a creative way as I apply them to my product design?

Lesson 7 Rubric: Evaluating Student Research and Product Development

Performance	Novice	Competent	Expert
Evidence What evidence have I gathered? How well have I evaluated and analyzed the primary sources?	Inadequate use or absence of primary and secondary sources; no variation in types, perspectives, or opinions of resources.	Some evidence drawn from primary and secondary sources; adequate use of opposing and varied resources; refers to analyses of several available sources.	Detailed evidence gathered from primary and secondary sources; evaluation of opposing and varied resources; effective analysis of all sources.
Organization How well have I organized my research? How well have I supported my questions or ideas with evidence?	Organizing idea may be ill-defined, too broad, or absent; evidence may be present but does not support any particular idea, thesis, or set of questions.	Has clearly defined organizing idea, thesis, or questions; most evidence is connected to the organizing idea, and the reader is able to make the connection.	Has clearly defined organizing idea, thesis, or questions; complex argument is clearly presented and supported by specific and relevant evidence.
Connections How well have I made connections between my research findings and the questions I have generated? What do I now understand?	Limited or no connections are made to a larger context; shows limited or no understanding of student knowledge or development of new ideas, even at a personal level; use of research findings in the story is not connected to the story.	Recognizes patterns and can make accurate generalizations; explains and applies the relationship between the concepts and issues beyond the work.	Demonstrates relationship between main idea and larger context; analysis of issues reveals well-developed, original ideas and new understanding.
Style and voice Does my voice or the subject's voice come through in my writing? How well have I communicated my ideas?	Writing is unclear with no particular style, voice, or originality; uses research findings in the overall story idea.	Writing is clear but lacks focus; style is straightforward, but attempts have been made to add original touches to the story; student voice is present but inconsistent; research findings are used within the story, but rationale for their use is not clear.	Writing is confident; the story is clearly intentional; student voice is evident; writes with lively and engaging language; research findings enhance the story; the book has a distinct personal identity.
Conventions Have I communicated my ideas effectively? Have I edited my work? Have I used the proper mechanics for documenting sources?	Communication is impaired by errors; little or no use of conventions for publication.	Some mechanical errors, but communication is not impaired; demonstrates knowledge of accepted conventions for publication.	Mechanical errors are rare or nonexistent; follows appropriate conventions for publication.

Comparative Analysis Charts

Round 1—Identifying Distinguishing Traits, Skills, Dispositions, and Products/Services of the Individual

You are to generate a list of personality and environmental traits, as well as the skills and dispositions that you feel contributed to your subject's ability to achieve high levels of accomplishment. Personality traits are behavioral or co-cognitive behaviors that are inside people, in their minds and in their hearts. Environmental traits might be defined as those elements in a culture that may encourage certain behaviors. Also consider the skills that they used to carry out their work, the dispositions they possessed that may have contributed to their success, and the types of products or services that they provided to humanity.

To guide your brainstorming, ask yourself, "What did it take for this individual to make a difference in peoples' lives?" "What positive characteristics helped shape his or her sense of self, and what influence did his or her work have on humanity?" Explain why the person engaged in the work that he or she did.

Individual Represented _____

Personality Traits	Environmental Traits	Skills	Dispositions	Types of Products or Services
Examples	Examples	Examples	Examples	Examples and Influences

Round 2—Identifying Distinguishing Traits, Skills, Dispositions, and Products/Services of Individuals in a Particular Discipline

During this round, you will sit with other students who have studied the lives of people who shared the same disciplinary field as your subject. You will use your lists to compare and contrast the similarities and differences in the traits, skills, dispositions, and products and/or services to see if any commonalities exist among these individuals. You are trying to find out if they share something in common with each other and identify distinguishing traits that made them different from one another.

Disciplinary Group Represented _____

Comparison	Personality Traits	Environmental Traits	Skills	Dispositions	Types of Products or Services and Influences on Humanity
Similarities					
Differences					

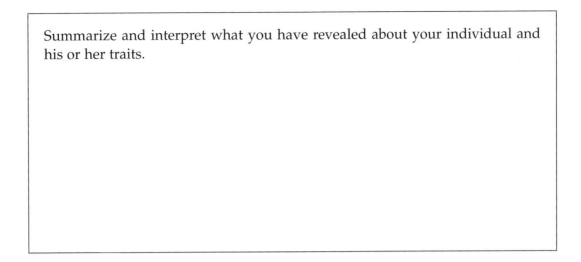

Summarize and interpret what you have revealed about your individual and his or her traits.

Round 3—Identifying Distinguishing Traits, Skills, Dispositions, and Products/ Services of the Individuals Across All Disciplines

Directions to the Teacher:

The teacher should use this chart to record the students' responses to identify a pattern of behaviors and traits that all the individuals shared across the discipline.

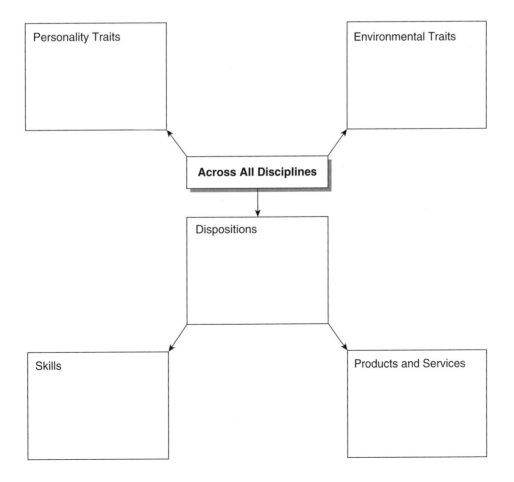

Personality Traits

Environmental Traits

Across All Disciplines

Dispositions

Skills

Products and Services

Taking Action: Interest Development Centers

Center 1: Photo-Essays/Biographies to Reveal
Concerns, Heighten Awareness, Offer Suggestions

When trying to identify a project that reveals issues of personal concern, it is often the case that those with artistic dispositions pursue their work differently by bringing to our attention the issues or problems we face through photographing the concerns. These artists often capture our concerns and document the awareness of a need to take action through the photographs they select and the narrative text that they use to explain the importance of the photo selected. Through the photographs they take, they make metaphoric connections to help us think about the things that we wish not to discuss in the open or reveal something that is ignored. They make us sit up and take notice, which does prompt us to become more aware, more sensitive, and perhaps reconsider how we will change our lives. In the book *Abandonings: Photographs of Otter Tail County, Minnesota*, Maxwell MacKenzie (1995, Preface) stated the following:

In the year that I turned forty, I returned to where I was born, though not raised, and was drawn to make photographs of the remnants of an earlier life there, now all but passed away. Otter Tail County lies northwest of Minneapolis-St. Paul, close to the North Dakota border, on the edge of the Great Plains. Europeans first settled there in 1865, and over the next fifty years, thousands came, primarily Norwegians and Swedes. Among them was my great-grandfather, Lars Erick Lundeen, who came in 1880 at the age of twenty-one. Most of the immigrants were farmers who took advantage of the free land, rich black earth, and abundant water. By the 1930s, many of the pioneers had already begun to leave the land, forced by dust storms and the Depression to desert the very homes they had struggled so hard to build. I felt the need to document some of what remains before all traces disappear and we have no reminders of what went before. I wanted us to remember their brave efforts and the graceful shelters they built, even in ruin so pleasing to the eye. To me, this landscape and these buildings— sad, empty, silent houses and falling-down barns—possess a profound beauty, not merely for their spare, simple designs and weathered boards, but as monuments to the men and women who, like my own ancestors, made long journeys and endured great hardships to reach this remote part of America and build in it a new home.

MacKenzie's photos chronicle those abandonings, and he has selected the words and poetry of other writers to express his thoughts and emotions about his reactions and remembrances about these places.

Use this example to consider the possibility of identifying the type of project you would be interested in pursuing. Does the book *Abandonings* provide you with any ideas for a project that would be of personal concern? Are there any human issues or concerns you would like to profile or use to raise awareness? Is there a personal journey that you wish to explore through the creation of a photo biography?

Center 2: Recording Important Lives—Personal Memoirs

Our lives are often enriched by the lives of others who have in some way shaped who we are. These individuals may be our family members, a grandfather who has helped us understand who we are, or another family member who displayed great acts of courage in the face of difficult challenges. Friends, who are devoted us, who help bring out the best in us on a daily basis, can enrich our lives. These lives often may go unnoticed, and our words of gratitude may go unspoken. The same is true of teachers whom you may have had in school. In the memoir *Tuesdays With Morrie* (1997), written by Mitch Albom, a professor's life is profiled by one of his students prior to his death. Albom tells the professor's story after spending considerable time with him, making observations, interviewing him, and recording his actions, which help identify the importance of this man in the author's life.

Use this example to consider the possibility of profiling a life of someone who has influenced you. You will need to interview this person, perhaps chronicle the life through the stories that he or she shares with you, and then reveal how this life is personally meaningful to you. In the final analysis, you will be asked, "How did your work on this project parallel the work of biographers and the lessons you learned from individuals who create?"

Center 3: Taking Action—What Kids Can Do Projects

View the Web site *What Kids Can Do* (www.whatkidscando.org) and read through the list of projects these students are pursuing. *What Kids Can Do* documents the value of young people working with teachers and other adults on projects that combine powerful learning with public purpose for an audience of educators, policymakers, journalists, community members, and students. Read through the list of featured stories that reveal how students your age and from across the country are interviewing members of their own communities to retrieve and preserve—in written, audio, and video form—the memories of local elders' histories. Notice how they are pooling their efforts to take on a cause and making contributions to their school, community, and state through the actions they take.

Use these examples to consider the possibility of identifying the type of project you and your peers can pursue together. As you decide, consider the influences (political, cultural, social, etc.) that had an impact on the actions that your subjects took to serve humanity and how these parallel the actions these students pursued. Also look at the types of products and services that these students created and published as compared with the subjects you read about to increase the awareness of the type of product you would like to prepare.

Center 4: Focus on the Discipline

In the following chart, consider the types of projects that may be based on your areas of interest and strength. These ideas should help you consider options for your work. There may be others in the class who may wish to take on a project with you. Use the list to brainstorm your ideas.

Examples by Subject	Project Ideas
Mathematics	Assist with the design, measurement, and construction of a wheelchair ramp for a building that does not have one.
Science	Engage in a project that addresses an environmental issue in your community or design hands-on science activities to teach science concepts to younger students.
History	Archive your community's history or the oral histories of community members.
Music	Provide music for those in waiting rooms at the hospital or determine how to select the appropriate music for a nursing home.
Language	Translate community bulletin boards into other languages.
English	Write letters to Congress supporting an important issue, or fight against an issue of local, state, or national importance.
Computer science	Design a Web page for a not-for-profit organization that does not have one.
Art	Paint murals on the walls of a dilapidated school or create photo-essays to reveal issues of personal and/or societal concern.

Action Planning Guide

An action plan is an outline or description of a project that serves as a step-by-step guide to making your project a success. Complete the following steps as you organize your project.

Step 1: Define the Type of Project

Determining the type of problem to solve will provide the focus you or your team needs to make it happen. You can identify some of the problems by researching local, state, and national issues by reading your local paper, discussing issues of concerns with adults, going to town meetings, and so forth. List all the problems you can think of that are facing you, your peers, families, or the community at large and that you feel need to be addressed.

_____

_____

_____

_____

Step 2: Choose Team Members

Solving problems or addressing an issue is a tough job. You can complete this project on your own, especially if you select an issue or concern that is of personal interest. You can also do the project with others. With the added support, new ideas, and the special talents of others, you may find that having other members on your team can enhance your project. Look around. See if you can find anyone else to help you in your quest.

_____

_____

_____

_____

Step 3: Establish a Goal or a Mission

What are you going to do for your project? A proper mission statement not only says what you are going to do but also tells who and how you will complete this mission.

_____

_____

_____

_____

Step 4: Ask Questions

Finding out the important questions related to your topic ensures that you will have a set of guidelines for taking action in accomplishing your mission.

_____

_____

_____

_____

Step 5: Design Activities, Create Timelines, and Assign Roles

Describe the actions that will help you or the team answer the questions you developed in the previous step. Put together a step-by-step outline or plan for each task associated with each activity. This plan should include which team members will participate, when the activity will take place, and where it will happen.

Action	Who	When	Where

Step 6: List Materials and Costs

List the materials and resources you or your team members need to complete the project.

Human Resources	Materials	Equipment	References

Step 7: Implement Your Plan

Begin your plan by implementing the activities that you listed in Step 5. Keep track of your progress by recording findings in your research notebooks, taking photographs that record the actions you took, and securing taped interviews if your project requires this type of information.

_____

_____

_____

_____

Step 8: Develop the Product

Determine the type of product that is best for the type of project that you selected. In some cases, some of you will be creating photo-essays or photo biographies as products, while others will want to share the findings from their projects as they implement a solution that addresses a concern or an issue. Describe the type of product you will create.

_____

_____

_____

_____

Step 9: Reflection

Don't wait until the last minute to evaluate your project. Take time to reflect along the way. This way you can revise your plans and make the necessary adjustments to ensure success.

_____

_____

_____

_____

Worksheet: Assessing My Project

Please fill in the information about your project. Then read each of the following questions. Rate yourself on a scale from 1 to 5, with 1 being the lowest and 5 being the highest. Explain your answers.

Name: _____

Project title: _____

Describe what you accomplished:

1. How well did you achieve your goals?   1   2   3   4   5

2. How well did you learn new information and ideas?   1   2   3   4   5

3. How well did you learn new skills?   1   2   3   4   5

4. How well did you learn new things about yourself?   1   2   3   4   5

5. What part of your work makes you the most proud?

6. If you had to do your project over again, what would you change and why?

7. How does the project you worked on relate to the life of the individual you studied? What are the analogies and metaphors?

8. How does your project show that you have grown or improved in some way?

Bibliography

(Books 1 and 2 Combined)

Albom, M. (1997). *Tuesdays with Morrie: An old man, a young man, and life's greatest lesson.* New York: Doubleday.

American Association for the Advancement of Science. (1993). *Benchmarks for science literacy.* Oxford, UK: Oxford University Press.

Ammeson, J. (2002, January). The lens of time. *Northwest Airlines World Traveler, 34*(1), 38–43.

The @rtroom, www.arts.ufl.edu/art/rt_room/index.html

Arts EdNet. (1999). *National standards for visual arts education.* Retrieved December 5, 2004, from www.getty.edu/artsednet/resources/Scope/Standards/national.html

Bandura, A. (1993). Perceived self-efficacy in cognitive development and functioning. *Educational Psychologist, 28,* 117–148.

Barton, E. (1997). *Peppe the lamplighter.* New York: HarperTrophy.

Berriault, G. (2002). *Stone boy by Gina Berriault in "The Stone Boy": A Study Guide from Gale's "Short Stories for Students"* (Vol. 7, Chapter 15). Farmington Hills, MI: Thompson Gale.

Betts, G. (1985). *Autonomous learner model for the gifted and talented.* Greeley, CO: Autonomous Learning.

Bloom, B. S. (1956). *Taxonomy of educational objectives: Handbook 1. The cognitive domain.* New York: David McKay.

Bransford, J. D., Brown, A. L., & Cocking, R. R. (2000). *How people learn: Brain, mind, experience, and school.* Washington, DC: National Academy Press.

Brookhart, C. (1998). *Go figure!* Chicago: Contemporary Books.

Brown, M. W., & Weisgard, L. (Illus.). (1990). *The important book.* New York: Harper Trophy.

Bruner, J. (1977). *The process of education.* Cambridge, MA: Harvard University Press.

Budzinsky, F. K. (1995). "Chemistry on stage": A strategy for integrating science and dramatic arts. *School Science and Mathematics, 95*(8), 406–410.

Burns, D. (1993). *A six-phase model for the explicit teaching of thinking skills.* Storrs: University of Connecticut, National Research Center on the Gifted and Talented.

Burns, K. (Director). (2002). *The civil war.* Alexandria, VA: PBS Home Video.

Chapman, C. S. (2003). *Shelby Foote: A writer's life.* Jackson: University Press of Mississippi.

Clavell, J. (1989). *The children's story . . . But not just for children.* New York: Dell.

Cooney, B. (1999). *Elenore.* New York: Puffin Books.

Creech, S. (2001). *Love that dog.* New York: HarperCollins.

Csikszentimihalyi, M. (1990). *Flow: The psychology of optimal experience.* New York: Harper Perennial.

Dahl, R. A. (2002). *How democratic is the American Constitution?* New Haven, CT: Yale University.

Deci, E., & Ryan, R. M. (1985). *Intrinsic motivation and self-determinism in human behavior.* New York: Plenum.

Dewey, J. (1933). *How we think.* Boston: D. C. Heath.

Divine, D. (Director). (1999). *Monet: Shadow and light.* Los Angeles: Steeplechase Entertainment.

Divine, D. (Director). (1999). *Rembrandt: Fathers and sons.* Los Angeles: Steeplechase Entertainment.

Earhart, S. (2001). *VITAL: Visual impact in teaching and learning.* Charleston, SC: Carolina Art Association.

Educational Web Adventures, www.eduweb.com

Eighmey Ltd. (2005). *Eighmey's think tank.* Retrieved December 5, 2004, from http://kancrn.kckp.k12.ks.us/Harmon/breighm/zog.html

Eighmey Ltd. (2005). *Eighmey's think tank: Reading and understanding a legal case.* Retrieved December 5, 2004, from http://kancrn.kckps.k12.ks.us/Harmon/breighm/case.html

Emory University. (2004). *Amendments never ratified for the U.S. Constitution.* Retrieved December 4, 2004, from www.law.emory.edu/FEDERAL/usconst/notamend.html

Erev, I., & Roth, A. E. (1998). Predicting how people play games: Reinforcement learning in experimental games with unique, mixed strategy equilibria. *The American Economic Review, 88,* 848–881.

Erev, I., & Roth, A. E. (1999). On the role of reinforcement learning in experimental games: The cognitive game-theoretic approach. In D. V. Budescu, I. Erev, & R. Zwick (Eds.), *Games and human behavior: Essays in honor of Amnon Rapoport* (pp. 53–77). Mahwah, NJ: Lawrence Erlbaum Associates.

Erickson, H. (1998). *Concept-based curriculum and instruction: Teaching beyond the facts.* Thousand Oaks, CA: Corwin.

Film Study Center, Harvard University. (n.d.). *DoHistory.* Retrieved December 5, 2004, from www.dohistory.org/

Franchere, R. (1970). *Cesar Chavez.* New York: Crowell.

Franklin Institute Online, http://sln.fi.edu/franklin/statsman/statsman.html

Fritz, J. (2003). On writing biography. In D. E. Norton, S. E. Norton, & A. McClure (Eds.), *Through the eyes of a child: An introduction to children's literature* (6th ed.). Upper Saddle River, NJ: Pearson Education.

Gardner, H. (1993). *Creating minds: An anatomy of creativity seen through the lives of Freud, Einstein, Picasso, Stravinsky, Eliot, Graham, and Gandhi.* New York: Basic Books.

Giraffe Heroes Project. (n.d.). *Welcome to giraffe country.* Retrieved December 5, 2004, from www.giraffe.org/

Glaser, R. (1984). Education and thinking: The role of knowledge. *American Psychologist, 39*(2), 93–104.

Goleman, D. P. (1995). *Emotional intelligence: Why it can matter more than IQ for character, health and lifelong achievement.* New York: Bantam Books.

Gregory, J. M. (1971). *Frederick Douglass, the orator: Containing an account of his life, his eminent public services, his brilliant career as orator, selections from his speeches and writings.* New York: Crowell. Available from http://docsouth.unc.edu/neh/gregory/menu.html

Haines, K. (n.d.). *The exponential growth/decay WebQuest.* Retrieved December 5, 2004, from www.web-and-flow.com/members/khaines/exponents/webquest.htm

Hearn, B. (1997). *Seven brave women.* New York: Greenwillow.

History Matters, www.historymatters.gmu.edu/

Housen, A. (1979). *A review of studies in aesthetic education.* Unpublished manuscript, Harvard Graduate School of Education, Cambridge, MA.

Hughes, L. (1991). *Thank you m'am* (Creative Short Stories). Saint John's, Newfoundland, Canada: Creative Company.

Igus, T. (1992). *When I was little.* East Orange, NY: Just Us Books.

International Reading Association. (2004). *IRA/NCTE standards for the English language arts.* Retrieved December 5, 2004, from www.readwritethink.org/standards/

Irons, P. H. (1990). *The courage of their convictions: Sixteen Americans who fought their way to the Supreme Court.* New York: Penguin Books.

ISTENETS. (2004). *Technology Foundation standards for all students.* Retrieved December 5, 2004, from http://cnets.iste.org/students/s_stands.html

Johnson, S. (1750). *The rambler #60.* Retrieved December 5, 2004, from www.samueljohnson.com/ram60.html

Joyce, J., & and Weil, S. (1996). *Models of teaching.* Boston: Allyn & Bacon.

Kaplan, S. (1994). *Differentiating core curriculum and instruction to provide advanced learning opportunities.* Sacramento: California Association for the Gifted.

Khun, D. (1986). Education for thinking. *Teachers College Record, 87*(4), 495–512.

Knowledge Network Explorer. (2004). *Lessons, WebQuests, information for teachers and librarians.* Retrieved December 5, 2004, from www.kn.pacbell.com/

Kohlberg, L. (1964). Moral education in the schools: A developmental view. *School Review, 74,* 1–29.

Krathwohl, D. R., Bloom, B. S., & Masia, B. B. (1964). *Taxonomy of educational objectives: The classification of educational goals: Handbook 2. Affective domain.* New York: David McKay.

Kunhardt-Davis, E. (1987). *Pompeii . . . Buried alive!* New York: Random House.

Lauber, P. (1998). *Painters of the caves.* Washington, DC: National Geographic Society.

Library of Congress, www.loc.gov/

Library of Congress. (2004). *How to read a poem out loud.* Retrieved December 5, 2004, from www.loc.gov/poetry/180/p180-howtoread.html

Library of Congress. (2004). *Section 2: Analysis of primary sources.* Retrieved December 5, 2004, from http://memory.loc.gov/learn/lessons/psources/analyze.html

Lyon, G. (1992). *Who came down that road?* New York: Orchard Press.

MacKenzie, M. (1995). *Abandonings: Photographs of Otter Tail County, Minnesota.* Washington, DC: Eliott & Clark.

Mahoney, A. (1998). In search of gifted identity: From abstract concept to workable counseling constructs. *Roeper Review, 20*(3), 222–226.

Maker, J., & Nielson, A. (1996). *Curriculum development and teaching strategies for the gifted and talented.* Austin, TX: Pro-Ed.

Montana Heritage Project, www.edheritage.org/

Moser, R. (Director). (1999). *Goya: Awakened in a dream.* Los Angeles: Steeplechase Entertainment.

Moser, R. (Director). (1999). *Mary Cassatt: American impressionist.* Los Angeles: Steeplechase Entertainment.

Nash, G. B., & Crabtree, C. (Project Codirectors). (1994). *National standards for United States history: Exploring the American experience.* Los Angeles: University of California, National Center for History in the Schools.

National Academy of Sciences. (1995). *National science education standards.* Retrieved December 6, 2004, from www.nap.edu/readingroom/books/nses/html/

National Association for Gifted Children. (2000). *The parallel curriculum model: A model for planning curriculum for gifted learners* (Pilot version). Washington, DC: Author.

National Center for History in the Schools. (1996). *National standards for history, Basic edition.* Retrieved December 5, 2004, from http://nchs.ucla.edu/standards/

National Council of Teachers and Mathematics. (2000). *Principles and standards for school mathematics: An overview.* Available from http://standards.nctm.org/document/

National Council for the Social Studies. (2004). *Curriculum standards for social studies: 2. Thematic strands.* Retrieved December 5, 2004, from www.socialstudies.org/standards/strands/

National Research Council. (1999). *How people learn: Brain, mind, experience, and school.* Washington, DC: National Academy Press.

Phenix, P. (1964). *Realms of meaning: A philosophy of the curriculum for general education.* New York: McGraw-Hill.

Plumley, E. (2004). *The exponentials WebQuest.* Retrieved December 5, 2004, from www .web-and-flow.com/members/eplumley/exponentials/webquest.htm

Presseisen, B. Z. (1987). *Thinking skills throughout the curriculum.* Bloomington, IN: Pi Lambda Theta.

Raylman, D. (2004). *The exponentials WebQuest.* Retrieved December 5, 2004, from www.srsd .org/~kcornelius/raylman/webquest.htm

Renzulli, J. S. (2002). Expanding the conception of giftedness to include co-cognitive traits and to promote social capital. *Phi Delta Kappan, 84*(1), 33–58. Retrieved from www.sp.uconn .edu/~nrcgt/sem/expandgt.html

Renzulli, J., Leppien, J., & Hays, T. (2000). *The multiple menu model: A critical guide for developing differentiated curriculum.* Mansfield Center, CT: Creative Learning Press.

Renzulli, J., & Reis, S. (1997). *The schoolwide enrichment model: A how-to guide for educational excellence* (2nd ed.). Mansfield Center, CT: Creative Learning Press.

Roberts, T., & Billings, L. (1998). *The Paideia classroom: Teaching for understanding.* Larchmont, NY: Eye on Education.

Rossetti, C. (1872). *Who has seen the wind?* Available at www.recmusic.org/lieder/r/rossetti/ wind.html or http://www.grc.nasa.gov/WWW/K-12/Summer_Training/Elementary97/ WhoHasSeenTheWind.html

Roth, A. E., & Erev, I. (1995). Learning in extensive-form games: Experimental data and simple dynamic models in the intermediate term. *Games and Economic Behavior, 8,* 164–212.

Ryan, P. M. (1999). *Amelia and Eleanor go for a ride: Based on a true story.* New York: Hyperion.

Ryan, T. J. (Director). (1999). *Degas: Degas and the dancer.* Los Angeles: Steeplechase Entertainment.

Schaefer, C. L. (2001). *The copper tin cup.* New York: Walker Books.

Schelby, A. (2000). *Homeplace.* New York: Orchard.

Shinew, D. M., & Fischer, J. M. (Eds.). (1997). *Comparative lessons for democracy: A collaborative effort of educators from the Czech Republic, Hungary, Latvia, Poland, Russia, and the United States.* Calabasas, CA: Center for Civic Education in cooperation with Ohio State University.

Smith, G. B., & Smith, A. L. (1992). *You decide: Applying the Bill of Rights to real cases.* Pacific Grove, CA: Critical Thinking Press & Software.

Southern, T., & Jones, E. (1991). *The academic acceleration of gifted children.* New York: Teachers College Press.

Sternberg, R. J. (1985). *Beyond IQ: A triarchic theory of human intelligence.* New York: Cambridge University Press.

Sternberg, R. J., & Grigorenko, E. L. (2000). *Teaching for successful intelligence: To increase student learning and achievement.* Arlington Heights, IL: Skylight.

Strickland, C. A., & Hench, E. (2003, March). *Affective differentiation.* Paper presented at Association for Supervision and Curriculum Development Annual Conference, San Francisco.

Strong, M., & Strong, D. M. (1997). *The habit of thought: From Socratic seminars to Socratic practice.* Tonowanda, NY: New View Publications.

Swartz, R. J. (1994). *Infusing critical and creative thinking into content instruction.* Pacific Grove, CA: Critical Thinking Press & Software.

Tomlinson, C. A. (1996). Good teaching for one and all: Does gifted education have an instructional identity? *Journal for the Education of the Gifted, 20,* 155–174.

Tomlinson, C. A. (1999). *The differentiated classroom: Responding to the needs of all learners.* Alexandria, VA: Association for Supervision and Curriculum Development.

Tomlinson, C. A., Kaplan, S., Renzulli, J., Purcell, J., Leppien, J., & Burns, D. (2002). *The parallel curriculum: A design to develop high potential and challenge high-ability learners.* Thousand Oaks, CA: Corwin.

VanTassel-Baska, J., & Little, C. (Eds.). (2003). *Content-based curriculum for high-ability learners.* Waco, TX: Prufrock Press.

Ward, V. (1980). *Differential education for the gifted.* Ventura, CA: National/State Leadership Training Institute for the Gifted and Talented.

Wenger, E. (1998). *Communities of practice: Learning, meaning, and identity.* Cambridge, MA: Cambridge University Press.

What Kids Can Do, www.whatkids cando.org

Wiggins, G., & McTighe, J. (1998). *Understanding by design.* Alexandria, VA: Association for Supervision and Curriculum Development.

Zeller, B. (2000). *Civil war collection: Artifacts and memorabilia from the war between the states.* San Francisco: Chronicle Books.

Zuo, L., & Cramond, B. (2001). An examination of Terman's children from the theory of identity. *Gifted Child Quarterly, 45,* 251–259.

Index

**CORWIN
PRESS**